Thomas Pringle

Frontispiece Thomas Pringle, attributed to James Struthers Stewart (1791–1863), engraver of Glen Lynden scenes in *African Sketches*. The portrait is in the possession of the descendants of Pringle's sister Jessie, wife of William Ainslie, who settled at the Cape in 1833, as did Stewart and his family the following year.

Thomas Pringle

South African Pioneer, Poet and Abolitionist

RANDOLPH VIGNE

JC JAMES CURREY

James Currey
is an imprint of Boydell & Brewer Ltd
PO Box 9, Woodbridge, Suffolk IP12 3DF (GB)
www.jamescurrey.com

and of

Boydell & Brewer Inc.
668 Mt Hope Avenue, Rochester, NY 14620-2731 (US)
www.boydellandbrewer.com

British Library Cataloguing in Publication Data
A catalogue record for this book is available
on request from the British Library

ISBN 978-1-84701-052-0 (James Currey cloth)

Typeset in 10.5/12 Monotype Garamond
by Avocet Typeset, Chilton, Aylesbury, Bucks
Printed and bound in Great Britain by
CPI Group (UK) Ltd, Croydon CR0 4YY

To James and Clare Currey

Contents

Contents

List of Illustrations and Maps

Preface

Thomas Pringle was a lively, high-spirited man of many friends and engaging personality, a much published poet and an ultimately successful editor, campaigner against oppression in South Africa and slavery in the world beyond. After his death in 1834 at only 45, his fellow writers and friends Josiah Conder and Leitch Ritchie left glowing pictures of his three lives – in Scotland until 30, then South Africa and his last years in London. These were appended to Pringle's *Narrative of a Residence in South Africa* and *Poetical Works*[1] respectively. Ritchie had had the enormous advantage of access to Pringle's papers before his widow Margaret sent them to the Cape for his great friend and chosen biographer John Fairbairn's use. Their disappearance is unexplained.

A full biography, by Jane Meiring, did not appear until 1968 and a second, by John Robert Doyle, in 1972.[2] More than forty years after the appearance of the latter, we should look at Pringle from a standpoint different from that reached by the succession of earlier assessments of his life and work. That is the object of the book before you.

A year after his death came a review of his *African Sketches* by, or partly by, John Gibson Lockhart in the *Quarterly Review* (December 1835), which praised his work and character while mean spiritedly belittling his background and achievements. His reputation in Britain faded rapidly and by the end of the century Mrs Oliphant's *William Blackwood and His Sons* (1897) had set the tone for the disparagement of the founding co-editor of *Blackwood's Edinburgh Monthly Magazine* which has persisted right up until his entry in the *Oxford Dictionary of National Biography* in 2004. Mrs Oliphant called Pringle and his co-editor James Cleghorn 'incompetent' and 'pseudo-literary men' and this denigration took root, though researchers like E.L. Strout must have found that no such charges were made at the time. Lockhart and John Wilson, succeeding mainstays of *Blackwood's*, ridiculed them, in the libellous 'Chaldee MS' and later, for their personalities, lameness and quarrels with both the rival Edinburgh publishers Blackwood and Constable but never for their literary ability.

Coleridge wrote to Pringle of his discovery of the latter's 'Afar in the Desert' and his captivation by it as, with small changes, 'among the two or three or four most perfect lyric poems in our language'.[3] His poem 'The Nameless Stream' predicting his future obscurity roused the young Tennyson to write to him, of his collection *Ephemerides* in 1832: 'The man who could write it will not flow an altogether nameless stream through the nineteenth century'.[4] Yet he is not included in twentieth-century works on Scottish poetry and his close connection with Coleridge as editor and friend is not mentioned in E.K. Chambers's standard life of Coleridge.[5] The *Narrative of a Residence in South Africa* last appeared in print in Britain in 1864 and but for a small luxury edition called *South African Sketches. Poems by Thomas Pringle* from the Abbey Press, Edinburgh in 1902, all has been silence.

If Britain forgot Thomas Pringle, South Africa claimed him and a series of editions of his poems, with biographical notes, have appeared between John Noble's in 1881 and Chapman and Pereira's[6] in 1989. The *Cape Monthly Magazine,* in 1860, in the heyday of the Cape liberalism he had played his part in inspiring, pronounced that his 'influence would endure for all time' and associated him 'with the foremost efforts in the history of the emancipation of the coloured race from personal political thraldom under which for near two centuries it has groaned'. The *Narrative*[7] reappeared in 1966 and J.R. Wahl's abridgement of it in 1970 as did his edition of the South African poems[8] the same year but little was added to his life story.

Valuable work by English literary scholars has not reached beyond its appearance in learned journals or in doctoral theses, pre-eminently in the latter category, by Patricia Morris and Damian Shaw.[9] J.V.L. Rennie's magisterial four-volume study of *The Scottish Settler Party of 1820* was informally printed and privately published in 1991.

It is hoped that *Thomas Pringle: South African Pioneer, Poet and Abolitionist* will put Pringle's status as editor and poet in Britain in a more positive light than before and convey a fuller picture of his character than previous biographers have given us. His initiation of the campaign for press freedom, now enshrined in the United Nations Declaration of Human Rights but always at risk, is re-examined. In South Africa the 'emancipation of the coloured race', to use the language of 1860, has reached its apogee. May this book also accord Pringle recognition of his devotion to his 'great cause', the achievement of a first stage towards what we now call human rights for indigenous South Africans and slaves from many countries. The final stage of Pringle's political work in South Africa was reached with the enactment of democratic rule in 1994. Slavery in its many new forms in the world remains a cause to which Pringle's example may recruit successors to those great abolitionists of which he was one.

NOTES

[1] First published as two parts of Pringle's *African Sketches* (London, 1834), without the biographies.

[2] *Thomas Pringle. His Life and Times* (Cape Town, 1968); *Thomas Pringle* (New York, 1972).

[3] Coleridge to Pringle, endorsed 20.3.1828, Griggs, E.L., *The Collected Letters of Samuel Taylor Coleridge,* vol. 6 (Oxford, 1971), p. 732.

[4] Tennyson to Pringle, 13.12.1832, Sotheby's Catalogue, 2910.1969.

[5] Chambers, E.K., *Samuel Taylor Coleridge. A Biographical Study* (Oxford, 1938).

[6] Noble, J., *Afar in the Desert, and Other South African Poems* (London and Cape Town, 1881), Chapman, M. and Pereira, E., *African Poems of Thomas Pringle* (Durban, 1989).

[7] Pringle, T., ed. Robinson, A.M. L., *Narrative of a Residence in South Africa* (Cape Town, 1966).

8 Wahl, J.R., *Thomas Pringle in South Africa, 1820–26* (Cape Town, 1970); Pringle, T., ed. Wahl, J.R, *Poems Illustrative of South Africa, African Sketches Part I* (Cape Town, 1970).

9 Morris, P., 'A Documentary Biography of Thomas Pringle', Ph. D. dissertation, London University (1982); Shaw, D.J., 'The Writings of Thomas Pringle', D.Phil. thesis, Cambridge University (1996).

Author's Note

There are many aspects of Thomas Pringle's life in Scotland, South Africa and England that need explaining to readers unfamiliar with one or more of these environments as they were in Pringle's time. Happily, there is a wide range of information available on all of them and the Bibliography on pp. 250–6 identifies many sources of such information.

A note will be added here on the indigenous peoples of the Cape Colony, on the Bantu-speaking nations largely beyond it, and on the state of the eastern frontier of the colony where Pringle's party of Scots settlers, and the English settlers near them were located.

Within the colony, and in smaller numbers outside it, were the pastoral Khoikhoi, bondsmen of the colonists until 1828 and the hunter-gatherer Bushmen, now also known as San, the underclass of these ancient occupiers of the land, known jointly today as Khoisan. The Griquas and other mixed-race groups like the Bergenaars and the urban 'Cape Coloured' people were widely spread. The slave population, imported from Indonesia, India, Madagascar and other parts of Africa were mainly in the western Cape.

On the frontier and to the north-east were the Bantu-speaking nations and clans, known as the Nguni (as distinct from the Sotho-Tswana to the north and north-west): the amaXhosa (amaGqunukhwebe, amaRharhabe, amaNgqika among them), closest to the Albany settlers and the abaThembu (including the amaNdungwane and the amaTshatshu), neighbours of the Scots settlers. Invaders from further to the north-east, a mass movement known as the Mfecane, brought the Hlubi and others, and the fugitive Mfengu, allies of the Cape government. Their origins, like those of the 'Mantatees', invaders from the Sotho-Tswana regions, are still the subject of debate among historians. Further north-eastwards were the amaZulu, led by their warrior king, Tshaka, who was a cause for alarm in the distant colony until his death in 1828.

The situation on the frontier was the result of a struggle for the land that had begun with the First Frontier War of 1779, between the Xhosa and Boer commandos, and after forty years of intermittent conflict had culminated in the 'ethnic cleansing' of the Zuurveld by the British and Boer commandos in 1812, followed by the Fifth Frontier War of 1819 and the defeat of Ndlambe's people led by the prophet-warrior Makhanda at the Battle of Grahamstown. Governor Somerset declared the 10,000 kilometres between the Fish and Keiskamma Rivers an unpopulated 'neutral belt'. In Pringle's time, Boer and British were allowed to farm in the northern sector of what was now the 'Ceded Territory', while the Xhosa king Ngqika and his son Maqoma were not allowed to return, a major grievance of the Xhosa, as was the loss of the Zuurveld.

The eastern frontier was the most perilously unsettled part of the colony, where the struggle for possession of the land was bedevilled by frequent theft of cattle from unfenced settler farms, and reprisal raids, which Pringle termed the 'commando system'. Perhaps inborn from his awareness of the Scottish border raids of the English, his sympathy was with the dispossessed rather than the dispossessors.

Acknowledgments

A major source of the materials from which Thomas Pringle's life story can be found is his letters, and I thanked many people and institutions for making these available to me for my edition of *The South African Letters of Thomas Pringle* (Cape Town, Van Riebeeck Society, 2011). I repeat my thanks to them here, add Anne Westoby, cartographer, to the list and reiterate the names of those who, in varying degrees, have helped me write Pringle's life. They are: Alan Bell Esq., Professor William Christie, Mrs Sheila Clare, Ms Marianne Gertenbach, Zolile H. Keke Esq., Professor Hugh Macmillan, Dr Patricia Morris, Ms Cora Ovens, Professor Jeff Peires, Professor Howard Phillips, John Rennie Esq, Professor Christopher Saunders, Dr Damian Shaw, Professor Robert Shell, Mrs Sandy Rowoldt Shell, Professor Sue Thomas, Professor Tony Voss, and two computer wizards who made the production of the final electronic text possible, Sean Moriarty in England and Nick Sartini in South Africa.

I ask forgiveness of the many librarians and archivists who have been particularly helpful for not naming them again. Their institutions are listed on p. xvii. My thanks go also to my friends of many years, James and Clare Currey, who advised me to submit my manuscript to the publishing house founded by James and which, now part of Boydell and Brewer, still rightly bears his name. I thank also Lynn Taylor and Jaqueline Mitchell of James Currey, publishers who have been a pleasure to work with.

Finally, I heartily thank my wife Gillian, who has encouraged me, travelled with me to the Scottish Borders, Edinburgh, Baviaans River and Pringle's Cape Town and London, and has also checked the text and advised changes and corrections, which was invaluable.

Abbreviations

ACC	*African Court Calendar*
BL	British Library, London
Bodl. Lib.	Bodleian Library, Oxford
CA	Western Cape Archives and Records Service, Cape Town
Cory Lib.	Cory Library, Rhodes University, Grahamstown
CUL	Cambridge University Library
EUL	Edinburgh University Library
J. Rylands Lib.	John Rylands Library, Manchester
Lib. and Arch.	Canada Library and Archives, Canada
LP	Library of Parliament, Cape Town
LUL	Leeds University Library
NELM	National English Literature Museum, Cape Town
NLS	National Library of Scotland, Edinburgh
NLSA	National Library of South Africa, Cape Town
ODNB	*Oxford Dictionary of National Biography*
OED	*Oxford English Dictionary*
RCC	*Records of the Cape Colony*
RH	Rhodes House, Oxford
SACA	*South African Commercial Advertiser,* Cape Town
SRO	Scottish Record Office
TNA	The National Archives, Kew
UCL	University College, London
VOC	*Vereenigde Oostindische Compagnie*
WUL	Witwatersrand University Library, Johannesburg

Part I

Scotland

Border Farm to Literary Edinburgh
(1789–1820)

1

The Elfin Band

It was – still is – a magic land. A green, rolling landscape, westwards from the east coast off Holy Island, with the English border dipping southward along the Cheviot hills, past Flodden Field where King James IV and 9000 of his Scottish subjects were slaughtered by Henry VIII's shock troops, to Kelso with its twelfth-century abbey and on into 'Walter Scott country' – Melrose, Abbotsford and Selkirk, where for 33 years Scott, 'the Great Unknown' for most of them, sat as Sheriff in his courtroom, and to Ettrick Forest.

In Lanarkshire and west towards Glasgow and Clydesdale surroundings change. The people of Berwick, Roxburgh and Selkirkshire look north and south, to Edinburgh and beyond, and to the lands of the Five Abbeys, St Cuthbert's Way, which leads to Jedburgh, and the smugglers' route over the Cheviots.

The land was fertile – marsh and lochs in ancient times – but the English border was close and enough blood was shed there to give those north of it a very strong sense of their Scottishness. It was the land of the reivers, making cattle theft endemic so that Thomas Pringle, born on the farm Blaiklaw, also known by its earlier name of Easterstead, four miles south-east of Kelso, on 5 January 1789, was less surprised than he might have been in his later years at endemic cattle theft from both sides of an African border.

It was a land of dissenters – 'Secessionists' like Pringle's own family, gypsies, whose Scottish 'capital' was almost on the border, at Town Yetholm (*yett* = gate) and poets. Sir George Douglas, Bart., of Springwood Park, Kelso, anthologist of minor Scots poets, in 1891, found them 'as thickly sown as stars in heaven on a frosty night'. The 'flower of Scotland's poetry', he wrote, was also in 'her anonymous ballad literature'.[1] Both were found throughout the borders – from the old minstrels, modernized by Scott, Britain's most popular poet until another Scot, Lord Byron, eclipsed him, to the old woman, the mother of that phenomenon of Scottish literature, James Hogg, known as the Ettrick Shepherd. Old Margaret Laidlaw chided Scott unmercifully when he declaimed to her his version of an ancient ballad. Hogg, a self-taught peasant farmer in the ancient royal forest of Ettrick, south-west of Abbotsford, had become a noted poet and novelist with the publication of The Queen's Wake in 1813. His and Pringle's paths were to cross and recross in the years ahead.

James Thomson, son of the minister at Ednam, just north of Kelso, was a Londoner from his twenties. He was, after Pope, the most widely read – and sold

– poet of the mid-eighteenth century. His great nature poem, *The Seasons*, was the first to break with the neo-classicism of Pope and the Augustan age, opening the way for Wordsworth and the romantics. They turned away from the artificiality of Thomson's phrasing, which hindered enjoyment of such as John Leyden, born in 1775 at Denholm, on the Teviot, and of Thomas Pringle himself. Scott was, of course, the great poet of the borders. With *Waverley,* in 1814, he came also to dominate the English novel for the rest of his life.

Thomson, Leyden, Hogg and Pringle all took the 'high road that leads to England', mocked by Dr Johnson, leading some like Leyden and Pringle, to faraway places. Scott stayed. Growing up in Edinburgh where what seems to have been poliomyelitis in infancy caused permanent lameness, he was sent to his grandfather's farmhouse beside the fifteenth-century Smailholm Tower, which the Scotts had acquired from the Pringles in 1645. From the farm Sandyknowe Walter Scott drew the lore and minstrelsy, the stories of the reivers from Northumberland (who plagued Smailholm) and of 'battles long ago' which became his inspiration as poet and novelist.

The Pringles of Smailholm had suffered a long decline, from the deaths at Flodden in 1513 of four brothers, the sons and the heir of the Laird, David Pringle of Smailholm. These Pringles, originally Hoppringill, with lands in the Royal Forest of Ettrick, were the senior branch of the prolific Pringle surname in the borders. A great-grandson of David Pringle, bereaved at Flodden, Sir James, married his eldest son and a daughter to children of Sir Walter Scott's direct ancestor, another Walter, known as 'Auld Wat' Scott of Harden, who died in 1613.

There were Pringles in all the eastern Border districts, in Edinburgh and beyond. Their name originated in the village of Hoppringle (so spelt today), in the parish of Stow in Midlothian, five miles from Galashiels in Selkirkshire and six from Melrose. But the Pringle heartland of our time is a 40-mile stretch of the Tweed basin, radiating from Melrose, and is coterminous with 'Scott country' centred round Abbotsford. There were many Pringle 'houses' – Clifton, Haining, Smailholm, Whytbank and Yair among them.

James, the third Laird of Whytbank (pronounced Whitebank, less than three miles west of Galashiels) had a natural son, William, born before 1640 who became the tenant of his father the fourth Laird at Yair, an estate to the south of Whytbank, on the right bank of the Tweed, near its confluence with Ettrick Water. Yair in due time became the seat of the Laird of Whytbank and the link between the baseborn William and his descendants farming at Blaiklaw was recognized when, in 1830, at the age of 41, Thomas Pringle, somewhat of a celebrity, back from South Africa, visited Alexander Pringle of Whytbank and Yair, who regretted that 'our dear Thomas' had stayed so short a time.[2]

Thomas himself, great-great-great grandson of the third Laird, made no claims for his family as gentry. He wrote of them as 'for four generations at least plain, respectable Scottish husbandmen'[3]. He wrote to his brother William in South Africa of the Pringles of Whytbank that his immediate family still held 'a sort of feudal or patriarchal regard for that house as the chief of our ancient Scottish name and Clan'. He wrote elsewhere that 'of my grandfather's seven sons, three were bred to farming, two were cabinet makers, one became a clothier and one of them was educated for the Secession Church, of which my grandfather was an Elder'.[4] The clothier was the youngest, the merchant, Adam, who moved north to Perth where he became Lord Provost in 1833–6 and the Secessionist minister was Alexander who served in Perth from 1777 until his death in 1839. Revd Alexander Pringle was awarded an honorary doctorate of divinity by Marischal College, Aberdeen in 1819.

Thomas's grandfather, William Pringle, had become tenant of Blaiklaw in 1759, a farm of 500 acres owned by the Wauchopes of Niddrie, still today a landowning family in Roxburghshire. His fifth son Robert, Thomas's father, took over the tenancy. He was a quiet man, defeated in his late fifties by a succession of bad farming years in a period of general agricultural decline, and willing in his late sixties to leave the organizing and leadership of the family in their migration to Africa to his third son and fourth child Thomas.

Thomas dedicated his account of that migration, first published with his poetry in *African Sketches* in 1834 and in 1838 as *Narrative of a Residence in South Africa*, with a sonnet to Robert Pringle 'with many a prayer of reverential love' as 'a recreation to thine honoured age'. Robert, 'sprung from a stalwart line of Scottish sires', was to become the patriarch in Africa.

of a young race, who with their fathers' fires
Shall warm the heart of their adopted land.

Robert had been widowed when Thomas was six, remarried, and had left Blaiklaw with his second wife Beatrice Scott and two children for a farm near Bishop Auckland in Co Durham, which he rented from, or managed for, General Sir Gordon Drummond. The general had distinguished himself fighting Napoleon in Egypt and served in 1812 against the Americans. The seat of the Drummonds of Megginch was near Perth and the general had married a wife from Co Durham. It is possible that either the minister Alexander or the future Lord Provost Adam arranged Robert's move.

The children of Robert Pringle's first marriage, to Catherine Haitlie, a Berwickshire farmer's daughter (the name was spelt Heatlie in later years by her South African relatives) were already scattering. The daughters, Mary and Isabella, were in Jedburgh and Kelso, respectively, Isabella as a teacher. Sons William and John were both on the land and it seems William was employed by the new tenant of Blaiklaw. Alexander, the youngest was preparing to move to Wilmington, Delaware in the United States, and Thomas living and working in Edinburgh. Thomas's first great cause was to settle and reunite his scattered family in a new country.

The account he gives of his childhood is idyllic, and is echoed by the close friend of his student and later life, Robert Story,[5] son of the schoolmaster at Yetholm and factor to Mr Wauchope of Niddrie. Robert Story became minister at Rosneath in today's Argyll and Bute and a power in the Church of Scotland. Story was Thomas's companion on a few days holiday at St Mary's Loch which the latter recorded in his long poem, published in 1819, 'The Autumnal Excursion'. It is filled with word pictures of the surroundings of the poet's childhood and youth amid

> The scented heath, the sheafy vale,
> The hills and streams of Teviotdale.

The poem, 572 lines in 31 stanzas, vividly portrays Teviotdale, in which lay the parish of Linton with Blaiklaw near its centre, two and a half miles north of the now vanished Linton village, where Pringle's mother and others of the family lie buried in the hilltop churchyard, beside one of Scotland's oldest church sites. The poem is also charged with the high Scottish patriotism of the young Pringle and shows early signs of the passion for liberty and justice which was to give him a place in history which his poetry, at least in his native land, did not.

He recalls the bloody suppression of the Covenanters for whom, as a Secessionist, he clearly felt great sympathy, by John Graham of Claverhouse and his dragoons:

> Tyrants! Could not misfortune teach
> That man had rights beyond your reach?
> Thought you that torture and the stake
> Could that intrepid spirit break,
> Which even in woman's breast withstood
> The terrors of the fire and flood!

He reaches the climax of this transport of praise for heroic defenders of their freedom:

> Aye! – though the sceptic's tongue deride
> Those martyrs who for conscience died;
> Though modish history blight their fame
> And sneering courtiers hoot the name
> Of men who dared alone be free
> Amidst a nation's slavery;
> Yet long for them the poet's lyre
> Shall breathe its notes of heavenly fire.

Scott's *Old Mortality* tells us more of the foolish zealotry of the Covenanters than of the misdeeds of 'bloody Graham'. Pringle's poem had first been published in 1811, five years earlier, and Pringle annotated it with a two-page exposure of Claverhouse's cruelties and a stinging rebuke to 'his most eloquent apologists' and 'certain historians' for their 'canting language'.[6] The writer was his 'old and reverend friend', the Revd Thomas McCrie, the Secessionist minister whose services he and Story were to attend in their early days at the University of Edinburgh, where he had the chair of Divinity. McCrie was the noted biographer of John Knox and of Andrew Melville, 16th-century Presbyterian leader and scholar.

Another theme is the recollection of Pringle's own happy childhood in that 'lovely land'

> By Teviot's lone, historic strand,
> By sylvan Yair, by Ettrick's glens
> By haunted Yarrow's 'dowie dens';
> Till, with far-circling steps we hail

Thy native Bowmont's broomy dale,
And reach my boyhood's birchen bowers
'Mong Cayle's fair cottages and towers.

Here, within the sound of the river Kale's 'mountain melody' he would enjoy 'schoolboy rambles free\And heartfelt young hilarity!' Or would, in summer, lie reading of 'Roman and Grecian glory' or of 'Scotland's champion – Wallace bold':

Of Scotland's ancient 'lune and lee'
And Southron's cruel treachery
Till I have wept in bitter mood
That now no more, in English blood
My country's falchions might atone
The warrior's fall and widow's moan.

His account of the family home at Blaiklaw is Arcadian, though always with a sense of times past, as his historical fancy imagines:

Lone Blakelaw, on whose trenchéd brow
Yet unprofaned by ruthless plough,
The shaggy gorse and brown heath waves
O'er many a nameless warrior's grave.

The clashes with the English reivers and invading armies fill his memory of childhood games, when, the 'elfin band at play', his siblings, 'tilled each his tiny field':

Or proudly ranged in martial rank
In rival bands upon the bank
With rushy helm or sword of sedge
A bloodless Border war to wage.

Yet it is tinged with deep sadness as he remembers his long dead mother, 'that gentlest human Friend' who

No more her anxious eye could bend
On one by young affliction prest
More close to her maternal breast.

The 'affliction' was, of course, the other tragedy of Thomas's early life, when, by his own account, at a few months old, his nurse let him fall, dislocating his hip and concealing the accident so that he was to spend the rest of his life on crutches. Like Sir Walter Scott, whom he encountered first in Edinburgh in 1816, he was lame but wonderfully active, a horseman, walker, even climber, and man of action. In his last London years he would walk from Pentonville to his office in Aldermanbury and later, when living in Highgate, his friend Leitch Ritchie recalled that 'when wandering with him … among the gentle hills of Highgate, I rarely remembered that my buoyant minded friend was on crutches'.[7]

Pringle recalled being 'tormented by doctors' and made to wear, to no avail, 'a red morocco boot, with steel bandages', soon 'superseded by a pair of crutches'. He learned to use them 'with such ease and adroitness, that ... I felt little incommoded by my lameness'.[8]

Scott walked with a stick only and never suffered, as Pringle did, the humiliation of being taunted for his lameness in the midst of his troubled literary life in Edinburgh that lay ahead.

Leitch Ritchie felt that 'the useless limb, which he was to drag laboriously about for the rest of his life' made him 'send his thoughts back to himself'.[9] It may also have made him send his thoughts out to others who were made to suffer through no fault of their own. First his own family in their time of decline, then the social ills of South Africa and finally slavery were to provide all the scope needed for him to engage with others' problems.

He wrote light-heartedly enough about his journeys to school, which he started making, with his brothers William and John, at the age of five:

> We rode, all three of us, on one stout galloway, the foremost guiding our
> steed, and the other two holding fast, each by the jacket of the one before him.
> We carried our noon-tide meal ... in a wallet; and my crutches were slung, one
> on each side, to the pommel of the long-padded saddle.[10]

His first school, near Blaiklaw was closed by 1795 so the brothers continued at Linton until he and John went on to Morebattle. They boarded there with their old nurse, Mary Potts, who had been held responsible for his accident and about whom he wrote 'I met with an accident in the nurse's arms, by which my right limb was dislocated at the hip joint'. Despite this, and presumably long forgiven by his parents, he lived with her in Morebattle until, like Sir Walter Scott twenty years earlier, he went on to Kelso Grammar School at the age of 13.

His friend Story visited Morebattle after Pringle's death and met Nanny Potts. She had little to say of Pringle except praise for his 'affectionate disposition'[11] and personal kindness, recalling that 'when a collection was made in 1793 (the year of the dearth), he proposed to give half of all the pocket money he had.' He also, she said, repeatedly gave his porridge 'to provide a supper for a poor lad who was in the habit of doing work for him'. Until 'having watched, [she] discovered it'. She told Story that, though, 'very devout', he preferred history to divinity for reading, specially 'books that had battles in them'. Claiming to have been strict with her charges' religious observance, especially on the Sabbath, to Thomas she gave Bunyan's *Holy War,* which would hardly have enlivened long evenings in Morebattle.

Story came away with two letters written by Pringle in 1833, the year before his death. They both give glimpses of his schooldays without the hindsight of Story's own much-quoted account of his first meeting with Pringle, when they set off for Edinburgh together.

To the old nurse Pringle sent with his letter of 1833 'a small piece of gold under the seal' – a half-sovereign it must have been – 'to cheer your little board on New Year's Eve', the cold Christmas weather having made him think of her '"wee bit ingle" and ill-stocked cupboard'. He told her he had heard from 'my friend Mr Pringle of Clifton' that he had, asked by his now celebrated kinsman Thomas, sent 'a cartload of old sticks from the park to keep your little room warm through the *lowe* of the winter.' The Laird had also sent 'a few shillings for tea and tobacco'.[12]

Clifton Park, then the great house of the parishes of Linton, Morebattle and Hounam, passed by marriage in 1845 to the Elliots, Lairds of Harwood, when the ancient Pringle line came to an end. Here had been a grand connection for Thomas, once the infant lamed in the care of Nurse Potts. She, however, had a different version of the accident: 'It seems', she told Story, 'when gambolling in the arms of his mother, she had grasped him suddenly, from some momentary fear of his falling, by the thigh, and the distortion which was produced was not detected till some months after, when too late for remedy'.[13] Thomas himself believed that Nanny Potts was to blame: the accident happened 'in my nurse's arms' and she 'unfortunately concealed the incident at the time'.[14] He gave the lie, too, to the old nurse's claims of strictness towards him: she 'never forgave herself' and indulged him 'in every caprice. I consequently ruled her with despotic sway, requiring strict discipline on the part of my parents to prevent me from being quite spoiled'. Whatever the cause – a congenital defect discovered late has been suggested – the victim bore no grudge and nor did the parents. Poor Catherine Pringle died only a year after Thomas had started school, making the nurse's care more necessary than ever.

Pringle in these same letters of 1833 asked Nanny Potts to write to him about her 'health and circumstances', for news of his 'worthy old friend John Turnbull, who, he wrote, 'was getting frail (honest man)' and his wife Peggy ', how the Morebattle minister who had instructed him, the Revd James Morrison, and his wife fared, and 'of Mr Hoy'. He gave her news of his father, brothers and sister, especially of 'your old favourite' William, 'always delicate but not more'. He wrote of John's beautiful estate at the Cape, and 'likely to be the richest of the family some day', unlike Thomas himself, who had wished that the 'mite' he had sent her were 'ten times as much, but I am not yet rich, nor likely ever to be, though (thank God!) I have enough for all necessary wants.'

The 'honest man', John Turnbull, was the inspiration of much of the burning sense of glory and shame the young Pringle felt for Scotland's sad history, and England's turpitude. He wrote of Turnbull, shepherd to both Robert Pringle and his father, as 'one of the worthiest and, in his humble sphere, one of the most generous-hearted men I ever knew.'[15] After reciting his virtues – piety, humour, delicacy of feeling, propriety of demeanour, he recalled that Turnbull had also 'some of the hereditary prejudices of his rank and nation ... a determined detestation of the Southron of ancient times, and a sovereign contempt for those of the present'.

The second 1833 letter acquired, or copied, by Robert Story on his visit to Morebattle, was to Mrs Morrison, widowed daughter-in-law of the aged minister, 'poor Mr Morrison' and written only eleven months before Pringle's early death. He is saddened by the disappearance of so many school friends and 'entire families', which he had noticed on his 'last hasty visit' (in 1830). It may serve as an epilogue to what had been a carefree time, with:

my recollection of the happy days I spent in your father's house and garden, and all poor David's plays and mine still fresh in my recollection. I remember the planting of the camomile beds and of growing shrubs from the hedges at Marlefield and Clifton Park, and the herrying of mavis's nests, and all your poor father's and mother's kindness to us in our troublesome pranks. These were in many respects pleasant days, before we knew of the great world and the sterner duties of life. I still love to look back on them.

From Morebattle, 'loveliest village of the plain' between the Cheviots and the Eildon hills, once beside the now almost vanished Linton Loch, Thomas moved to the busy market town of Kelso, for three more serious years at Kelso Grammar School. Despite his love of gardening and evidence of his mechanical skill, he was thought to be physically unequal to the farming life and must be prepared for a profession. Almost nothing is remembered of his Kelso schooldays, except that he was taught Latin by John Dymock, later at Glasgow High School and, a modern touch, the author of lucrative Latin text-books for the Edinburgh publishers Oliver and Boyd. The buildings are gone and Kelso High School, now on a different site, has no records of the period.

'The Autumnal Excursion' is equally silent, except for its recollections of the poet's long, long thoughts of youth, as the 'elfin band at play' grow older and

As childhood's gamesome mood gives place
To manly thought and maiden grace.

In Linton churchyard, at his mother's grave, he pondered 'Man's mysterious mortal state'.[16] May there still be, when life is over, 'some mystic link between the Living and the Dead'? This is not the mind of a convinced Calvinist, however devout at his prayers. But his thoughts are still full of battles long ago, recalled for him by the old shepherd Turnbull, as 'with ancient grudge his wrath would glow', of the haunted beauty of the landscape, its winding rivers and hills where 'amid the mountain thyme's perfume …boundless heaths of purple bloom'. Above all, 'that home of early love' where, returning, he hears 'kind voices on the breeze' and

The sire – the kindred band I see –
They rise with smiles to welcome me!

This was perhaps his greatest early passion, thwarted when the family left Blaiklaw. Even when 'The Autumnal Excursion' was written, in August 1811, 'ungentle hearts and strangers rude' had taken their place

The hearth is cold, the walls are bare
That heard my grandsire's evening prayers.

Perhaps William was employed at Blaiklaw – Thomas writes of his being there in January 1812, of his father's move to Bishop Auckland in Co Durham, and of his youngest full brother Alexander's intention to visit Willie before leaving for America. He did so, never to return. When the opportunity came to gather the family together and move them to a wild and distant country, Thomas seized it.

Pringle's childhood had ended in November 1805 when, as arranged by their fathers, young Robert Story arrived at Blaiklaw to travel with 16-year-old Thomas to Edinburgh, where they were to share lodgings and read respectively Latin and Greek, and theology. Story, who gave us the only outsider's view of Pringle's youth, writes vividly of the boys' excitement at comparing their learning and interests at that first meeting, when they shared Thomas's room in the old Blaiklaw farmhouse. They talked far into the night as they ranged over their reading, quoting in Latin 'whenever it was possible to bring in a sentence or two'.[17] Story was deeply impressed by his new friend's knowledge of natural history, quoting from Bernardin de Saint Pierre's *Studies of Nature* (1788), and its stories, especially his masterpiece, the tragic romance *Paul et Virginie*, set in an idyllic Mauritius, but above all by what he knew of the African journeys of another lowlander, Mungo Park of Selkirk, who was to die on the Niger river the following year. A friend of Sir Walter Scott's, Park's *Travels in the Interior Districts of Africa* had been published in 1799.

It was surely selective memory, hindsight indeed, that led Story to highlight his 'remembrance of the wonder excited in me' by hearing Pringle talk of Park and Bernardin de Saint Pierre. Pringle also quoted 'some of the most splendid passages' from Thomas Campbell's *Pleasures of Hope* (1799), on the downfall of Poland and its heroic leader, General Tadeusz Kosciusko, well known in Europe, and in America, where he had fought under Washington. He was captured by the Russians in 1794:

Hope for a season bade the world farewell,
And Freedom shriek'd as Kosciusko fell!

'Often since', Story wrote, 'I have been struck with the half-prophetic indications his predictions then gave of his future history. His love of liberty, his Whiggish predilections wherever he was, even when most to his disadvantage, and unceasing energy, were this early shown to have possessed his boyish view.'

In simplest terms Whig meant liberal and Tory conservative and it was Pringle's loyalty to the Whig tendency that was to lead to his own downfall in South Africa but not that of his cause.

Story considered that Pringle's keen interest in African scenes may have made 'the idea of emigration to the Cape less repulsive to him'. (This from the minister of Rosneath on Clydeside, who had moved only that short distance from Yetholm). Despite his sometimes ponderous tone, Story was amused by the comparison of what 'Park hazarded amid the lions and tigers of the African wilderness' with the boys' setting off next morning, 'amid the merriment and jest of his younger kindred …not with a tiger but together on the back of a small Highland Sheltie' on their two-day journey to Edinburgh, 37 miles distant. And to their new lives.

NOTES

[1]   Douglas, Sir George et al., *Poems of the Scottish Minor Poets from the Age of Ramsay to David Gray* (1891), p. 123.

2   Alexander Pringle to L.J.S. Cunninghame, 29 January (?1832), SRO GD 149/37/6. Morris, Patricia, 'A Documentary Biography of Thomas Pringle'. PhD thesis, University of London (1982), p. 27.

3   Pringle, Thomas, *Narrative of a Residence in South Africa. To which is prefixed a Biographical Sketch of the Author by Josiah Conder* (1835, 1966 ed.), p. xxii.

4   *Op. cit.,* p. 22.

5   Story, Robert H., *Memoir of the Life of the Rev. Robert Story* (1862), pp. 10–11; *The Cape,* Cape Town (13 January 1922), p. 22 (20 January 1922), p. 22.

6   Pringle, Thomas, *The Poetical Works of Thomas Pringle with a Sketch of his Life by Leitch Ritchie* (1838), p. 216.

7   Pringle (1838), p. xv.

8   *Op. cit.,* p. xiii.

9   *Op. cit.,* p. xiv.

10 *Op. cit.,* p. xiv.

11 *The Cape. An Independent Review of South African Life and Politics,* Cape Town, No 338, 20 January 1922, p. 22.

12 Vigne. Randolph, 'Additional Letters to *The South African Letters of Thomas Pringle*' (2011), www.vanriebeecksociety.co.za, p. 25.

13 *The Cape,* 20 January 1922, p. 22.

14 Pringle (1838), p. xii. Pringle (1966), p. xxii.

15 Pringle (1838), p. 217.

16 Pringle (1838), *The Autumnal Excursion,* p. 120. [The reference is to the book the poem appeared in.]

17 *The Cape,* 27 January 1922, p. 22. Library of Parliament, Cape Town, Fairbairn Papers, 1, 11.

1. The Borders region of Scotland showing Thomas Pringle's boyhood home, Blaiklaw farm, south-east of Kelso, where he attended the grammar school and Linton and Morebattle where he spent his early schooldays. See also Abbotsford, home of Sir Walter Scott, Edinburgh, Pringle's home from university days, and East Lothian, home county of Margaret Pringle's Brown family, the Rennies and Sydserffs. Ettrick forest, home of James Hogg, lies south-west of Selkirk.

2
Edinburgh

The Shallows

We know of Thomas Pringle's student days mostly from what his friend and fellow lodger Robert Story tells us and from the letters Story found at Morebattle. We can guess the impact of the metropolis on these country boys, sons of a Roxburghshire tenant farmer and of a neighbouring parish schoolmaster. Their metropolis had been Kelso, which Walter Scott, brought up in his barrister father's Edinburgh household and briefly near Kelso, saw as

> The most beautiful if not the most romantic village in Scotland, presenting objects not only grand in themselves but memorable for their associations.[1]

Beautiful, even made grand and memorable by its Abbey ruin, but a village. Edinburgh, a teeming city, half 'Auld Reekie', half the Athens of the North, squalid slums side by side with Robert Adam's New Town, was a place where a rural somebody would feel himself an urban nobody. Pringle took a long time to make the leap. When fame finally made him, briefly, a household name there, it was as a figure of controversy, a victim in a world of sharp tongues and sharper pens. It took 15 years of penurious toil, some achievement but ultimate disappointment, to lead him to hope for a better life and an early dream to be brought to reality.

The first years of study at the university were filled, as Story tells us, with talk, argument, seeking after truth (mainly of religious belief, accepted without question at Blaiklaw and Morebattle but a subject of intense debate with his student friends) and of a gradual absorption in literature, rather than in the classics, theology and the other subjects he studied. 'The tickets of the lectures he attended', wrote Leitch Ritchie, who had seen records perhaps preserved by Pringle's widow and now lost, were for 'chemistry, logic, and metaphysics, Scottish law, anatomy and surgery, &c.'[2] Keeping 'a watchful eye upon the progress of English literature', Pringle told a friend, unnamed by Ritchie, 'of the *début* of a Mr Wilson, a new recruit of the Lake bards' – this was John Wilson, who, as 'Christopher North', was to be at the centre of the highly unpleasant brouhaha which awaited him and was a factor in his decision to start a new life in a little known and distant country.

Story's assessment, presented in the biography by his son, who became Principal of Glasgow University, mixed admiration of Pringle's character and personality with a sad shaking of the head at missed opportunities and misused talents. Story expressed 'great delight' in Pringle's

> inflexible integrity, his openness of heart, his lively fancy, his eloquent trust, the sunlight and rainbow cast of his character.[3]

Among his father's student friends, Pringle stood at the centre:

> He had a singular capacity for attracting friends, and this in a playful humour, with all his tenderness and pathos of mind, which very effectively enlivened the intercourse he had with them.

Two of the friends he shared with Story, Thomas Cannan and James Morton, became Church of Scotland ministers, though Morton was later ordained in the Anglican church and became vicar of Holbeach, Lincolnshire, where he wrote the biography of John Leyden. Pringle sought to review a later book of Morton's, *Monastic Annals* (1833) in the *Literary Gazette*, then edited by William Jerdan, another Kelso man, but one who had spent his adult life as a journalist in London. Cannan became minister at Carsphairn in Wigtownshire.

Among the eleven sonnets in Pringle's own first collection of verses, *The Autumnal Excursion*, published in 1819, is, number IX, 'On Parting with a Friend Going Abroad'. The friend has been identified as Cannan. His journey 'o'er the wild and trackless sea' was only to the Continent and the sonnet dwells on the comparison between parting 'with the friends we leave ... as parting spirits look to earth once more ... from the dim ocean of eternity'. The poem says nothing of Cannan himself. He and Pringle corresponded after leaving the University, as did Pringle and Morton.

In a letter of 1813 Morton shared with Pringle his indignation at an attack on Charles James Fox in the Tory *Quarterly Review* and agreed with Pringle's Whig view that 'it had been better if peace had been made long since' as the Whigs 'had always recommended' but had failed to bring about. Morton proposed 'some little excursion to some classic ground upon the Borders where none of us has yet been'.[4]

There was also Henry Inglis, a man of letters like Pringle, or perhaps a Grub Street hack, whom Pringle helped in his later literary life in London. Another, John Donaldson, a law student, was called to the bar in 1826 and became Read Professor of Music at Edinburgh University later in life.

Story writes of Pringle's organizing a small, weekly club, the Philomathic, where members would read their prose or verse and criticize each other's work. According to Ritchie, he was 'much more conversant with English poetry and criticism at this time than students of his student generation generally were'.[5]

There was the rub. While his friends applied themselves to theology, medicine or the law he was not drawn to any of these – certainly not to the church, while, wrote Story, he had an 'unconquerable antipathy' towards the practice of law, 'some pettifogging anecdotes in his neighbourhood having taken hold of his mind'. He thought 'the bodily labour ... of a country surgeon beyond his capabilities', yet he did not lack physical hardihood: Story several times remarks on the gruelling walks they took together and his 'passion for ascending hills'. 'Specially consecrated ground from which he could command such prospects of the traditionary country' was the top of 1472-foot Hounamlaw, south of Morebattle and Town Yetholm. Story recalled also an exhausting walk from Kelso to Edinburgh in a single day. Story arrived nearly blind with fatigue, and next morning his 'hair was here and there streaked with grey.'[6] It turned completely white not many years later.

This difficulty of fixing on a profession caused him, according to Story, 'considerable pain and anxiety' from early on in his university career. 'It became,' wrote Story, in his finger-wagging mode, 'manifest that the great error of his life was in having fixed on no profession.'[7] Or may Providence, or the 'divinity that shapes our ends' have held him back from entering on a career that would have bound him to a way of life, a confinement of his spirit and ideas that might have led to professional success, money in the bank, and total obscurity?

The 'pain and anxiety' were to stay with him, from one cause or another, for a dozen years before the path he was to follow became clearer.

The University of Edinburgh was a loose corporation of teachers and students, even the townsmen and their wives attended lectures in fair numbers. It was without the rigid class structure of Oxford and Cambridge, where undergraduates ranged from menial 'sizars', through middle-class men improving themselves, 'tuft-hunters' among them, to the wearers of those 'tufts', young noblemen with golden tassels on their mortarboards. Edinburgh, Glasgow (the senior Scottish university) and Aberdeen were nothing like that, and, it has been estimated, cost only one-tenth in fees and living expenses. Thomas Pringle could appear to better effect at Edinburgh than he would have done at Oxford or Cambridge, where a sharper cutting edge would have been needed for a young Scot to make his way. Two of these he was to encounter in the years ahead (John Wilson being one of them and John Gibson Lockhart, Scott's son-in-law, the other) to his great cost.

His academic career was undistinguished. Story recalled that he was:

> of studious habit and attended diligently to the duties of his different classes, and although he did not make a brilliant figure, his appearance was already respectable when examined by the professor. His studies, when not engaged in preparation of the lessons for the day, consisted chiefly in the *belles lettres* of his mother tongue

and did not 'extend, as he might have done, his classical knowledge'.

Unlike his friends, Pringle seems not to have taken his degree and his name last appears in the university's records in 1808, in which the subjects studied are not stated. (He had registered for his first year, 1805, to study Latin and Greek). He was a regular attender at the meeting house at which the Revd Thomas McCrie preached and they maintained a literary friendship, sharing, among other things that strong partisanship in favour of the Covenanters.

McCrie, though a Secessionist, was awarded a doctorate of divinity by the university in 1813 and became Professor of Divinity in 1816. He was acquainted with Thomas Thomson, an Ayrshire minister's son and a learned lawyer, who in 1804 was appointed to the newly created post of Deputy Clerk Register to the Record Commission.[8] The Commission had been set up only two years earlier to reform the whole system of public records, the history of which tells the story of Scotland's troubled past. Edward I, 'the hammer of the Scots' and victor over Wallace, had taken the records to England at the start of the 14th century, as, in part, did Cromwell in 1651. Much was lost but, says the renamed National Archives of Scotland of itself: 'The appointment of Thomas Thomson ... laid the foundation of the modern Record Office. His 35-year term of office saw a programme of cataloguing and repair of the older records and the start of record publications'.

The Clerk Register, Lord Frederick Campbell, who held the office for 48 years, had set up the post of Deputy and had found the money to pay for the building of a General Register House, a masterpiece by James and Robert Adam in 1774, at No 2 Princes Street. Today, the Victorian buildings of New Register House and the Back Dome standing behind it, the old General Register House contains the genealogical and family history material which make it, at its own assessment, 'arguably the best national genealogical resource in the world'. The National Archives of Scotland in New Register House accommodate over 60 Km of Scottish records (its work today largely financed by the fees paid by the ceaseless flow of genealogical researchers).

How different it all was when Thomas Pringle was taken on some time in 1808 after leaving the university. Thomson had soon found that the Clerks of Session he could command were quite inadequate for the great volume of document copying he was putting in hand and Thomas Pringle was taken on, having a sound knowledge of Latin. Thomson instituted the keeping of daily progress books by his staff. Pringle's begin in January 1809 and continue until 1815, followed, as we shall see, by a break and a resumption of full-time work until the end of 1819 when he was taken up with the planned family emigration to South Africa the following year.

The number of Pringle's fellow assistants varied, averaging about six, most of them transcribing for six hours a day six days a week, with a fortnight's annual leave and three one-day holidays. Pringle's task was transcribing and abridging, and later collating and printing 'retours of service'. These were documents for collection and return ('retour') to Chancery so that heirs' claims to landed property could be recognized. Those published by Thomson from the mid-sixteenth century, in 1811 and 1816 have become indispensable to today's genealogists, which would have surprised Pringle and his fellow clerks.

The copying was largely mechanical drudgery, on poor pay (averaging £4 per week he told Sir William Campbell in 1817 – Thomson's salary was £500 a year). Yet he retained deep respect and admiration for Thomson, even dedicating *The Autumnal Excursion* to his 'esteemed friend' Thomas Thomson. Pringle was, wrote Story, 'a diligent and faithful servant to his employer, whose kindness and consideration he often spoke of.'[9]

We know of only one refreshing break in the routine of his working life at the General Register. He was selected by Thomson to inspect and transcribe the muniments at Marchmont House, near Duns, in 1816 and spent seven or eight weeks there, continuing the work with four documents of major interest and value he was allowed to bring back to Register House. Sir William Campbell of Marchmont House had asked Thomas McCrie, by then Professor of Divinity at Edinburgh University, to find a student to work on the documents but McCrie recommended that one of Thomson's assistants take on the task. His young friend Thomas Pringle was duly assigned to it.

Sir William had succeeded to the baronetcy on the death of his father Sir Alexander Purves, descended from Charles II's solicitor-general for Scotland. Sir William's paternal grandmother was the daughter of the Earl of Marchmont, a title since extinct, and for various dynastic and inheritance reasons, had become Sir William Home-Purves-Hume-Campbell. Despite his ancestry, Sir William's muniments proved disappointing but Pringle did find among them a letter written by Lady Grizel Baillie (daughter of an earlier Earl of Marchmont) to her exiled brother Patrick Hume in Holland, with his father, then Sir Patrick, who had escaped from imprisonment in Scotland for supporting the Covenanters. Also with them was her future husband, George Baillie, son of Robert Baillie, whose execution in 1684 had caused Sir Patrick to flee.

The romantic story of her father's hiding in the charnel house at their home, then Redbraes Castle, Berwickshire (or, in another version, in a churchyard), where the 12-year-old Grizel brought him food, is told in her daughter Lady Murray's then unpublished life of Lady Grizel. Sir Patrick returned to Britain with William of Orange in 1688, became Lord Chancellor of Scotland and was rewarded with an earldom.

Lady Grizel is remembered today as 'supposedly … the first aristocratic writer of the late 17th century to become interested in national songs'[10] Very few of her own are extant. It was one of these, though only a fragment, that Pringle found in the letter to her brother. The opening eight lines of Pringle's poem, 'Lady Grizzel's Lament', in his first collection, *The Autumnal Excursion*, are taken from the fragment. Pringle added a note to the poem about Lady Murray's memoir and mentioned that 'copious extracts' from it had appeared in 1818 in writings by Samuel Rose in the *Edinburgh Magazine* and elsewhere. Thomas Thomson wrote to the Edinburgh publisher Constable in 1822 about the publication of Lady Murray's MS:

> It will make a pretty little volume. The whole has been finished for some time except an article for the Appendix containing some account of Lady Murray herself. I should like to be able to say something of her husband, Sir Alexander, who was a remarkable person, though a most uncomfortable bedfellow.[11]

The volume duly appeared as *Memoirs of the Right Hon. George Baillie of Jerviswood and of Lady Grissell Baillie by her daughter Lady Murray,* with Thomson named as editor. It was published first privately by Register House and in 1824 commercially by Constable, Thomson paying the printer on both occasions. Pringle, the discoverer of Lady Grizel's letter and the song in it, had no part in the publication of the memoir and only a single poem of his own came out of his discovery. 'O the ewe-bughting's bonny' was published as were others of Pringle's 'songs' with a specified 'Air' – 'The yellow-hair'd laddie' in this case. As with Scott's *Minstrelsy of the Scottish Border* and many such collections, there was no fixed demarcation between poem and song. Lady Grizel's opening verse sets the joyful bringing of the ewes to the sheepfold ('bughting') amidst the shepherdess's heartbreak. It ends:

> O the shepherds take pleasure to blow on the horn,
> To raise up their flocks i' the fresh summer morn:
> On the steep ferny banks they feed pleasant and free –
> But alas! My dear heart, all my sighing's for thee !

He also attempted to continue the story but unlike Scott he was no storyteller and we do not learn what became of 'young Sandy' who 'bood gang to the wars wi' the laird, To win honour and gowd – (gif his life it be spared !)'.

Pringle had moved on from the beginning of his drudgery, albeit under a kindly master, at Register House eight years earlier. He had become known in Edinburgh and its literary world, and was a published poet in *Albyn's Anthology*. He was still, as Story tells us in his account of their holiday journey round St Mary's Loch and its hinterland in 1810, deeply immersed in the history and legends of the Border.

Thomson, later to be a founder and vice-president of the antiquarian Bannatyne Club, was close to Scott, the giant of Scottish literature of that time and the Bannatyne Club's founding president. This was a moment of great interest in Scotland's past and its heroes, a rising tide, which Scott and his publishers had taken at its flood with *Waverley* in 1814. A year later came *Guy Mannering*, in which Pringle had a hand, in an important part of its subject matter, the character Meg Merrilies and her Gypsy community.

The work at Register House was time consuming but still left Pringle space for a life of his own. Leitch Ritchie's gives no source for the story, which he must have heard from someone who was present at this 'little instance of [Pringle's] hatred of oppression'. The instance arose from a rumour that the performing in Edinburgh of the Scottish playwright Joanna Baillie's *The Family Legend* was to be attended by 'the Edinburgh Reviewers and their disciples'. They were to 'assemble at the theatre that fateful night and damn the play'. Their object was to vindicate the journal's cutting criticism of Joanna Baillie and her works.

The *Edinburgh Review* which first appeared in 1802 was the Whig forerunner of Constable's *Edinburgh Monthly, Blackwood's* and those other journals that were a late flowering of post enlightenment Scottish culture and a model for their successors in London, like the *Quarterly Review*, founded in 1807, and abroad. With the *Edinburgh Review*, Jeffrey, Horner, Brougham and even the founder, the kindly Revd Sydney Smith, established a school of criticism which spared none whose work or views fell below their high standards. Byron had hit back the year before with his *English Bards and Scots Reviewers* (though himself a Scots bard).

> To Jeffrey go, be silent and discreet,
> His pay is just ten sterling pounds per sheet:
> Fear not to lie, 'twill mean a sharper hit,
> Shrink not from blasphemy, 'twill pass for wit,
> Care not for feelings – pass your proper jest,
> And stand a Critic – hated yet caress'd.

The *Edinburgh Review* was a feared voice but later comers like the *Quarterly* and, under Wilson and Lockhart, *Blackwood's*, were to care even less for the feelings of their victims.

Joanna Baillie's supporters sought another weapon against her 'oppression'. Pringle organized forty or fifty young men 'to fill the pit and shout down every murmur of disapprobation' from the *Edinburgh Review* faction. Above the uproar 'the sound of their leader's heavy crutches was heard'. Hardly conducive to attentive enjoyment of the play but, says Ritchie, to be thanked for 'the fortunate career of a drama by no means worthy of the genius of Joanna Baillie'. The play was dedicated to Walter Scott, who wrote the prologue and epilogue, and printed by James Ballantyne, who had been at Kelso Grammar School with Scott, for his brother John as publisher (and, of course, for Scott, the secret partner).

The Edinburgh Theatre, where it was performed, was managed by another of Scott's protégés, Henry Siddons, son of the 'Tragic Muse', who with his wife Harriet played the leading roles. *The Family Legend* tells a story dating back to the fifteenth-century feud between the Campbells and Macleans. She was pleased by the 'affectionate reception of the piece … in my native land', however. Pringle's *claque* seems to have had a clear victory over the Edinburgh Reviewers.

Joanna Baillie had long been a local celebrity. The daughter of the parish minister of Bothwell, South Lanarkshire, later Professor of Divinity at Glasgow University, she was a poet but her fame rested mainly on her published plays rather than on their success in the theatre, *The Family Legend* as much as the others. She had moved to London in 1782 and her Hampstead home was much visited by the literary giants of the day, Scott among them on his visits south.

A letter, written in 1828, in which she expressed the hope that Pringle would visit her in Hampstead has survived, but has no reference to the uproar in her defence that night in 1810.[30]

Scott, the 'Wizard of the North' and after 1814 the 'Great Unknown' author of *Waverley* and its successors, was a man of the broadest humanity, a romantic conservative and traditionalist, vehement opponent of parliamentary reform which he saw, rightly, as the end of the old order, yet a supporter of women writers and aspiring young Whig poets like Thomas Pringle.

In the small, intimate circles of Edinburgh's cultivated literary circles of those days, with its numerous clubs and ceaseless gossip, the role of Thomas Pringle must have reached Scott's ears, if he was not already aware of his young fellow Borderer, whose ancestors were closely connected with the Scotts of Harden. To Thomas McCrie goes the credit for having made the introduction, despite the wide gulf between the pro-Covenanter Whig Secessionist and the Tory whose sceptical view of the Covenanters was yet to be shown in *Old Mortality*. McCrie and Scott were to disagree sharply a few years hence, with Pringle siding with McCrie. McCrie's son and biographer described Pringle in 1840 as his father's 'amiable and lamented friend',[31] despite Pringle's having embroiled the great man in his painful *Blackwood's* troubles to come.

More active than McCrie or Thomson in forming Pringle's relationship with Scott was James Hogg, the Ettrick Shepherd, already a noted if controversial poet and essayist well known in the literary world of Edinburgh. A mixed blessing his role proved to be as events to come were to prove.

The link between McCrie and Pringle – 17 years younger – was at its closest in their membership of the Secessionist church, founded in 1733 to maintain strictly the principles of the Reformation. The Secessionists had split again in 1774 into Burghers and Anti-Burghers, which latter faction included the family of Thomas Pringle's grandfather, an elder, at Blaiklaw, and his venerable uncle Alexander, the Secessionist minister at Perth. Thomas and his friend Robert Story followed Dr McCrie after his expulsion in 1809 from the Anti-Burgher meeting house in Potterrow. McCrie had led four fellow ministers in forming their own presbytery (one of them was the Revd James Hogg, parish minister of Kelso), followed by protracted litigation. An obscure chapel in Carrubber's Close was succeeded by McCrie's own specially built meeting house, the McCrie Free Church in West Richmond Street.

The parting of Story from his friend Pringle was marked by the publication of *The Institute,* a verse satire they had composed together, apparently a teasing account of the Philomathic, their student society which sought to spread knowledge and enlightenment through funding an institution for the purpose. Its jingling rhyming couplets are pleasant enough but its target is lost to us today (and was when Story's son recorded it in 1862). The poem describes the society's 'snug apartment thirteen feet by eight' where 'crazy seats around the walls extend, \ And tattered mats the well worn floor defend ... \ Here bugs from time unknown a fortress held \ And many a tribe of orators expell'd.'

At what became the Edinburgh Institution and then the Forum, would-be learners, Hogg among them, paid for lectures and debating in its rooms in Carrubbers Close. Fifty might attend a debate, impossible in the Institute's tiny apartment. Yet a link is suggested by 'The Institute's' dedication to the august Edinburgh Institution.

It may have amused a few of their friends and contemporaries but it sold few copies and made no money for the authors. Ritchie quotes a lost letter of Pringle's to Story in which, 'after retailing some of the encomiums he had heard',[32] Pringle went on

> but alas! *'Pecunia quaerenda primum laus post nummus'*; I now long to see
> the solid pudding, for printers will not be paid with praise alone. But surely, my
> good fellow, there is some stuff in both our craniums capable of being beaten
> into something of higher temper and polish than the 'Institute'.

Praise there was, and Robert Chambers and Charles Rogers, writing forty or fifty years later, take Ritchie's word for it. *The Institute* 'obtained a considerable share of public favour' wrote Rogers in 1856 and Chambers saw evidence that the Register Office 'left Pringle's mind unencumbered for the literary occupation of his leisure hours. The first of these was *The Institute* which ... was abundantly lauded.'[12] The extreme rarity of the book in today's antiquarian booktrade suggests otherwise, however.

Ritchie had the advantage of reading many of the vanished letters of Pringle's in this period. Pringle debated his religious beliefs with Story, Donaldson and others and 'seems to cling to religious hope with almost a convulsive grasp'. He suffered from 'dyspepsia, his constitutional enemy', was 'harassed by incessant labour' and went through bouts of depression. Story deplored Pringle's employment in the Register Office at 'a trifling salary'[13] as 'not conducive to his mental improvement', though he found it 'occasionally interesting'. Story 'could conceive of no employment … less fitted to develop what was in him', yet 'his fancy was ever buoyant and it had delights of its own'.

Story seems not to have followed Pringle into this wilderness, a political environment Pringle was to endure later in South Africa and for which the schisms of the Church of Scotland was some preparation. Story left Edinburgh in 1811 and after a succession of posts tutoring the sons of lairds and noblemen he became, briefly, a minister at Kelso. He and Pringle kept up a flow of lengthy and deeply introspective letters, often filled with criticisms of each other's versifying. In 1815 Story's long ministry at Rosneath on Clydeside began and his close intimacy with Pringle was at an end.

Ritchie wrote of this period that Pringle 'made numerous acquaintances and more than the common number of friends. … his bland yet sprightly manners, and his kindliness of disposition … attracted at once respect and affection wherever he went.' Story found that Pringle's 'ardent and enthusiastic temperament' enabled him, despite exhaustion after the daily labour of transcription, to continue 'his reading and writing in prose and verse', the fruit of which would appear 'in the various knowledge and information he would cast into the circulation of every literary party'.

Overriding the world of letters, however, was 'his passionate love of nature and rural scenery which he could but seldom gratify'. This was the dawning of the age of the Lake poets, of Wordsworth and Coleridge's *Lyrical Ballads,* the worship of nature and of the grandeur of mountains and forests. Pringle was not a late coming copyist of this school: his 'Autumnal Excursion' predated Wordsworth's 'The Excursion' by three years. Originally to be called 'The Recluse', might Wordsworth's masterpiece have been renamed as an unconscious repeating of the title of Pringle's much slighter work?

Pringle was away from Register House for the whole of August and most of September 1810, when his Progress Book reports him as 'absent in the country on account of indisposition'. During his convalescence he made his St Mary's Loch visit with Story, who wrote:

> His joy was intense as we rode over to Branxholm and then over the mountains
> to the lovely loch of St Mary and downward along the lovely vale of Yarrow.
> Never shall I forget the kindling of his spirit during the whole period that
> seemed to irradiate all we looked upon.[14]

It was this 'happy wandering' that inspired 'The Autumnal Excursion', which Story felt to be 'but a faint adumbration of his spirit' during their long ride together.

The poem itself has had a life not unlike its author's: of unrecognized merit. He wrote an early draft under the title 'Paterna Rura: a poem addressed to a friend'. In the summer of 1811 and the following year he met James Hogg, the Ettrick

Shepherd, who was in search of money to be made from his own great creative gifts and also of revenge for the belittlement he had received from the Scottish journals. Pringle wrote to Story that he had read from his 'Paterna Rura' to Hogg, who had 'strongly pressed me to print, and flattered me so well that I have set to and finished them.' The flattery led to Pringle's allowing Hogg to include the poem in a yearly or half-yearly 'repository' of poems by Britain's poets, scaled down to a single volume, to be called *The Poetic Mirror*. The second of its 19 poems was 'Paterna Rura', retitled 'Epistle to Mr R. S****', an easily penetrable disguise for Robert Story. The new title compounded Pringle's difficulties with the poem.

Hogg asked Byron and Samuel Rogers for poems. Both agreed to contribute but failed to deliver. Wordsworth sent a poem and then reclaimed it, Southey and Coleridge did not reply and Scott, who, though he was Hogg's greatest supporter, refused. For all the rare qualities of the 'great and good' as Ritchie called him, Scott had a well-developed money sense and saw no reason why someone else should take all the profit from his own writing.

In the end, it was only Pringle's 'Epistle to Mr R. S****' that appeared and all but three of the rest were clever pastiches of the poets he had invited, written by Hogg himself, in, so he claimed, three weeks. John Wilson, friend and neighbour of the Wordsworths and later a thorn in Pringle's side, wrote three, two posing as Wordsworth's and the third a parody of his own work. The book was anonymously published by Longman, but Hogg's role, both as editor and parodist, was soon detected. The 'Epistle to Mr R. S****', without some of the autobiographical lines in its later existence as 'The Autumnal Excursion', was thought to be by Scott, or a fine pastiche, and dedicated to another R.S., the poet laureate, Robert Southey.

Hogg, unpredictable, mischievous and untruthful as he was, seems to have maintained his love of Pringle's poem. In 1819, Pringle asked him if he might reprint the poem in his own collection of that year, to be called *The Autumnal Excursion, or Sketches in Teviotdale; and Other Poems*. Hogg agreed, and told Pringle: 'I never met with anyone who thought more of the poem than I did. There are but few that can appreciate such a poem and Mr Scott is one of them.'[15] He went on to warn Pringle, from his own bitter experience (though not with *The Poetic Mirror*), not to be 'very sanguine' about sales: 'it is not very fashionable now to read poetry and high as I value the thing I am sure I am right'.

Thirteen years later Hogg wrote in his autobiographical *Altrive Tales* that of all the poems in *The Poetic Mirror* 'the most beautiful and ingenious piece of work is not mine. It was not mine and was not meant to be an imitation of Mr Scott's manner at all.'[16] Was it his particular devilry that prompted him to add: 'There is likewise another small secret connected with that work which I am not yet able to unfold, but which the ingenious may yet discover'? Surely 'that work' was the book itself, not Pringle's 'Epistle', and the 'secret' may have been Wilson's three contributions.

Leitch Ritchie's variant of the story was that Scott was asked to 'revise'[17] the poem, which he understood to be 'an imitation of the strains of the Wizard of the North' and declared that he 'wished the original notes had always been as fine as their echo'. The comparison with Scott was made in London by the *Quarterly*

Review, to whose anonymous reviewer it was 'in the tone of the admirable introduction to the several cantos of *Marmion*'[18]. Constable's *Scots Magazine* reprinted several extracts from the poem, and made the same comparison with the introduction to the cantos of *Marmion* and also of *The Lay of the Last Minstrel*, finding it 'an uncommonly pleasing little poem, both as to sentiment and description. It adheres also pretty closely to its model, to the best specimens of which it is little inferior.'[19]

The lengthened version published in 1819 doubtless suffered from the early confusion as to its authorship and its supposed parodying of Scott, but even more from its publication just as Pringle was leaving for South Africa. He was unable to promote the book, an essential action as he had published it at his own expense and Constable, the publisher, had no incentive to make it known. A few years earlier Pringle's friend William Blackwood would have done so but the years between *The Poetic Mirror* and emigration were turbulent and unhappy, estranging him, for a time, from Blackwood. They were made so not least by the hand of the Ettrick Shepherd.

It is not now possible to compare 'The Autumnal Excursion' with the 'Paterna Rura', a holograph copy of which was deposited in the library of Rhodes University, Grahamstown in 1944. It had belonged to a grandson of Thomas's much loved sister Mary Williams, who had followed the main party to the Cape in 1822. Most unfortunately it disappeared from the library in later years. Bound in the same cover were notes to the poem, which included genealogical material. Luckily this had been transcribed by Professor Rennie of Rhodes University in 1944 and made great use of in his exhaustive study of the Scottish settlers of 1820.

The publishing history of *The Autumnal Excursion* typifies the confusion that Hogg wrought in his dealings with Pringle. He named Scott as the author of the poem in the table of contents of *The Poetic Mirror*, which removed from Pringle for some time to come all credit for a singularly beautiful poem.

At 25 Thomas Pringle, the Border tenant farmer's son, whose passion was English writing and who had failed to enter a profession, living instead the life of an ill-paid drudge copying ancient documents, had little to show for all his reading and his literary friendships in a great centre of European culture. Most of his published satire, *The Institution*, was written by his friend Story, his contribution to James Hogg's *Poetic Mirror* was attributed on the contents page to Walter Scott, and his long years at Register House had borne no literary fruit except the opening eight lines of his yet unpublished poem 'Lady Grizel's Lament'.

In 1815 he was in print once more when Alexander Campbell published the first of three planned volumes entitled on its sumptuously engraved title-page *Albyn's Anthology, or, a Selected Collection of the Melodies and Vocal Poetry Peculiar to Scotland and the Isles ... written by Walter Scott, Esq., and other living poets of the first Eminence.*

The anthologist, Alexander Campbell, was well known in the Scottish musical world as organist and music master in Edinburgh, where the young Walter Scott had been his unmusical pupil. As a collector of songs, music and poetry, he would have been known to Pringle and his friends in their student days. Pringle wrote of him familiarly as 'Sandy Campbell' in a letter to his friend John Fairbairn many years later.[20]

Here, in the two volumes (the second appeared in 1818 but, despite their success, there was no third) were four of Pringle's songs, with their music scores, three to appear as poems in later years, all with slight changes. Alexander Campbell tells us how they were acquired for his collection. 'I'll bid my heart be still' was 'taken down by the Editor'[21] when sung 'to a sweetly rural and plaintive air' from an ancient melody by 'Mr Hogg and his friend Mr Pringle'. We learn that Pringle received

> from his sister, Miss M[ary] Pringle, Jedburgh, these stanzas of the original
> Border ditty which was chanted to the melody here alluded to … It is to the
> obliging zeal of this young lady from promoting this work that the Editor is
> indebted for the admirable Melody to which Mr Walter Scott has written 'Jock
> o' Hazeldean' and likewise the fine original Air to which her brother has
> written 'The Banks of Cayle'.

Mary, who was Robert and Catherine Pringle's first-born and four years older than Thomas, was very close to him and shared his love of Scottish vernacular music. They had spent their childhood in the very region where Walter Scott had collected the Border ballads, from Upper Tyneside to the Cheviots and Eildon hills, and fashioned them into *Minstrelsy of the Scottish Border*, its successors and finally *The Lay of the Last Minstrel*. These had launched Scott as Burns's successor in Scotland and the most popular poet in the English language. By 1816 he had become the Laird of Abbotsford and a great figure in the land, while clandestinely producing the novels attributed to 'the author of *Waverley*'. The linking of himself and his protégé James Hogg with Pringle should have helped to establish the young Register Clerk in the pantheon of Scottish writing.

Campbell claimed that his contributors included 'living poets of the first Eminence'[22] and with himself, Hogg and John Wilson, were such as Alexander Boswell (son of the great biographer), James Morton (Pringle's university friend), Elizabeth Grant, James Gray and Robert Jamieson. But who were James Douglas and William Smyth? Was 'Mrs Gray' the schoolmaster poet's second wife, whose sister Margaret was to make an unlikely but happy marriage with James Hogg? Another contributor, 'Mr Fairbairn', was John, brother of Pringle's university friend James Fairbairn from Legerwood, Bewickshire. John Fairbairn, younger by five years than Pringle, was at this time teaching at Bruce's Academy in Newcastle-upon-Tyne.

John Fairbairn had read medicine from 1812 to 1815 at Edinburgh University, without taking his degree. In 1813 Pringle had written a light-hearted letter to James as 'His Worship the Lord Provost', typical as a former fellow student's little joke, and by 1818 he was corresponding with John, who was to join him in South Africa, to become inextricably linked with him in the central events of his struggles there. John Fairbairn was a keen versifier and his poems, admired by Pringle, found their way into print in South Africa. Several were published in the Christmas annual, *Friendship's Offering*, Pringle was to edit in his last years in England.

The handsome folio volumes of *Albyn's Anthology* must have made their mark among lovers of music and Scottish tradition rather than in the wider world of literature. Pringle's songs – the other two are 'O sweet is she who looks on me', which Campbell noted, in 1818, to have been 'expressly written for this work by the original ingenious projector, the late editor of what is now entitled *Blackwood's Magazine*' (it was later published as 'The Dark-Haired Maid') and 'O lovely Mary', later titled 'Mary of Glenfyne'. The latter was disowned at first by Pringle, who scored out his name in the copy of the volume he presented to his sister Mary. As well as the dedication 'To Mrs Williams from her affectionate brother, Tho. Pringle, Cape of Good Hope, Oct. 1st, 1824' he wrote in the book, still in her collateral descendants' possession, in place of his name: 'The Revd. Mr Campbell, altered by T.P.' He published it nevertheless in his *Ephemerides* (1828) and it appears in his posthumous *Poetical Works* (1839). Alexander Campbell was never ordained though described as a church musician. This clerical namesake has not been identified.

All three are very pleasing and certainly 'pathetic' in the old sense. 'I'll bid my heart be still' was written shortly after the Battle of Waterloo, fought on 18 June 1815, and mourns 'the untimely and lamented fall of a distinguished officer, in that sanguinary conflict'. The Air to which it was sung was the ancient 'Farewell, ye fading flowers'.

His sonnet written in 1813 and published in *The Autumnal Excursion* 'To Sir Thomas Graham (Lord Lynedoch) on his return from Spain, March 1813' is another inspired by the wars against Napoleon.

The ills of old Scotland at the hands of the Southron still aroused him. 'The Banks of Cayle, or, the Maid of Lerdan's Lament' is sung by the lady of Corbet Tower, still standing near Morebattle. Edward I forced her, the last of her line, into marriage with his knight Warwick, her lover, 'the gallant Lord of Yair' having been killed at Biggar. It reappeared in *The Autumnal Excursion* as 'Lament of the Captive Lady' but shorn of its lilting chorus, which places it even more precisely where Thomas must have heard the traditional tale from old John Turnbull, the shepherd, or another who kept the folk memory alive:

O bonny grows the broom on Blaikla knowes
And the birk on Lerdan vale
And green are the hills o' the milk-white ewes
By the briery banks of Cayle.

William Hay, in his Pringle biography and poetry collection of 1912, annotated the poem: 'The song was omitted from the 1839 edition, but I have inserted it to show that the sentiments expressed in South Africa animated the poet from his youth up.'[23] These 'sentiments' inform the last two of the 13 stanzas:

And Edward, Scotland's deadly foe,
Has pledged my captive hand
To him who wrought my kindred's woe
And seized my father's land!

But though the treacherous Tyrant's yoke
My country still must bear,
A Scottish maid his power shall mock –
He cannot rule despair!

His own struggle against what he saw as a 'treacherous Tyrant's yoke' in South Africa, lay ahead and he had to go through his own baptism of fire, and be tempered in the process, while putting the romantic, tragic dream of old Scotland and 'Blaikla knowes' behind him.

NOTES

[1] Crockett, W.S., *Footsteps of Scott* (1905), p. 26.
[2] Pringle (1838), p. xxix.
[3] *The Cape,* 13 January 1922, p. 22. LP, Fairbairn Papers, 1, 11.
[4] Morton to Pringle, 4 November 1813, EUL MSS Gen. 1790, no. 90. Morris, p. 42.
[5] Pringle (1838), p. xix.
[6] Story, pp. 5–6.
[7] *The Cape,* 13 January 1922, p. 22.
[8] Morris, p. 35.
[9] *The Cape,* 20 January 1922, p. 22.
[10] Morris, p. 59, n. 2.
[11] Constable, T., *Archibald Constable and his Literary Correspondents*, 3 vols (1873), vol. 2, p.175. Morris, p. 60.
[12] Baillie, Joanna, *The Family Legend: a Tragedy* (1810). Baillie to Pringle, 12.3.1828, Leeds University Library, Brotherton Library, 2488.
[13] McCrie, Thomas, *The Life of Rev. Thomas McCrie by his Son* (1840), p. 228.
[14] Pringle (1838), xxvi.
[15] Rogers, Charles, *The Modern Scottish Minstrel, or the Songs of Scotland in the past Half Century*, 6 vols (1855), vol. 6, p. 131; Chambers, Robert, *The Scottish Songs, Collected and Illustrated,* 2 vols (1829), vol. 2, p. 256.
[16] *The Cape,* 13 January 1922, p. 22.
[17] *The Cape,* 20 January 1922, p. 22. LP 1, 11.
[18] Hogg to Pringle, 1 February 1819, Bodl. MS Montagu 1.4.260. Morris, p. 55.
[19] Hogg, James, *Altrive Tales* (1832), p. lxvii. Morris, p. 54.
[20] Story, p. 34; Morris, p. 55.
[21] Pringle (1966), p. xxvii.
[22] *Scots Magazine,* 17 (January 1817).
[23] Pringle to Fairbairn, 5 October 1825. Vigne (2011), p. 252, LP, Fairbairn Papers, 1, 84.
[24] Campbell, Alexander, *Albyn's Anthology* … , 2 vols (1816, 1818), vol. 1, p. 41. Morris, pp. 57, 58.
[25] Campbell, A., vol. 1, title page.
[26] Hay, W., *Thomas Pringle, his Life, Times and Poems* (1912), p. 135.
[27] Baillie, Joanna, *The Family Legend: a Tragedy* (1810). Baillie to Pringle, 12.3.1828, Leeds University Library, Brotherton Library, 2488.
[28] McCrie, Thomas, *The Life of Rev. Thomas McCrie by his Son* (1840), p. 228.
[29] Pringle (1838), xxvi.

3
Edinburgh

At the Flood

Among Thomas Pringle's wide Edinburgh circle in his years at Register House, James Hogg, already famous in Scotland and beyond as the Ettrick Shepherd, was probably the most active in his interest, albeit with side effects that must have given Pringle much pain. To have published the 'Letter to Mr R. S****'and attributed it to the most celebrated living English poet of the time was the first such injury. Another was to claim the credit for the major step Pringle took the year after *The Poetic Mirror* had appeared. Pringle's love of literature and the antiquarian knowledge he had acquired through his work for Thomas Thomson encouraged him in forming a plan to found and edit a new journal of literature and politics. It would include antiquarianism, a new interest much advanced by Scott.

Since the great days of the Scottish Enlightenment, when the economist Adam Smith and the historian David Hume were household names in Europe, Edinburgh had become a major centre of publishing and printing. Its journals, above all the Whig *Edinburgh Review*, set a new standard for literary and political analysis and debate, with poets as heirs to Robert Burns and a poet and novelist Walter Scott, a colossus of early nineteenth-century literature. It is all the more remarkable that an obscure young clerk with no grand connections should bring back to Edinburgh and Britain a major competitor of the *Edinburgh Review* to be published by William Blackwood, a Tory bookseller of great ambition.

Pringle came together, somehow, with the unlikely figure of James Cleghorn, a former Berwickshire farmer who had become editor of Constable's *Farmer's Magazine*, working also as an actuary and accountant, with business interests in the insurance field. Like Pringle he was incurably lame and could walk only with crutches. They were an improbable pair. Robert Pearse Gillies, Pringle's contemporary and an impecunious would-be man of letters like himself, wrote:

> Among the Shepherd's acquaintances and cronies from the Forest was the late Thomas Pringle, author of divers meritorious poems, a young man of excellent literary tact, and of most amiable disposition, mild, persevering, patient and industrious, on the strength principally of his own patience [and] fortitude without fortune, determined to publish a new Edinburgh magazine.[1]

Cleghorn he describes as 'a burly man with a strong voice and very dictatorial manner'. Other than having come from a tenant farming background to the battleground of early nineteenth-century literary Edinburgh they had only one thing in common: their lameness. Even here Gillies found them opposites, 'Pringle skipping briskly about on crutches; his friend, I think, seldom moved from his chair.'

By what must have seemed good fortune at the time, the bookseller William Blackwood, a man of high ambitions, strong will and excellent contacts, had the same idea and took to Pringle and his plan as soon as it was put to him. Hogg, ever the Munchausen-like imposter, for all his real achievements, claimed that:

> I had the honour of being the beginner, and almost sole instigator of that celebrated. work, *Blackwood's Magazine*, but from the time that Pringle had taken in Cleghorn as a partner I declined all connection with it, farther than as an occasional contributor.[2]

Pringle must often have had to scotch this particular unwarranted fancy of the Ettrick Shepherd's. In a letter to William Jerdan, his fellow editor from Roxburghshire, he wrote in his London years:

> As to Hogg's being the projector of *Blackwood's Mag.*, he is mistaken; at least I am sure Mr Cleghorn and I were the persons who proposed it to Mr Blackwood, and concocted the whole matter. But it is likely enough that Hogg might have had a similar idea in his head previously, for it was a project we had been talking of in literary parties at James Gray's, Grieve's, Wilson's &c., for a year or two before it actually started. Hogg and Wilson and Gray were among the earliest contributors, but the scheme as far as it was realized in the first six numbers (which were Whiggish) was mine.[3]

The letter gives us a glimpse of Pringle's social life, with the friends of the respected James Gray (he declined the editorship of Constable's *Edinburgh Magazine* in years to come), of John Grieve, poet, and Hogg's friend and collaborator, and the larger than life John Wilson, who was to join with Hogg, John Gibson Lockhart and Blackwood in Pringle's later humiliation. It suggests also that Pringle saw the projected magazine as a vehicle for Whig ideas, a scheme that was not to be realized. Blackwood's *Edinburgh Monthly Magazine* under Pringle and Cleghorn was a serious, scholarly publication which research has shown to have been a satisfactory publishing venture in commercial terms. After a detailed analysis of the sales figures for each of the first six issues, Patricia Morris summed up: 'It is thus impossible to accept the legend that the magazine was a faltering concern under poor editorship, until Lockhart and Wilson salvaged it.'[4]

Nor is it true, as even the *Oxford Dictionary of National Biography* (2004) entry for Pringle asserts, that, 'disappointed with his editors' lack of inspiration and commissioning zeal Blackwood dismissed them.'[5]

The lengthy and, to the uninvolved reader, tedious correspondence between Blackwood and his first editors, with the belligerent but businesslike Cleghorn doubtless taking the lead for his side, contains much evidence of Blackwood's attempts to get rid of Cleghorn, towards whom he felt strong antipathy, and to keep Pringle on as sole editor. Blackwood did assert that he had procured most of the material in the first four issues, a claim he would scarcely have made if the magazine was 'a meek and mild miscellany', 'a weak and washy production' (Margaret Oliphant, Blackwood's historian), 'weak and unpromising' (S.C. Hall) or 'as limping as its editors' (A.L. Strout).[6] Hogg wrote merely of the disagreement between publisher and editors:

> I received a letter from Mr Blackwood [in July 1817] soliciting my return to Edinburgh, and
> when I arrived there I found that he and his two redoubted editors had gone to loggerheads,
> and instead of arguing the matter face to face, they were corresponding together at the rate
> of about a sheet an hour.[7]

When its crisis came that same month, Blackwood, who delighted in what he called in his heavy Scots accent 'my maa-gaz'n', hence *Blackwood's* sobriquet during its 160-year run, 'Maga', wrote to a London agent to inform him that he had been 'obliged to resolve upon stopping the Magazine with No 6'.[8] He had, he reported to Messrs Baldwin, Cradock & Co. in July 1817 entered into

> a negotiation with Mr Pringle, the editor, whom I wished to retain, both on account of
> personal friendship, and that I expected he would soon become much more useful when he
> had more experience and when the editorial duty devolved on himself alone. ... Instead,
> however, of Mr Pringle acting in the friendly way he had professed, he joined Cleghorn.

Blackwood found it 'most vexatious stopping the magazine which was doing so well'. He reassured his agents that he had ready in the wings a new editor, 'a gentleman of first-rate talents by which I will begin a new work of a far superior kind'. Not that he thought ill of the work in hand: 'I shall take good care to have the two numbers we are yet to publish equal, if not superior to, the preceding ones.'

Pringle had clearly sacrificed a promising career with Blackwood out of loyalty to his co-editor, Cleghorn, whom he must have felt was in the right in Cleghorn's quarrels with Blackwood, which seem mostly to have been about Blackwood's constant interference in the editorial process and their financial arrangements with him.

The quarrels went on, both sides had recourse to arbitrators – Pringle and Cleghorn's was the able George Combe, Edinburgh Writer to the Signet (or solicitor, in the English legal system) and later a major authority on the new and popular, but all too evanescent, science of phrenology. Pringle was later, in 1823, to send him two Bushman skulls from South Africa, for the study of character rather than for promoting the 'scientific racism' which involved describing the Khoikhoi as 'the nearest approximation to the lower animals',[9] a bogus 'scientific' judgment which would have horrified Pringle.

Arbitration could not reconcile the determined and devious Blackwood with the stubborn and demanding Cleghorn, however. The editors eventually received a small settlement from Blackwood.

Nowhere does Blackwood specify any objections to the content of Nos 1 to 6. It has been assumed that the amount of Whig material was anathema to the high Tory Blackwood, who hoped that it would prove a counterblast to the dominating Whig journal, *The Edinburgh Review*, begun in 1802 by a brilliant coterie: Henry Brougham, Francis Horner, Francis Jeffrey, second editor after a year by its originator, the Revd Sydney Smith. What Blackwood thought when the first issue of his own magazine opened with a eulogistic obituary of Francis Horner is unrecorded.

One of those who might have been expected to ridicule his predecessors' efforts was the other half of those 'gentlemen of first-rate talents', John Gibson Lockhart. In fact, Lockhart said only, in his monumental life of his father-in-law Sir Walter Scott, that Pringle was 'for a time Editor of *Blackwood's Magazine'*, that 'the publisher and he had different politics, quarrelled and parted'.[10]

It becomes clear that the abuse of the first editors of *Blackwood's* was uttered by writers who were not on the scene when it was being produced. A study of Lockhart, using contemporary sources, however, pronounced that Pringle:

> a young Borderer who had been a clerk in the Register House, had real merits … He was a friend not only of Hogg (whom he had helped with the *Poetic Mirror*), but of Will Laidlaw, whom he promptly added to the staff of the magazine, hoping thereby to bring in Scott as an occasional, perhaps a regular, contributor. While Scott could never be induced to write for the magazine, he more than once supplied it with very valuable material.[11]

Laidlaw was given by Pringle, 'a Teviotdale man and an old acquaintance … the care of the *Chronicle department*'[12] wrote Lockhart. The son of a Selkirkshire farmer who had employed the young Hogg as a shepherd, Laidlaw had introduced Hogg to Scott, whose steward, in 1817, and amanuensis for the novels of 1819–20 Laidlaw became. His work for Blackwood ceased with the end of Pringle's editorship and 'Maga' losing its Whig content. 'On the retirement of [Pringle] … and the magazine assuming a high Tory character, Laidlaw's Whig feelings induced him to renounce the alliance', with the approval of Scott who, though a staunch Tory, had 'no kindness for Blackwood personally'.

By whatever means it was gained, Scott's most valuable contribution was the information on Gypsies, much of which, too ill to write down himself, he dictated to Pringle in some form. 'Notes concerning the Scottish Gypsies' appeared in the April, June and September 1817 issues. There has been much debate about the authorship of these 30 pages. The allegation by most who accepted Blackwood's version of events, which discredited Pringle, has been that Pringle edited Scott's dictated words and published them. Pringle's authorship, using Scott's information is as likely.

In his introduction to the 1829 edition of *Guy Mannering,* however, written when he was no longer 'the Great Unknown' but the author of the Waverley novels, Scott revealed that 'the prototypes of the principal characters in the book'. Meg Merrilies, the Amazonian Gypsy woman was based on 'Jean Gordon, an inhabitant of the village of Kirk Yetholm in the Cheviot hills, adjoining the English border', stories of whom Scott had heard from his father and grandfather. He remembered in his early childhood seeing Madge Gordon, the supposed grand-daughter of Jean. 'of whom an impressive account is given in the same article *(Blackwood's,* vol. 1, p. 56) *but not by the present writer*'[13] [my italics]. If not by Scott, the passage about Madge Gordon must have been contributed by Pringle, most of it quoted from 'a letter of a friend who for many years enjoyed frequent and favourable opportunities of observing the characteristic peculiarities of the Yetholm tribes'.[14] The Yetholm schoolmaster's son, Robert Story, among Pringle's friends, had these opportunities, growing up in Yetholm as he did.

Pringle wrote in a third-person footnote that the Spaewife of his eponymous poem blended the features of the gypsies of the same name and vocation. ... well known to him in his boyhood – Madge Gordon, grand-daughter of the famous Jean Gordon, the proto-type of Meg Merrilies of whom a description was given in the first number of *Blackwood's Magazine*, which has recently had the honour of being quoted by Sir Walter Scott in his intro-duction to the tale of Guy Mannering. .. the younger Madge Gordon may possibly be still alive.[15]

Story recalled that 'every week she paid my father a visit for her *awmous* [alms] when I was a little boy, and I looked upon Madge with no common degree of awe and terror'. Alan Lang Strout, in his detailed study of the whole affair, is contemp-tuous of Pringle's role as editor, yet described these notes on the Scottish Gypsies as 'perhaps the most important of all in the six numbers'.[16]

The savaging happened in the first issue of *Blackwood's* edited by Blackwood in 1817 and succeeding years, with Wilson and Lockhart as his unnamed associates, and Pringle was one of many under attack. By replacing Pringle and Cleghorn with these two, Blackwood saw to it that his first editors' reputations would be ruined, by ridicule rather than by serious denunciation. He appointed these two young men who had treated, as he wished, his Princes Street offices as yet another club.

John Gibson Lockhart, with his Oxford 'first', sophisticated manners and pene-trating intellect – handsome, sardonic and a merciless critic, was a perfect companion for John Wilson. Poet and friend of the Lake Poets, Wilson was a prolific writer and as ferocious a critic as Lockhart. He was a giant, physically and in his personality, but never a gentle one. With a brilliant Glasgow and Oxford academic career behind him, a briefless barrister, he had suddenly found himself in urgent need of money, which Blackwood was willing and able to provide. Both were Tories, both felt themselves well above the common herd of men, not least the Scottish educated classes, even those maintaining the high traditions of the Scottish Enlightenment.

Sadly for Pringle and, as it turned out, for Hogg, both Wilson and Lockhart revelled in sarcasm and contumely, not sparing even their friends. Wilson grotesquely and hurtfully caricatured James Hogg:

a stout country lout, with a bushel of hair on his shoulders that had not been raked for months, enveloped in a coarse plaid impregnated with tobacco, with a prodigious mouthful of unmeasurable tusks, and a dialect that sets all conjecture at defiance.[17]

This was in the days of Wilson's pseudonymous role for *Blackwood's* as 'Christo-pher North', a character in the 'Noctes Ambrosianae' series in the journal, where biting wit verged on the abusive.

The first targets for their scorn were, however, Pringle and Cleghorn. Lock-hart told how they combined to fashion the tool that was to do so much damage when it appeared in the October 1817 issue. It was a satirical pseudo-Biblical spoof, in the form of a fable about animals, called 'The Translation from an Ancient Chaldean Manuscript'. Universally known as the Chaldee MS, Lockhart wrote to a friend that it had excited prodigious noise here – it was the sole subject of conversation for two months. ... Hogg, the Ettrick Shepherd set up an attack on Constable, the bookseller, respecting some private dealings of his with Blackwood. Wilson and I liked the idea of introducing the whole panorama of the town in that sort of dialect. We drank punch one night from eight till eight in the morning, Blackwood being by with anecdotes, and the result is before you.[18]

It has been calculated that they added 140 verses to Hogg's original 40 and the venom and scorn were of their making. The result told the story of Blackwood's conflict with Pringle and Cleghorn and of their defection to his hated rival Constable, and brought in a large cast of the characters thronging Edinburgh's cultural life, mostly held up to ridicule.

Pringle and Cleghorn appear in the first passage:

And I turned my eyes and behold two beasts came from the land of the borders of the South; and when I saw them I wondered with great admiration. The one beast was like unto a lamb and the other like unto a bear, and they had wings on their heads; their faces also were like the faces of men, the joints of their legs were like the polished cedars of Lebanon, and their feet like the feet of horses preparing to go forth into battle; and they arose and came onward over the face of the earth, and they touched not the ground as they went.[19]

The lameness of the Lamb and the Bear is mocked several times. While 'the Crafty' (Constable's sobriquet before the Chaldee MS) spoke 'it seemed as if he trembled and was afraid of the beasts and the staves wherewith they skipped'. Pringle could not repeat his successful Gypsies article, they parodied, Pringle the Lamb saying: 'Lo! My legs are weary and the Egyptians which were wont to carry me are clean gone and wherewithal shall I go forth to make war upon the man whose name is Ebony'. The Crafty complains at having Cleghorn as one of his editors: 'They have given me a horn which is empty and a horn which hath no feet', and more of the same.

The story of Pringle and Cleghorn's move from Blackwood to Constable is told entirely to the advantage of Blackwood and the Tories. Blackwood is 'Ebony', Constable 'the Crafty', Scott 'the great magician who dwelleth in the old fastness, hard by the river Jordan, which is by the border'. Scott is spared gibes at his lameness. Many who were pilloried were easily recognized, as were those who were favoured, like Wilson 'the Leopard' and Scott. Lockhart was depicted, accurately, as 'from a far country [Oxford], the Scorpion, which delighteth to sting the faces of men, that he might sting sorely the countenances of the man which is crafty, and of the two beasts.'

Hogg's somewhat rough, peasant manner, fondness for whisky and his prominent front teeth were laughed at. He was 'the great wild beast from the forest of Lebanon, and he roused up his spirits, whetting his dreadful tusks for the battle'. Yet Gillian Hughes depicts Hogg as a man of good appearance, well dressed, and socially at ease despite the class difference which to some extent made him more acceptable to such as Wilson and Lockhart than the likes of the middle-class Pringle.

Strout found the Chaldee MS 'well worth reading today' and the first chapter in particular, which 'starts amusingly with a narrative of the recent quarrel between Blackwood and his former editors'. Most readers today can only wonder why the

Chaldee MS, as Gillies recalled, 'raised such a commotion in Edinburgh, that nothing like it was on record in our literary annals. ... Never had there been such an uproar made about a scrap of literary *babillage* since the days of Jonathan Swift, and scarcely then'.[20] Lockhart and Wilson went into hiding, Hogg on his farm was too frightened to come to Edinburgh, Blackwood scarcely dared to leave his house and was assaulted the one time he did so. There were libel actions, even a duel.

Pringle sued 'William Blackwood, bookseller in Edinburgh' for damages, with results that are not known. In 'a profane mimicry of the language of the Holy Scriptures'[21]

> (Blackwood) had done everything in his power to cast ridicule on the person of the pursuer, to hold up to ridicule those personal infirmities under which, without any fault of his, the pursuer has the unhappiness to labour; to degrade and vilify his character as a man of integrity, to outrage his feelings and injure him in private and public esteem; and to deprive him of that reputation to which alone he must be indebted for the means of his subsistence, and that of his family.

Pringle sent the April 1818 issue of the *Edinburgh Magazine* to his great friend and later close collaborator in South Africa, John Fairbairn, then teaching in Newcastle-upon-Tyne. Exhibiting his lamb-like qualities of those years and a degree of *amour propre,* Pringle wrote, with it:

> B. has been sent to Coventry since you left Edinb. by his brethren of the trade. He has indeed been so completely degraded that we hesitate about pushing forward our prosecution lest it appear like tormenting a dead dog.[22]

The dog was very far from dead. Blackwood and his friends were soon back on their feet and more than capable of depriving Pringle of his reputation as editor and man of letters. In their histories of *Blackwood's*, Mrs Oliphant in 1897 and F.D. Tredrey in 1954 perpetuated the judgment that the *Monthly Magazine* was

> a jumbled, meek and mild miscellany and when the proprietor tried to strengthen its second number, the Editors complained piteously of interference. The magazine limped on its way through the remaining four issues, recording births, marriages, deaths, markets, corn fairs, village wisdom, civilizing Greek drama and speculating of the wonders of animal migration. ... The sales never exceeded more than 2000 copies per month,[23]

To appreciate the falseness of this condemnation one need only realize that the contents of the renamed volume 2 and its successors, edited by the Leopard and the Scorpion, contained very much the same sort of mix – and many articles commissioned by or submitted to their predecessors. The new editors' injection of lethal criticism and personal abuse gave *Blackwood's* notoriety but, after that first issue – reprinted, without the Chaldee MS – did not, as Dr Morris has shown, sell more copies than it had done under the Lamb and the Bear. Blackwood also saw fit to reprint those first six issues and named the volume *Blackwood's Edinburgh Monthly Magazine*, though the title is usually taken as beginning only with Lockhart's and Wilson's editorship.

What 'family' had Pringle to provide for, as his libel writ claimed? On 18 July

1817, the day after he and Cleghorn had contracted with Constable to take over the aged and ailing *Scots Magazine* under a new name, the banns were called in St Cuthbert's Church in Edinburgh for his marriage to Margaret Brown, 37-year-old spinster daughter of the late William Brown, farmer, of Papple, East Lothian. They were married, with 'James Gray of the High School' as witness, next day, neither at St Cuthbert's nor the Browns' own parish church at Whittinghame. In the November 1817 issue of Constable's *Edinburgh Magazine,* which Pringle and Cleghorn had edited since September, appeared the notice: 'July 19, At Edinburgh by the Reverend Henry Garnock, Mr Thomas Pringle to Margaret, daughter of the late William Brown, farmer, of Papple, East Lothian.'

Garnock had served as minister at the Canongate Kirk since 1815. Was the announcement made to substantiate Pringle's claim that he was a family man when libelled by his successors at *Blackwood's*?.

A lost, undated letter quoted by Ritchie tells us, however, that, despite his employment by both Blackwood and Constable, and his marriage, he was living as a bachelor, and as poor as ever, though the word has its non-monetary sense:

> I am in a strange and curious state but I cannot explain it except in generalities. I am supposed to be prosperous and getting forward in the world, and yet I am one of the poorest men I know. I have no regularity of hours and am often out all night, and yet I am perfectly sober and given to no dissipation. I am well known to half the people in Edinburgh, and might spend all my time in pleasant company if I chose, and yet have not a friend in it – at least a *male* friend. I am the editor of two magazines, which are direct rivals. I am supposed to be a bachelor, and to live in an attic four stories high, with a cat on my mantel-piece, and yet I have a house with a street door, and though not a wife in it, one ready to take there as soon as I am able.[24]

Margaret did not join him, at 6 Drummond Street, for six months – Margaret, nine years older, with no dowry, and Thomas, poor, unqualified and crippled but a published poet and joint editor of Constable's new journal. The future looked brighter, though the timing of his marriage and his unlikely choice of a bride suggests a tendency to precipitate action not always to his best advantage, which so affected his later life and career.

His toil was harassing nevertheless. Josiah Conder tells us that 'for some time before and after his engagement with Blackwood Mr Pringle edited the *Star* Newspaper, then almost the only liberal paper in Scotland.'[25] The Whig-inclined twice-weekly *Edinburgh Star* launched in 1808 by the Aikman brothers, publishers of Hogg's unsuccessful literary weekly, *The Spy,* was edited from 1817 by Pringle. *The Star* had 'a not unmeritable career' and was 'quoted respectfully in the Glasgow papers'. Under Pringle it 'took pride in its law reports'. Eclipsed by *The Scotsman,* founded in 1817, it was absorbed by the *Edinburgh Observer* in 1825.

Perhaps it was getting this paper out that kept Pringle up all night, as he complained. More demanding still was his and Cleghorn's struggle to make a success of *The Edinburgh Magazine and Literary Miscellany, a New Version of the Scots Magazine,* which they edited for Archibald Constable from October 1817 until March 1819, longer than their 12–month contract had stipulated. Their appointment was conditional on their achieving monthly sales of 2000 copies within twelve months.

Constable's motive was largely to outdo his rival Blackwood, and Pringle, at a half-way stage, felt that they were holding their own. He sent his friend Fairbairn the June 1818 issue and wrote: 'Our next will be better. The enemy still go on with a great deal of *birr* and ability, but we expect to turn them out at length.'[26] 'Maga' did the turning out ten months later and survived, much changed, until 1980.

Pringle's and Cleghorn's *Edinburgh Magazine* took second place to the jewel in Constable's crown, the *Edinburgh Review*, and competing also with *Blackwood's Magazine*, lacked contributors of top quality. An exception was Hazlitt, who sent Constable a telling letter regretfully refusing a book review for fear of losing his footing with Jeffrey of the *Edinburgh Review* (he sent them instead a notice of Benjamin West's picture 'Remarks on Mr West's picture of death on the Pale Horse and on the descriptive catalogue which accompanies it', which appeared in the issue of December 1817). Constable solicited material for his new journal but Hazlitt clearly favoured the old, despite its high-handed way with him. Eventually he agreed to send a monthly article, for a fee that was high even by Constable's generous standards, and a heavy charge against the journal.

Hazlitt, arguably the most brilliant essayist of the age, made some memorable contributions to the *Edinburgh Magazine*: 'On the question of whether Pope was a poet', 'On the effects of war and taxes', 'Thoughts on Taste' all appeared in 1818, and 'Thoughts on Taste' Part 2, after Pringle and Cleghorn had handed over the editorship to the Revd Robert Morehead. There were lesser pieces too: 'On respectable people', 'On fashion' and 'On nicknames', also all in 1818. The magazine reviewed favourably Hazlitt's *Characters in Shakespeare's Plays*, which the *Quarterly* criticized harshly, and praised his *Lectures on the English poets*, for his treatment of Wordsworth. Hazlitt was not always favoured: the reviewer, perhaps Pringle, defended Thomas Campbell against Hazlitt's strictures (July 1818).

Throughout this period Hazlitt was the butt of sneering hostility from Wilson and Lockhart in *Blackwood's*. 'Hazlitt cross-questioned' in August 1818 by Lockhart at his most aggressive and personally insulting. Hazlitt sued for libel and won damages. *Blackwood's* thus kept up its early reputation for what Hogg called its 'deevilry'. With the Chaldee MS in the October 1817 issue Wilson and Lockhart had also published the libellous 'Letter to the Lord High Constable, from Mr Dinmont', which, since it mocked yet again the transfer of Blackwood's first editors to Constable, Pringle had included in his claim for damages. The first of its contributions on 'The Cockney School of Poetry', mercilessly attacked Leigh Hunt. Later studies battered Hazlitt and poor John Keats who, 'was killed by one critique', as Byron put it in *Don Juan* (Canto IX): ''Tis strange the mind, that very fiery particle, Should let itself be snuffed out by an article.'

The mauling of Pringle and Cleghorn by Wilson and Lockhart continued. The pretext was a laudatory article about Hogg, whose friendship with Pringle continued to prove both a boon and a curse. The author is unknown but may well have been Pringle, whose hand can be detected in the lyrical passages about Ettrick Forest and Yarrow and in some familiar favourite themes, such as the sufferings of old Scotland at the hands of the English and the high virtues of the Covenanters.

Hogg and Pringle were specially derided by Wilson (or Lockhart) in two linked

'Letters to Mr James Hogg', the second by 'Timothy Tickler', an elderly, strongly Tory character based on Wilson's uncle, Robert Sym, in whose house 'Southside' in Gough Square the 'Maga' contributors often met. The letters poured scorn on both Hogg – for his dress, lack of education, vanity and his claims to greatness (though 'a man of genius') – and on the writer of the offending article, who was thought to be an 'old gentleman' with no Latin or Greek:

> It would seem that the Writer had sat down with the intention of trying to show how ridiculous he could make both you and himself. ... the Essayist's efforts upon himself have been crowned with success... he has made himself the subject of very general and sincere merriment.[27]

It was at this time (February, March 1818) that Pringle's libel action against *Blackwood's* was to be fought. The letter from Timothy Tickler ends thus:

> P.S. At a party at Southside last night a young gentleman gave the following toast: Messrs Cleghorn and Pringle, and the Trial by Jury

The point is lost to us today but it is as if it was felt that not enough hurt had been caused by the 'Letters' and the names of the editors of the *Edinburgh Magazine* must be brought in, since the 'old gentleman's' anonymity had been preserved.

The *Edinburgh Review* and *Blackwood's* profited mightily by their merciless ways but this was not Pringle's style and Hogg's prediction to Blackwood of Maga's supremacy was borne out: 'the original part of C's will be nothing enriched by his editors and that yours will suffer slight loss by the change'.[28] He continued, cryptically, 'Crafty will have the advantage at first. He has a number of *great guns* about him. .. but who will disdain to write for a two shilling magazine?' It was noticeable that Wilson and Lockhart did not disdain to proclaim their pride in securing Pringle and Cleghorn's writers. They listed in their first issue 96 articles in hand or in preparation, 'among whom we are happy to announce almost all the distinguished contributors to the late Edinburgh Monthly Magazine'.[29]

Despite Pringle's tenacity and Cleghorn's arguments over sales and payment, reminiscent of the dispute with Blackwood, though without the latter's malice, the end of their editorship became inevitable. Mrs Grant of Laggan, observing the Edinburgh social and literary scene, noted in her memoirs, 'The Revd Mr Morehead has undertaken Constable's magazine, the Crafty having as usual quarrelled with the editors and dismissed them.'[30]

Cleghorn had the *Farmer's Magazine* and his growing insurance interests to fall back on but for Pringle there was only his place in Register House, which Thomson had kept for him. Constable's *Edinburgh Magazine* failed under Pringle and Cleghorn and had an intermittent and hesitant run under their successors but had published some gems nevertheless. Here in profusion was Hazlitt, not only the most penetrating of 19th-century critics but certainly the most readable. Here too was Walter Scott's 'Jock o' Hazeldean', the first of its four stanzas having been learned by Pringle from his mother's singing and the rest added by Scott. It had appeared in the first volume of *Albyn 's Anthology,* with music supplied by Mary Pringle, but the *Edinburgh Magazine* made it a favourite of thousands.

Lady Grizel Baillie's memory was revived by Pringle in the April and May 1818 issues, with the quotation of extracts from 'the interesting memoir of her eventful and exemplary life'[31] left in manuscript by her daughter Lady Murray, as he footnoted her 'Lament' in his *Autumnal Excursion*. He acclaimed Lady Grizel as 'the patroness of the poet Thomson who was said to have been encouraged chiefly by her recommendation to try his fortune as a literary adventurer in London'. Grizel Baillie is barely remembered today except as someone who influenced both Allan Ramsay and James Thomson. She 'ought to have greater recognition today' wrote a contributor to the masterly *Scottish Literature in English and Scots* (2002), which in its 1069 pages finds no space to mention her promoter Thomas Pringle. The extracts from Lady Grizel's 'Lament': 'O the ewe-bughting's bonny' are quoted, presumably by Pringle, who wrote four of the five stanzas, in the article entitled 'Some particulars of the sufferings of the families of Polwarth and Jerviswood, prior to the Revolution of 1688, with extracts from Lady Grizel's narrative'.[32]

From Lincolnshire Pringle's university friend the Revd James Morton contributed, also in May 1819 but doubtless commissioned before that, 'Remarks on the Life and Political Services of the late Dr John Leyden'. Leyden's *Historical Account of Discoveries and Travels in Africa*, published by Constable in 1817, had already been reviewed. Other old associations produced 'Remarks on the plays on the passions by Joanna Baillie', showing Pringle's old interest still alive. *Scottish Literature,* quoted above, noted that 'she was admired by Scott, Lord Byron and others' and is now, with wonderful circumlocution, 'coming for serious reassessment' in the 'modem cultural context which scrutinizes issues of gender'.[33]

Pringle's own poems were published. 'O sweet is she that thinks on me' (a 'Highland song: Air Mo Nighead dhu'), which was 'written expressly for *Albyn's Anthology,* in the second volume of which will appear the original words and music, early next winter' (October 1817). Coleridge and Byron both appear, as does Keats, whose *Poems* were published in March 1817, paid for by himself, as Pringle was soon to do with *The Autumnal Excursion*.

Lockhart's attack on Keats, Leigh Hunt and Hazlitt in 'On the Cockney School of Poetry' appeared in *Blackwood's* in the autumn, and the *Quarterly Review* joined the chase, with its dismissal of *Hyperion* in 1819. Pringle's *Autumnal Excursion* was ignored rather than attacked by *Blackwood's*, but was favourably reviewed by Morehead's *Edinburgh Magazine,* in the month of *Blackwood's* derisive 'Letter to Mr James Hogg', Part 1. Who would have thought, Morehead's reviewer asked, that Pringle's poems 'could have proceeded from no other than a mind of great delicacy and refinement'? 'To Sir Thomas Graham (Lord Lynedoch) on his return to Spain, March 1813' is quoted in full ('this is very good') as is 'To a female relative'. Both would be well into the lower half of a modern reader's list of favourites. Fearing most critics might ignore so small a book, the reviewer went on 'We do not venture to speak of this as very great poetry, but perhaps it is something better … It grows directly from that inspiration which our poet so beautifully intimates when he says [quoting 32 lines from 'The Autumnal Excursion', including these]:

Nor shall the enthusiast dreams decay
Which charmed the long and lonely day,

When, wrapt in chequered Border cloak,
On Blaiklaw's ridge I watched the flock.
'Twas there amid the woodland wild,
A Fairy found the mountain child
And oped to its enchanted eye
Imagination's Paradise.

The reviewer's valediction, speaking for the journal, was some compensation for this well-meant yet faint praise:

We trust that Mr Pringle, who has just retired from an employment not very congenial to a poet (our readers must have perceived from this notice of his poems that he is no longer an Editor of the Journal) will now be visited by many more of these happy moods, and that his elegant genius will be at no loss for better and more suitable occasions for displaying itself.

Cold comfort for Pringle at his desk in Register House, copying manuscripts. Constable did pay both editors £250 after prolonged wrangling, but only in April 1820 when Pringle was on the high seas bound for the Cape of Good Hope.

The magazine continued under a succession of editors, with changes of name to *The New Scots Magazine* and *Scots Weekly* until it 'folded' in 1834, having survived Constable's undeserved bankruptcy and Scott's with it, in 1826. Scott, at 54, considered ways of finding the £120,000 to be paid and said, probably apocryphally, 'No, this right hand shall work it all off.'[34] The Crafty seems somehow to have jumped clear and was producing 'Constable's Miscellany' of books on literature, art and science the following year.

The *Farmer's Magazine* did go down in 1826 and Cleghorn went on to found the Scottish Provident Institution. There is no trace of any communication with Pringle despite their joint editorship and it remains a mystery that Pringle worked with him for so long, losing his business link with Blackwood thereby, though not, in the longer term, Blackwood's friendship.

Josiah Conder, a fellow editor in his London days and Congregational church hymn writer, in a biographical sketch preceding Pringle's posthumous *Narrative of a Residence in South Africa,* quoted Pringle's feelings at the end of his literary life in Edinburgh: 'My connexion with the journal had been prejudicial, rather than otherwise, to my views in life, and has given me, moreover, a decided aversion to literature, or at least to periodical literature'.[35] This from the man whose intense love of the poets comes through so clearly in 'The Autumnal Excursion'. Conder himself added:

His love of the country was not a sentiment of the fancy, but a craving of the heart after the native element of his tastes and affections; and, though one of the most social of human beings, the free desert, where 'man is distant but God is near', seems to have been more congenial to his spirit than the sickening warfare of envious competition and mercenary rivalry connected with a literary life.

James Hogg's words about him mark his unsuitability for the backstabbing and quarrelling he was to leave behind. In 1835, unaware of Pringle's death, he wrote to a mutual friend 'Compts. to kind-hearted, honest, pragmatical Pringle'.[36] Even the grudging Strout conceded 'he makes, on the whole, an attractive figure.' [37]

Dr Morris gave a detailed account of Cleghorn's successful later career in the insurance business, and wrote: 'Until his death in 1837 Cleghorn's life was as eventful as Pringle's'.[38] This must be a minority view: their later lives were as different as were their characters and personalities; one in the counting house, the other, as succeeding chapters will show, packed with action 'afar in the desert' and with participation in a great historical event at its end.

Though back copying documents in the Register Office he was not free of the febrile and underpaid literary life of Edinburgh and was still embroiled in legal action against both Blackwood and Constable. His major preoccupation, as Conder quoted him, was 'the consolatory prospect of re-uniting my father's family, which fortune had so widely dispersed, into one circle and society, in my immediate neighbourhood'.[39]

With the drudgery of producing the bi-weekly *Edinburgh Star* and the frenzy of editing first for Blackwood and then for Constable a monthly magazine of serious and wide-ranging content behind him, Pringle might have thought that ahead lay quiet, a hearth and home, more poetry and time for his family at large. His letter, written as he moved from Blackwood to Constable in late 1817, tells of his 'strange and curious state', of his bachelor life and hard work, yet with a wife and a house 'ready to take there as soon as I am able'.[40]

Margaret must have joined him at 6 Drummond Street at the end of 1817, perhaps early in 1818. The background to the marriage is scarcely known. The mother of the Pringles' Rennie cousins who accompanied them to the Cape in 1820 was born Brown and related to Margaret's family, her sons having been born at Westmains, near Papple. One James Brown, tenant of Westmains, sponsored five of Margaret's brothers and sisters at their baptisms. Margaret's address for the banns called at St Cuthbert's in Edinburgh was 27 Clyde Street: perhaps the couple met in Edinburgh through the family connexion. However it came about, the match seems an odd one, Margaret being 37 and with no dowry, and Thomas 28 and financially precarious.

If there was trouble it came early and was to do with Thomas's seeming lack of religious conviction. Story was called in as a peacemaker, and Margaret, whom Story's son called 'a somewhat morbid religionist',[41] received heartfelt advice from her husband's dearest friend.

> You are anxious, you are unhappy, when the idea of his being deficient in religious principle or feeling agitates your mind, and you obtrude the subject on him when necessary cares may occupy his attention. Now, my dear madam, this is not prudent.[42]

Story recalls later in the letter his loving intimacy with Pringle:

> I am ignorant as to whether there be anywhere in the world so much affectionate fidelity left. Never since we knew each other did a day or an hour of coldness interrupt the vehement exchange of friendly regard, and the profoundest secrets of our spirits, without hesitation and without fear, were deposited in each other's bosoms.

Pringle had longed for a close companion to replace what the absent Story had been to him in their student days and after. Margaret seems to have supplied this want. We have glimpses of her from his writing and from others in later years but there is no evidence to make one doubt his assertion that

> amid all my difficulties and harassing toil since my marriage … I have never for a single moment had reason to repent of my decision.[43]

He had married at a time when his future looked bright and he needed only a home to complete his happiness. 'I am in better health at present than I have enjoyed for many years', he wrote in an undated letter quoted by Leitch Ritchie.[44] 'The magazine at present is going on very prosperously.' And now, to complete the trio of 'health, competence and peace', he could enjoy the third, which 'I can confidently count upon at my own fireside, whatever may occur elsewhere', for Margaret had 'qualities which compensate to me a hundredfold the want of fortune'.

The second year of their marriage was as crowded as 1817 had been. But both 'competence' and 'peace' went to the wall, with the unremitting and ultimately unsuccessful struggle to establish Constable's *Edinburgh Magazine*, litigation against Blackwood after the public scandal of the Chaldee MS. and always the struggle for a better income, to support Margaret and himself, in Drummond Street. Story may have healed the rift over Thomas and Margaret's religious differences, but 'whatever may occur elsewhere' covered much unhappiness. The wounding gibes of Wilson and Lockhart contributed to it.

They were part of the continuing vendetta, four months after the Chaldee MS, by Wilson and Lockhart, with Hogg added to their victims. In the detail can be seen the malicious content of Edinburgh's 'periodical literature' which Pringle came to detest.

Pringle's and Hogg's friend James Gray was commissioned to produce a series of biographical articles about Hogg for the *Edinburgh Magazine*. 'The Life and Writings of James Hogg' ran from January to March 1818. *Blackwood's* went on the attack when the first article appeared, with a 'Letter to James Hogg' in February 1818 and continued in March with 'Letters of Timothy Tickler to Various Literary Characters. Letter II – to the Ettrick Shepherd'. The letters to Hogg on the 'Life and Writings' articles have a clear ring of Wilson at his most contemptuous and personally insulting about them. (A.L. Strout is undecided as to whether Wilson or Lockhart was the perpetrator.[45]) Poor Hogg was thus pilloried by a man thought to be his friend. He was further humiliated, on his own account, by Archibald Constable, who, he alleged, stepped in and stopped the fourth and final article in the 'Life and Writings' series.

Pringle and Cleghorn had confounded the Tory Blackwood by publishing a eulogy of Horner of the Whig *Edinburgh Review*, the very journal he was attempting to rival. This time they upset the Whig Constable by adulatory articles on Hogg, a major figure among the Tory writers in *Blackwood's*. Hogg's 4000-word riposte to Timothy Tickler was probably written for publication in *Blackwood's* but exists only in draft among his papers. It affects humour and a bantering tone but is the cry of a deeply injured man:

The truth is, Mr Tickler, envy is the leading trait of your character. – the prevalent passion that acts as a mainspring to every movement of your mind … you had this very powerful motive for the publication of these two letters. In the first place you saw that it was an attempt to place me in a light that you could not endure … in the second place you saw that the critical letters themselves were the best and most original things in Constable's magazine. Therefore it was a galling business to you in every respect, and so you determined to knock it on the head.[46]

Hogg defended the other victims of Timothy Tickler's 'spleen', specifically Jeffrey of the *Edinburgh Review,* James Gray (unnamed) and Pringle.

Pringle and Cleghorn had brought their libel action against Blackwood the previous month and Wilson confined his gibes at them to a reminder of their role in the Chaldee MS. He derided Gray for comparing Hogg favourably with Terence. Making a point lost to us today (were Pringle and Cleghorn thought to have fallen out? Or merely such an ill-assorted pair?), Wilson wrote:

There are no more points of resemblance between you and Terence than between a lamb and a bear and the very thought of you and Terence (were that gentleman still alive amongst us) sitting together over a bowl of punch at Young's is not more absurd than would be the herding together of the above-mentioned animals.[47]

The poet and playwright Publius Terentius Afer, originally a north African slave, had died in 159 BC. His famous line: *Homo sum humani nihil a me alienum puto* [I am a man. I consider nothing human alien to me.] seems to fit Pringle rather better than Hogg.

Hogg wrote affectionately to Pringle on 21 August 1818 apologizing yet again for his instigation of the Chaldee MS:

I am sorry to say that my hands have not been altogether clean of the literary persecution that has been raised against you and your friend for … I have been, as it were the beginner of the whole mischief.[48]

He made a stout defence of Pringle in the draft letter of 3 August 1818. Timothy Tickler had written in a letter published in July 1818: 'It amazes me that Mr Constable should have preferred Cleghorn and Pringle to Hugh Murray, the former Editor.' Hogg responded:

You know nothing of Mr Pringle if you suppose Hugh Murray superior to him in *taste and genius*. There are very few in the British empire with whom I would degrade Pringle by comparison. I am sorry that his circumstances have induced him to become a retailer of literary trifles, for which I think him in no way calculated … give Pringle time to consider a subject so as to mature it in his own mind, to amplify and correct it at pleasure, I know no man – not one – who can write with more beauty and elegance.[49]

He brought in another 'King Charles's head' – the claim that he had been the first to mention to Blackwood the idea of 'setting a magazine on foot',[50] though conceding that this was 'the consequence of a letter I had from Pringle.' He again dissociated himself from Cleghorn –

a self-important gabby kind of a body, rather ill-natured and impatient of opposition. In literature he is nothing save what Constable has made him.

He was critical of Pringle too for 'sticking Maggy Scott [the *Scots Magazine*?] and the law [his libel action against Blackwood], in which he has been ill-advised by proud, passionate people'. He condemned 'all persecution of Pringle as unjust and illiberal':

> Were it not that I am bound to support my publisher [Blackwood], who in a great measure supports me, I would spend every hour that I have to spare in assisting Pringle, and I am sorry, for his sake only, that casualties which he might have averted [the libel action] but could not, have thrown us into opposite scales.

The letter appears never to have to have been addressed or posted. It was not Hogg's custom to keep drafts of letters that he actually completed and dispatched, and it is not in Wilson's papers, though he would very probably have destroyed a letter so injurious to his *amour propre*.

Hogg's relationship with Pringle was a complex one in which the latter was the more sinned against. The confusion, an unhappy one for Pringle, over the 'Epistle to Mr R. S****' in the *Poetic Mirror*, Hogg's claim that he originated 'Maga', and most culpably the Chaldee MS seems not to have marred their friendship. In the Edinburgh days Hogg would write to Pringle as 'Tam', who was to prove a true friend at the end of their lives. He saw fit to ask Hogg's permission to reprint 'Epistle to Mr R. S****', which he took to be Hogg's copyright. In his reply Hogg warned his 'dear Tom' (in this instance), the less experienced author, of the risk he was taking:

> It is not however very fashionable to read poetry and high as I value the thing and I am sure I am right you must not be very sanguine. Pray do not forget Mickle and the authors of all the beautiful and original ballads in the Border Minstrelsy[51] [Scott's 1802–03 collection, the composers of the imitations among its ballads, already forgotten].

Hogg wrote 'I approve entirely of your plan' to include 'your beautiful poem', the 'Epistle', adding 'I hope the two affecting episodes are restored'. He again asserted his great admiration for the poem and quoted 'Mr Scott' as 'one of those few who gave it all due praise'.

The 'Epistle' was to appear, renamed, in the little book Pringle called *The Autumnal Excursion, or Sketches in Teviotdale: with Other Poems*. He found time to put it together and see it through the printer's. The book, which appeared in January 1819, was well received but brought in as little 'solid pudding', in his thirtieth year, as *The Institute* had done in his twenty-second.

It is a pleasing little collection, mostly sonnets and songs, to accompany the 'Autumnal Excursion' itself. When it came from the printer he was already back in Register House with Thomas Thomson, to whom he dedicated the book. Delicacy, refinement, 'we do not venture to speak of this as very great poetry', 'elegant genius'[52] – the *Edinburgh Magazine* review probably expressed the view of most readers.

The Autumnal Excursion gave momentary pleasure to Pringle at a time of despondency and dissatisfaction with the literary world of Edinburgh. He was soon to find a way out, for himself, and new lives for his family.

NOTES

1. Gillies, R.P., *Memoirs of a Literary Veteran*, 3 vols (1851), vol. 1, p. 231.
2. Hogg (1832) in Strout. Alan Lang, 'The "Noctes Ambrosianae" and James Hogg', *English Studies in Africa*, (January 1937).
3. Pringle to Jerdan, – April 1832. *Notes and Queries, a Medium of Inter-communication*, 3 November 1855. See also Morris, P., 'A Periodical Paternity Claim: Pringle v. Hogg', *English Studies in Africa*, 25.1 (1989).
4. Morris, p. 122.
5. Blackwood to —, 23 July 1817. Oliphant, Margaret, *Annals of a Publishing House: William Blackwood and his Sons, their Magazine and Friends*, 2 vols (1897), vol. 1, p.104. *Oxford Dictionary of National Biography*, 60 vols (2004), Thomas Pringle.
6. Oliphant, vol. I, p. 100. Hall, S.C, *Retrospect of a Long Life, from 1815 to 1883* (1883), p. 331. Strout (1950), p. 696.
7. Hogg (1832), p. lxxv.
8. Blackwood to Baldwin, Cradock & Co, 23 July 1817. Oliphant (1897), vol. I, pp. 104–05
9. Fabian, Ann, *The Skull Collectors* (2011), quoted in *The Times Literary Supplement*, 27.1.2012, p.8.
10. Lockhart, J.G., *The Life of Sir Walter Scott, Bart.*, (1844 ed.), p. 640n.
11. Carswell, Donald, *Sir Walter Scott, a Four Part Study in Biography* (1930), pp. 226–7.
12. Lockhart (1844 ed.), p. 346.
13. Scott, Sir Walter, *Guy Mannering* (1819, 1860 ed.), vol. 3, p. 15.
14. *Ibid.*
15. Pringle (1838), p. 214.
16. Strout, A.L. *James Hogg's, Forgotten Satire, John Paterson's Mare* (New York, Publications of the Modern Language Society of America, 52 (1937, 1967 ed.), p. 432.
17. *Blackwood's*, vol. 10 (August-December 1821), p. 44.
18. Lang, Andrew, *The Life and Letters of John Gibson Lockhart*, 2 vols (1897), vol. 1, p. 107. Strout (1950), p. 22.
19. *Blackwood's*, 2 October 1817, pp. 88–96, *passim*.
20. Hughes, Gillian, *James Hogg, a Life* (2007), Strout (1937). Gillies, vol. 1, pp. 233, 235.
21. Summary of damages, 28 January 1818, NLS 5.143. Morris, p. 113 (facsimile).
22. Pringle to Fairbairn, 20 May 1814, LP, Fairbairn Papers, 1, 11
23. Tredrey, F.D., *The House of Blackwood 1804–1954. The History of a Publishing Firm* (1954), p. 23.
24. Pringle (1838), p. xxxiv.
25. Pringle (1966), p. xxvii; Cowan, R.M.W., *The Newspaper in Scotland. A Study of its Expansion, 1815–60* (Glasgow, Outram, 1946), pp. 37–8.
26. Pringle to Fairbairn, 20 June 1818. Vigne, Randolph, *The South African Letters of Thomas Pringle* (2011), p. 2. LP, Fairbairn Papers, 1, 2.
27. *Blackwood's*, March 1818, p. 656.
28. Hogg to Blackwood, 24 September 1817. Morris, p. 123.
29. *Blackwood's*, 2 October 1817.
30. A. Grant to Cogswell, 24 May 1819. Grant of Laggan, Anne, *Memoir and Correspondence of Mrs Grant of Laggan* (1844), vol. 2, p. 244. Morris, p. 128.
31. *Edinburgh Magazine*, April 1818.
32. *Edinburgh Magazine*, May 1818.
33. Gifford, D. M. et al. (eds), *Scottish Literature in English and Scots* (2002), p. 201.
34. Scott to Lady Louisa Stuart, 6 February 1826. Scott, Sir Walter, ed. Sir Herbert Grierson, *Letters of Sir Walter Scott*, 12 vols (1932), vol. 9, p. 418.

35 Pringle (1838), p. xl.
36 Hogg to —, 14 January 1835. Strout (1937), p. 433.
37 Morris, p. 131.
38 Strout (1937), p.433.
39 Pringle (1966), p. xxviii.
40 Pringle (1838), pp. xxxiv-v.
41 Story (1862), p. 77.
42 *Ibid.*
43 Pringle (1966), p. xxvii.
44 Pringle (1838), p. xxxvi.
45 Strout (1946), pp. 141–2.
46 Hogg to Wilson (draft), 3.8.1818, Hogg (2004), p. 461.
47 *Blackwood's,* 2:12, March 1818, p. 655.
48 Hogg to Pringle, 21.8.1818, Pringle (1838), cxlviii.
49 Hogg to Timothy Tickler (draft), 3.8.1818, Hogg (2004), p. 372.
50 *Ibid.*
51 Hogg to Pringle, William James Mickle (1735–88). Scottish poet.
52 *Edinburgh Magazine,* April 1819, pp. 319–23.

4
A Long, a Last Adieu!

At 30 Pringle was back where he had been at 20, after an experience of literary life that had been unhappy and financially unrewarding. He wrote to a friend:

> My present occupation is inadequate to the support of my family in the most moderate way I can devise; I see little or no prospect of materially improving my circumstances in this country and I have already incumbrances on my shoulders which threaten every day to become heavier, and at last to overwhelm me in hopeless debt. Now this is a state of life the most intolerable that can well be imagined, and which one must experience fully to estimate. It paralyses the very blood and heart of man; and I cannot and will not endure it while a prospect remains of extricating myself by my exertion, or sacrifice, that can be made with honour and a good conscience.[1]

Along with extricating himself he held to his great hope, that the family of Robert Pringle could be held together as economic decline shattered the unity he had treasured in the Blaiklaw days. They had begun to scatter when the lease of Blaiklaw was coming to an end, before 1812.

Thomas's letter to his father of 17 January 1812 shows him to have been, even then, the leader among his full and half- brothers and sisters. It shows also that John, 21, and Alexander, 19, were already employed away from home, John, we know, was living with a cousin, John Riddell, son of Robert Pringle's eldest sister Isabella, a corn miller, before moving on to the management of 'a Gentleman's estate for several years', according to Robert Hart, who was to employ him in the Cape Colony in 1821. Alexander already wanted to emigrate to the United States, to 'the settlement on the Ohio river where his uncle and cousin William are' (These two are unidentified. Thomas wrote in an account of the family the previous year that his maternal grandfather's family had all died, 'except for one cousin, if still alive'). William, Robert's eldest son, who seems to have stayed on to wind up affairs at Blaiklaw in 1812, married Anne Scott of Coldstream, Berwickshire, before joining his father in Co Durham.

The unsettled, precarious state of the family can be seen further in Robert's move back to Scotland, where by 1816 he is found living at Haughhead, Penicuik, near Edinburgh. A Secession church had been built in Penicuik in 1750 and its minister gave Robert a reference recommending 'Robert Pringle and Mrs Pringle his spouse, members of his congregation' to a congregation at the Cape of Good Hope and testifying to their 'unblemished character as Christians'.[2]

The Cape of Good Hope? Parliament in London intervened in the fortunes of the Pringle family – and hundreds of others – as a *deus ex machina,* offering them settlement *as a family* on their own land in a new, distant colony.

Colonial emigration had never, before this time, been planned and executed by the government of Britain. With the end of the Napoleonic wars, the introduction of machinery and the closing of old industries, bad harvests and drought, unemployment rose, as did the price of bread, while that of corn fell as did wages. It was feared that distress and discontent would play into the hands of radicals and some alleviation was sought. The 'Peterloo Massacre' of July 1819, when troops were called in to quell a Chartist rally, killing 11 and wounding 400 in the crowd, was a symptom of this fear rather than a means of dispelling it. Removing unemployed workmen from the scene seemed a better means. With little advance discussion, but for some consideration by a parliamentary Poor Law commission earlier in the year, or publicity, the Chancellor of the Exchequer, Nicholas Vansittart, won parliamentary approval that same month for a grant of £50,000 to finance the emigration of such unemployed workmen and their families to the Cape of Good Hope.

Between 1815 and 1826 there were six such experiments in state-aided emigration. There was little precedent for them nor did they continue into the future. Nor yet make any impact on over-population or unemployment: as they undoubtedly did on the histories of the colonies in Canada, South Africa and, latterly, Australia where they were conducted. Many thousands of Scots had made their way to Nova Scotia, Cape Breton and Prince Edward Island since the 1760s but the Cape had become a possession of the Crown only after the Congress of Vienna in 1814. The British immigrants had been individuals with local connections and the party of fewer than two hundred Scots and their families had been brought out in 1817 by a laird of Orkney, Benjamin Moodie, without government assistance.

The far eastern part of the colony had been identified in 1816 by Colonel John Graham (ninth Laird of Fintry in Forfarshire) as a healthy and fertile destination for settlers from the Scottish highlands, both to develop the region (which he had cleared of African migrants from across the colonial boundary in a bloody campaign in 1812) and to defend it from cattle raiders and invaders from across the border. In 1816 the Governor with whom Pringle was to do battle, Lord Charles Somerset, pressed for Graham's scheme to be considered by the long-serving Secretary for War and the Colonies, Henry, third Earl Bathurst. It received no such consideration[3] but Graham's promotion of the idea (which he also advanced in a tour of the Highlands) would have been known to Thomas Pringle, whose uncles were prominent figures in Perth: the merchant Adam (later Lord Provost) and Alexander, Church of Scotland minister from 1777 until his death in 1839. Thomas's only poem celebrating a living soldier and patriot was his sonnet to Thomas Graham, Lord Lynedoch, MP for Perth, cousin and military patron of Colonel John Graham, who had served under him in the Austrian army at the start of his military career and later in the Peninsula against Napoleon.

Much less likely is the possibility that the Hon. East India Company's agent at the Cape, from 1797 until his death in 1815, John Pringle, of the Haining family in Selkirkshire had, when in Britain from 1804 to 1808, spoken of the Cape to informants of his very distant and socially lower ranking kinsman Thomas.

Pringle wrote of his family in *African Sketches* that:

> The change of times, however, and the loss of capital, had completely over-clouded their prospects in our native country; and therefore when the Government scheme of colonizing the unoccupied territory at the Cape was promulgated, I called their attention to that colony, and offered to accompany them, should they determine to proceed thither as settlers. After maturely weighing the advantages of the Cape, as compared with other British colonies, they made their election, and empowered me to apply on their behalf to the Colonial Department.[4]

He set out his 'two distinct objects' in emigrating to the Cape:

> One of these was to collect again into one social circle, and establish in rural independence, my father's family, which untoward circumstances had broken up and began to scatter over the world. To accomplish this, emigration to a new colony was indispensable.

The other object was to 'obtain through the recommendation of powerful friends some moderate appointment, suitable to my qualifications in the civil service of the colony, and probably in the newly settled district.'

It was Thomas who offered to lead the party of emigrants to the Cape, and he thus succeeded in taking with him his father Robert, stepmother, brother John and half-brothers and half-sister William Dods Pringle (Dods was Beatrice Pringle's mother's name), Catherine Heatlie Pringle and Beatrice Scott Pringle, 11, 10 and 4 respectively.

Of the 24 who sailed to South Africa in 1820 only these eight were of Thomas's immediate family. Seven more were Margaret's Rennie cousins and her sister Janet and the remaining nine from outside the family circle. Six more of the Blaiklaw Pringles, spouses and children joined them in the succeeding 13 years, as did John Riddell, the corn miller cousin and his family, and 21 others, clergymen and their families, the artist James Struthers Stewart and his family, and (the first of these to arrive), the schoolmaster John Fairbairn, to succeed Story as Thomas's bosom friend and close confidant and to be linked with him forever in the history of South Africa.

Professor Rennie, descended from the East Lothian settler family related to Margaret Pringle, wrote that 'much of the correspondence relating to the building up of the party survives, at any rate from the beginning of September 1819 until the submission of the final embarkation list in the following January'[5]. And they set sail for the Cape the same month. In truth, however, none of the family correspondence nor that with the non-family element of the party is extant. Only Thomas's official correspondence with the Colonial Office survives, as does the earliest on the subject, with the patron whose 'interest' pointed the way – Walter Scott of Abbotsford. The party was formed and ready to sail after only four months – an astonishingly short time to have conceived and organized the transportation of 24 Scots men, women and children to their *ultima Thule* in southern Africa.

Thomas exhibited a very uninformed awareness of the Cape through the travels of his cousins, George and Thomas Haitlie, who had found their way there from India. George, who died at Klapmuts, near Cape Town, in 1813, is remembered in Pringle's poem of that year, 'Lines, written on hearing of the death of an early friend'.[6] The title gives 'friend' its old secondary meaning of relative. The poem makes references to an imagined Africa very unlike the Mediterranean, vine-growing Western Cape landscape where George Haitlie was 'to gain – in a drear distant clime, A nameless grave before thy prime!' His killer was 'the Fiend Ambition ... Who scatters wide her victim's bones O'er blighting swamps – o'er burning zones'. Seven years later Pringle was to experience a different Africa. The poem ends with a touch of the essential Pringle, who was several times in his life to survive blows that would have laid low a lesser man. We are urged to

> Confide, while we submissive bow,
> That He will cheer who chastens now;
> And to a loftier faith give scope,
> Nor mourn as those who have no hope.

He was to meet Thomas Haitlie by happy chance in Cape Town on arrival there in April 1820.

The July 1819 parliamentary grant of £50,000 received great and instant *éclat*. John Barrow wrote in the *Quarterly Review* in November 1819 that the measure was 'hailed with great applause in every part of the house'. Barrow had experience of the Cape as Private Secretary to the first British governor, Lord Macartney. Barrow's *An account of Travels into the Interior of Southern Africa in the Years 1797 and 1798* (2 vols, 1801, 1804) had done more to make the Cape known to the British public than any other work. It had also led to his becoming one of the most prolific contributors to the *Quarterly Review*, founded in 1809 'with the design', wrote Barrow 'of counteracting the more than Jacobinical poison scattered most industriously through the pages of the *Edinburgh Review*'.[7]

Pringle had no need to wait for the *Quarterly* to learn of the Cape emigration scheme. It was advertised in the *Caledonian Mercury* on 22 July as well as in the *Morning Post* and other London papers a few days earlier. *Blackwell's* acclaimed the scheme in its August 1819 issue. It had been put forward 'not because that colony is too thin of inhabitants but because the mother country is too full'.[8] It was designed also to stop

> emigration to the frozen shores of Canada and the United States, or divert and encourage it to the finest colony in the world. We surely have learned enough of North America to convince us of the degraded and miserable condition of its people. South Africa, on the other hand, has every advantage to repay the sacrifice of quitting the land of our forefathers.

Three pages of eulogy of the Cape follow, of the landscape, especially in the hinterland of Knysna, of Constantia wines, of the prospects of English settlement, such as at Saldanha Bay – 'the finest harbour in Africa' – and the low cost of living. All this despite the lack of churches, the absolute rule of the governor, and the severity of the Dutch legal system still in force. All in all,

There is no country under heaven, where the poor may find a safer asylum, and where activity, economy and good conduct will meet with so certain and full a reward.

Pringle was unlikely to have read *Blackwood's*, from sheer disgust at its treatment of him, nor the very Tory *Quarterly*, but Walter Scott, a founder of the latter and a friend of its contributors John Wilson Croker and Barrow at the Admiralty would have known much of the Cape scheme, enough indeed to advise Pringle to consider it. He was to help him in every way to take full advantage of it.

In October 1819 *Blackwood's* somewhat modified its eulogy and in another six pages set about correcting the misinformation in the '*Guide to the Cape of Good Hope* &c., &c. and the *Cape of Good Hope Calendar*, a mere reprint',[9] both of them 'puffed and placarded with the most audacious quackery in every corner of the town'. *Blackwood's* this time dwelt upon 'some points which we had not then leisure to discuss and, moreover, as the subject is becoming hourly more extensively popular and seriously important', it reproduced in full the two circulars issued from the Colonial Office to prospective emigrants to the Cape.

The Colonial Office circulars laid out the deposit (£10 per family of parents and two children under 14, or per individual adult, £5 for children between 14 and 18), 100 acre plots, rent-free for 10 years, arrangements for victualling, for the paying of ministers (one per 100 families) and much else, ending 'in order to ensure the arrival of the settlers at the Cape at the beginning of the planting season, the transports will not leave the country until the month of November'.[10]

The second circular offered a little more guidance: 'the settlers will be located in the interior of the colony, not far from the coast',[11] agricultural implements could be brought with the settlers or bought 'at prime cost' on arrival, seed corn purchased in the colony and – a sobering touch – 'The settlers will not find habitations ready for their reception'. More generally, the land grants were to be given out thus :

If any parishes in which there may be a redundancy of population shall unite in selecting an intelligent individual to proceed to the Cape with the settlers under his direction such an individual would apportion the grants of land to families and individuals in his party.

That person, in the party he had recruited, was Thomas Pringle.

As the overwhelming majority of the 4000 to 5000 settlers who were accepted as settlers were poor and uneducated there are few accounts from them of their response to the scheme. Those who did write of it were leaders like Thomas Pringle or the Pembrokeshire country gentleman Thomas Philipps. One of the humbler settlers , 18-year-old Josiah Goldswain, of Marlow in Buckinghamshire, recaptured the moment:

Nothing purticler ocured in my life until October 1819 when thear was Great talk about the Cape of Good Hope and that thear was a Gentleman coming down from London to make up a partey ... At the latter end of the Month Mr Wm Weait [Wait] ... down to Great Marlow he came ... we were all worned to meet at the Grayhown Inn at seven o'clock the same evening wen to my Great astonishment I fond they Market room quit ful ...sum of those wich ware in the winter ceason depentent on the parish for support but Mr Wait assured them that it wold be thear hone faltes if they that did not make up thear minds to go to the Cape of Good hope if they did not make a little fortune in a verey short time.[12]

Contemporary estimates of the number who applied to go to the Cape under the leadership of such as William Wait and Thomas Pringle range from 50,000 to 90,000, of whom 4000 to 5000 went to the Cape.

The circulars had nothing to say about the proximity of the frontier with the lands of the amaRharhabe, the abaThembu and others stretching eastwards. In its August 1819 issue *Blackwood's* added a mild *caveat* to their description, the Zuurveld or Albany district between the Sundays and Great Fish Rivers, as 'one of the most fruitful parts of the colony'.

> The Kaffers have made frequent and destructive incursions along these luxuriant though now almost deserted tracts. However, there is little to be dreaded from this barbarous people, should the country be well stocked with British farmers. Though a cruel, the Kaffers are a cowardly people; and the military efforts that are at this moment directed against them by the colonial government will doubtless drive them beyond the frontier of the colony (the great fish river).[13]

A recent cattle raid on the Theopolis mission station was referred to: 'If these marauders are not subdued by main force, there will be no end to their excesses'. Main force was indeed used to subdue the 10,000 Rharhabe followers of Chief Ndlambe led by the messianic Makhanda in their attempt to overwhelm Graham-stown on 22 April 1819. The firepower of the 400-strong colonial and Khokhoi defending force was enough to defeat them, as Pringle would have read in the *Edinburgh Magazine* shortly after the end of his editorship. They were not defeated by their cowardice but by the muskets and fieldguns in the hands of trained British and colonial troops ranged against their spears. In later years George Thompson's *Travels and Adventures in Southern Africa* (1827), edited by Pringle, stated that:

> from the bloody defeat they met with [at Grahamstown], it is obvious what a vast superiority the use of fire-arms confers, and how weak an enemy the Caffers are, when encountered by Europeans in the open plain.[14]

The Battle of Grahamstown was only the most recent of a series of eastern frontier conflicts, going back to 1779 and now recorded in a numbered sequence of frontier wars (or, to African nationalists, wars of dispossession). The Fifth Frontier War had been fought in 1818–19 but was not mentioned in the promo-tion of the settlement scheme.

The Pringles and Rennies must have been cheered by the quotation from William J. Burchell's *Hints on Emigration to the Cape of Good Hope* published in 1819, three years before his major work, the rightly admired *Travels in the Interior of Southern Africa*. He found 'the Zuure Veldt (Albany) a beautiful and delightful country, issued with every diversity of scenery and surface, abounding in herbage, wood and water; and having a soil capable of feeding large herds of cattle, and of producing corn and vegetables more than sufficient for the supply of a numerous population'.[15] It was Burchell whose evidence to the Poor Law commission of 1819 may have influenced the choice of the Zuurveld for settlement of emigrants to the Cape of Good Hope. He was praised by *Blackwood's* but in its November 1819 article the *Quarterly* published Barrow's criticism of Burchell's *Hints*. Burchell in turn wrote unsympathetically of Barrow when his own *Travels* appeared in two volumes in 1822 and 1824. Through all this sparring, the Zuurveld remained Burchell's 'most beautiful and delightful country'.

It may seem strange that no one queried the name Zuurveld, 'sour fields', as the herbage turned out to be. It must have been a disappointment to Pringle's party to be told that they and the two other projected Scottish parties were to be placed north of the Arcadian tracts of the Zuurveld in the harsher, though well watered, Baviaan's River valley, in the foothills of the Winterberg mountains. Colonel John Graham, his military career on the frontier ended, had been granted a farm in the same region, which he called Lynedoch. He died, aged 46, before occupying it and left it to his Cape-born widow, born Johanna Catherina Cloete, of the Westerford Cloete family.

If it was good enough for Colonel Graham, the Colonial Secretary at the Cape, Colonel Bird, who apportioned the locations according to the settlers' national groups, thought it would serve well Graham's Scottish compatriots.

The bulk of the settlers were to be placed in the Zuurveld or Albany district, and Thomas Pringle, though settled beyond it, was to become their pre-eminent spokesman in the early and desperate struggles of the settlement.

It is not clear from what Pringle tells us what step it was that began his many-thousand mile journey, from failed though not discredited literary journeyman and archival scribe to leader of pioneering settlers in a remote and untamed colony. The *African Sketches* (1834) is a distillation of the journal, letters and documents of his leaving home and his years at the Cape, all of them lost despite Margaret's wish that they be used for his biography. He sums up the family situation, as already quoted, and their decision which 'empowered me to apply on their behalf'[16] for the 'Government plan' and emigrate to the Cape. Linked with this was his own involvement in 'literary concerns' which had given him 'a decided aversion … to Periodical Literature as a profession' and decided him to seek a civil service post in the new colony. He wrote:

> Having explained these views to my respected friend Sir Walter Scott, in the autumn of 1819, that illustrious and benevolent man entered into them with his characteristic cordiality and promptitude.

Joanna Baillie, to whose support Tam Pringle had rallied his student friends ten years earlier, wrote that Scott's face 'if I had been in a crowd and at a loss what to do, I should have fixed upon among a thousand, as the sure index of the benevolence and the shrewdness that would and could help me in my strait'. He was to help Pringle and his family in theirs – perhaps the more remarkably since their acquaintance had been quite brief – after 'The Epistle to Mr R.S****' in 1816, in fact. Pringle was a Whig editor supplanted by Scott's Tory son-in-law Lockhart, and there was a clear class difference.

Whether, in his strait, Pringle went to Scott or the reverse is unknown, but Scott immediately wrote to some of his ministerial friends in London, in behalf of myself and my party of emigrants, and obtained our ready admission among those selected by Government for the new settlement, from the vast number of applicants.[17]

Scott appears to have lacked much feeling for Pringle, for whom so many felt deep affection. He used the word 'conceited' for him in later years, though perhaps in its older sense of having fanciful notions. William Blackwood, of whom a modern critic wrote that he 'had the spirit of a guttersnipe [and] was a dirty fighter but a game one',[18] preserved a letter from his brother Robert, who described Pringle's visit to Abbotsford after his return from South Africa thus:

> There is another very good joke of Sir Walter's. Pringle, the Lamb of the Chaldee MS, has been to Scotland lately [1830] and was on a visit to Abbotsford. Sir Walter got very tired of him (he is a great *bore* – that's my own) and told Lockhart that he had just turned the Lamb out to grass on the holm.[19]

What may have been an inoffensive aside was repeated by Scott to Lockhart, to Robert Blackwood and on to his brother William, from whom it found its way long after into Mrs Oliphant's authorized *Annals of a Publishing House*.

Pringle did not disown the Lamb sobriquet despite its malicious origin. When Scott, generous as ever, sent £15 to Pringle, awaiting embarkation in worsening financial straits, the grateful recipient wrote on the cover of his letter of thanks 'The lamb is exalted!'

Scott first secured the Pringle party's place in the 'Government scheme', though not at 'ministerial' level. On 4 September 1819 Scott wrote:

> I have by post forwarded the memorial to Mr Croker of the Admiralty , with whom I am intimate, requesting him to put it in the proper train without delay. I think I can rely on his intercession with Lord Bathurst and Mr Goulburn, neither of whom I myself know, and that you will be put on as good if not a better footing than any who go out to the Cape.[20]

John Wilson Croker, first secretary to the Admiralty, a mainstay of the *Quarterly Review* and founder of the Athenaeum Club, indulged himself with a little sport in his letter to the kindly Henry Goulburn, under-secretary for war and the colonies under the longest serving secretary, Henry, third Earl Bathurst:

> Dear Goulburn
>
> 'Accept a miracle instead of wit'. I send you a very dull and almost illegible piece of Walter Scott's composition, but dull and difficult as it is, I hope his name and my request will induce you to wade through the enclosed packet.
>
> The argument of this new 'Tale of my Landlord' is as follows:
>
> One Pringle, a Scotch Tory born lame, dedicates himself to literature – sets up a magazine – quarrels with his publisher – is turned off, abused and ridiculed. Sets up a new magazine in opposition to the former, engages with the new publisher for a salary for five years, on the strength of which he marries, computing, it would seem, that his marriage and all its consequences must be ended before five years. The new publisher is as bad as the old – another dismissal – the wife breeds copiously – the little all of the increasing family 100£, which, however, is but to last two years – present difficulties – dreadful prospects – desperate

projects – emigration to Canada or the Cape – prefers Canada – changes his mind – prefers the Cape – how to get there? Applies to Walter Scott, for whom he has done some little literary jobs – and on whose family he has some kind of dependence – sets forth his wishes and his means – the former a grant of land, the latter 500£, and a dozen experienced farmers and their wives, his own relations or servants. Walter Scott receives the proposal, and conveys it to the first lord of the Admiralty. His Lordship advises Scott to interest Mr Croker, who can interest Mr Goulburn, who can interest Lord Bathurst, who can interest Lord Charles Somerset to do something for the interest of the intended colony of the Pringles.

Croker, who was himself bored with reading three long letters and one short one on the subject, writes a longer letter than any of them to Goulburn, and bores him with the whole galiamatias. Goulburn in a rage writes a hasty refusal without reading the letters; next day dreadfully wet; can't go abroad; thinks he may as well decipher Walter Scott's letter, and wade through Pringle's. Does so in two hours, ten minutes, fifteen seconds. Writes a favourable answer to say the proposal promises reasonably well, and that he will do all he can, Croker acquaints Scott – Scott tells Pringle. Pringle in ecstasies of joy runs to tell his wife, big with child – rapture accelerates her labour. She is brought to bed of a fine boy, who is christened Henry-Scott-Bathurst-Goulburn Pringle.

Finis of the 1st volume,
Yours ever.
J.W.C.[21]

The letter was dated 8 September 1819. The promptness of the action taken by Croker showed his respect for the 'Wizard of the North'. It made up for his carelessness with the facts and the almost Lockhart-like sarcasm. Thomas was no Tory, he and Margaret Pringle had no children and they were in no way dependent on the Scotts, the First Lord on the Admiralty, Viscount Melville, had not, so far as is known, been approached, though Scott knew him. He would certainly have known of the family's Cape connexions. His father, Henry Dundas, the 1st Viscount Melville, having been, when Secretary for War and the Colonies, the recipient of many of Lady Anne Barnard's letters when she was Lord Macartney's unofficial hostess during his Governorship of the the Cape in 1797–9. Henry's nephew, Francis, was Acting Governor in the first British occupation of the Cape (1795–1802) and at loggerheads with Lady Anne and her husband Andrew Barnard, the Governor's secretary.

Croker's letter is both as a period literary curiosity – the opening quotation from Edward Young on Chesterfield, the revelation that Scott was no longer 'the Great Unknown' to Coker as early as 1819; the comic, Mr Jingle-like anacoluthon with its string of dashes, the French word for gibberish – and as a jesting summary of what Scott must have written to Croker, mixed with what Pringle himself contributed to the packet. With all its raillery, Croker's letter does show a carefully hidden sympathy for Pringle's case and his hope that Goulburn will act accordingly.

Croker and his son-in-law John Barrow were both deeply involved with the *Quarterly Review*, as was Scott. Bathurst and Goulburn were outside Scott's range, unlike Melville, who had been his friend. Goulburn, almost overwhelmed with sorting out the scores of thousands of applicants and making plans for their settlement in South Africa, all to be done inside six months, with a tiny, augmented staff, nevertheless found time for a special concern for the Pringle party.

Goulburn had favoured helping poor families to emigrate to Canada but came to appreciate both the better living conditions at the Cape and the advantage of settling the skilled rather than the unskilled. The character of the Pringle party must have pleased him and the four surviving letters he received from Thomas Pringle suggest a warm though entirely businesslike relationship. When Pringle received copies of *The Autumnal Excursion and Other Poems* he presented a copy to Goulburn.

Sadly he was to clash, in the 1830s, with Goulburn, whose income came from West Indian sugar estates, made profitable by slave labour. This troubled Goulburn deeply, for he, like his fellow Tories Bathurst and even the authoritarian Cape governor, Lord Charles Somerset, did all they could to ameliorate the conditions of slavery. Was not the victorious abolitionist of the slave trade in 1807, William Wilberforce, himself a Tory? When Pringle returned from the Cape and battle lines were drawn between abolitionist and slave-owner there was to be no quarter.

The letters to Goulburn of 1819–20 are written in Pringle's rather stilted, cap-in-hand style. Croker had clearly sent word that he should petition Lord Bathurst, via Henry Goulburn and on 22 September 1819 he did so with a letter to Goulburn, from 24 Salisbury Street, Edinburgh. He wrote proudly, though he called his claim 'humble', that, as the scheme called for 'persons possessed of some small capital' who had also 'steadiness, enterprise and agricultural skill', his father and brothers 'who form four of the party [though only three embarked], are allowed to be as good farmers as any in the county of Roxburgh', and had also 'the other qualifications above mentioned'.[22]

He was more self-effacing when it came to his own needs. He wrote in the *Narrative* that Scott had performed a second great service: 'He also exerted himself with the utmost zeal to obtain an appoinment for myself in the colony'[23] Having neither capital nor farming experience and being disabled he trusted to obtain, he wrote, 'some moderate appointment, suitable to my qualifications, in the civil service of the colony, and probably in the newly settled district'. In the 22 September letter he merely refers to Scott's telling him 'that he has mentioned something of my own individual situation and wishes to Mr Croker'. Scott's 'candid explanations ... will have infinitely more weight than I can presume to urge'.[24] He was very much the Lamb in signing off: "I will not further intrude upon your time, except that it will exceedingly oblige me if you will be so good as to inform me as soon as your convenience will admit, whether I may hope for success in this double application ...'

On 5 October he wrote again, this time about the composition of the party, just joined by two 'young men of most respectable connections and good character'.[25] They were Charles Sydserff, 'a nephew of the late Baron Hepburn, and related to Lord Dalhousie' and 'a brother of the Rector of the High School of Edinburgh'. The latter is not heard of again, but Sydserff ('Syd' pronounced 'side') is an interesting recruit of whom we shall have more to say. Pringle is anxious to know if the application has been successful and, if so, when they will embark. 'Mr Scott, whom I had the pleasure of seeing at Abbotsford a few days ago, told me it would be Spring before any of the emigrants to Algoa Bay would sail, but I presume he has been mistaken'.[26] He again ventures to 'hope humbly for your favourable consideration of my request, and … your attention to my personal wishes so far as agreeable to the views of Government'.

His next letter, from 43 Princes Street, Soho on 27 November, where he and Margaret are staying while 'the rest await your further directions in Edinburgh', sets out his case for an appointment at the Cape, for which he has 'but humble qualifications'.[27] Can this be the man Scott called 'conceited' (see p. 225), assuming he used the word in its modern sense?

> My pretensions are not lofty, indeed I can neither boast of scientific knowledge nor of much experience in affairs, I may only venture to lay claim to some little literary experience, and … to habits of attention and accuracy formed during ten years employment under the super-intendence of Mr Thomson, the Deputy Clerk Register of Scotland, and in the management of a newspaper and magazine for more than two years … I have had little or no practice in figures or accounts and cannot therefore pretend to any great expertness in matters where they are principal requisites. For the rest, I understand French and Latin, and am at present acquiring some knowledge of the Dutch language.

It was his 'personal infirmity and want of capital' that ruled out farming and made him so anxious for employment 'in the service of the colony'.

More than six weeks later, he and Margaret were still at the Princes Street address, with funds running low. On 12 January 1819 he wrote to John, the younger of the two Fairbairn brothers, friends of his early life in Edinburgh, whom he had tried and failed (*pro tem*) to recruit. He told John Fairbairn that he had come to London a fortnight before to make embarkation arrangements with the Colonial Office 'and to solicit Government patronage for myself. I had a very promising letter from Walter Scott to your old friend Croker, but Croker is a cold-hearted, indifferent political intriguer and I made nothing of him'.[28]

With 'the other Admiralty Secretary', John Barrow, he had 'better success' and judged him 'a fine frank friendly man. He has promised me recommendatory letters to the Colonial Secretary in Cape Town, and gave me much agreeable and encouraging information. He thinks there is no fear of our ['not' omitted?] doing well'.

Scott had introduced him also to Major-General Francis Dundas, Lord Melville's nephew and Acting-Governor of the Cape in 1798–9 and 1801–03 who was also *bête noire* there of Lady Anne Barnard who called him 'a stupid, pettish, arrogant, *tow stuffed* general'[29] (tow: wads of flax used to ignite guns, i.e. touchy and irascible.). Pringle fared better with him and was given letters, though Scott wrote that he did not expect them to be of much consequence 'as many of his friends have died or left the Cape'.[30] In the same letter Scott informed Pringle that he would be in London in early January and would then 'take care to get from Lord Sidmouth better letters of recommendation than I could do … by writing'. He had no doubt that he would interest Sidmouth –'an exceedingly good man' – on Pringle's behalf 'when I have the opportunity of seeing him'. Pringle would get 'a packet of letters from me very shortly after your arrival at the Cape, if not before'. With this letter came a generous gift of £15, for which Pringle expressed heartfelt gratitude. He ended:

> The recommendations you intend for me are higher than anything I have ventured to hope for … But the privilege of calling you *my Friend* is what I prize still higher.[31]

Though ill-health kept Scott from London until March, after the Pringle party had sailed, Thomas wrote to George Combe, his adviser during the wrangles with Blackwood, that his future prospects were favourable:

> though I have neither succeeded in finding temporary employment here nor obtained any appointment at the Cape. I shall however carry out letters of recommendation from Lords Bathurst and Sidmouth to the Governor and from Mr Barrow of the Admiralty and others to the inferior Colonial Authorities. And I have received from several persons who have resided in the Colony much encouraging information both in regard to my own prospects and to those of my friends. Mr Barrow who knows the country as well as any man says he has no doubt both of their success and mine.[32]

So the Pringles set off with Thomas as the leader of the party. He had no job to go to and no money, but was in high hopes, raised by Scott's wonderfully active benevolence and by his own plans of literary success. He also planned a collaboration with Fairbairn, when the latter came to join him, and and would have, as his literary agent, Thomas Underwood, the bookseller son-in-law of his revered friend, the Revd Alexander Waugh.

He made other friends in London, among them the Moravian minister, the Revd Christian Ignatius Latrobe, who had visited his church's missions at Genadendal, Mamre and also Enon which he had founded, five years before. Latrobe's *Journal of a Visit to South Africa in 1815 and 1816* was published in 1818. His introductions to the Moravians at the Cape were as useful to Pringle as were those, to the London Missionary Society members and others at the Cape, given to him by Alexander Waugh, of the United Secession Church, and minister of the Wells Street congregational church in London. Waugh, a minister near Melrose in Selkirkshire before moving to London in 1782, took a lasting interest in the Pringle party which Pringle repaid with his 'Lines to the Memory of the Revd Dr Waugh', written on his death in 1827. He also helped the Secessionists Henry Belfrage and J. Hay to edit Waugh's memoirs, which appeared in 1830. Waugh had been a founder of the London Missionary Society in 1795.

> And ye far habitants of heathen lands,
> For you he raised his voice and raised his hands
> And taught new sympathy to start
> With generous throb through many a British heart.[33]

The L.M.S. had sent Dr John Philip to South Africa to inspect its missions and he had stayed on as Superintendent. An introduction from Waugh put Pringle on the best possible footing with Philip, a major figure in South Africa's troubled history in those years. Bathurst's letter to Somerset having the same intention, Pringle was well served to make himself known to the leaders of what turned out to be the opposing forces at the Cape.

The months in London had been filled also with much correspondence over the composition of the party, his responsibility as leader. There were many changes to the numbers and names of its members. His brother William and sister Mary were among those who dropped out, to join the family later. The most significant gain was the 22-year-old Charles Sydserff, who added £1,500 to the party's capital, and must have impressed the Colonial Office with his noble and professional connections.

Remote and obscure though the Cape must have seemed before the first British occupation, its use as a place of furlough for East India Company civilians and soldiers created many links. Captain Alexander Grant, who, with his fortune, had escaped the Black Hole of Calcutta, met and married in Cape Town Margaretha Hendrina Beck, daughter of a wealthy brewer and cattleman, Johan Zacharias Beck, an immigrant from Saxe Gotha. On Grant's death she married a kinsman of his, Brigadier-General Simon Fraser, whose death in action at Saratoga in 1779 was the subject of a celebrated battlescape by Benjamin West. Her third husband was Sir John Buchan-Hepburn, Bt, Baron of the Exchequer.

Professor Rennie quotes a letter from Charles Sydserff's elder brother John, written in 1818, refusing Charles's request for money 'in order to your accepting Lady Hepburns kind offer of Cadett-ship in the Company's service' since if he did so 'I should remain in debt untill my death. I am determined to enter by and by into strong measures to liquidate the debt *my Father* and his *Friends* and their Dice Boxes have intailed upon Ruchlaw[34] [the family property in East Lothian]'. The circumstances suggest that it was Lady Buchan-Hepburn (née Beck, of the Cape) who put up the funds that enabled a young kinsman of her husband's (he died in 1819) to settle in the distant colony where she had married her first husband, Captain Grant.

On 13 January 1820 Pringle wrote to acknowledge Henry Goulburn's letter of three days earlier and explained the delay in returning the letter he had been given to the Governor of the Cape, Lord Charles Somerset, so that 'the full and final list of my whole party'[35] could be included. This was due to his having 'experienced some difficulty in getting it out of a trunk which my friends had left at the wharf on their arrival'. The plea for employment had had some results, albeit only a recommendation to the Governor.

The rest of the letter listed the names of the eight who had withdrawn and of the five men, one woman and two children who had replaced them. The last of them, William Elliott had joined since the supposed final list of alterations had been sent to Goulburn a few days before. The party was now complete.

With Thomas, 30, was his wife Margaret, 40, her sister Janet Brown, 44, Thomas's father Robert, 65, his second wife Beatrice, 49, and children William Dods, 11, Catherine Heatlie, 9 and Beatrice Scott, 3, and Thomas's youngest full brother, John, 28. The six Rennie, cousins of Margaret Pringle and Janet Brown, were Elizabeth, 44, and her children Elizabeth Kirkwood, 17, and Charles, 9 with George, 21, John Brown, 20, and Peter, 19, all three farmers. Late recruits like Charles Jervis Buchan Sydserff were James Ekron, 25, ploughman, Alexander Mortimer, 23, baker, and James Souness, 21, ploughman. The party was completed by Ezra Ridgard, 29, saddler, his wife Elizabeth, 23, and children Andrew, 3, and Mary Ann. With them came, at the last minute, Ridgard's cousin, William Elliott, 27, bookseller's assistant, on his way to a missionary appointment but useful to make up the numbers.

After a long, frustrating delay the 24 settlers of Pringle's party embarked at last at Deptford on the 330-ton brig *Brilliant* and sailed from Gravesend a fortnight later, on 15 February 1820.

NOTES

1. Pringle (1838), p. xxxvii.
2. Lynedoch Papers. Pringle, E. et al., *Pringles of the Valleys. Their History and Genealogy* (1957), pp. 2–3. Rennie, J.V.L., *The Scottish Settler Party of 1820,* 4 vols (1991), vol. 1, p. 104, vol. 4, p. 1508.
3. I.E. Edwards's case in *The 1820 Settlers in South Africa* (London, Longmans, 1934) that Somerset's plan to use the settlers as a 'buffer' against the advance of the Nguni into the colony was secretly behind the settlement scheme is unsupported by any evidence. See H.J.M. Johnston, *British Emigration Policy 1815–30* (Oxford, Clarendon Press, 1972).
4. Pringle (1966), p. 3.
5. Rennie, vol. 1, p. 13.
6. Pringle (1838), pp. 161–3.
7. Barrow, Sir John, *An Auto-biographical Memoir of Sir John Barrow, Bart.* (1847), p. 494.
8. *Blackwood's* 5, p. 523.
9. *Op. cit.,* p. 526.
10. Cory, G.E., *The Rise of South Africa,* 5 vols (1910–30), vol. 1, p. 13.
11. *Blackwood's,* 5, p. 80.
12. Goldswain, Jeremiah, *The Chronicle of Jeremiah Goldswain, Albany Settler of 1820,* 2 vols (1946, 1949), vol. 1, pp. 1–2.
13. *Blackwood's,* 5, p. 81.
14. Thompson, George, *Travels and Adventures in Southern Africa,* 2 vols (1967, 1968 eds.), vol. 2, p. 199.
15. Burchell, W.J., *Hints on Emigration to the Cape of Good Hope* (1819), p. 20.
16. Pringle (1966), pp. 3–4.
17. *Ibid.*
18. Carswell, p. 227.
19. Oliphant, vol. 2, p. 117.
20. Scott to Pringle, 4.9.1819, Pringle (1966), pp. 4–5.
21. Croker Papers, vol,. 1, pp. 47–8. Nash, M.D., *Quarterly Bulletin of the South African Library,* 33 (September 1972), pp. 57–8.
22. Pringle to Goulburn, 5.10.1819, Vigne (2011), p. 5. *Records of the Cape Colony,* 12, pp. 335–6.
23. Pringle (1966), p. 4.
24. Pringle to Goulburn, 22.9.1819, Vigne (2011), p. 3. *RCC* 12, pp. 317–18.
25. Pringle to Goulburn, 5.10.1819, Vigne (2011), p. 4. *RCC* 12, pp. 335–6.
26. *Ibid.*
27. Pringle to Goulburn, 27.11.1819, Vigne (2011), p. 7. *RCC* 12, p. 337.
28. Pringle to Fairbairn, 12.12.1819, Vigne (2011), p. 9. LP, Fairbairn Papers, 1, 1.
29. Barnard, Lady Anne, *The Cape Diaries of Lady Anne Barnard, 1799–1800,* 2 vols (1999), vol. 2, p. 187 and n. 8.
30. Scott to Pringle, 10.12.1819, Pringle (1966), p. 5.
31. Pringle to Scott, 13.12.1819, Vigne (2011), p. 11. NLS MS 3890, f 239.
32. Pringle to Combe, 29.1.1820, Vigne (2011), p. 16. NLS MS 7202 f 99.
33. Pringle (1838), p. 208.
34. Rennie, vol. 4, pp. 1552–3.
35. Pringle to Goulburn, 13.1.1820, Vigne (2011), p. 13. *RCC,* 12, p. 502.

1. *Blackwood's Edinburgh Magazine*, vol. 1. Cover of the first six issues, edited by Pringle and Cleghorn, reprinted with 'Blackwood's' added to the original name. (*London Library*)

2. Title-page and dedication of *The Autumnal Excursion*. The quotation is from Virgil's Eclogue 1, with omissions ('Here, by familiar streams and hallowed springs … you tune wooded musings on a delicate reed'). The dedication is to Pringle's employer at the Register Office. (*National Library of South Africa, Cape Town*)

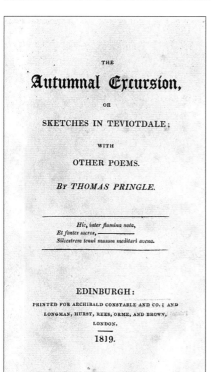

3. Sir Walter Scott (1771–1832) in his study at Abbotsford, by Sir William Allan (1782–1850), with named possessions, including, under his feet, the Cape lion skin sent to Scott by Pringle in 1822.
(National Portrait Gallery, London)

4. Thomas Pringle's farm Eildon, on the Baviaans River, painted in 1849 by the artist Thomas Baines as a guest of William Pringle, Thomas's eldest brother, who took possession of the farm in 1822.
(*A.W. Pringle. Photographed by Steve Bailey*)

5. John Fairbairn (1794-1864), close friend of Pringle's and fellow campaigner for Press freedom, editor of the *South African Commercial Advertiser*, 1824-49, proprietor from 1835, and founder of the 'Old Mutual' insurance company.
(*Western Cape Archives and Records Service, Cape Town*)

6. Lord Charles Somerset (1767–1831)as a regimental officer, aged 22 (after Cosway), Governor of the Cape of Good Hope, 1814–26. Pringle's adversary over the freedom of the Press at the Cape, relief of the Albany settlers and other issues.
(National Library of South Africa, Cape Town)

Part II

The Cape Frontier
Pioneer, Settler Leader
(1820–1821)

5

Settler Leader

Arrival

Pringle had little to say of the 72-day voyage to the Cape, other than that it was 'pleasant and prosperous'.[1] So he wrote in *African Sketches* and also in a letter to Sir Walter Scott five months after his arrival.[2] His party of 24 shared accommodation – he called it 'a good deal crowded' – in the 330-ton *Brilliant* with 95 settlers from Gush's, Sephton's and Erith's parties, London artisans, Methodist tradesmen, and a group of Surrey farmers. Gush and Sephton were carpenters and Erith a baker. There was also the eight-strong Caldecott family, independent settlers.

In the way of shipboard affairs on a long voyage a quarrel developed between the head of the family, Dr Charles Caldecott, and the coachbuilder George Bray in Gush's party. Pringle described the outcome of the 'polemical discussions'[3] that took place with a pleasing detachment, even humour.

> … under the guidance of two local preachers, – a tall, grave Wesleyan coachmaker and a little dogmatic Anabaptist surgeon – they soon split into two discordant factions of Arminians and high Calvinists. Heated by incessant controversy for three months, many of them, who had been wont formerly to associate on friendly terms, ceased to regard each other with sentiments of Christian forbearance; and the two rival leaders, after many obstinate disputations, which became more intricate and intemperate every time they were renewed, had at length parted in flaming wrath, and for several weeks past had paced the quarter-deck together without speaking or exchanging salutations.

The quarrel had a most unhappy end. Dr Caldecott died on board ship in Algoa Bay and Bray a few days later. Pringle wrote that the deaths were seen by the survivors as 'a solemn rebuke for the indulgence of that human pride and wrath.'[4] With which, a touch sceptically, he failed to concur and commented only on the 'moral lesson' as 'a striking one'. The effect of it was to reconcile the two factions who together founded the village of Salem, 16 miles south of Grahamstown. Five years later, he tells us, the splendidly named Alfonso Torkington Caldecott, eldest son of the doctor, who had Spanish connexions, married a daughter of Bray.

There was no such easy unity to be achieved at the Cape between the old Dutch and new British communities. Britain had seized the Cape during the Revolutionary Wars with France, in 1795, returned it to the Dutch – then the Batavian Republic – in 1803, after the Peace of Amiens, and taken it again in 1806. It was seen as of vital importance to secure the crucial half-way house on the voyage to and from India, and before 1820 British settlers had arrived in small numbers – merchants, soldiers, officials, missionaries and only one organized group, some 200 Scots led by a laird from the Orkneys, Benjamin Moodie, in 1817. The 1820 scheme brought the first – and last – substantial number of settler families. They came, not to the occupied territory post-1795 or 1806, but to a colonial possession of King George III. The Treaty of Paris transferred in 1814 the Cape of Good Hope to the Netherlands government – and the British government paid £6 million to the Netherlands' creditors among the nations of Europe.

In Cape Town itself the Dutch officials worked well with their new British counterparts but inland the Afrikaner farming community showed resentment towards the newcomers, whose government recognized the indigenous Khoisan people as equal under the law, though it took eight years to bring this to the statute book. The British brought new rules with them that sought to mitigate the hardships of slavery. The Scots party were to find themselves occupying land from which Afrikaner rebels had been expelled, and their leaders executed, after the Slagtersnek affair, a grievance kept alive into the twentieth century.

A new governor had arrived only months before the Cape of Good Hope had legally become a British possession, Lord Charles Somerset, whose absence on leave so affected Thomas Pringle's hopes of early employment in government service. Eldest of the five younger brothers of the fifth Duke of Beaufort, Lieutenant General Lord Charles Somerset, PC, MP, was a courtier, close to the Prince Regent, whose coronation as King George IV he was to attend in 1821 before returning to the Cape, with his own regiment, the 103rd Foot, former Joint Paymaster of the Army, Comptroller of the King's Household – at 47 a very considerable public figure and grandee.

The Acting Governor who met the 1820 Settlers at Algoa Bay, Major-General Sir Rufane Donkin, was a minor figure by comparison. Donkin's bitter chagrin at the Governor's behaviour towards him and his actions at the Cape was to become a lifelong obsession and to dominate his later career as Whig member of parliament.

It was an explosive mix: Dutch-British hostility, a quarrel between the Governor and his surrogate in his absence, opposed views on the status of the indigenous Khoisan in the colony. It is a relief to most modern readers, to find almost no religious argument or discussion in Pringle's writings in the years to come. Though he held regular services for the Khoi and 'Bastaard' (mixed race) people of the Baviaans River when settled at Eildon, and was responsible for recruiting and dispatching Scottish ministers to the Glen Lynden Church, he kept clear of the sort of doctrinal factionalism which had split the Scottish church of his forebears into competing fragments. Perhaps it was this calm, unquestioning acceptance of the Gospels, and the liturgy on offer, that had upset Margaret in the early days of their marriage.

The *Brilliant* put in first at Simon's Bay on 30 April 1820. Party leaders alone were allowed on shore. 'While our vessel lay at anchor here a few days', taking on provisions, he wrote, 'I paid a visit to the capital of the colony' about 25 miles distant. To Sir Walter he wrote that from Simon's Town he 'rode up to Cape Town'.

The new Thomas Pringle begins to emerge, a hardy, determined, horse-riding figure who makes light of what was in those days a difficult journey along the False Bay coast, beside lakes and marshes to the outlying farms south-east of Cape Town. In the years ahead he rode great distances over the wildest country.

From the start he was working towards two objectives: the settling of his party on a location still to be decided, and the pursuit of a career for himself once the former had been achieved. He came ashore at Simon's Town with Goulburn's letter to the Governor, only to learn that Lord Charles had set sail for England on 13 January, while the settlers were awaiting their sailing instructions. With Lord Charles, a widower for the past five years, were his two daughters, one of whom needed medical treatment. Lord Charles, despite the succession of highly unpleasant incidents that marred his time as Governor, was normally the soul of duty and it seems strange that he should have left his post at this time. The ailing daughter recovered her health on the voyage, but the 23 months he was to spend in England were not so much, as he had expressed the hope, of use to the settlers, as to himself. He returned to the Cape in November 1821 with a new Lady Charles.

The Colonial Secretary at Cape Town Castle, Colonel Christopher Bird, knew well Lord Charles's acute sense of his position and understandably refused to open the letter Goulburn had written him, with Pringle as the bearer. The acting Governor, Lieutenant-General Sir Rufane Donkin, was away from Cape Town and Bird, stating that Donkin could not open the letter either, as it was marked 'Private', sent it back to England for Lord Charles himself to read. Thus was the course of Pringle's life changed. He would not be able to deposit his party at their location and after a decent but brief interval head for Cape Town to take up the appointment that Walter Scott's far-reaching influence would secure him. The consequences were of great importance to his role in South Africa.

His week in Cape Town was not entirely wasted. 'Almost by accident'[5] (his own oxymoron) he met in the street his cousin Thomas Haitlie (now Heatlie) who at once rode to Simon's Town to see his Pringle uncle and cousins, bringing them farm produce and advice about their lives ahead. Heatlie was one of the small army of angry colonists who had their own personal quarrels with Lord Charles Somerset. Pringle was to add Thomas Heatlie's to his list of official complaints against the Governor in later years.

Of far greater significance was Pringle's meeting with Dr John Philip, 'the Elijah of South Africa', and his friend and supporter, the worthy H.E. Rutherfoord, Cape Town merchant and philanthropist. He had letters of introduction to Philip from Scotland and from the venerable Dr Alexander Waugh.

Waugh was a pioneer supporter of mission work in Africa and India, a movement still young in 1820. He had petitioned the University of Aberdeen for an honorary doctorate for John Philip in 1813. It was refused on sectarian grounds but granted by both Columbia and Princeton. Though Pringle wrote only that he 'formed an acquaintance'[6] with Philip at this first meeting, it was to have a profound effect on Pringle's life in South Africa, followed as it was by his visit to Bethelsdorp, the London Missionary Society's station near Algoa Bay, a few weeks later, doubtless encouraged by Philip, superintendent of L.M.S. missions in South Africa.

Philip 'dominated the racial politics of southern Africa from the 1820s to the 1840s' writes a present-day historian. He 'contended for the equal legal rights of Khoisan and whites within the Cape Colony and advocated strengthening African chiefdoms against the advance of white settlement. With this he earned the century-long enmity of white settlers, including some who desired to trek from the Cape Colony'. Many did in 1837, later to form independent republics across the Orange and Vaal Rivers, to distance themselves from racially egalitarian rule. Philip's was 'the clearest missionary voice for racial equality' and his 'moderate Christian liberalism' was an inspiration to Pringle and to 'white and black opponents of white domination until the 1950s'.[7]

Pringle's sanguine, hopeful nature comes across clearly in his account of Algoa Bay, where he again was allowed ashore ahead of his party, who had a weary 29–day wait, after one premature, short-lived disembarkation. He had already seen the Tsitsikamma forest lining the shores of Knysna lagoon: 'there was the grandeur and the grace of nature, majestic and untamed'. To the Scots 'the sublimely stern aspect of this country' aroused 'stirring recollections of their native land',[8] whereas, 'so different from the rich tameness of ordinary English scenery' it struck the English 'with a degree of awe approaching consternation'. Pringle exhibits a marked feeling of superiority over his 'southron' fellow settlers here and later in his experience of them.

He gives a vivid word picture of the 'animated and interesting scene' at Algoa Bay – the thatched government buildings, storehouses and, near the Market Square of Port Elizabeth today, endless rows of army tents housing the settlers, with parties of them 'moving off in long trains of bullock wagons' to the interior, their places immediately taken by 'fresh bands hourly disembarking from the vessels in the bay'. William Shaw, a young Methodist minister, saw 'an array of barren sand hills behind and close to which appeared a series of rugged and stony declivities, and, in the distance … the dark and gloomy range of the Winterhoek Mountains frowned upon us, shutting us out, as it seemed, from the Paradise of which we had … dreamed'.[9] To Pringle these were 'the heights over the Zwartkops River, covered with a dense jungle, … the picturesque peaks of the Winterhoek and the dark masses of the Zureberg ridge far to the northward, distinctly outlined in the clear blue sky'[10]. From his first landing in Algoa Bay he saw beauty, as 'we passed some sand-hills covered with beautiful shrubs such as are found among the rare exotics of our European green houses; and aloes and other strange plants were … trodden underfoot as carelessly as thistles and burdock in an English barn-yard.' Henry Dugmore, then a boy of 10, in Edward Gardner's party, recalled 'the desolate sand-hills and salt-marshes' of the landing place where 'a dreary barren looking waste met many a disappointed eye'.[11]

Pringle was excited too by the human activities around him:

Tall Dutch-African boors, with broad-brimmed white hats, and huge tobacco pipes in their mouths, were bawling in Colonial-Dutch. Whips were smacking, bullocks bellowing, wagons creaking; and the half-naked Hottentots, who led the long teams of draught oxen, were running, and hallooing and, and waving their long lank swarthy arms in front of their horned followers, like so many mad dervishes.[12]

At the lower end of the social scale, Jeremiah Goldswain had no thought of his surroundings but recorded that he could earn for himself two Rixdollars a day during the six weeks before leaving for Wait's location: 'our time of service did not commence until we rived on they Land that was alotted for ous'.[13] As for the Khoikhoi leaders of the wagons, they were 'the most dispisable creatours that ever I saw: most of them were half-naked having nothing more to cover them with but six or eight sheep skins'. The settlers were soon experiencing the tensions of the racial mix their arrival had added to. John Ayliff, of Willson's party, asked a Khoikhoi passer by if some berries he had picked were edible ('good for skof'[14]) he addressed the man as 'Hottentot' and was rebuked: 'What for ye call me Hottentot?' 'Well,' I said, 'you are a Hottentot ain't you?' He replied, 'Ja ik is, but we don't like to be called Hottentots'. Ayliff, a Methodist missionary, published in 1846 his *Vocabulary of the Kafir Language*).

Pringle's experience encompassed the Bantu-speaking Africans when he rode the nine miles to Bethelsdorp, guided by 'a Hottentot boy ... [who] trotted along at a goodly pace by the side of my pony'.[15] This boy and the 'mad dervishes' leading the wagons gave Pringle his first impressions of the indigenous people he had come to live among. His view was to expand considerably during the Bethelsdorp visit, which was to have a far-reaching impact upon his view of human relations in South Africa.

Bethelsdorp had a sad history. The pioneer missionary, Dr Johannes Theodorus Van der Kemp, a man of learning and dedication but impossibly out of step with the colonists and officials around him, had been given a site not of his choosing, with serious disadvantages in its infertility and lack of water, and most seriously from 1806, the proximity of Jacob Glen Cuyler, the magistrate at Uitenhage eight miles away, who had authority over him. The James Reads, father and son, of lesser calibre but devoted to their Khoikhoi flock, also found Cuyler and the surrounding Boer farmers hostile and unaccommodating and it is a credit to their work that Pringle was to find much to admire, in the people of the mission if not in their station. Attending the evening service in their 'rustic chapel', where the large congregation was 'attentive and devout and their singing ... singularly pleasing and harmonious", he saw before him 'the remnant of an aboriginal race, to whom this remote region now occupied by white colonists, had at no distant period belonged'. The older people among them

> had probably spent their early days in the wild freedom of nomadic life, and worn out their middle life in the service of the colonists, it was pleasing to think that *here*, and in a few other institutions such as this, the Christian humanity of Europe had done something to alleviate European oppression.

Here, if '*a few* of the race were enabled to escape from personal thraldom' it was to 'emerge from heathen darkness into the glorious light and liberty of the Gospel' rather than to any hope of a return to a lost autonomous polity, which to Pringle simply meant 'the indolent habits of nomadic life'. If Pringle was to dedicate himself to relieving the oppression of the many Khoikhoi whose land had been taken from them, restoration of it was not even a dream.

His Bethelsdorp visit also revealed to Pringle the inhumanity of colonial rule.

An African woman with a little daughter and a baby on her back had been 'made prisoner by order of the Commandant on the frontier', with other women, for crossing into the colony without leave. She had been brought from magistrate Cuyler in Uitenhage to Bethelsdorp by a black constable, with orders to the missionary, the Revd George Barker, to send her on as a servant to a farmer 20 miles to the west. The woman pleaded passionately for freedom and justice for herself and her children, 'in the Amakosa dialect', translated into Dutch by the mission people who had gathered round. Barker could do nothing but try to console her. This was the start of Pringle's sympathy for the dispossessed amaRharhabe section of the Xhosa-speaking peoples on the frontier. He

> could not help beginning to suspect that my European countrymen, who thus made captives of harmless women and children, were in reality greater barbarians than the savage natives of Caffraria.

Back at Algoa Bay he went back on board the *Brilliant* until 25 May when the party was at last allowed ashore. He visited Uitenhage, 16 miles way, and 'one or two other places', while awaiting the arrival of the Acting Governor and had much time to observe his fellow passengers with a sharp eye.

The 'higher class of settlers' in their pavilion tents with their 'elegant arrangements and appliances … appeared rather unfitted for *roughing it* (to use the expressive phraseology of the camp)'. Indeed the diary of 15-year-old Sophia , daughter of Major George Pigot and grand-daughter of Lord Pigot, a former governor of Madras, described those first days on shore as if the family were still with the county set in Staffordshire or even taking the waters at Bath. She had no qualms about her new surroundings: 'Went on shore at Algoa Bay – very much delighted. There were dinners and teas'. 'Captain Charlton sent me a tart'. 'Delightful walk and very beautiful country … walked down the hill to seek for a man to tune the Piano.'[16] Sophia later married Donald Moodie, the laird's son from Orkney, bore him 14 children and lived an eventful life in the Cape Colony and Natal until her death in 1881.

The Pringles escaped Sophia's attention, which was focused entirely on her own kind and on the young officers from the sloop *Menai* in the bay and such as Lieutenant Gowan of the 72nd Foot, stationed at Fort Frederick, on the hill above the landing place. Like Thomas Philipps, gentleman farmer and former banker from Pembrokeshire, she would have seen the Pringles as 'very honest plain Scotch people'.[17] Colonial life was a great leveller: Sophia's brother-in-law John Wedderburn Dunbar Moodie was to be Thomas and Margaret Pringle's house guest in London when on his way to Canada many years later.

In the Settlers' Camp Pringle found 'respectable tradesmen and jolly farmers … watermen, fishermen and sailors …numerous groups of pale-visaged artisans and operative manufacturers from London and other larger towns , [the] far larger proportion [of whom] were squalid in their aspect, slovenly in their attire and domestic arrangements, and discontented and uncourteous in their demeanour'. With parties of pauper agricultural labourers, they formed 'a motley and unprepossessing collection of people' – the very sort – 'idle, insolent and drunken, and mutinously disposed towards their masters and superiors' – of which the Albany scheme was designed to rid England.

These settlers set off for their locations in long trains of wagons – Philipps's five wagons were part of a train of 19 and were deposited with their boxes and implements in the open veld to start making their homes. None was far from another family or group in their stretch of the Zuurveld running down to the sea. For the Scottish party a different scene waited.

They had to bide their time at the Bay for three weeks before the Acting Governor, General Sir Rufane Donkin and the deputy colonial secretary, Henry Ellis arrived. That same day, 6 June 1820, Sir Rufane named the new town-to-be after his young wife, born Elizabeth Markham, daughter of the Dean of York, who had died in India shortly before. Pringle's real business followed when he presented Sir Walter Scott's letter to Donkin, which Scott was told, 'made a very favourable impression and I received assurances of friendship and goodwill'.[18] Donkin was described by Dr Thomas Calton, leader of the Nottinghamshire party, as 'a man of the most easy and pleasant access I ever saw; delighted the settlers by his affability and polite attention to their several petitions'. Pringle wrote home that from both Donkin and Henry Ellis, deputy to Colonel Bird, Colonial Secretary in Cape Town, he 'experienced then and since, the most zealous and friendly attention'.[19] Barrow's and other letters (about Pringle's need for employment) Pringle had already left for Ellis. He learned that the Scottish settlers were to be placed in the upper part of the Baviaans River valley, adjacent to the frontier with 'Caffer' territory, far to the north of the English in Albany. 'The highland Emigrants under Captain Grant and General Campbell'[20] were to be beside them, the town of New Edinburgh would be established with a magistracy and a Scottish clergyman. The Highlanders would form 'a local militia for the defence of that part of the frontier'. Tragically, however, the *Abeona* carrying the Highlanders to the Cape caught fire off the Guinea coast five months later, over a hundred perished and the 27 saved did not join their fellow Scots in the Baviaans River valley. Pringle's party were to be the sole British settlers in what must have seemed a most perilous location.

They moved off a week later, having spent four weeks in the Settlers' Camp. Pringle's liberal awareness of and sympathy for the indigenous people, the slaves and others brought to the Cape by the Dutch from their eastern possessions was already marked. He took pains to note in *African Sketches* that a house in the new town was being built for 'a Malay named Fortuin' who later became 'one of the wealthiest and most respectable inhabitants of the place'.

It took a week from the meeting with Donkin before seven ox-wagons were available for Pringle's party and on 13 June 1820 the 16-day journey to the Baviaans River began. It was slightly prolonged by Pringle's decision to divert the wagon train, through thick bush, to the Zwartkops salt pan he had read about in Barrow's *Account of Travels*, where a year's supply of 'culinary salt' was collected.

The 16–day journey inland was a revelation. Pringle was captivated. His word-picture of their travelling party at the evening outspan – the Scots, Afrikaners, Khoikhoi and Bushmen ('for there were two or three of the latter tribe among our wagon leaders') equals that of the Settlers' Camp and surpasses the paintings of the frontier artists Thomas Baines and Frederick Timpson I'Ons. The night sounds made the Scots realize that 'we were pilgrims in the wilds of savage Africa'. They travelled on through the Zuurberg with its 'dark jungle', through park-like scenery and the 'desolate sterility of savage mountains' over 'parched and desert plains' seeing only a handful of far-separated farm houses, huge herds of springbok and scarcely a human being.

After eight days they reached the army post of Roodewal (today's Cookhouse) on the Great Fish River. Lieutenant Charles Lennox Stretch of the 38th Foot, in command, recalled that midwinter night 57 years later:

> About 8 o'clock in the night the sergeant on duty reported to me that a number of wagons had arrived, and the people [had] requested to be allowed to remain for the night. I immediately went to the wagons. It was very dark and a person spoke to me. I asked him from whence he came and his name. It was ... Thomas Pringle, the head of a party of settlers from Algoa Bay ... en route to the location assigned to them ... on the Bavians River ... It was a bitter cold night and ... I requested Mr Pringle to accept whatever accommodation I had for the party.[21]

After crossing 'one of the wildest and least inhabited tracts of the frontier districts',[22] wrote Pringle, they 'were received by the officers of the garrison and their ladies with the utmost kindness and hospitality' and found the 'cordial hospitality and English comforts ... altogether delightful.' Of more lasting advantage was the fact that such men as Stretch shared Pringle's liberal sympathies towards the indigenous people as did Stretch's father-in-law Robert Hart, who rode over from the colonial government's Somerset Farm which he had managed since leaving the army three years earlier. Despite his 'iron look and rigid nerve' Hart was moved to tears when he heard the Scots accents of the women in Pringle's party 'fresh and unsophisticated from the banks of the Teviot and the Lothian Tyne', which he had last seen in 1795. He became a firm ally of Pringle's in the years ahead. Pringle wrote:

> He was extremely well informed respecting the capabilities of the country and the character of the inhabitants. His information and advice ... were highly important and were communicated with much kindly feeling, and with a certain shrewd sagacity which we found to be one of his characteristic features.[23]

More remarkably still, the magistrate of the Graaff-Reinet district where their location was situated, was a man of firm liberal convictions, though of a more abrasive and mercurial temperament. Lieutenant Andries Stockenstrom had succeeded his father, after a four year 'interregnum', as magistrate, Anders Stockenstrom having been killed by Rharhabe tribesmen while in a parley with them during the campaign to drive Ndlambe's people out of the Zuurveld in 1812. Andries Stockenstrom had a low opinion of many among the settlers, who were 'capable of any species of crime that can be traced in the police records ... who have done more towards the demoralization of South Africa than the conquest and domination of [by?] the Kafirs could have done'.[24] The Pringle party, he wrote, 'were consigned to me' and were part of the 'enterprising, intelligent, industrious mass'. He was to write later: 'From what little I knew of Mr Pringle ... I entertained a warm liking for his person and a great respect for his character'.[25]

A sub-magistracy had been established in 1819 in the hamlet of Cradock, where Captain William Walter Harding, 'an old soldier and a perfect gentleman' in Stockenstrom's view, held office. He formed a close bond with Pringle and did all in his power to assist his party. Harding had served against Napoleon in Egypt and in the Peninsular War before the taking of the Cape in 1806. He 'had never seen a more spirited little action'[26] than the Battle of Grahamstown on 22 April 1819 and doubtless enlivened Pringle's account in his edition of George Thompson's *Travels and Adventures in Southern Africa* (1827). Harding spoke with unusual admiration for Makhanda's and the British ally Boesak's actions. Ndlambe's warriors were not the cowards the *Edinburgh Magazine* had labelled them.

The contrast with the magistrate at Uitenhage, Jacob Glen Cuyler, who had made life impossible for the pioneer missionary Van der Kemp at Bethelsdorp, was palpable. The settlers in Albany were to suffer under the authority of Henry Rivers, as unsympathetic to them as was the Governor, Lord Charles Somerset on his return from England in November 1821.

After their welcome at Roodewal, which ended with a dinner in the officers' mess, the last eight days, transported by fresh wagons and oxen and with a new guide for the final stage, P.A. Opperman, Field Cornet of Baviaans River, were of a different order altogether.

After a relatively easy first day they reached the farm of Opperman, who had been a loyalist in the Slagtersnek rebellion against British rule five years before, and that of 'Groot Willem' Prinsloo, who gave them a warm welcome despite his having been on the wrong side at Slagtersnek. The really hard going began as they entered the narrow cutting of the Baviaans River and were 'literally obliged to *hew* out our path up the valley'. For five days more they made their way 'up this African glen … with the handsaw, the pick-axe, the crow-bar and the sledgehammer, and the lashing of the poor oxen to force them on (sometimes 20 or 30 in one team) … through such a track as no English reader can form any adequate conception of.' At last, 'after extraordinary exertions and hair-breadth escapes' the wagons reached a ridge overlooking 'a beautiful vale about six or seven miles in length … like a verdant basin'.

> The bottom of the valley, through which the infant river meandered, presented a warm, pleasant, and secluded aspect … with groves of mimosa trees, among which we observed in the distance herds of wild animals – antelopes and quaggas – pasturing in undisturbed quietude.

It was this prospect of which Field Cornet Opperman said, as they stood on an elevated ridge: 'And now, mynheer, *daar leg uwe veld* – There lies your country.'[27]

'*Uwe veld*' must have seemed beset with hazards, perils and a wildness that called forth all their courage and pioneering spirit. Some of the Slagtersnek rebels, five of them hanged by magistrate Cuyler five years before, had run their cattle and lived here in their crude reed huts, known as *hardbieshuisies*. The land just below the ridge had been occupied by Hans Bezuidenhout, the rebel leader killed in a final shoot-out with Cuyler's troops. It became, as it still is, Craig Rennie. Other frontier Boers had been expelled from near-by farms. The location itself stood on the very frontier of the Colony, proclaimed by the Dutch governor in 1786, and now beside the so-called 'Neutral Territory' from which the amaRharhabe had been driven eastwards, over the Keiskamma River, only the previous year.

A further danger was presented by the armed bands of mixed-race and Khoikhoi *banditti*, some of them deserters from the colonial forces, who could attack an unprotected settlement with impunity. Many more descendants of frontier Boers and Khoikhoi, Bushmen or slave women lived among the Boer farmers, most in a state of abject dependence. Their plight stirred Pringle's human feelings. It was the treatment of one of these by his master, Freek Bezuidenhout, that had led to the Slagtersnek rebellion in 1815, when Boer malcontents rose up against the new British colonial power whose forces had sought in vain to bring Bezuidenhout to trial and had killed him when he fired upon them. The explosive mix into which the Scots settlers had ventured included the Rharhabe people under their chief, Ngqika who had scorned their approach to him to join them in driving out the British. It was Ngqika whom the British recognized as paramount chief on the frontier and his uncle Ndlambe whom they attacked in defence of Ngqika's interests and their own land claims.

The caves and ravines of the Winterberg were a refuge also for nomadic Bushmen, the hunter-gatherer underclass of the Khoikhoi. The sworn enemies of the colonizers who had taken their hunting grounds, they would slaughter their sheep, cattle and horses, regardless of their need for food. Pringle's 'Song of the Wild Bushman' expresses respect for his subject's refusal to 'crouch beneath the Christian's hand and kennel with his hounds', and proclaims that 'the brown Serpent of the Rocks \ His den doth yet retain'. He was to employ a Bushman boy whom he called Dugal after Dugald Dalgetty, a much loved character in Scott's *A Legend of Montrose*, published in 1819, which Pringle must have read or acquired before leaving Scotland. Scott's Dugald was a mercenary who did not make up his mind whether he was for King (whites?) or Covenanters (Nguni Africans?) until the end of the book. Pringle mistakenly calls Scott's Dugal a 'son of the mist' in a footnote to his poem 'The Lion Hunt'. Dugal the Bushman boy would occasionally go off to the wild but return after a few days. Though unnamed, he was immortalized in Pringle's classic 'Afar in the desert' in which each of the five stanzas begins:

Afar in the Desert I love to ride,
With the silent Bush-boy alone by my side.[28]

Pringle was prepared to go out on commando against Bushman marauders during his last 12–month stay in Baviaans River, incurring at a later stage the disapproval of his friend Fairbairn in Cape Town, to whom he replied: 'Your denunciations against my Bushman Commandoes do not alarm me … I am no quaker to turn my cheek to the smiter, and if attacked will resist even to slaying the aggressor, be he who he may'.[29] He took a milder tone in his official correspondence, arguing against bloodshed in routing out Bushmen attackers, and showing a pragmatic attitude to the contradictions of the liberal's role in South Africa's racial conflicts.

All this lay in the future. Apart from the Bethelsdorp incident, Pringle had no commitment to his later crusade for decency towards the indigenous people, nor any fear of them, despite the advice of Captain Harding, who arrived, with a land-surveyor, to meet them that first day, 'to take careful precautions to avoid being surprised by our wild neighbours, the Bushmen and Caffers'.[30] That first night on their location:

> At about midnight we were suddenly roused by the roar of a lion close to our tents. It was so loud and tremendous that for a moment I actually thought a thunderstorm had burst upon us. But the peculiar *expression* of the sound – the voice of fury as well as of power – instantly undeceived me: and instinctively snatching my loaded gun from the tent-pole, I hurried out …[31]

There follows in the *Narrative* a memorable, precise description of the nature of the lion's roar and its terrifying effect 'on our thus hearing it for the first time in the heart of the wilderness'. He manages a touch of humour in imagining the 'laughable array of pale or startled visages' they would have presented after they had been 'thus hurriedly and fearfully aroused from our slumbers'. Lions were seen by day and in time Thomas Pringle was to join the lion hunt when, the following April, a lion, seen near his farm Eildon the day before, killed his favourite horse. Several versions of his account of the hunt were published, the most spirited his poem 'The Lion Hunt'[32] with the party of Bezuidenhout, Coetzer, Muller, Lucas van Vuur[en], the mixed-race Arend, Eckhard and Groepe, the 'Hottentot lads' Slinger, Allie, Dikkop and Dugal [the Bush-boy], with George Rennie and Pringle himself, the crutches unmentioned, in at the kill. The poem ends:

> What a glorious lion! What sinews – what claws -
> And seven feet ten from the rump to the jaws!
>
> His hide, with the paws and the bones of his skull,
> With the spoils of the leopard and the buffalo bull,
> We'll send to Sir Walter. – Now, boys, let us dine,
> And talk of our deeds o'er a flask of old wine.

The skin, to be seen at Sir Walter's feet in Sir William Allan's portrait of 1831 (see Illustration no. 3, p. 62), has long since disintegrated. The skull of the now extinct Cape black-maned lion, *Leo leo melanochitus*, which stood on his study mantel shelf at Abbotsford was later, according to Scott family sources, sent to the British Museum – a link between Pringle's kindly patron and that day in the Baviaans River valley in April 1821. Regrettably, it was recorded as transferred to the Natural History Museum in Kensington, which has no record of it.

The day after that first night of the lion's roar Opperman and the armed escort set off with the wagons, some of them shattered by their journey through that almost impenetrable track 'leaving us in our wild domain to our own courage and resources.'

NOTES

[1] Pringle (1966), p. 2.

2   Pringle to Scott, 22.9.1820, Vigne (2011), p. 27. NLS MS 874, f 43–6.
3   Pringle (1966), pp.18–19.
4   *Op. cit.*, p. 19.
5   Pringle (1966), p. 6.
6   *Ibid.*
7   Elphick, Robert, 'The Impact of Foreign Missionaries', *New History of South Africa,* ed. H. Giliomee and Bernard Mbenga (2007), p. 99.
8   *Ibid.*
9   *Souvenir in Commemoration of the Centenary of the 1820 Settlers of Albany* (1920), p. 137.
10 Pringle (1966), p. 8.
11 Dugmore, Henry, *Reminiscences of an Albany Settler* (1871. 1958 ed.), p. 15.
12 Pringle (1966), pp. 9–10.
13 Goldswain, vol. 1, p. 19.
14 *Souvenir,* p. 137.
15 Pringle (1966), p. 13.
16 Pigot, Sophia, ed. M. Rainier, *The Journals of Sophia Pigot, 1819–1821* (1974), pp, 50, 58.
17 Philipps, Thomas, ed. A. Keppel-Jones, *Philipps, 1820 Settler. A Selection* (1960), p. 300.
18 Pringle to Scott, 22.9.1820, Vigne (2011), p. 27. NLS MS 867 f 43–6.
19 Pringle to unknown, 30.9.1820, Vigne (2011), p. 33. *The Courier,* 23.5.1821.
20 Pringle to Scott, 22.9.1820, Vigne (2011), p. 28. NLS MS 867 f 43–6. See p. 85.
21 Stretch, C.L., MS, 1877. Pringle Letterbook, NELM.
22 Pringle (1966), p. 27.
23 *Op. cit.,* p. 28.
24 Stockenstrom, Sir Andries, ed. C.W. Hutton, *The Autobiography of the Late Sir Andries Stockenstrom, Bart.,* 2 vols (1887), vol. 1, pp. 168–9.
25 *Op. cit.,* p. 201.
26 Thompson (1967), vol. 1, p. 36.
27 Pringle (1966), p. 33.
28 Pringle (1838), p. 8. See pp. 84, 152.
29 Pringle to Fairbairn, 5.8.1825, Vigne (2011), p. 200. LP, Fairbairn Papers, 1, 56.
30 Pringle (1966), p. 35.
31 *Op. cit.,* p. 39.
32 Pringle (1838), p. 21.

6

At Glen Lynden

They spent the night where Field Cornet Opperman left them and next morning 'leaving a sufficient guard to protect our little camp, we proceeded on foot, well armed, to inspect our new domain'.[1] They found it 'sprinkled over ... with beautiful clumps and groves of mimosa trees, interspersed with open grassy pastures, while the river, a gurgling mountain-brook, meandered placidly through the fertile meadows'. Almost a scene from 'The Autumnal Excursion' but for the troops of quaggas, the hartebeest, duiker, rietbok and wild hog, all named and described in his *African Sketches* (1834), based on the lost journal he kept all those years.

At last they chose a spot three miles up river from that camp for their first settlement. They called it Glen Lynden, a name of Pringle's invention rather than from the map of Scotland. It was later given to their whole location and now denotes only the glebe of their church and its Dutch Reformed neighbour. It became the farm of Pringle's father Robert, now called Lower Clifton, and he and Beatrice, Thomas's stepmother, are buried there.

Captain Harding, that 'very intelligent and agreeable man',[2] as Pringle described him in a letter to Scott, arrived with the government surveyor H.J.H. Azerond, to define their boundaries and formally hand over the location to Thomas. Then came a rude shock. Harding and his party left next morning (1 July 1820) 'after strongly advising me to take careful precautions to avoid being surprised by our wild neighbours, the Bushmen and Caffers'. Nightly sentinels were posted and 'this precaution we still continue',[3] he wrote in a letter home a month later.

In *African Sketches*, their first Sunday service, the day after Harding's departure, ended with 'an excellent discourse from a volume of sermons presented to me on parting by a revered relative, the Revd Dr Pringle of Perth',[4] his uncle in fact, Alexander, brother of Robert. 'While we were singing our last psalm in the afternoon, an antelope (*oribi*) ... stood for a little while on the opposite side of the river, gazing at us in ... amazement as if yet unacquainted with man, the great destroyer'. They did not feel themselves to be in a leafy corner of Roxburghshire for the river 'shaded here and there by the graceful willow of Babylon vividly reminded us of the pathetic lament of the Hebrew exiles: "By the rivers of Babylon there we sat..."'

That same letter to Scotland soberly described their perilous state, until 25 July when ten armed Khoikhoi guards arrived by ox-wagon from Harding's Cradock sub-magistracy:

> Placed in a remote corner of mountainous country, far from all roads, and at least 20 miles distant from the nearest Boor's house, exposed to prowling beasts of prey, and more savage men, with only 10 men able to bear arms, and half of these but little experienced in the use of them, we felt the necessity of constant vigilance …

While the able-bodied men cut reeds and carried timber on their shoulders for the building of their huts, Pringle 'was sometimes left the only guard to the women and children at our camp; and often their frighted fancies conjured up Bushmen and Caffers moving over the hills, or skulking among the rocks …'

In *African Sketches* he quoted directly from his journal in those first days:

> *Monday 3 July*: All hands mustered this morning to begin erecting our temporary huts at Clifton, three miles up the valley. One party appointed to cut willow-poles, another to cut reeds by the river, a third to carry the materials to the spot. Peter Rennie and I left to guard the camp, for fear of a surprise from native banditti. Some large baboons among the rocks, on the hill tops, at first mistaken for Bushmen. The evening comes on wet. Our camp alarmed by a lion at midnight.[5]

In those first four weeks sowing and planting filled their days, when the *hardbies* huts had been built of willow, reeds and clay. Two of the men set off for Roodewal for supplies and with a letter asking Captain Stretch to buy 'a horse or two'. A horse was sent six days later and next day a load of flour from Robert Hart at Somerset farm which, wrote Pringle with nice understatement, 'was somewhat damaged by the wagon having been overturned in the river'[6] The two Khoikhoi men with the flour brought also a letter from Hart inviting Pringle to accompany him on 'an excursion into Cafferland … but must stick to my post at present.' They had reached their location only a fortnight before. Much travelling was to come later, his first departure from Glen Lynden taking place three months after their arrival.

Pringle wrote much about the wildlife – most of all about the lions, a constant threat to their livestock as their flocks and herds grew in number, through trading with their Boer neighbours, and to their horses. The communities about them are even more closely observed and described. Among them were 'the boor Engelbrecht' and his family, squatting nine miles down river on the farm Lynedoch and hired to transport with his wagon the party's goods to Lower Clifton. Lynedoch had been allocated to Colonel John Graham, whose headquarters, when his troops were clearing the Zuurveld, now Albany, of Ndlambe's people in 1812, became the settler capital, Grahamstown. From Simon's Town where Graham was the magistrate he was appointed to the new magistracy of Albany 700 miles to the east but was too ill to move and died in 1821, aged 42. Lynedoch had earlier been farmed by one of the Slagtersnek rebels. We glimpse its squatting occupier Adriaan Stephanus Engelbrecht and his way of life in a brief word picture in Pringle's journal:

> He cultivates no ground, but with his family, lives entirely, without bread or vegetables, on the milk and flesh of his flock, and what he kills in hunting. He appears to be very ignorant and uncultivated, but is civil enough, and has a shrewd eye to his own interest…. Purchased a few sheep from him for slaughter.[7]

His November 1820 letter to a friend in Scotland judges the Afrikaners by the likes of Engelbrecht.

> The upper part of the river had only recently been inhabited by civilized men, if we can apply the epithet *civilized* to the rude African colonists, who had settled here among the Caffres, without any grant or permission of the Government.[8]

His words grew harsher still:

> The Dutch Boors ... are out of the question in regard to society. In manners and information they are scarcely equal to the rudest peasantry of England and far inferior to those of 'Auld Scotland'.

This view was much tempered when he, Margaret and her sister Janet stayed at the farm house of Schalk Burger, an 'affluent grazier' in the Sneeuberg on their way to Cape Town nearly two years later.

> I left them in the afternoon, much pleased with the good humour and good sense that seemed to prevail among these rustic inhabitants of the mountains. There was nothing *Arcadian* certainly about them, but their appearance was decent and comfortable, and their manners frank, hospitable and courteous.[9]

A week after employing Engelbrecht, Pringle and his brother John and 'the free Negro Black William' who had been sent from Cradock with letters from Stockenstrom and Harding, rode out to survey the location more closely. There was 'nothing to be seen from the tops of the nearest hills but other mountains, higher and more desolate, behind them'[10] They visited 'Engelbrecht's kraal' only to find that 'he, with his wagon, family, flocks and herds has moved off (perhaps from fear of the Bushmen), to some other *squatting* place. Now our nearest neighbour down the valley is Groot William, about 25 miles distant'. Adriaan Stephanus Engelbrecht had in fact been banned from the area for seven years as a Slagtersnek rebel. Perhaps he felt, with the Scots party, and now Black William, in the offing it was time to move on.

It was on this ride that 'Black William gave us some details of the insurrection of the Boors in this quarter in 1815 and showed the cave where Frederick Bezuidenhout fired on the party sent to arrest him'. Perhaps hearing the story of Slagtersnek from such a narrator helped form Pringle's view of what he called 'this wicked and foolish rebellion'.[11] In his own account of the rebellion he describes the former rebels as 'very submissive subjects to the Government and inoffensive neighbours, as far as *we* [Pringle's emphasis] were concerned.'

Andries Stockenstrom had been appointed magistrate (or Landdrost) in May 1815, when, in his words, 'this knot of desperadoes [had] set all law at defiance'[12] Many years later he credited *African Sketches* with 'an admirably detailed account of this sad rebellion and tragedy ... compiled from the official records and from the accounts given by the magistrates and many of the Boers themselves'. Even Sir George Cory, whose seminal *The Rise of South Africa* supports the colonists' case throughout, found Bezuidenhout and his confederates 'misguided', yet he dismissed Stockenstrom's words as 'evidently ... inspired by Pringle' and Pringle's as 'so permeated with anti-colonial prejudice and so coloured to suit party purposes that it is difficult to regard it as better than an actual falsehood' albeit 'in the main in agreement with the evidence taken at the trials'.[13] Cory ends this bitter contumely:

> Though Mr Pringle has written much in connection with South Africa which, regarded purely and simply as writing, is beautiful, the Eastern Province has little for which to thank him.

Yet Pringle, unlike most contemporary European observers of the rural Afrikaners, who either liked or loathed them, was tolerant in his view, after that first outburst quoted above. The frontiersmen, those 'rude African colonists' he first encountered, were treated with humour. He and his neighbours found themselves 'somewhat teased by Sunday visits from our Dutch-African neigh-bours'[14] from further down the valley or the Tarka region to the north. The hosts were obliged to share their dinner with these uninvited guests, whose object was 'either to gratify idle curiosity or with a view to commercial dealings'. After advising them that 'secular business' could not be conducted on a Sunday, Pringle offered them 'a seat among my Hottentot audience and invited them to read aloud the Sunday service' he held in Dutch. Embarrassed by their semi-literate state and finding it 'a shocking degradation to sit down amidst a group of Hottentots' the Sunday visitors came no more. 'In other respects we found them generally, however uncultivated, by no means disagreeable neighbours ... civil and good-natured and, according to the custom of the country, extremely hospitable.'

Pringle found himself in those early months 'a sort of civil and military officer, of a medical practitioner, religious instructor, engineer, architect, gardener, plas-terer, cabinet maker and, I might add, *tinker*.'[15] He had enjoyed and become quite skilled at both carpentry and gardening as a boy and was thus able to 'act the Robinson Crusoe in a small way'. Not an apt analogy as he had Margaret and her sister with him, and, besides his father, the family, their ploughmen and the rest of the party, the 'Hottentot guard', the 'ten poor ignorant natives under my tempo-rary direction'.[16] They had relieved the men from 'keeping up nightly sentinels' and of the fear of being 'surprised by marauders from the waste country to the east-ward'. Though 'well-armed and skilled in the use of the musket', the men were not soldiers but contract workers on the farms of the Agter-Sneeuberg and Tarka regions, drafted by the magistrates, presumably Harding at Cradock, who paid for their sustenance.

Though he identifies none of them as individual characters, he writes of them with a general benevolence. 'Intelligent Mulattoes' or 'of the Bushman blood', all were 'respectful, faithful and strictly honest' – a sad contrast with Sandy Mortimer, 23, Charles Sydserff's servant to whom Pringle gave a pass, countersigned by Harding, to leave the settlement. Mortimer, who had been destitute when Sydserff engaged him, and Sydserff's other servant James Souness, seemed from the start 'disposed to mutiny'[17] and on 1 October 1820 Pringle wrote in his journal that he had sent Mortimer off 'with the Somerset wagon towards Grahamstown. This lad has turned out to be at once a fool and a blackguard, and utterly irreclaimable'. He was not heard of again.

Those first guards were relieved every three of four weeks and Pringle found no cause to complain 'except in a very few instances, of neglect of duty or misconduct … during the eight months we were thus guarded.' It was they who were his congregants at the Sunday services Pringle held for them in Dutch. He found them earnest worshippers and anxious for instruction. 'One poor fellow, to whom my wife had given a New Testament, several months afterwards sent her, from his master's place, a hundred miles distant, the present of a milch goat with twin kids, as a testimony of gratitude'.[18]

From the start Pringle had urged Harding to find Khoikhoi who would help the party work the land, and, though the guards took on a minimum of herding and farm work, their mixed-race kinsmen were soon to be a source of both. An aged German settler, Johannes Stolz, at Swaershoek, a few miles north-east of Somerset farm, had received, Pringle learned later, 'a favourable report … of the treatment the Coloured caste had received at Glen Lynden' and wrote to Pringle in August 1821 asking him to take in 'certain families of his Hottentot vassals'.[19] The letter was followed by an urgent message from Stolz urging Pringle to help protect his dependants as he was about to die. Pringle and George Rennie rode the 70 km to Swaershoek and arrived only to find that Stolz had died two days before. The funeral dinner reminded Pringle 'of some of Sir Walter Scott's graphic sketches'.

But how different! 'The only real mourners were the coloured people, who were not admitted to the feast, and only permitted to follow the funeral at a humble distance'. Stolz's considerable property quickly 'fell into the hands of covetous strangers and the Mulattoes, who had occupied a large part of it as tenants and cottagers, were speedily dispossessed.' Pringle took in a dozen or more stock-owning families as tenants and others as farm servants and herdsmen. Thus 'we greatly strengthened our own hands, while …. protecting and benefiting those oppressed and despised people.'

A month after the arrival of the Mulattoes, Field Cornet Opperman called up six of them for a commando raid into the bushman country. Pringle had not been notified and complained strongly to Harding, who exempted the men. In a rare reference to his lameness, he told Harding of his particular need for such labour: 'From bodily infirmity, you are aware that it is impossible for me … to give my personal assistance whether in agricultural labour or the charge of cattle'.[20]

His need for help and the link with his disability is revealed also in a letter to Stockenstrom in February 1821. Unable to obtain any Khokhoi servants he asked Stockenstrom to find a Bush boy to be put in his charge:

> I am frequently obliged to ride alone which from my late accident I find to be dangerous from other causes than Bosjesmen or Caffers. On the day that I had my fall … had I not been luckily very near home at the time I must have lain till I perished, for my collar bone being fractured I could not use my crutches and our horse galloped off from me.[21]

The boy Dugal arrived four months later. Pringle mentions in a note to 'The Lion Hunt' that 'I named him Dugal after Sir Walter Scott's "son of the mist" of that name'. Like so much of the wild Winterberg and Mathole regions, there were constant reminders of the Highlands of Scotland. Scott describes the 'children of the mist' as living, like the Bushmen, in a place 'well suited to their name and habits. It was a beetling crag, round which winded a very narrow and broken footpath.' Like the Bushmen, 'they considered the forester's hunting in their vicinity an aggression'.[22]

Pringle's Dugal was 'but partially *tamed*, poor fellow, and used to take himself off to the wilds, occasionally, for two or three days at a time; but always returned when he tired of the *veld-kost* (country food, i.e wild roots)'.

In Glen Lynden the Bushmen were the aggressors and Pringle made no objection to the sending out of commandos against these marauding *banditti,* the original possessors of the land. In October 1821 he wrote to Harding of the action of Second Lieutenant Pettingal, R.E., surveying the river, who, leading an armed party against a large band of Bushmen 'came upon a party of these wild marauders in one of the most savage recesses of the neighbouring mountains. They were at breakfast on a grey horse, which they had slaughtered ... Pettingal, enraged by the loss of his best horse, poured in a volley upon them, but apparently without effect for they all scrambled off, with inconceivable agility, among the rocks and bushes. ... he did not succeed in killing or capturing one of them'.[23] He was to ride out himself against the Bushmen on his return to Glen Lynden from Cape Town, a fact made much of by his detractors among censorious South African historians.

His note to the 'Song of the Wild Bushman' in *African Sketches* predated the theorizing of anthropologists and linguisticians, who saw the Bushmen as a separate species (between men and apes, according to Gustav Fritsch in 1880). To Pringle they appeared to be 'the remains of Hottentot hordes ... driven, either by the gradual encroachments of the European colonists, or by internal wars with other tribes, to seek for refuge among the inaccessible rocks and deserts of the interior'.[24] His was a mixture of sympathy for their fate and realism about the effect it had had on their character: 'Having descended from the pastoral to the hunter state ...from a mild, confiding and unenterprising race of shepherds, they have been gradually transformed into wandering hordes of fierce, suspicious and vindictive savages.' These 'South-African "children of the mist" have been constantly found in a state of precarious truce, or of bitter hostility with the colonists.'

Their likeness to Scott's 'children of the mist' fits with so much else of Pringle's overlaying of the Scottish landscape and people, and of Scott's depiction of them, on to this remote corner of Africa. They are 'a small sept of banditti, called, from their houseless state and their incessantly wandering among the mountains and glens, Children of the Mist, ... a fierce and hardy people, with all the irritability, and wild and vengeful passions, proper to men who have never known the restraint of civilized society', wrote Scott in *A Legend of Montrose.*[25]

Outstanding among the new Mulatto tenantry who would help protect Glen Lynden from marauders were the Groepes, offspring of a German settler and former Field-Cornet of Swaershoek who 'now in extreme old age was considered to have *lost caste* from his associating with his own children by a Hottentot woman'.[26] They were tenants of Robert Pringle on a four-year contract which obliged them also to help build the road out of the settlement. Two of the sons, Christiaan and Karel, owned stock equal in quantity to 'many of the poorer Boors'.

Even Harding, though 'a humane man and an able and upright magistrate', had 'considerable doubts whether the colonial laws would sanction our receiving them on our grounds as *tenants*'.[27] Stockenstrom, Harding's superior at Graaff-Reinet, who in coming years was to draft, with the help of Dr Philip, the Magna Carta of the Khoikhoi and their mixed-race kin, Ordinance 50 (1828), 'decided in favour of the more liberal interpretation and thus the Mulattoes of Zwagershoek became our tenants'.

Pringle now likened himself to 'a petty "border" chief, being able to muster upwards of thirty armed horsemen, including our own party and the six Hottentot soldiers at an hour's notice'.[28] The Corporal and five privates of the Cape Corps regiment, formed by Colonel John Graham from the old Pandours of VOC rule, had replaced the 'Hottentot guard' in March 1821. Pringle reported to the Colonial Secretary, Bird, that the soldiers were 'very sober and well-behaved men and much preferable to our former guard of Provincial Hottentots',[29] whose unwillingness to perform farming tasks or to help build the clay fort Pringle planned (but did not, in the end, need) had become irksome to the settlers.

The arrival of the Cape Corps men raised morale in the party, much lowered by a long summer drought followed by the failure of their first crop at the start of 1821 from 'rust', as with the settlers in Albany, and by the news that neither of the Scottish parties expected to share the Baviaans River valley with them would arrive. Captain Grant's 500 Highlanders had withdrawn – many had gone instead to Canada, destination of 600 Highlanders in June 1820 and 2000 in spring 1821 – and the 126, many of them unemployed weavers, from Glasgow and the west of Scotland had suffered a fire in their vessel the *Abeona* in mid-Atlantic near the Equator on 11 November 1820. Only 27 emigrants survived and journeyed on to the Cape, to be settled there, a few of them in Albany, on the Kowie River.

The new tenantry, with Pringle and Stockenstrom as landlord and magistrate, found themselves in vastly improved conditions of life. When in 1828 Stockenstrom's idea of settling such people on their own land was realized, in the Kat River Settlement, Christiaan and Karel Groepe were among the leaders, Christiaan becoming one of the three Field Cornets. He had come a long way from the helotry of Swaershoek, where he was not allowed to marry his wife of 12 years because, poor unlettered woman, she could not repeat the Catechism correctly.

The Kat River Settlement won praise even from those who had had no good word for 'Hottentots' and 'Bastaards' but it inevitably fell victim to the demand for such fertile and well watered land from the British settlers and Afrikaner farmers. The Kat River people were wholly loyal to the Government through the wars of 1834–5 and 1846–7 that broke the frontier peace that had existed in Pringle's time there. Their sufferings under two successive unjust and harsh magistrates (Biddulph and Bowker) appointed by a misinformed and prejudiced Governor, Sir Henry Pottinger, led them eventually, in 1851 to join with the Xhosa insurgents in Mlanjeni's War, the longest and bloodiest of the frontier conflicts. The most reluctant of the rebels was Christiaan Groepe, doubtless bound in his old loyalty to Stockenstrom, Philip and Pringle.

In a speech to the Cape Parliament, in his sixties, at the end of Mlanjeni's War, Stockenstrom told the story of Kat River, with great eloquence, ending:

> Let no one tell you that the Frontier is out of danger …There is not a black man south of the tropic who trusts you, or who would not turn against you as soon as he should see a chance of crushing you. Every friend you have you have turned into an exasperated foe.[30]

Pringle was spared the horrors of the wars that resumed on Christmas Day 1834, three weeks after his death in distant London. The news of his death came to another sympathetic to the African cause, Captain Stretch, his host at Roodewal and his friend Hart's son-in-law, while on service in the Amatola (Mathole) valley in what is known as the Sixth Frontier War:

> John Pringle, G. Rennie and Mr Scott [married to Pringle's half-sister Beatrice] slept at our camp. Read a letter informing John of his brother's death and his happy end …[31]

Happy to meet his maker but less so had he lived to know how his high hopes for peaceful progress for the indigenous people of South Africa had been brought to a halt.

In the little world of Glen Lynden, with his thirty armed horsemen he 'considered our location perfectly secure from any serious attack of the wild natives in the vicinity'.[32] These 'wild natives' were the Bushmen families still living in the Winterberg and some robber bands of Cape Corps deserters and Khoikhoi who had escaped servitude on Boer farms. The least feared at the time were the Bantu-speaking Africans who had occupied the Neutral Territory on the borders of Glen Lynden and the Baviaans River before the Bezuidenhouts, Fabers and Oppermans had come there.

Of the Thembu community on the border there was little to fear, though the Afrikaner farmers complained of stock theft. Their chief, Bawana of the ama-Tshatshu, was well disposed and Pringle's light-hearted verse picture of his life in Glen Lynden, 'The Emigrant's Cabin' (1822) includes a visit from 'Powana' and a councillor, who are invited into the Pringles' beehive hut, 'my rustic cabin, thatched with reeds':

> Ha! Arméd Caffers with the shepherd Flink
> In earnest talk? Ay, now I mark their mien;
> It is Powana from Zwart Kei, I ween,
> The Amatembu chief. He comes to pay
> A friendly visit, promised many a day
> To view our settlement in Lynden Glen,
> And smoke the Pipe of Peace with Scottish men.[33]

'With Powana and his clan of the Amatembu Caffers,' Pringle notes, 'we had friendly intercourse on several occasions; but the scene in the text is a poetical fiction'. The posthumous *Poetical Works* (1838) has a title-page vignette by W. Purser, engraved by Pringle's friend J.S. Stewart, showing groups of figures with the *hardbies* hut and *witgatboom* in the background. In the group Bawana and 'his gay consort Moya' can be seen, with the shepherd and others, on the Baviaans River bank. Pringle's warm feelings towards these African neighbours are expressed in prophecy:

Yet let us not these simple folk despise;
Just such *our* sires appeared in Caesar's eyes:
And, in the course of Heaven's evolving plan,
By TRUTH MADE FREE, the long-scorned African,
His Maker's image radiant in his face,
Among earth's noblest sons shall find his place.[34]

The Thembu, whom J.H. Soga described as 'the least warlike of the South African tribes'[35] had lived around what is today Mthatha for some 400 years, and Bawana's people, the amaTshatshu, had moved westwards, nearer the colony, into lands claimed by the amaXhosa. They were attacked by the son of Ngqika, Maqoma, who himself moved his people into the Kat River section of the Neutral Territory, thus defying the colonial government. They were later expelled to make room for the Kat River Settlement.

Maqoma's amaNgqika made inroads into the Pringle location after Thomas had left the settlement, stealing cattle and sheep and also attacking the ama-Tshatshu. Worse was to come with the arrival in 1827 of the Mfecane invaders, displaced by Tshaka's wars in what is now KwaZulu Natal, and laying waste the country as they moved west. Bawana himself, escorted for his safety by John Rennie, brought to W.M. Mackay, Harding's successor at Cradock, a letter from George Rennie at Glen Lynden endorsing Bawana's call for help from the colonial forces. All his cattle had been stolen and five of his children killed by the Mfecane. Help was not forthcoming.

According to J.H. Soga who, being part-Xhosa, had unrivalled oral sources, Bawana eventually moved east and took what is now the Queenstown district from the Bushmen. He was, wrote Soga, 'of considerable importance'.[36] His people, known as the Emigrant Thembu, settled around Queenstown and further into the Transkei, where their descendants still reside.

With such friendly neighbours as Bawana's Thembu, Pringle did not develop the inveterate hostility towards the amaXhosa that possessed most Albany settlers. At the same time as Pringle was versifying so favourably in 'The Emigrant's Cabin' about Bawana and his people, young Jeremiah Goldswain in Albany was chronicling a grim event. This was the death of Richard Freemantle and his 15-year-old son John at Mahoney's clay-pits in the far north-eastern corner of the Albany district near the Fish River boundary. He wrote: 'they Kaffers sprung out of the wood and sum of them thrue ther Asigies and others sprung on they men. Mr Richard Freemantle was stabed to death: Samul Freemantle was wounded and his brother John had an Asigie throne at him wich went allmost thrue his bodey'.[37] This was a revenge killing and far worse was to come upon the Albany settlers, in both peace and war.

Along the Baviaans River, despite drought, 'rust', Bushmen, lions, the smallness of their land allocations (greatly increased by Pringle's negotiations) and their remote isolation, the Scots settlers had, by the end of the second year, 'begun to feel quite at home on their respective farms'.[38] Pringle was able to write that at the end of two years 'the state of our little settlement was, on the whole, prosperous'. Wheat and barley had been reaped, gardens and orchards were well stocked with vegetables and fruit. Flocks and herds were considerable in number and gradually increasing'.

To Pringle the establishment 'in rural independence of my father's family' was only 'one of two special objects in view… in emigrating to the Cape'.[39] Precluded from farming by both his disability and his lack of capital, he had also sought from the start 'some employment under Government'. A third object had been put to his friend John Fairbairn in a letter from his Soho lodgings in December 1819. Fairbairn was told that he was 'engaged to write some account of the Colony, at least the New Settlement, by the advice of Sir Walter Scott, and Barrow has promised that it be published here for me on liberal terms'.[40] With a characteristic mixture of generosity and optimism he offered to share authorship and profits with Fairbairn, adding 'I am almost certain it will pay us handsomely'.

The lost journal seems to have provided the basis for the book, which he did not write until his return to Britain. As *African Sketches* it was published first in combination with his poetry, including some of his best-remembered verse, written in the beehive hut at Eildon. Of the 28 African poems 'Evening Rambles' and the sonnet 'Enon' are the only two dated: 'Glen Lynden 1822' and '1822' respectively. 'An Emigrant's Song', 'The Desolate Valley' and 'The Lion Hunt' were all clearly written in 1820–2. 'The Emigrant's Cabin', in the form of a letter in verse to John Fairbairn, which gives such a light-hearted yet illuminating picture of his and Margaret's life on Eildon, was worked up from a contemporary draft, as Pringle told Fairbairn when sending him a copy of *African Sketches* in 1834.

'Evening Rambles' offers a lyrical, romantic picture of 'our Lybian [*sic*] vale', contrasting 'sterile mountains rough and steep \ Heaving to the clear blue sky \ Their ribs of granite bare and dry' with the 'shaggy Glen' below, 'Its sheltered nooks and sylvan bowers, \ Its meadows flushed with purple flowers'. But, picturesque and pastoral as it is, the poem evokes also the plight of the indigenous people, for the mountain's 'crest o'erhangs the Bushman's Cave \ (His fortress once and now his grave.)' Even the fate of the 'brown Herder' … no shepherd he from Scottish fell' is bemoaned. 'His look is dull, his soul is dark' for, 'born the White Man's servile thrall, \ Knows that he cannot lower fall.'

'The Desolate Valley' also mixes his evocation of landscape and fauna with his feeling for the dispossessed amaXhosa. The 'billowy waste of mountains, wild and wide, \ Upon whose grassy slopes the pilgrim spies \ The gnu and quagga by the greenwood side', from where 'how wildly beautiful it is to hear \ The elephant his shrill *reveille* pealing' … 'And see those stately forest-kings appear, \ Emerging from their shadowy solitudes'. But there was no sign of man 'save the old Caffer cabins crumbling round' \ In 'the long grass (Sicana's [Ntsikana, an early Xhosa Christian] ancient ground)'. But 'all is silent now. The Oppressor's hand was strong.'

Unlike this mingling of the picturesque and the elegiac, 'The Lion Hunt' is a cheerful and lively *jeu d'esprit* in the style of 'The Emigrant's Cabin', made so perhaps by Pringle's delight at the comradeship of Boer and Scot ('Muller and

Rennie') with Khoikhoi, mixed-race and even Dugal the Bush boy in their life-and-death struggle with the lion 'at bay in the brushwood preparing to fight':

Call our friends to the field for the lion is near!
Call Arend and Ekhard and Groepe to the spoor,
Call Muller and Coetzer and Lucas van Vuur'
Side up Eildon-Cleugh, and blow loudly the bugle:
Call Slinger and Allie and Dikkop and Dugal;
And George [Rennie] with the elephant gun on his shoulder

Despite the excitements, the joys of the pioneering life and the satisfaction of the success of their settlement, 'suitable employment' was always in Pringle's mind. The post at the new South African Public Library in Cape Town, suggested to him first by Ellis at Algoa Bay, was at last in his reach. Six months after his return from long leave in England, Lord Charles Somerset offered him the sub-librarianship (the librarianship was an honorary post) – at a modest £75 per annum – in May 1821. Enraged by Donkin's actions in his absence, feeling nothing but contempt for the struggling settlers in Albany, he nevertheless smiled on the Scottish party and cannot fail to have been impressed by Pringle's letters of recommendation, chiefly by Sir Walter Scott, a confirmed Tory like himself. He was to chide Pringle, when their quarrel was at its bitterest, for his ingratitude, recalling his favour at that time.

Partly to collect material for his book and also to advance the fortunes of his party Pringle made three journeys out of Glen Lynden during those first two years, and a fourth which took him, with wife and sister-in-law, on the 700-mile ox-wagon trek across the Karroo to Cape Town to take up his 'employment under Government'.

Pringle's contact with the world beyond Glen Lynden did not come only from these journeys. The party received their first mail from Britain in October 1820. One letter in particular stirred unhappy memories of his mistreatment by William Blackwood, Lockhart and, in particular, John Wilson. And, quite the opposite, a military visitor revived his recollections of the literary life in London, and, unintentionally, turned Lord Charles Somerset against him.

These first two years 'afar in the desert' were physically beneficial: there are no references to the ill-health which plagued his later years. They also detached him from the painful events of 1817–19 in Edinburgh. Most fruitfully, however, they taught him the nature of the racially mixed South African society, his interaction with Stockenstrom and Philip and even with Harding and Stretch winning him over to his later dedication to 'the final emancipation of South Africa'.[41] This cause he was able to pursue after leading the fight for democratic rights for his own people against absolute colonial rule by an autocratic governor.

NOTES

[1] Pringle (1966), p. 34.
[2] Pringle to Scott, 22.9.1820, Vigne (2011), p. 31. NLS MS 867 f 43–6.

3   Pringle (1966), p. 35. Pringle to – , 25.11.20, Vigne (2011), p. 95. *The Courier*, London, 23.5.21.
4   Pringle (1966), p. 38.
5   Pringle (1966), pp. 40–1.
6   *Op. cit.*, p. 43.
7   *Op. cit.*, pp. 42–3.
8   Pringle to – , 25.11.1820, Vigne (2011), p. 34. *The Courier,* London, 23.8.21.
9   Pringle (1966), p. 162.
10 *Op. cit.*, p. 43.
11 *Op. cit.*, pp. 43–4.
12 Dracopoli, J.L., *Sir Andries Stockenstrom(1792–1864). The Origins of the Racial Conflict in South Africa* (1969), p. 30.
13 Cory, vol. 1 (1910), pp. 367–8.
14 Pringle (1966), pp. 48–9.
15 *Ibid.*
16 Pringle (1966), p. 51.
17 Pringle (1966), p. 63.
18 Pringle (1966), p. 48.
19 *Op. cit.*, p. 108.
20 Pringle to Harding, 8.9.1821, Vigne (2011), p. 57. *RCC* 14, p. 150.
21 Pringle to Stockenstrom, 7.2.1821, Vigne (2011), p. 44. CA 1/GR/10/2/59
22 Scott (1819, 1860 ed.), p. 245. Pringle (1838), p. 83.
23 Pringle (1966), pp. 107–08.
24 *Op. cit.*, p. 224, 225.
25 Scott (1819, 1860 ed.), p. 97.
26 Pringle (1966), p. 109.
27 *Op. cit.,* p. 109.
28 *Op. cit.,* p. 110.
29 Pringle to Bird, 22.4.1821, Vigne (2011), p. 49. CA CO 1568/155.
30 Dracopoli, p. 187.
31 Stretch, C.L., ed. Basil le Cordeur, *The Journal of Charles Lennox Stretch* (1988), p. 58.
32 Pringle (1966), p. 110.
33 Pringle (1838), pp, 31, 88.
34 *Ibid.*
35 Soga, *The South-Eastern Bantu (abe-Nguni, abaMbo, amaLala)* (1930), p. 479.
36 *Op. cit.*, p. 478.
37 Goldswain, vol. 1, pp. 42–3.
38 Pringle (1966), p. 156.
39 *Op. cit.*, p. 3.
40 Pringle to Fairbairn, 12.12.1819, Vigne (2011), p.10. LP, Fairbairn Papers, 1, 1.
41 Pringle to Fairbarn, 10.11.1825, Vigne (2011), p. 289. LP, Fairbairn Papers, 1, 122.

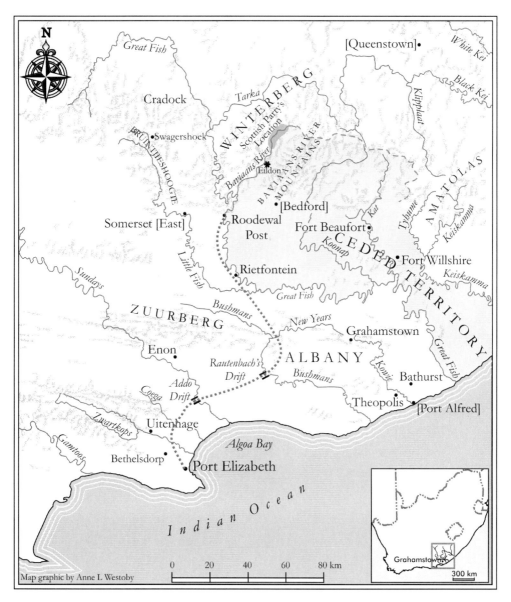

2. Eastern frontier of the Cape Colony in the 1820s, showing the territory ceded to the colony by Ngqika, king of the Rharhabe section of the amaXhosa king, by treaty in 1819. The Scottish party's location is on its north-western border. The dotted line indicates the Scottish party's route from Algoa Bay to the Baviaans River in June 1820. The English settlers shared the route as far as the Bushmans River before turning eastwards into the Albany district.

7

Beyond Glen Lynden

Pringle's travels during these 16 months at Glen Lynden achieved much for him – a wide knowledge of the country and its people, with a slow growth of his commitment to raising up the oppressed indigenous groups, and absorption of its varied beauty: forested mountains beside the bleak harshness and sterility of parched plains and their teeming animal life, which found its way into his poetry when 'recollected in tranquillity'. No poet before him had translated his romantic, Arcadian view of nature to the wilds of southern Africa.

In his *Narrative of a Residence in South Africa* there is writing of descriptive power not to be found in Barrow, Burchell or Lichtenstein and of a beauty acknowledged even by Cory, who saw Pringle as an enemy of the colonists he so admired.

The first of his three major journeys was made for a hard practical purpose. In July and August 1820 it had become clear that cattle and sheep rather than crops must provide the party's livelihood. The market – the infant Port Elizabeth – was too far and the roads towards it execrable. There was sufficient water to irrigate only 50 or 60 acres. Every effort was made to grow barley and wheat, and orchards were planted but it was quickly realized that vastly more than the 1100 acres allotted to the whole party would be essential to their survival. One hundred acres per adult male in such a landscape was derisory and 'even a thousand acres per family was an inadequate allotment'.[1] It was inescapable that this was cattle country and unfit for dependence on agriculture

It was curious – and never explained by Pringle or his official correspondents – that Sydserff was told on arrival at Algoa Bay that he had been granted an extra 500 acres. His informant was Abraham Josias Cloete, of the Groot Constantia wine-growing family, who had been commissioned, at the age of 15, in the 15th Hussars. As a half-pay Captain he had been sent to Algoa Bay as deputy Assistant Quartermaster to assist at the arrival of the settler ships in 1820. Had Sydserff's rich aunt, Lady Buchan-Hepburn, born Margaretha Hendrina Beck of Newlands paid for the extra acreage? Yet even that was far too little for profitable sheep and cattle farming.

On 12 September 1820 a letter was brought (with that damp flour) from the Colonial Secretary, Henry Ellis, in Cape Town, replying favourably to Pringle's application for more land. The party were offered either 'a considerable extension of our present boundary'[2] or a new and larger location further down the valley. It was decided that Pringle would consult 'our new friends, Captain Harding and Mr Hart'. He set off with Peter Rennie, youngest of the three sons of Margaret's cousin, the widow Elizabeth Rennie, and a young Khoikhoi guide, Oray Dikkop, 'who knew every pass of the mountains, and every bridle path through bosky dell and barren waste, for at least a hundred miles around'. They rode in a straight line, direct for Cradock.

Their route took them over 'the ridge which divides the valley of Glen Lynden with its acacia groves and verdant meadows ... a little Goshen of beauty and fertility', downward into the Tarka. He displays a panoramic picture of what lay before them:

> Before us, to the westward, the Tarka opened up in dim perspective, with wild, savage glens winding down to it through ridges of gloomy hills, which, as they approached the main valley, broke off into separate peaks, steep, sterile and rocky, but assuming, in many instances, curious conical forms, at once singular and monotonous. ... there were no trees excepting the fringe of willows and thorny mimosas ... Of anything like grass there was little or no appearance, excepting in some of the recesses and declivities of the hills. The whole country appeared like a cheerless desert; and even the alluvial soil along the banks of the river had the aspect of a brown heathy waste.

They reached Cradock after spending a night at the relatively prosperous farm of Winzel Coetzer, 'our nearest neighbour', about 25 miles north of Glen Lynden. Of its 6,000 acres 20 were under cultivation – the rest were for his 700 head of cattle and 6,000 sheep and goats. Walking over the farm, Coetzer 'pointed to a distant cloud of dust moving up the valley: "*Maar daar komt my vee – de beste tuin!*" (But there come my cattle – the best garden!)' His account of Winzel Coetzer with his large, extended family 'assiduously occupied about the place ... , while the herds and flocks were folding' and of their hospitality, is kindly and favourable. They won Pringle's approval in a way that the frontier Boers did not. He had written to Sir Walter Scott: 'We are at present entirely isolated from the rest of the English population, with the Caffer Frontier close to us on one side, and our only neighbours the most uncivilized and worst affected Boors in the whole Colony'.[3]

Winzel Coetzer's wife even boasted a little social superiority. Born Jacoba Jourdan, she was of Huguenot descent. 'Her father, she said, spoke French but she knew no language but Dutch. Her manner and address, however, retained something of French urbanity and politeness, which contrasted agreeably with the Batavian bluntness of her husband.' Her father may have been a grandson of one of the two male Jourdans who came to the Cape as Huguenot refugees in 1688, both of them from the Luberon region of Provence.

Next day, after passing Cradock, with its 30 houses, 'decent-looking church'[4] and two small shops where such things as tea, coffee and sugar 'could *sometimes* be purchased', they reached Harding's home at Driefontein, an hour's ride from the village. Here were 'the refined hospitality and domestic comforts of an English home', where Pringle and Rennie and their guide stayed from 16 to 18 September 'with our intelligent magistrate and his family', hearing his opinion about their location and learning much about the frontier and its people.

He rode on to the farm of a large-scale horse-breeder, Paul du Plessis, at Swaershoek while Rennie returned to Glen Lynden. Though he had been Pringle's companion on those first nights guarding the camp and on this long ride, he appears hardly at all in the *Narrative*. We learn, in a letter to Fairbairn, of his painful death five years later from an exploding rifle – part of the lock lodged in his skull – as he prepared to pursue Bushman thieves who had stolen horses from the location. He was the first casualty of the founding 24 (though Mortimer was not heard of again after departing) .

Pringle saw the superiority of the homes of the farmers well inside the colony compared to 'those of Winzel Coetzer and other Boors nearer the frontier line, the country having been longer settled and property considered more secure'.[5]

At Somerset Farm he was struck by the setting between the Little Fish River and the Bosberg range: 'a magnificent front clothed with hanging woods of forest timber, and diversified with hoary rocks and steep buttresses of green turf'. He found it 'superbly beautiful' when, after good rains 'a number of little cascades appear, flashing over the wooded cliffs'. The farm, formerly a *vlei*, with 600 acres under cultivation, impressed him as a credit to Hart's 'talent and perseverance'. After a week with 'my friendly countryman and his family', they did the ten-hour ride directly back to Glen Lynden 'through one of the best peopled and wealthiest tracts of our pastoral district'.

The decision to extend their location three miles down river was decided after Hart had visited Glen Lynden, very soon after Pringle's week with him. Perhaps he was needed to persuade some of the party against moving but Pringle does not hint at divisions among them. This 'able and active man ... aided us very beneficially with his experienced counsel'. Divisions came four or five months later, after drought had dried up their springs and withered young trees and plants, rust had blighted their crops and the bad news had reached them of the wreck of the *Abeona*.

> These concurrent disasters, crowding upon us all at once, greatly disheartened most of our party; and I was urged by some of them to apply to the government to remove us to Albany ... I prevailed upon all the families, however, to give the place a longer trial.

The drought broke in March, and the corporal and five men of the Cape Corps sent for their protection by the sympathetic Acting Governor Donkin 'contributed not a little to the restoration of confidence and satisfaction'. This last 'feeling of security' enabled Pringle, 'desirous of extending my knowledge of the colony and of the various classes of the population ... to leave the location at this period to accompany Mr Hart ... through a part of the colony very seldom traversed even by the colonists'.

There was clearly a bond between the bookish, lame young Pringle, at 31, and the hardy ex-soldier, 12 years his senior, who had come to the Cape in 1795. Hart had fought through the frontier war of 1811–12, serving with the Cape Corps as adjutant to Colonel John Graham, when the Zuurveld, now Albany, was cleared of Ndlambe's people. Pringle wrote, probably in London after his return from the Cape:

> I have now lying before me a journal kept during that campaign by my friend Mr Hart, who was then a lieutenant in the Cape Regiment [with] many details ... which illustrate in a very

striking manner the misery inflicted by dispossessing these clans in the summary and violent manner pursued.[6]

Pringle takes pains loyally to exonerate such 'men of high character as Colonel Graham and Colonel (then Captain) Fraser' at least from an 'execrable transaction' recorded by Hart whereby an envoy of Ndlambe's was forced to betray the whereabouts of his people 'for fear of his life'. Yet he found Fraser had made use of the information obtained.

The same extracts were quoted by 'Justus' in his *The Wrongs of the Caffre Nation* (1837) but they may have been taken from Pringle's *Narrative* rather than from a reading of Hart's lost journal. The disappearance of Pringle's papers after his death may have put paid not only to his journal but to Robert Hart's as well, though this may have been kept during the Zuurveld campaign only. Pringle would surely have made use of other parts of the journal had it been in his care.

Eight months after Hart's original invitation to accompany him 'upon an excursion into Cafferland'[7] he happily agreed to travel with Hart to the Enon mission station some hundred kilometres ride to the south. Starting from the Somerset Farm Hart, Pringle and 'a Hottentot attendant' rode south over drought-stricken plains, and, near the Little Fish River, through vast herds of springbok which 'literally *speckled* the face of the country as far as the eye could reach', perhaps 20,000 of 'these beautiful animals' in view. Pringle refers the reader to the much fuller description of migrations of perhaps 100,000 Springboks by Stockenstrom which he himself had included in both the *South African Journal* and in his editing of George Thompson's *Travels*.

After some 40 kilometres over waterless plains they reached the foothills of the Zuurberg and slept the night in a lonely Boer farmer's 'wigwam' beside a stream, shared a supper of 'mutton and potatoes dressed with wild honey' and slept on a mat of rushes … , covered by a blanket of tanned lamb skin with the wool on it.' Their host was their sole human contact in their ride over the almost uninhabited Zuurberg and the journey thus provided scarcely any extension to Pringle's knowledge of 'the various classes of the population'.[8]

He learned much about the way of life of the Moravians when they reached Enon, which confirmed his opinion formed of them after meeting Bishop Latrobe in London: 'I admire them and their labours more than almost any other sect'.[9] The first in the field in South Africa (see p. 132) they trained their mission people in artisanal skills as well as religious and moral conduct in mission villages which have survived, from Mamre and Genadendal in the western Cape to Shiloh in the upper Kei valley in the eastern Cape.

Hart having gone on to Algoa Bay, Pringle took a ride on his own and heard from his Khoikhoi guide a graphic account of the attack on the mission during 'the irruption of the Caffer clans, after the invasion and devastation of their country by the colonial troops in 1818'. He tells the story well, without favouring Ndlambe's dispossessed people. Cory's version is wholly on the side of the colonists – the Moravians were simply caught in the crossfire. Pringle recounts also the memorably tragic event of the 1812 campaign – the killing of Anders Stockenstrom, father of Andries, while parleying with a party of Rharhabe spokesmen. Hart 'related to me the circumstances of this melancholy affair as we rode along'. The details, he wrote in the *Narrative*, were later confirmed 'by other competent authorities'. Andries Stockenstrom, a 19-year-old ensign in Colonel Graham's Cape Regiment, later satisfied himself that his father's murder and that of his 14 companions, 'pierced by innumerable wounds', had not been 'premeditated treachery' but a sudden strike when the white men's duplicity was suspected with the arrival of news that the British had already attacked and blood had been shed.

Andries Stockenstrom's autobiography, edited and supplemented by his grandson C.W. Hutton (1887), describes Pringle's as 'a most accurate and interesting account of the terrible tragedy of 28 December 1818',[10] so full an account, indeed, that the autobiography recounts the tragic event relatively briefly. Pringle drew on a variety of sources, official records and in all probability such an eyewitness as Paul du Plessis, the Swaershoek horse-breeder whose farm Pringle had slept at after his first visit to Somerset Farm. Du Plessis was one of the few Boers who had escaped death with Anders Stockenstrom.

A biographer of Andries Stockenstrom in 1969 commented:

> Anders Stockenstrom had great tact and wisdom and his advice in the difficult years ahead might well have tempered his son's often acrimonious relations with the British. The young man did inherit some of his father's character, for he was able to forget the horror of the murder and look sympathetically at the plight of the natives in their battle against the settlers.[11]

Pringle himself repeats the missionary Stephen Kay's quotation of Andries Stockenstrom's words about this 'melancholy affair'. Addressing a gathering of chiefs at Wesleyville mission in 1829, Stockenstrom said:

> We do not now seek each other with the musket or the assegai to shed each other's blood. When we meet it is to shake hands and to be good friends. The bad times have passed away. The Caffers killed my father, and some of you were near at the time. The Boors killed your father (old Kongo) [Chungwa, the Gqunukhwebe chief]. Those were bad doings but now all is changed. You have received missionaries; you have now the same word of God that we have. The only difference between us is the colour of our skins; but though you are black and we are white, yet God has made of one blood all the nations of the earth.[12]

Idealistic but vain words. Only five years later 'bad doings' by both sides provoked the horrors of the Sixth Frontier War, known to the settlers, some of whom lived through three more, as 'the Kafir War'.

Recalling the killing of Anders Stockenstrom at Doorn Nek, Pringle expressed his regret that 'not even a rude stone has been erected to mark the grave of this meritorious magistrate'.

Such a thing would be rendered minuscule by the incomparable magnificence of the surroundings. The mountains struck Pringle most forcibly, with their 'wild and savage sublimity'. He saw 'a billowy chaos of naked mountains, rocky precipices and yawning abysses that looked as if hurled together by some prodigious convulsion of nature … in some pre-adamite conflict of angelic hosts', while below 'a dark impenetrable forest spread its shaggy skirts'.

It was early morning when we traversed this savage scene, and the mists which hung upon the mountains, lifting or lowering their fleecy folds as we advanced, partially revealed and again enshrouded the chaotic labyrinth which extended around and beneath us – presenting sometimes glimpses of wild sylvan beauty almost elysian, and then, on a sudden, enfolding just beneath us a gulf of black rocks and forests scathed by fire … The scenery of the Zuurberg far surpassed anything of the kind I had either witnessed elsewhere or formed a conception of from the descriptions of others.

To make their descent they

entered at the head of a glen by a path … an alley made by the elephants when they issue forth from their sylvan recesses to ascend the mountain. It was about six feet wide and arched over like a summer alcove, for the elephant, forcing his way through the thickets, tramples down or breaks off the larger branches that obstruct his passage, while the lighter and loftier, yielding to the pressure of his huge body, meet again like a Gothic arch when the monarch and his troop have passed through … a pathway, when once broken out, is soon trodden by them as bare, if not so smooth, as a gravel walk. Indeed, but for the services of the elephant as a pioneer, these dense and thorny forests, choked up with underwood and interlaced with rope-like creepers, would be almost utterly impenetrable.

Despite such paths and the skill of their Khoikhoi guide ('the memory and adroitness of this race in such circumstances are most remarkable') and Hart having once travelled by this route, they lost their way and became 'entangled among the thickets and gullies of one of those frightful ravines'. At last they gained the grassy banks of the Witte River and reached the mission station of Enon 'before the night closed in'.

They had feared both elephants and buffaloes, a constant menace, as Pringle learned from both the Moravian missionaries and a farmer's wife he encountered at 'a solitary farm-shieling' on a ride he took with a Khoikhoi companion from the mission. She told him of the 'wanton malice' with which they destroyed crops and fruit trees, which 'they could neither devour or totally destroy' and of the threat they posed to life itself.

Despite the terrifying days of the attack in April 1819 and the mission's withdrawal – 150 of them – to Uitenhage for 'several months' by Cory's account,[13] Pringle found Enon a calm, well-ordered place, with 'a sort of pleasing pastoral quiet'. Its small European staff, led by the venerable Johan Heinrich Schmidt and his English wife, the sole European woman on the mission, welcomed Hart and Pringle, 'with an affectionate and patriarchal cordiality'. Pringle brought a letter and a parcel of books from their bishop, the Revd Christian Ignatius Latrobe, who had founded the mission during his tour of the colony in 1815–16, the subject of his *Journal of a Visit to South Africa* (1818).

Enon was the inspiration of a Ngqika woman, known as Wilhelmine, who had made her way from the Langekloof to Genadendal, where she pleaded for a Christian mission to her people, and won Latrobe's agreement. The frontier turbulence made a Xhosa mission impossible and Enon became the Khoikhoi settlement Pringle and Hart visited. Its subsequent history is somewhat obscure. Archdeacon (later Bishop) Merriman, passing by the Moravian mission of Clarkson in the Tsitsikamma forest in 1851, 'found there some of the Moravian missionaries from

Enon, who had come away with part of their people, that station … not being considered safe from marauding Kafirs'.[14] (This was during Mlanjeni's War, the eighth, longest and bloodiest of the frontier wars). A local historian referred in 1904 to the destruction of Enon and its re-establishment in 1819, adding that 'Enon has had a somewhat chequered career and, strange to say, the authorities seem anxious to keep its history a profound secret … the present missionary, Rev. F. Rauh, has persistently refused to supply us with any information for this work'.[15]

We know that Wilhelmine and her Khoikhoi husband Carel Stompjes were instrumental in establishing the Moravians' first successful mission, Shiloh, among the Thembu, in 1828. Pringle mentions it with approval in an article about Christian missions to the Xhosa peoples, written when he was in London in 1833.[16] The Enon mission buildings still stand and its story and that of the remarkable Wilhelmine remain to be told.

Pringle's sonnet 'Enon'[17] captures the emotion he felt at the mission, after the gruelling ride and what he had learned of the frontier conflicts. Dated April 1821, it must have been written during his week at the mission or very soon after, and compares the Moravians' 'pious toil' where 'beasts of prey and men of murder roam' but where now 'a garden blooms and savage hordes grow mild', with

> … the guilty heart when Heavenly Grace
> Enters, it ceaseth not till it uproot
> All Evil Passions from each hidden cell;
> Planting again an Eden in their place
> Which yields to men and angels pleasant fruit;
> And God himself delighteth there to dwell.

If the journey to Enon taught Pringle little at first hand about the lives of the peoples of the Cape, his next expedition, only a few weeks later, seems to have been a source of understanding of the landscape of the Zuurveld, now Albany, and of a general view of the English settlers' progress. Again with Robert Hart, he toured the whole area of settlement in July 1821. They visited Bathurst, the seat of the magistracy, Grahamstown, soon to supplant it, on a whim of Lord Charles Somerset, determined to undo all Sir Rufane Donkin had done in his absence, Port Frances (renamed Port Alfred in 1860 after the visit of Queen Victoria's second son, a young midshipman), Theopolis, the mission station sacked by Ndlambe's tribesmen in 1819, and the settler hamlet of Salem. They saw also 'all the principal locations of the English settlers from the Kareega to the mouth of the Great Fish River'.[18]

The settler farmers' homes intrigued him. There were neat, whitewashed wattle-and-daub cabins, with 'trim garden plot and wattled fence',[19] often looking 'extremely handsome and picturesque, as we suddenly came in sight of them peeping out from the skirts of the ancient forest, or embowered in some romantic wood or evergreen shrubbery'. Besides homesteads displaying 'that peculiar neatness which the English peasant displays', there were 'too frequent indications of the sloven, the sluggard, the drunken and the improvident'.

'At this point', he wrote, 'the settlers had only slightly experienced the effects of their mistakes and the pressure of their misfortunes'. After floods, the same blight which had destroyed the crops in Glen Lynden, the 'arrogance and incompetency' of 'certain local functionaries' (since replaced on the orders of the sympathetic Donkin) and the realization of the need for expert farming, had 'awakened even the most sanguine from the delusive dreams of wealth and ease'. Almost overwhelming calamities lay ahead, while Glen Lynden prospered, and Pringle took up their cause against the despotism of Lord Charles Somerset and his government in Cape Town.

Though much occupied with settling his 'Mulatto tenants' and farm workers at Glen Lynden, with fending off predatory Bushmen, and much correspondence about the enlargement of their location, Pringle had time for further 'exploratory excursions', this time 'into the waste country lying between our valley and the New Caffer Frontier, which had remained totally unoccupied since the native inhabitants were driven out of it in 1819'.[20] First called 'the Neutral Ground', it became 'the Ceded Territory'. His 'South African border-ballad', 'The Forester of the Neutral Ground'[21] suggests that Boer outcasts, as well as displaced Bushmen and some Xhosas in search of grazing settled in it. His 'forester' is Arend Plessie, who had defied his father and brothers, farmers in the Camdeboo, by marrying 'brown Dinah the bondmaid who sat in our hall'. Arend lives 'like old Ishmael, Lord of the Wild', fearing only 'what may befal when the turf's on my head; / I fear for poor Dinah, for poor Rodomond / And dimple-faced Karel, the sons of the *bond*'. Slavery awaits them as the sons of his father's slave, Dinah. But this is not a rare glimpse of life in the Neutral Ground. Pringle notes 'the story of the poem is founded on facts, which occurred some years ago in a different quarter of the colony.'

The *Narrative* half of *African Sketches* was written for a readership in Britain who would thrill to its stories of hunting and exploration and his evocation of the magnificent landscape. On one such journey he climbed the 6,000-foot peak of the Winterberg:

> Though steep, it is accessible on horseback to within 500 or 600 yards of the top, whence it is necessary to clamber up the shelving rocks on the western side; the tabular summit being surrounded apparently, in all other directions, by a perpendicular wall of basaltic rock, like the rampart of a fortification. In many places, gigantic natural columns abutted from this rocky rampart, like flanking towers and bastions, separated, in numerous instances, by deep chasms from the front of the cliff.[22]

Thomas Pringle, the cripple whose crutches Lockhart and Wilson had mocked in the Edinburgh days, was able to look down from the summit on 'these inaccessible turrets', where 'we observed the eyries of several species of eagles and vultures' and, always the amateur botanist, 'a belt of dwarf bamboo, not found in the country below', fringing the base of these rocks. Charles Stretch recalled his amazement at Pringle's 'rapid movements down the steep spur of the Winterberg, with greater swiftness than those who had two good pins to support them'.[23]

He explored the Mankazana valley, where 'the country though wild was rich and beautiful', saw deserted Bushman caves and 'the remains of Caffer hamlets … now fast crumbling to decay [which] excited reflection of a melancholy character'.

The contrast with Albany is palpable. There, though the elephants had retreated to impenetrable forests 'since the arrival of the settlers', buffaloes, hyenas and some antelope were still in the 'forest-jungle' along the rivers. But

> the herds of hartebeests, quaggas and other large game, described by former travellers as frequenting the open pastures, and adding so much life and beauty to the lonely landscape of Albany, had almost totally disappeared, and with them the lion. A few scattered flocks of springboks were all that we observed remaining of *ferae naturae*.

In the Mankazana and the lands beside 'the other chief branches of the Koonap River … for some years abandoned to the undisputed occupation of the wild animals, which flocked to it in great numbers', Pringle could say that 'In no other part of South Africa have I ever seen so many of the larger sorts of antelopes; and the elephant, the rhinoceros and the buffalo were also to be found in the forests'.

These expeditions were a source of real pleasure and even excitement to Pringle. He describes most vividly and at some length a tour into the Ceded Territory with two lieutenants of engineers, C. Rivers and F.W. Pettingal, and a newcomer to the colony, Captain R.C. Fox with 'six or eight men of the Cape Corps cavalry'. After a night in Pringle's reeded cabin they rode into the Ceded Territory and found themselves, on the second day, amid a herd of more than fifty elephants,

> scattered in groups over the bottom and sides of a valley two or three miles in length; some browsing on the succulent spekboom, which clothed the skirts of the hills on either side; others at work among the mimosas and evergreens sprinkled over the meadows. As we proceeded cautiously onward, some of these groups came more distinctly into view; consisting apparently, in many instances, of separate families, the male, the female and the young of different sizes; and the gigantic magnitude of the chief leaders became more and more striking. The calm and stately tranquillity of their deportment, too, was remarkable. Though we were a band of about a dozen horsemen, … they seemed neither to observe, or altogether to disregard, our march down the valley.

Captain Fox was keen to see an elephant hunt as were some of the Khoikhoi 'to attack a group browsing in a thicket about a quarter of a mile distant'. It would have been 'dangerous in the extreme' and their destruction was not attempted 'merely to furnish sport to the great destroyer, man, and I was glad when, after a brief consultation, it was unanimously agreed to leave them unmolested'.[24]

Yet here in the cabin and in the wilds along the Koonap river Pringle found himself brought back into the world he had known, both as participant and observer, and had abandoned. Perhaps with a touch of poetic licence he sets the scene in 'The Emigrant's Cabin':

> Sometimes a pleasant guest, from parts remote,
> Cheers for a passing night our rustic cot;
> As, lately, the gay-humoured Captain Fox,
> With whom I roamed 'mid Koonap's woods and rocks,
> From Winterberg to Gola's savage grot,
> Talking of Rogers, Campbell, Coleridge, Scott,
> Of Fox and Mackintosh, Brougham, Canning, Grey;

And lighter themes and laughter cheered the way –
While the wild-elephants in groups stood still
And wondered at us on their woody hill.

Charles Richard Fox was the eldest son of the third Baron Holland and his wife but born before her divorce from her first husband and so not the heir to the title. Nor would he inherit Holland House, the celebrated centre of Whig society, where the Hollands also entertained royalty, Tory leaders, men of letters, wits and distinguished foreign visitors. Charles was a much loved son and popular with a wide circle due to his charm of manner, good nature and generosity.

Commissioned as an ensign in the 85th (Duke of York's Own) Regiment at 18, then lieutenant, he seems to have bought his captaincy in the Cape Corps five years later, perhaps as a step-up, albeit in a low-ranked regiment, and also to see and enjoy the wilds of Africa. His time at the Cape was short. Lord Holland had arranged an exchange with a good line regiment, the 15th Foot, and he was back in England by October 1822. But not before he had dined with the Governor in Cape Town, Lord Charles Somerset having returned to duty at the end of November 1821.

On 25 June 1823 Pringle wrote from Cape Town, to Sir George Mackenzie, Bart., a distinguished man of science in Edinburgh who had encouraged him to write a 'history of the emigration to South Africa in 1820'. Perhaps the link was through Thomas Thomson, since Mackenzie was a leading Scottish antiquarian, or perhaps through George Combe, who had moved from the law to promoting the new science of phrenology. There is much correspondence between Mackenzie and Combe in the National Library of Scotland. Pringle, furthermore, having sent lion skulls to Scott had sent human ones – Bushman and Nguni – to Mackenzie, the latter brought over by 'Mr Stevenson' who promised also to present Sir George 'with an Indian skull which he has brought from Calcutta'.[25] There seems to have been no moral objection to such exhibits in that period.

Pringle had found the source of his Whig liberalism being the barrier to a better-paid government post, which he had bemoaned to Sir Walter Scott the year before. He told Mackenzie that he dared not write about the 1820 settlers since he could not 'write truly about the Colony without giving offence to those in authority on whom my success and even my subsistence depend' and went on

> … though I keep myself aloof from all political or party discussions, I have the misfortune of being a *Whigg* … partly because Capt. Fox (a son of Lord Holland's) with whom I got acquainted on the frontier happened to speak of me at the Governor's table as 'a good staunch Whigg'.

Like James Hogg, Fox was Pringle's friend, who (unwittingly in Fox's case) did him harm – but in years to come Fox was able to help Pringle, who had himself to come to Hogg's assistance at the end of his life.

The letter to Mackenzie suggested another reason why Pringle lost 'the management of the Government Gazette to which I had been recommended by the Colonial Secretary and which I came down from my location in full expectation of obtaining – but found it otherwise disposed of by his Excellency'. This was that his name had 'been bandied about in Blackwood's Magazine and the Scotsman (very little to my own liking certainly).' He begged Sir George to help undo some of this damage by writing 'a few lines in my favour to Lord Melville or Sir George Clerk'. Both were Scots at the Admiralty, Melville as First Lord.

The bitterness and hurt he had suffered in Edinburgh followed him to his pioneering life in the wilds when letters started to arrive from home. He had written to Scott on 7 March 1821, shortly before his journey to Albany with Hart, about his prospects of 'employment under Government' and asked for his help to obtain a free passage to the Cape for his brother William and the eldest of the family, his sister Mary (and Isabella, who travelled later). It was William, he wrote, from whom he learned of his being embroiled in another Edinburgh brouhaha, of as personal and vindictive a nature as that following the Chaldee MS commotion four years earlier.[26]

The Edinburgh intelligentsia were split, along Whig and Tory lines, over the election to the professorship of moral philosophy, a job for life at the University, and one of great prestige. The electors were the Town Council and the Tory candidate won, though by far the less suitable of the two. He was John Wilson, the 'beautiful leopard' co-author of the Chaldee MS, described by Stanley Jones, biographer of another of his victims, Hazlitt (1989) as 'an overbearing bully [who] did not care who the victim was or what the bystanders might feel … his moral insensibility was inveterate and his incapacity to understand or recognize carelessly inflicted suffering permanent'.[27] His main opponent in contesting the chair, Sir William Hamilton, was by far the superior scholar, a moral philosopher of distinction, and of an unblemished character. Hamilton was a Whig, however, and the majority of voters, members of the Town Council, did not want him. So Wilson won – an appointment described as the most remarkable since Caligula made his horse a consul, by one of his most implacable adversaries, *The Scotsman*. Founded in 1817, it had become Edinburgh's leading Whig newspaper.

The Scotsman waged war against Wilson from the start, using as its main charge against him the rancour and slander of his articles in *Blackwood's*, 'in which the private character of the most respectable individuals in the country has been most wantonly and foully traduced'.[28]

The Scotsman also attacked the political integrity of Wilson, who 'as late as 1817 avowed his contempt for the political creed of the party by which he is now supported for the purpose of defaming his intimate friend!' This was during Pringle and Cleghorn's editorship, when Wilson had sent Pringle an article pouring contempt on a pamphlet published anonymously by Wilson's friend M'Cormick. He urged Pringle to publish the article because M'Cormick was 'a horrible Tory and deserved to be cut up, and that it would be the means of selling a hundred additional copies of the magazine'.

Pringle was, remarkably, outraged by this use of his private correspondence as a weapon against the man who had so abused him. His words to Scott, a Tory and friend of Wilson's, overlong as is so much of his correspondence when his honour or principles are in question, is incomparable evidence of his generous, forgiving nature and his rock-solid personal integrity.

> ... it seems in a late contest for the chair of moral philosophy in Edinburgh my name has been used by a party hostile to Mr Wilson and even a letter of his to me quoted to his disparagement. As the letter in question with other papers connected with the Editorship of the two Edinburgh magazines was committed by me on leaving Scotland to the custody of certain friends, for a very different purpose, namely my own conduct as editor if it should ever be assailed. I am vexed and displeased that any such papers have been employed for a purpose I neither wished nor authorized. Had it been otherwise I should long ago have made use of them myself, or transferred them to the party that has found access to them on the occasion when they repeatedly and fruitlessly applied to me for the sight of them. But then as now I disdained to make use of an ungenerous advantage against an individual who has used me ungenerously.

He was determined that his papers should not be used again in the infighting among the Edinburgh intelligentsia and had, he told Scott, 'sent home positive orders to have *all the papers alluded to* committed to the flames'. Why tell all this to Scott?

> I take the liberty to mention this to you as a friend of Mr Wilson's – that, if you judge it proper, he may be informed of it. By so doing, however, I bespeak neither his favour nor forbearance should he or his friends condescend to assail me in my absence – but merely because I detest the Boschman's dastardly warfare and scorn to use his poisoned arrows, though I should render myself defenceless by destroying them.

He wished only to forget 'the party squabbles of Edinburgh' and to be forgotten by the squabblers:

> I ... would wish my name, if remembered at all, to have no connection with them. In leaving my native country (probably forever) I buried all my personal resentments and the memory of offences in the billows of the Atlantic, and having forgiven my foes (if I had any) I would willingly be permitted to forget and be forgotten by them.[29]

Wilson's career as professor of moral philosophy makes an extraordinary story, in which the poet, literary critic and mediocre novelist gave daily lectures for thirty years, all of them written by his philosopher friend, Alexander Blair. His magnificent appearance and powerful charisma made him a hero to generations of his students, most of whom must have been aware that he knew almost nothing of his subject. As John Wilson he is forgotten but as 'Christopher North', his nom-de-guerre, he has a continuing notoriety for the wit and scurrility of his contributions to *Blackwood's* long-running series, the '*Noctes Ambrosianae*'.

If Pringle's papers were later destroyed as he had instructed, he lost more than 'Boschman' poisoned arrows. The contumely of Wilson, Lockhart and Blackwood has stuck and author has followed author in expressing varying degrees of contempt for his editorship. To Professor J.F. Ferrier, editor of *Noctes Ambrosianae* when published in 1884 as a popular by-product of Lockhart and Wilson's *Blackwood's* 'Pringle and Cleghorn' were a couple of incapables' (p. 245). Even Wilson's eminently fair biographer Elsie Swann (1934) calls Pringle's and Cleghorn's seven issues of *Blackwood's* 'a meek and mild miscellany',[30] and Tredrey related, on no evidence whatever, that when Blackwood 'attempted to strengthen the second number the editors complained piteously of interference' while his 'Maga' limped on laboriously through the remaining four issues'.[31] Yet he reprinted all six issues, renaming the volume *Blackwood's Edinburgh Magazine*.

How different were those first two years at the Cape! In addition to the success of the settlement of which he was the leader, and the friends he had made there, Pringle's close and happy relationship with Henry Ellis and the approval of his successor as Colonial Secretary, Colonel Bird (who probably leaked to Pringle Fox's damaging 'staunch Whig' revelation to Somerset), the commendatory letters to Somerset from Scott, Goulburn and others gave Pringle every hope of a suitable and properly paid post in Cape Town. With the arrival of his brother William with his young wife and sister Mary, he was able to hand over the leadership of the party to William and to make the move to Cape Town.

He did so having succeeded in most of his aims. He had not written the projected book and he had not escaped the Edinburgh jungle but the family were reunited, except for Alexander who, despite hopes of his completing the family circle, remained in America. The Scots party, despite drought, 'rust', isolation intensified by the lost hope of numerous Scots settler neighbours, the threat to their livestock and themselves posed by Bushmen, lions and hyenas, had established their homes securely and profitably in greatly enlarged lands. He was able to share with his fellow Scot Sir George Mackenzie his satisfaction that

> My party of Settlers are doing well, being the only party of Settlers that appear to be enjoying any degree of prosperity in South Africa – which I hope is creditable to our National perseverance, we being the only Scotch party that came out in 1820.[32]

He had much to remember with pleasure of the two years at Glen Lynden. His poem 'Evening Rambles',[33] dated 1822, captures some of the wild beauty of the landscape. The 'low and languid' breeze that came with evening

> … seems to tell
> Of primrose-tufts in Scottish dell,
> Peeping forth in tender spring
> When the blithe lark begins to sing.

But this is South Africa and the eye ranges

> O'er prospects wild, grotesque, and strange;
> Sterile mountains, rough and steep,
> That bound abrupt the valley deep;
> Heaving to the clear blue sky
> Their ribs of granite, bare and dry
> And ridges, by the torrents worn
> Thinly streaked with scraggy thorn …

The poet surveys the scene from his 'wonted seat' on a hilltop, below the mountain

> Whose crest o'erhangs the Bushman's Cave
> (His fortress once, and now his grave,)
> Where the grim satyr-faced baboon

> Sits gibbering to the rising moon,
> Or chides with hoarse and angry cry
> The herdsman as he wanders by.

He follows with his eye the river bed, the willows and nests, animals ('the thievish porcupine \ Plundering my melon-bed, \ Or villain lynx, whose stealthy tread \ Rouses not the faithful hound'), the birds, the 'adder coiled upon the path', even 'the lion … that soon will prowl athirst for blood'. Yet it is the herder who prompts his deeper thoughts – first the Khoikhoi shepherd ('the Hottentot in his state of debasement', says Pringle's note):

> Sauntering languidly along;
> Nor flute has he, nor merry song,
> Nor book, nor tale, nor rustic lay.
> To cheer him through his listless day …
> … But born the White Man's servile thrall,
> Knows that he cannot lower fall.

The cowherd is a free man but a victim of the Mfecane ravages ('The Bechuana refugee' the note calls him):

> With bolder step and blither eye
> Humming low his tuneless song.
> Or whistling to the hornéd throng.
> From the destroying foeman fled,
> He serves the Colonist for bread
> Yet this poor heathen Bechuan
> Bears on his brow the port of man;
> A naked, homeless exile he –
> But not debased by Slavery.

J.M. Coetzee's essay 'Burchell, Pringle and the South African Picturesque' (1988) sees 'the procedure of picturesque painting (and viewing) at work'[34] in 'Evening Rambles' and identifies the 'traverses' of the eye in the poem, though he does not mention the inescapable intrusion of despised, hated Bushman, downtrodden Khoikhoi and Tswana (or Sotho) refugee into the panorama. Coetzee's awareness of Pringle's achievement in conveying Africa to Europe is simply put: 'The familiar trot of iambic tetrameter increasingly accommodates the foreign content.'

Pringle carried with him to Cape Town an acute feeling for the humble victims of colonization, of man's inhumanity to man, and of slavery, depicted in the shepherd and the neatherd in 'Evening Rambles'. In the metropolitan scene (albeit of a remote colony), however, his crusading zeal was to be engaged with the colonists themselves as victims of absolute rule.

NOTES

[1] Pringle (1966), p. 51.
[2] *Ibid.*

[3] Pringle to Scott, 7.3.1821, Vigne (2011), p. 45. NLS MS389 f 67–8.

[4] Pringle (1966), p. 61.

[5] *Op. cit.,* p. 62.

[6] Pringle (1835), pp. 291–2

[7] *Op. cit.,* p. 43.

[8] *Op. cit.,* pp. 77–8.

[9] Pringle to Fairbairn, 12.12.1819, Vigne (2011) p.10. LP 1, Fairbairn Papers, 1.

[10] Stockenstrom , p. 494.

[11] Dracopoli, p. 24.

[12] Pringle (1966), p. 100; Kay. Stephen, *Travels and Researches in Caffraria* (1833), p. 254.

[13] Pringle (1966) pp. 101, 95–6, 82–3. Cory, vol. 1, p. 385.

[14] Merriman, N.J., ed. D.H. Varley, *The Cape Journals of Archdeacon Merriman* (1957), p. 160.

[15] Sellick, W.S.J., *Uitenhage Past and Present. Souvenir of the Centenary 1804–1904* , p. 34.

[16] Ellis, William, *Missionary Annual for 1833* (1833), p. 134.

[17] Pringle (1838), p. 67.

[18] Pringle (1966), p. 103.

[19] *Op. cit.,* p. 106.

[20] *Op. cit.,* p. 115.

[21] Pringle (1838), pp. 54–7.

[22] Pringle (1966), pp. 115–16.

[23] *Cape Monthly Magazine*, 8.43 (July 1856), p. 56.

[24] Pringle (1966), p. 120.

[25] Pringle to Mackenzie, 25.6.1823, Vigne (2011), p. 86. NLS MS 3896.

[26] Pringle to Scott, 7.3.1821, Vigne (2011), p.46. NLS MS 3892 f 67–8.

[27] Jones, Stanley, *Hazlitt. A Life from Winterslow to Frith Street* (1898).

[28] *The Scotsman*, Edinburgh, 17.5.1820.

[29] Pringle to Scott, 7.3.1821, Vigne (2011), p. 46. NLS MS 3892 f 67–8.

[30] Swann, E., *Christopher North (John Wilson)* (1934), p. 80.

[31] Tredrey, *The House of Blackwood, 1804–1954*, p. 23.

[32] Pringle to Mackenzie, 25.6.1823 Vigne (2011), p. 88. NLS MS 3896.

[33] Pringle (1838), pp. 15–19.

[34] Coetzee, J.M., *White Writing. On the Culture of Letters in South Africa* (1988). pp. 47, 164.

Part III

Cape Town and Genadendal

The Stand Against Power
(1822–1825)

8
Westward

The, 'on the whole, prosperous' state of the Glen Lynden settlement, which compared so starkly with the calamitous fate of the English settlers in Albany, brought many favours with it. Thomas Philipps, promoting settlement in 1836,[1] recalled the first four years as having brought

> bitter disappointment, principally from the entire loss of the wheat crop by the rust, a malady scarcely remembered before … at the same time the Caffers made frequent incursions and robbed the settlers of numerous cattle … the inattention and want of feeling of the military and civil authorities.

Philipps saw fit not to mention the three-year drought followed by a great flood, which ruined so many in Albany and which, apart from drought, the Scots had escaped.

When Thomas, his Library appointment in Cape Town secured, heard of the imminent arrival of his eldest brother William and his companions in July 1822 he was able to make use of the *laissez passer* with which an indulgent Colonel Bird had furnished him. It read:

> By Command of His Excellency – Whereas the Bearer Mr Thomas Pringle is to proceed from Graaff Reinet to Cape Town on Public Service, all Landdrosts, Field Cornets, and other Inhabitants, being called upon by the said Officer, are therefore hereby required to afford him every accommodation in their power, and forthwith to provide him, from Farm to Farm on his route with Draught Oxen, and with every other necessary he may, for the better execution of his Commission, stand in need of and require.[2]

With William and his wife of a few months, Anne Scott, were his sisters Mary and Isabella. Many years later Anne Pringle, in her sixties, testified in a land dispute among their son's generation

> We met at Somerset the late Mr Thomas Pringle on his way to Cape Town. … [He] rode back on horseback to Eildon and gave my husband possession of the farm. … [We] reached Baviaans River in August 1822.[3]

Pringle himself wrote that 'having placed [William] in possession of the farm of Eildon, upon which I had resided for last nine months, I prepared myself to proceed to Cape Town … After a short stay at Somerset Farm I commenced my journey on 7 August in an ox-wagon, accompanied by my wife and her sister',[4] their possessions and provisions for the journey, there being no inn along their entire route of nearly 700 miles.

The wagon itself was bound for Cape Town to collect supplies for the Graaff-Reinet drostdy. We are not told how the Pringles, Janet Brown and their possessions travelled from Glen Lynden, only that they spent those few days at Somerset Farm, where Thomas's youngest full brother John was now 'agricultural superintendent' under Robert Hart. Near-by, farming at Melkrivier was their friend Captain Stretch, now married to Hart's daughter Anne. The wagon duly followed the very rough road over the plains of Camdeboo, behind Bruintjies Hoogte, taking two and a half days for the 75 miles. Thirty miles a day was good going for ox-wagon travel. Their rate in the drought-stricken western Karroo, where grazing and water were minimal and the oxen often exhausted, went down to 15 miles a day.

The *Narrative* says little about the scenic beauty of the Great Karroo, which Pringle had already glimpsed and noted on his first journey to Cradock. Graaff-Reinet, 'a handsome country town, situated at the southern base of the Sneeuw Bergen, [with its] 2000 inhabitants ... and streets planted with lemon trees',[5] is similarly passed over and the reader is referred to George Thompson's *Travels and Adventures in Southern Africa* for 'a good description of the place'. This was in part Pringle's work. The modern, 1966 edition of the book sets out 'the direct evidence which points to much of the writing having come from Pringle's pen'.[6] Thompson describes the wide streets, laid out at right angles, the lemon and orange trees 'which thrive here luxuriantly and give the place a fresh and pleasing appearance'. The 300 houses are almost all 'neat and commodious brick edifices'. How unlike Barrow's experience of the town 25 years earlier when it consisted of 'an assemblage of mud huts ... forming a kind of street. At the upper end stands the house of the landrost, built also of mud, and a few miserable hovels ... in a ruinous condition and uninhabitable'. The inhabitants were seen by Barrow as 'rude boors',[7] for whom the Governor, Lord Macartney, wished to provide a church as a step towards 'civilizing' them.

One such brick edifice provided a 'hospitable roof' for the Pringles and Janet Brown, their host being the military surgeon Dr Patrick McCabe whom they had met at Roodewal on their first journey to the Baviaans river. In their three days Pringle learned much about 'the northern districts of the colony and the wild tribes on its borders'[8] from Stockenstrom and 'other intelligent local functionaries', one of whom was the Revd Abraham Faure.

The meeting with Faure was serendipitous. Of a Cape Dutch family with strong official and church connections, Faure was descended from a Huguenot official who had come to the Cape with Governor de Chavonnes in 1715. After training under Dr David Bogue at the London Missionary Society's institution at Gosport in Hampshire, he read 'scientific theology' at the University of Utrecht and returned to the Cape in 1818. He married Geertruida Isabella Caldwell, daughter of a British army officer, whose sister Georgina Johanna married William Elliott, the member of the Scottish party who, with the best of goodwill, had moved to Cape Town from Algoa Bay to take up missionary work.

Further links with Pringle were Faure's establishment of South Africa's first church library, in Graaff-Reinet, on his arrival there as minister, in 1818 when only 23, and their shared sympathy for the sufferings of the oppressed Khoikhoi and the hunted Bushmen. The year after his meeting with Pringle, Faure and Stockenstrom set up a mission to the Bushmen north of the Orange River. They named it Philippolis, after the champion of the Khoikhoi and *bête noire* of most of the settlers, Dr John Philip.

Either at this meeting or shortly after it in Cape Town, where Faure was to settle, the two agreed to publish a literary journal, with editions in English and Dutch on alternate months. *The South African Journal* and *Het Nederduitsch Zuid-Afrikaansche Tijdschrift* were to play their part in the unfolding development of the colony, and the careers of the two founding editors were to diverge similarly.

The overland journey had been made, Pringle wrote, 'with the view of enlarging my acquaintance with the interior of the colony'.[9] Much of his account of the journey describes the people, not the landscape, though there are haunting passages which ring specially true to those who have encountered it.

> At the time of our visit no rain had fallen on the Karroo for upwards of twelve months, so that I saw it under its most desolate aspect. Not a vestige of green pasturage was to be descried over the surface of the immense monotonous landscape, and the low heath-like shrubbery apparently as sapless as a worn-out broom, was the only thing our cattle had to browze on. No wild game was to be seen: all had fled apparently to some more hospitable region. Not even a wandering ostrich or bird of prey appeared to break the death-like stillness of the waste.[10]

The farmers who housed them during the journey make more rewarding reading. Schalk Burger, 'an affluent grazier' high on the Sneeuberg had room for them though there were already 28 guests in the house. Pringle was able to share the opinion of 'the Sneeuberg farmers, a class of men of whom Mr Barrow ... gave so favourable a report.' He praised the sleeping arrangements , and even the table service and left them 'much pleased with the good humour and good sense that seemed to prevail among these rustic inhabitants of the mountains'.[11]

Barrow, so scathing about most of the Afrikaner farmers he encountered, had written:

> They are a peaceable, obliging and orderly people; a brave and hardy race of men. ... It is not in the men alone that their dangerous situation has called forth the active powers ... instances of great female fortitude have here occasionally been shown.[12]

Schalk Burger, whose family had shown loyalty to British rule, pleased Pringle by holding devout evening prayers in the hall, which 'the whole company' attended. He was glad to see 'what I had never witnessed on the frontier', namely the slaves and Khoikhoi servants among the worshippers.

Schalk van Heerden, at their next stopping place, misdirected them and they had to travel 'nearly two days' journey out of our way'. This obliged them to skirt the desert, through drought-stricken plains in 'the pathless depths of the parched Karroo', at one stage for fourteen hours without water. Pringle evoked it in verse as a

> … region of emptiness, howling and drear,
> Which Man hath abandoned from famine and fear,
> Which the snake and the lizard inhabit alone,
> With the twilight bat from the yawning stone.[13]

Poetic licence accounts for his reference to 'the bitter melon, for food and drink, … the pilgrim's fare by the salt lake's brink', which his note identifies 'as a species of *coloquintada*, … a prickly cucumber, which is considered edible'. He saw it, he writes, 'on the skirts of the Karroo' but Burchell, to whom he refers, places it also as growing on 'the Desert of Kalleghanny or Challahegah…lying between the countries of the Bechuanas and the Damaras', i.e. the Kalahari.[14] Is this 'prickly cucumber' the !Nara, still harvested by the Topnaar people in the south Namib desert, a very far cry from the Karroo?

They travelled on through the eastern Karroo

> Where sedgy pool, nor babbling fount,
> Nor tree, nor cloud, nor misty mount,
> Appears, to refresh the aching eye
> But the barren earth and the burning sky:
> And the blank horizon, round and round,
> Spread – void of living sight or sound.

They stopped 'at a boor's place on the Zout Rivier (Salt River)', the waters of which were 'so brackish as to be scarcely drinkable'. They were nevertheless much entertained by the farmer, Du Ploit, 'a frank, talkative fellow and a great Nimrod in his way',[15] who had a fund of anecdotes about the animal life of the Karroo. Perhaps he was the C.M. du Plooy who was one of the 'postholders' in the newly created Beaufort sub-drostdy, renamed Beaufort West in 1862.[16]

Then came their stay in the seat of the Deputy Landdrost of Beaufort, John Baird, recently retired from the Cape Regiment, and a nephew of General Sir David Baird, who had taken the Cape from the Dutch in 1806. They were 'most hospitably entertained by our Scottish countryman'. Thompson, a year later, was 'welcomed with much cordiality'[17] by Baird. Yet Pringle's visit to the village gaol, with yet another fellow Scot, the Revd John Taylor, from Scone in Perthshire, should surely have warranted a rebuke for their cordial host (who was later removed from his post for his oppressive and corrupt behaviour).

Taylor had arrived at the Cape with Moffat and Brownlee as London Missionary Society missionaries in 1817 and, having transferred to the Dutch Reformed Church, was sent to Beaufort the following year. He then succeeded another Scot, the Revd John Evans, at Cradock, the nearest church to Glen Lynden until, in 1829, the Revd John Pears inaugurated the new Glen Lynden church. These Scottish ministers served the Dutch colonists and their Reformed Church well but maintained a close link with the colonial authority. Taylor disapproved strongly of the 'emigrant farmers' who trekked into the interior in 1837–8 in the epic 'Great Trek', yet occasionally ministered to them across the Orange River. His flock included the Kruger family, whose son Paul he had baptised in Cradock in 1823. Taylor and his consistory took action against John Baird and achieved his dismissal.

It is curious that Pringle did not add his condemnation but Baird's disgrace happened eight years before the publication of *African Sketches*, with the first printing of the *Narrative* in it. Perhaps he felt that Baird, whom he would first have met as an assistant to Robert Hart at Somerset farm, had paid the price. Baird was succeeded as deputy landdrost by the Pringles' great friend and supporter, Captain W.W. Harding, himself promoted to divisional Magistrate before retirement in 1829.

Pringle did, however, record the awful scene he witnessed in Baird's gaol, the condition of which was 'dreadful'. Taylor held him back from entering until the door was briefly opened to give some momentary ventilation and reduce the stink. Crammed inside were runaway slaves, now shackled and 'sullenly awaiting their awarded punishment and the arrival of their owners to drag them back to the house of bondage'. Some Khoikhoi were held prisoner after complaining of 'fraud and oppression of the colonists to whom they were bound in servitude', others held while awaiting employment, some 'wild Bushmen', most having absconded from the service of farmers, and with them the perpetrators of serious crimes 'awaiting the arrival of the annual Circuit Court' – all 'crowded together without distinction into this narrow and noisome dungeon'.[18]

Pringle was most struck by the presence of three Xhosa men, a woman and child and a boy of about sixteen, accused of murdering a Swellendam farmer who had one of their party killed for stealing a sheep as they travelled out of the colony. He described their dress, demeanour and physical beauty, most of all of the woman and the youth, the latter 'truly a model of juvenile beauty', his figure displaying 'a graceful ease and symmetry of proportion', a handsome face, bespeaking 'confidence and good will'. Pringle found that, a year later, they were still awaiting sentence but learned no more of them.

He again avoided blaming Baird – 'with whom the fault lay I cannot say', and the two years that lay before him were filled with hard work for the white colonists rather than for the indigenous underclass. Pringle was no deluded adorer of the alien and despiser of his own. In the final part of the journey, which took a further three weeks, they stayed a night with a grazier named Nel, near today's Prince Albert, and judged the place 'very wretched and dreary, yet he found physical beauty to compare with the Xhosa youth in the foul gaol: 'A daughter of this boor's, a girl about fifteen years of age, was one of the comeliest females of European race I had seen in the colony'.[19]

From the Ghamka (or Lion) River to the Dwyka (or Rhinoceros), both water-less, the wagons made only fifteen miles a day – half their rate in favourable country, but they came to a swiftly flowing stream, the Buffalo river, near today's Laingsburg, and the parched and exhausted oxen were refreshed at last. Heavy rains had fallen six weeks before and from then on the water courses were running, wild flowers blossomed everywhere and 'even the broad wagon-road, usually as hard as a threshing floor, was here overrun with verdant creeping plants, as close as a camomile bed'. As they approached Cape Town, over the Hex River pass 'there were elegant and capacious dwellings, skirted by orange groves, vineyards and cornfields'.

By 25 September they were in Cape Town, with his 'female companions much less exhausted than might have been expected by our tedious and trying journey'. Pringle himself was buoyed up and ready for the great work ahead. After his successful leadership of the 'Scotch Party' he was ready to reinstate himself, his fortune, his reputation – putting behind him the humiliation of Edinburgh. He would also aim to serve the people of the Cape and beyond, both colonists and colonized.

> At the close of the month of September Table Bay is free from the prevalence of north-westerly gales, and the heavy rains have ceased. The verdure of the Lion's Hill, and of the luxuriant crops of oats and barley along its base, affords pleasure to the eye. The plain, enamelled with flowering bulbous plants of every colour of the rainbow, variegating the very margin of the bay, adorned with neat and elegant villas, and the singular appearance of the Table Mountain, combine to delight a stranger on his arrival … The houses, flat roofed and chiefly white, with green windows, are spacious and convenient … The private gardens … are of exquisite beauty, and the garden houses are the favourite abode of the Cape-Dutch inhabitants.[20]

Thus wrote William Wilberforce Bird, a cousin of the great abolitionist, Controller of Customs, merchant and confidant of the Governor, Lord Charles Somerset. W.W. Bird (no kin to the Colonial Secretary Colonel Christopher Bird) moved in the smartest Cape circles and gives a vivid account of the race meetings, theatre life, the 'Indians' on furlough and the social entertainments of Cape Town. He is not a little critical of the manners of the citizenry and their propensity for unfounded gossip. This was the Cape Town that the Pringles and Janet Brown arrived at, and in the month that W.W. Bird completed his *State of the Cape of Good Hope,* published anonymously. Cape Town was not all frivolity: on the title page an editor was named: H.T. Colebrooke, most distinguished of the Indians, a famous Sanskrit scholar and member of the Bengal Council, who had bought land at Saldanha Bay.

George Thompson, at a lower, yet successful, level of commercial activity than Bird's, and rarely, if ever, a guest at the Governor's table, refers his reader to W.W. Bird's study, 'so recently and so very well detailed'.[21] Perhaps this was Pringle's stratagem, in 'ghosting' Thompson's *Travels and Adventures in South Africa,* as he did in his last months at the Cape, to avoid a lengthy account of Cape Town. Thompson and Bird part company above all on the latter's criticism of the Cape Dutch population, characterized by Pringle as 'a frank and hospitable and at the same time a prudent and thrifty race',[22] their activities in trade 'less obnoxious to ridicule than that supercilious affectation of gentility, which not infrequently hides beneath an aristocratic garb as much avarice and meanness as can be found in the most sordid "*smous*" [pedlar] of the Colony'.[23]

Thompson (or Pringle) finds that habits and customs in Cape Town are 'becoming every day more English' and discounts Bird's views as 'taken from the elevated point of view which the author is supposed to hold in Cape society. But to those whose more humble station in life [such as Pringle himself] has placed them in closer contact with these people it will be a matter for regret that if they ever so entirely change as to lose some of their present characteristics'.[24]

The sub-librarianship, which Pringle took up at once, was shared with P.

Harmsen, in charge of the Dessinian Collection. The Mozambican slave Lendor, whose purchase by the Committee for cleaning the library and looking after the chemical apparatus was recorded in the 15 October 1822 minutes, was 'disposed of' – for 1400 Rixdollars – within three months 'on account of his bad behaviour'. On 21 January 1823 the sub-librarians were authorized to hire, not buy, 'a slave or servant' to replace Lendor. Was he the same slave Lendor whose escape and recapture was later reported?[2] The Librarianship itself was a non-executive, unpaid post, held, on Pringle's arrival, by the Revd R.F. Kaufman, minister of the Lutheran Church. Pringle and a later chairman, W.W. Bird, were to confront each other over the barricades in time to come.

The South African Public Library, funded by a wine tax, was a creation of Lord Charles Somerset's, prompted by the Colonial Secretary and Chaplain, Colonel Bird and the Revd George Hough, in 1818. Its own two-storey premises in the courtyard of the Supreme Court building, formerly the Slave Lodge, which Bird described as 'handsomely fitted up, both in point of taste and utility. It consists of two spacious library rooms, with apartments and apparatus for chemical experiments.'[26] He indulges himself in a humorous but laudatory account of the 3086 books (which grew to 4565) bequeathed on his death in 1761 by Joachim von Dessin, Secretary of the Orphan Chamber, and also gives praise for the Library's possession of 'the best ancient and most recent modern publications in religion, in the classics, in history, poetry, geography, chemistry and political economy; a most ample collection of essays, of voyages and travels; and dictionaries of all ages and languages.' The sting is in the tail: 'The thing that appears to be chiefly wanting, which Mr Dessin could not bequeath, is a collection of readers; for reading is not an African passion'.

An account of the Library by John Fawcett, an officer in the Hon. East India Company's Bengal army on furlough, and a zealous evangelist who took on many colonists in his support for Dr Philip and his friends, demonstrates its development in the decade after Pringle's charge of it. The Library, he wrote in 1835:

> would be an ornament to any town. The room is much too small to contain the number of books or afford suitable accommodation to subscribers. This will probably be rectified on some future day, when the people, tired of quarrelling with each other, shall have leisure and unanimity enough to seek the advancement of its interests.[27]

He praised Pringle's successor, Alexander Johnstone Jardine, for his 'minute knowledge of the management of the books' and the 'great readiness and civility with which he issued them to readers'. Jardine benefited by the catalogue compiled by Pringle during his all too brief period at the Library.

The quarrelling had sharply polarized opinion since Pringle's departure and Fawcett made a point of acclaiming a victim of the quarrels, unnamed but with Pringle's sonnet, 'The Caffer', as an apt example of the work of:

> a poet of no mean name and reputation, discarded though he be by those who ought to sympathize in his praise, and feel honoured that such a genius rose from among them. He knew South Africa well, and has sung, in glowing lines of poesy, many a faithful, though bitter, truth regarding its inhabitants.

117

The poem puts Pringle's case for sharing equally the blame for frontier cattle thefts: 'He is a robber? True, it is a strife / Between the black-skinned bandit and the white'. Fawcett changed Pringle's Scots 'cleugh' to the Afrikaans 'kloof'.

Fawcett demonstrates a three-way tension, or what he calls 'three distinct exhibitions of hatred: 'First the Dutch hate the English; next, the Dutch and English hate the natives; and lastly the natives hate the Dutch and English.' He omits what could have been the fourth: the English hate the Dutch. His five topics that 'excite the bitterness of colonial feeling' are 'the emancipation of the slaves; the eastern frontier policy; the vagrant laws; the conduct of Dr Philip and the London Society's missionaries; Mr Fairbairn and his politics'. In all of these Pringle was a champion of the minority and at loggerheads with most of the colonists, Dutch and English.

Pringle, whose death in December 1834 was not known to Fawcett when his pamphlet went to its Cape Town printer in 1836, was not yet a champion of any of the five when in Cape Town, though 'discarded' by many of the colonists by 1835.

In these early months at the Cape, at his first house at 21 Kloof Street, every prospect seemed to please. The Library committee's goodwill was made real by their granting him 250 Rixdollars – the equivalent of three months' salary – for the 'trouble and expense' of his translocation from the eastern Cape. At the Library his duties were undemanding. He wrote to Walter Scott: 'the situation is extremely agreeable to me. I attend from 9 till 4 o'clock, but have much time for reading and study'.[28] He set about compiling, in scholarly fashion, the catalogue of English books in January 1823 and doubtless had much correspondence with John Barrow at the Admiralty, who had agreed to buy and dispatch books for the Library.

Barrow evidently enjoyed the work. His letter from the Admiralty in February 1823 tells Colonel Bird to expect 600 books by the *Urania*. He asks for £500 'to make your library complete [with] a selection of new books on science and natural history'. The committee minutes of 4 October 1824 note a third payment of £500 to 'Mr Barrow'.[29]

Pringle had an urgent need to supplement his income. With the permission of the Colonial Office, he advertised in the *Government Gazette* of 30 November 1822:

> Mr Pringle begs leave to intimate that he has made Arrangements which will enable him to receive a few young Gentlemen Boarders, for private Tuition; the Number not exceeding six. Applications or enquiries may be addressed to Mr P. at The South African Library, Cape Town.

He had soon 'as many from the principal families of the place as I could conveniently attend to'.[30] There was more than a possibility that he would be asked to take over the running of the *Government Gazette* – at £100 per annum – and the Library appeared to be 'warmly patronized by the Governor, and by all the chief functionaries'.

He soon saw opening about him 'fields of public usefulness far beyond my own humble powers'. He wrote again to John Fairbairn, a very persuasive letter:

> You must understand my good friend that having tired of herding ... and hunting lions and Bushmen, I accepted of an appointment offered me lately by the Governor ... to take charge of a Public Library.[31]

He was taking pupils 'as the salary is rather small' and had seen that 'there is a great opening here at this time for making something very handsome' by teaching the children, like his existing pupils, 'of the most respectable families in the Colony' and 'to attract pupils from India ... altogether there is scope for both *you* and *me* to make our fortunes ... Now, my dear John, could you not make a bold push and join me here speedily?'

There was also, 'to amuse our leisure', a magazine to be produced. It was a chance too good to miss. Here was 'a fairer prospect of making me independent than I have ever before had before me'. He adopted an almost wheedling tone:

> You know I have no small regard and affection for thee and notwithstanding thy surly silence I flatter myself I am not indifferent to thee my dear Johnny, I think we would grow together – we might mutually assist and further each other's good fortune.

Allowing three months for the letter to reach Newcastle, Fairbairn must have decided almost at once, and on 2 March 1823 he told Pringle of 'the unspeakable pleasure' it gave him to find his friend 'once more among Books and Men'.[32] He felt Pringle's views 'well founded and cannot without some unforeseen mischief fail to be realized to a very satisfactory extent'. He committed himself: 'I will join you (D.V.) about six weeks after you receive this epistle' Fairbairn particularly took to the notion of their producing magazines and newspapers, and why not a history of the settlement, and natural history? 'Little or nothing has been done ... since Sparrman and Vaillant' (John Barrow would have been wounded by this, so proud was he of his *Account of Travels in South Africa,* written after the Swede and the Frenchman's accounts, as were Lichtenstein's, Burchell's and Latrobe's). There could be public lectures and the 'giving to song ... the unknown streams and nameless mountains ...'

Fairbairn was greatly excited – the prospect must have inspired him since 1819 or 1820 when he had decided against joining the Scottish party, perhaps out of a sense of duty to his ailing mother. Now he was ready (and his mother, in fact, lived on until 1837 in Berwickshire, where he visited her in 1827, during a year long visit to Britain). 'There are still unknown kingdoms, or at least provinces, for us to explore ... What should hinder us from becoming the Franklins of the *Kaap?'* Sir John Franklin returned from his great Arctic expedition in 1822 and published his account of it in 1823. It was an unhappy analogy as Franklin and his men were to endure terrible suffering before his death in 1847, still seeking (and finding) the North-West Passage. The light-hearted reference was to Sir John and not the American Benjamin, who was many things but never an explorer. This misreading has been repeated by many, critically of the two friends for their apparent overweening self-esteem. Fairbairn was to survive Sir John Franklin by seventeen years – and to outlive Pringle by thirty – after a long and fruitful career in South Africa.

After staying at the Pringles' old Soho lodgings and calling on Underwood and his father-in-law, Dr Waugh, Fairbairn set sail for the Cape and reached Table Bay on 10 October 1823.

NOTES

[1] Philipps, Thomas, *Advantages of Emigration to Algoa Bay and Albany, South Africa* (1836), p. 7.

[2] Bird to Pringle, 5.7.1822. Rennie, vol. 1, p. 378.

[3] Pringle v Pringle, Supreme Court, CSC 2/1/1/114 No 28. Rennie, vol. 1, p. 378.

[4] Pringle (1966), p. 159.

[5] *Ibid.*

[6] Thompson (1967), vol. 1, p. xviii.

[7] Barrow, Sir John, *An Account of Travels into the Interior of Southern Africa,* 2 vols (1802), vol. 1, pp. 113–14.

[8] Pringle (1966), p. 159.

[9] *Ibid.*

[10] Pringle (1966), p. 164.

[11] *Op. cit.,* p. 162.

[12] Barrow (1802), p. 251.

[13] Pringle (1838), pp. 10–11, 74.

[14] Burchell, *Travels in the Interior of Southern Africa,* 2 vols (1822, 1824), vol. 1, p. 243.

[15] Pringle (1966), p. 165.

[16] The drostdy was at Graaff-Reinet, the term denoting both the area under the Landdrost's charge and the magistracy building.

[17] Thompson (1966), vol. 1, p. 141.

[18] Pringle (1966), p. 169.

[19] *Op. cit.,* p. 172.

[20] Bird, William Wilberforce ('A Civil Servant of the Colony'), *The State of the Cape of Good Hope in 1822* (1823), pp. 145–6.

[21] Thompson (1968), vol. 2, p. 141.

[22] *Op. cit.,* vol. 2, p. 143.

[23] *Ibid.*

[24] Pringle (1966), p. 189.

[25] Bourke to Bathurst, 18.10.1826, enc. 2, 'Slave Imports and Exports'. South African Public Library Minutes, vol. 1 , p. 14.

[26] W.W. Bird, pp. 152.

[27] Fawcett, John, *An Account of Eighteen Months' Residence at the Cape of Good Hope* (1836), pp. 89–90.

[28] Pringle to Scott, 31.10.1822, NLS MS 3895 f 201.

[29] Barrow to C. Bird, – 2.23, *RCC* 17.

[30] Pringle (1966), p. 178.

[31] Pringle to Fairbairn, 4.11.1822, Vigne (2011), pp. 81–2. Fairbairn Papers, LP 1, 2.

[32] Fairbairn to Pringle, 2.3.1823, Pringle (1966), p. 176.

9

'An Arrant Dissenter'

The mischief that was Pringle's undoing might already have been foreseen, though Fairbairn was to survive it. For Pringle wrote to Scott, before sending off his effective letter to Fairbairn, that, despite Colonel Bird's having tried hard to obtain for him

> the appointment of Superintendent of the Govt. Press ... and to this he had almost succeeded but for an unlucky circumstance which it appears had prejudiced Lord Charles against me. Some person has informed him (or perhaps he has imagined from seeing my name, much to my regret, mentioned in newspapers and magazines) that I am a violent Whig and formerly a supporter of the democrat press (as it is called) in Scotland ...[1]

The identity of the 'some person' who had given Lord Charles the idea that Pringle was 'a violent Whig' became clear to him. He wrote to Sir George Mackenzie in Edinburgh on 25 June 1823, the day before Fairbairn had sailed from Gravesend: 'Though I keep myself cautiously aloof from all political or party discussions I have the misfortune of being grievously suspected of being a Whigg',[2] for which he blamed Capt Fox for labelling him 'a good staunch *Whigg*' at the Governor's table.

Charles Fox, who had transferred to the 15th Foot, sailed from Table Bay in August 1822, shortly before the Pringles and Janet Brown had arrived in Cape Town from Glen Lynden. A bitter irony for Pringle it was that, again, a good friend had done him serious harm: Hogg, perhaps with a touch of malice in the mischief he had made with both *The Poetic Mirror* misattribution and, far worse, initiating the 'Chaldee MS'. From what we know of him, Captain Fox can have had not the slightest malice aforethought in mentioning Pringle's Whig background, and perhaps had no knowledge of his troubles with Blackwood and even the use of his letter in the contest between Wilson and Hamilton for the chair of Moral Philosophy, of which Pringle had complained to Scott in March 1821.

Somerset had the good of the colony at heart and worked hard to make it prosper but he was an autocrat, by nature and by breeding, in a post which gave him absolute power. The same motive that helped to produce the 1820 settlement scheme – fear of a rising of the masses against the ruling class – led him to extremes of watchfulness against any sign of radicalism at the Cape and a deadly dread of the press as a fomenter of revolt. The squalid public row over the accession of George IV and the exclusion of his would-be Queen from the coronation in 1821 revealed the capacity of the popular press to execrate and revile the monarchy in the person of their new King and to champion poor, impossible Caroline (only to drop her as soon as the coronation was over).

Fox's disclosure put an end to Pringle's hopes of superintending the government press but there were other promising opportunities for success and prosperity. A fine building for school and residence, Harington House, stood on the corner of the Keizersgracht (now Darling Street) and what is now Harrington Street, with a view of the Castle. It accommodated Pringle and Margaret, and presumably Janet and Fairbairn, who does not appear with his own address in the *African Court Calendar,* their rapidly growing number of pupils and five or six servants.

The academy had been advertised in *The Government Gazette* as

> A Classical and Commercial Academy in which the education of Young Gentlemen will be conducted according to the methods followed in the most advanced Seminaries in England. A limited number of Boarders and Day Scholars will be received. ... at the Academy, Harington House, Cape Town.[3]

If this initiative soon revealed a need also for a 'Day-School for the Education of Young Ladies',[4] Janet Brown was ready for it and in January 1824 she advertised in English and Dutch the opening of such a school at 'No 3 Keizersgracht, Harington House'. In August 1824 she advertised that 'Miss Brown's Day-School for Young Ladies will be removed from the Keizersgracht to No 14 Berg Street, corner of Castle Street'.

The school became 'Miss Brown's Academy for Young Ladies' in January 1825 and continued at 14 Berg Street, 'her Personal Residence as well as School'. She evidently stayed on in Cape Town when Pringle and her sister returned to Glen Lynden for their parting visit. Berg Street did not become St George's Street until 1830, during the building of St George's Church (later Cathedral) at its south end from 1827 (the name being proposed by William Wilberforce Bird).

Affairs at Pringle's Academy were soon to be overshadowed by the journalistic activities that brought his growing conflict with the Governor to a crisis. Pringle wrote to Lord Bathurst in January 1825, in the gathering storm, that in mid-1824

> our new academy was flourishing, popular, and every day increasing in numbers; we had ten boarders and about forty other pupils ... In July last our little academy was the most respectable and prosperous school in Cape Town and was attended by a large proportion of the children both of the Civil Servants and the Military Officers in the Colony.[5]

We know from his later intervention in the turmoil over Pringle's affairs that the grandson of the Chief Justice, Sir John Truter, was one of the pupils.

It was Pringle's tragedy that his dream of becoming, with Fairbairn, the Blackwood or Francis Jeffrey of the Cape should have so upset Lord Charles Somerset as to deny him even the opportunity of editing the *Government Gazette*, which was to continue under Andreas Richert, an elderly German-born printer, as a dull purveyor of official notices, with a modicum of European news items.

Pringle told Sir George Mackenzie of his belief that it was partly 'from having my name bandied about in Blackwood's magazine and the *Scotchman* [*sic*]' as well as Fox's injudiciously calling him 'a good staunch Whigg' that lost him these posts.

The difficulties that lay ahead were due to more than Captain Fox's indiscretion or the press reports of the campaign for the chair of moral philosophy at Edinburgh. Pringle had, with the Revd Abraham Faure, issued in February 1823 a prospectus of the *South African Journal* and *Het Nederduitsch Zuid-Afrikaansche Tijdschrift*. They had agreed to publish in English and Dutch on alternate months. Pringle wrote that he 'was encouraged to prosecute this purpose by the most enlightened inhabitants of the Colony, both English and Dutch'.[6] He and Faure 'made no secret of their scheme', and while preparing a memorial to the Governor seeking his approval (permission was not strictly needed) and a prospectus, Pringle was visited by Daniel Denyssen, the Fiscal, the Dutch equivalent of the Attorney-General of the Colony, who tried to dissuade him from the project, which would seriously harm his prospects in the colony. The memorial and prospectus, typically of Pringle, were sent to Somerset nevertheless, on 3 February 1823.

Though a despot, Somerset had the sense to know that a formally recorded refusal of his approval might do great harm to his reputation and standing. He wrote to Robert Wilmot Horton, Goulburn's successor at the Colonial Office, asking for Lord Bathurst's view of this subject 'which a person in office finds it difficult to word a refusal to that can meet the public eye'. The hostile caricature of Pringle that he sent Wilmot Horton showed that he had found out more about his past than was clear to Pringle, who

> had heretofore been employed to scribble for a Magazine published in Edinbro' under the auspices of the Edinbro' Reviewers, whose political and religious opinions he of course adopts.[7]

Pringle had faced greater perils than a colonial governor's displeasure. It was he who had inspired his fellow settlers to stay on in their remote Baviaans River location when the loss of the *Abeona* consigned them to a permanent isolation on a dangerous outpost of the frontier such as they had never envisaged. His savaging at the hands of Lockhart and Wilson, egged on by his erstwhile friend Blackwood, inspired by his affectionate companion Hogg, dispelled any illusions he had about a life in 'periodical literature' but the chance of making a success of it at the Cape had been too good to miss.

Pringle's early admiration of Somerset's administration – the attempt to mitigate slavery, the promotion of education (in English), the benevolence of the Colonial Secretary Colonel Bird – was soon turned to concern about Somerset's fitness to rule and at last to mutual hostility. Somerset ended his diatribe against Pringle to Wilmot Horton by pronouncing the ultimate accusation from a High Tory Anglican: ' He is *an arrant dissenter*'.[8] In a contest between an absolute Colonial Governor with the most powerful family interest at home, in a period of secure Tory rule, and a penurious young Scottish Whig, armed only with a pen and a burning sense of wrong, the outcome was certain in the short term.

In the early months of 1823, despite Pringle's awareness of the Governor's disfavour, the prospect was as pleasing as it had been on his return to Cape Town from Glen Lynden six months before. The Academy would soon be launched, the *South African Journal* held great promise and there were new worlds to conquer – a 'Literary and Scientific Society', such as had occupied Fairbairn's leisure in Newcastle, the book about South Africa which both Barrow and Scott had encouraged, even a decent income to augment the pittance the sub-librarianship brought in.

An unexpected boost to that income was to come from a young man called George Greig, who arrived from England on 9 March 1823, while Pringle and Faure were preparing the prospectus of the *South African Journal* to put to the Governor. That same week in early March 1823 John Fairbairn wrote to accept Pringle's invitation to join him at the Cape. The two friends were in harness together in November, with Fairbairn fully occupied with the Academy and Pringle serving also at the library.

George Greig had arrived with printing equipment and a wide range of household goods for sale. The son of a Pentonville market gardener he had served his apprenticeship with a printer in the City of London and had, he said, worked for His Majesty's Stationery Office. He set about acquiring funds to finance the newspaper he had it in mind to publish, by opening at No 1 Longmarket Street, a general store selling household goods, stationery and books. In July he applied for the Governor's permission to operate his printing press and to publish a 'literary and commercial magazine', which would rigidly exclude 'personal controversy, and all discussion of matter relating to the policy or administration of the Colonial Government'.[9]

This was July 1823, but as early as February of that year Somerset's antipathy to Pringle began to make itself felt. In the fifteen months that followed Somerset's negative response to Pringle's *South African Journal* project the struggle between Somerset and Pringle, joined soon after by Fairbairn, then Greig, was waged on several fronts. The outcome for Pringle was financial ruin, but for the causes at issue – freedom of speech and the ultimate defeat of absolutism – there was victory in the longer term.

Greig was a young man – only 23 on his arrival – of spirit and determination, said to be a radical, but was without Pringle's and Fairbairn's active, reforming zeal and liberal spirit, when these interfered with business. Though unschooled in the late Enlightenment ideals of late Georgian Edinburgh, he stood side by side with Pringle and Fairbairn in the struggle for Press Freedom, though their ways were to part in later years.

In that struggle it was Greig who first confronted Somerset at every point. Pringle's and Fairbairn's part of the campaign concerned only their *South African Journal,* which, though a commendable bi-monthly production, had none of the immediacy or political relevance of Greig's *South African Commercial Advertiser.* Though from the third issue they were the editors, with editorial powers secured under an agreement which showed that Pringle had learned a lesson from his treatment by Blackwood. This same agreement also guaranteed the secrecy of their positions as editors. In the engagement between the *Advertiser* and the colonial government it was Greig and Greig alone who was at the parapet.

His relations with Somerset had been uneasy from the start. His request for approval of his printing and publishing plans had first been ignored, then answered negatively, until a directive from Bathurst compelled Somerset, contrary to his strongly expressed views, to allow the *Advertiser* to appear.[10] The process and his trading affairs took more than six months and issue No 1 of the Cape's first independent newspaper appeared on 7 January 1824, two months before the launching of Pringle and Fairbairn's *South African Journal.* It was an instant success and filled a very real gap in the needs of the young, growing, thriving, mainly English mercantile community. It gave them the commercial information and advertising, and local and 'home' news lacking in the *Gazette,* edited by the elderly, pedestrian Andreas Richert, who had come to the Cape in its Batavian days and was Consul for the King of Prussia.

Greig's agreement with Pringle and Fairbairn enabled them to edit the *Advertiser* from its third issue. They wrote leaders that may have dismayed Somerset. On 7 April 1824 the anonymous Pringle attacked despotism and called for 'open discussion of differences' which could be achieved 'by means of a Free Press, its liberty (not licentiousness)' protected by law. The second issue of the *South African Journal* appeared the day before and must have been in Pringle's mind as he wrote his leader. Less than a month later despotism was to have its way with liberty and Press Freedom challenged by absolute power, sanctioned from distant London.

The *casus belli,* the Edwards libel case, was but one of a horrid array of ills which were to torment Somerset and must have affected his judgement, never his strongest suit, in his dealings with Pringle in 1824–5.

Somerset's biographer quotes a private letter in which Lord Charles wishes 'a Happy New Year' 1824 to the recipient and adds: 'There is something awful at all times entering upon one. ... It makes one shudder to think of what has happened to me in the last twelve months ... and it is not the least Calamity to me to reflect that I have been robbed of my good name'. The recipient was the lawyer John Thomas Bigge, who arrived at the Cape with his fellow Commissioner of Inquiry, Major W.M.G. Colebrooke, later a distinguished colonial governor, to conduct an investigation of affairs of the new colonies of Mauritius and Ceylon, to which parliament later added the Cape of Good Hope.

They were to 'inquire into the state of the settlements at the Cape of Good Hope, the Mauritius and Ceylon, and also into the administration of justice in the Leeward Islands'. Of particular importance were the courts and the introduction of the English legal system, the English language, the state of slavery (and the bondage of the Khoikhoi at the Cape) and, far down the list, 'the settlements lately formed and the probability of their success and advancement'.

The indulgent, sometimes admiring tone of A.K. Millar's biography of Somerset was influenced by his reading letters of Somerset to Bigge during the Commissioners' time at the Cape, July 1823 until 1825, which found their way to Rhodes House Library in Oxford in 1947.[11] They reveal a suffering 'Somerset agonistes', a kindlier, less confident figure than the overbearing patrician experienced by Pringle and many others. It was, of course, in Somerset's interest to show his best side to Bigge but even here his judgement was at times at fault. His persistent and pressing invitations to Bigge to ride with him to his pack of foxhounds, or to set off on long horseback journeys, must have greatly irritated this nervous and unskilled horseman. Nevertheless, there seems to have been a bond of friendship between the two.

The Commissioners were well disposed too to Pringle and Fairbairn. Pringle, and less often, Fairbairn, put their case to the Commissioners in great detail and repeatedly. The secretary to the Commissioner, John Gregory, allowed Pringle to use him for the conveying of confidential letters and even as a source of inside information. We are able to consider their case against Somerset and his officials in detail that is possible due to their presence at the Cape during these days of wrath.

Somerset's *anni horribiles* are summed up by Millar, quite fairly, thus:

> Looking back, Lord Charles Somerset must surely have regarded the period from 1823 to 1825 as the most harassing and anxious of his whole life. Not a week seemed to pass without the eruption of some new and disturbing development involving the press, the judiciary, aggrieved settlers or trouble caused by some downright rascals. The whole scene became turbulent and confused … in a morass of litigation, prosecutions and banishments.[12]

The presence of the Commissioners was a restraint on Somerset, who had to temper his authoritarian instincts under their watchful eyes. His conciliatory attitude towards them helped Pringle and Fairbairn in the early months of their clash with the Governor, and the Commissioners' receptive attitude towards their case against the Government enabled it to be fully documented. Pringle had good reason to hope that their report would in the end favour his case against Somerset's rule and his own claim for compensation.

Among the slings and arrows that hit Somerset in these years was the accusation of corruption brought by a senior official, Charles Collot d'Escury, from which he was absolved after a long and painful investigation by the Commissioners; the unceasing war on his administration waged by the embittered Sir Rufane Donkin, whose measures as Acting Governor he had insultingly repudiated; the treachery, as he saw it, of the Revd William Geary, whom Lord Charles's sister-in-law, the Duchess of Beaufort, had wished on him as a supposed defender of the Established Church against Dissenters like Philip and Pringle, who were no threat at all; and the fury of the Albany settlers aroused by their cavalier and hurtful treatment by Harry Rivers, the Landdrost Somerset had appointed to assist them in their early years of blight, drought, floods and cattle thefts. More damaging in the end were the attacks of an independent malcontent settler, Bishop Burnett, a half-pay naval officer, from whom Pringle took pains to distance himself.

Most personally wounding, however, was the criticism by Pringle and others of the 'commando system' (Pringle's phrase) to deal with the cattle thefts, which the Frontier troops seemed to provoke rather than prevent. In 1824 Somerset's favourite, his eldest son Henry, had taken command of the cavalry section of the Cape Regiment (he was to command the Regiment as a whole in 1828). Donkin's quarrel with Henry Somerset in his father's absence in 1820 had led to implacable enmity between Lord Charles and Donkin. Perhaps Pringle's stance against Colonel Henry Somerset put him similarly beyond the Somerset pale.

Pringle's point of no return with Somerset was reached on 18 May 1824 when he was summoned to the presence of the Governor, who had the Chief Justice,

Sir John Truter at his side, and berated in 'a most haughty and overbearing tone' for being 'one of those who think proper to insult me and oppose my government'.[13] Furthermore, as became apparent, the attacks on government by the Cape Town-based Society for the Relief of the Distressed Settlers of Albany, of which Pringle served as secretary from late 1823, had cut deep. His *Some Account of the Present State of the English Settlers in Albany,* 1824, did not spare Somerset's officials and some of its contents were to reappear in the second issue of the *South African Journal*, which Somerset had before him at the climactic meeting.

The meeting over, Pringle at once resigned his library post, since Somerset had 'considered insulting' his closing the *Journal* and signing the 'Memorial for a Free Press in the Colony' (together with 208 'most respectable inhabitants' on 14 May 1824). He ignored Somerset's charge that he had broken the terms of the prospectus of the *Journal* which Somerset considered binding. To Pringle the issue was purely one of censorship and press freedom.

Pringle, it may be said, felt that he had spared Colonel Somerset's father other harsh criticisms of his son and brother officers on the frontier. He reported to the Commissioners that at the 18 May meeting he had avoided 'raking up old scores' with the Governor over the troops that his son was commanding on the frontier and did not tell him that when he 'lived on that frontier in constant peril and alarm from the Caffres and never went to sleep without a loaded gun at my side … the officers on the Frontier were building Parade Forts, or pretty cottages, shooting Partridges, or smoking segars, or flogging Hottentot soldiers until they deserted in droves, doing everything useless or mischievous, but not defending the Frontier'.[14]

Pringle's honour was to suffer grievously as a result of a quarrel in which he had no part which led to the writing of extremely abusive letters to the Governor and the consequent criminal libel action, brought on Somerset's insistence, against a local merchant, Lancelot Cooke, and a recently arrived mystery man and self-styled attorney, William Edwards. The proceedings offered entertainment of a high order, the court was packed day after day as Edwards performed in his own defence, earning himself a month in gaol for contempt, before acquittal. Somerset was humiliated and hardly appeased when 'Edwards' was put on trial a second time. He was later found to be a convict escaped to the Cape from New South Wales, a fraudulent attorney believed to be called Alexander Low Kay (though there is some doubt as to his real identity), and sent back to gaol awaiting transportation. Even from gaol he was able to throw very nasty mud, which not only hit its target but splashed Pringle in the process. This was in June 1824, but the case itself had already led to the central event of the struggle for Press Freedom which Pringle and Fairbairn espoused with such passion.

Among other scurrilous placards put up by persons unknown in the streets of Cape Town was one very briefly displayed accusing Somerset of a homosexual relationship with his physician, Dr James Barry, who was also Colonial Medical Inspector. Barry, who had a distinguished later career in what became the Royal Army Medical Corps, was alleged to have been found, on his death, to have been a woman and one who had borne a child. The evidence was shaky, however, and his or her sexual make-up remains a mystery.

A copy of the placard was found in the cell of the infamous Edwards, who had previously, in court, referred to Somerset as having a black woman servant in his household as his concubine. Edwards, with his gaol alibi, was able to blame another escaped convict, one Haynes, for affixing it, but Haynes had made a second flight and was not apprehended.

There had been an all-out search for co-conspirators in this outrage against His Excellency, and it reached Pringle's ears, through the sub-librarian who had succeeded him, Alexander Johnstone Jardine, that Pringle's name was on a list of persons whose papers were to be searched. Pringle was appalled by this impugning of his honour and rectitude and, after an immediate confrontation with the Fiscal, Denyssen, an inquiry was held and later the Commissioners of Inquiry made their own report to Bathurst in London

Neither was able to establish the source of the information Jardine had passed on to Pringle. The Commissioners were sure that there had been no search warrant with Pringle's name on it. Denyssen maintained official secrecy over the whole matter. So charged with rancour and hostility against the Governor's enemies, imagined or otherwise, had the atmosphere become by June 1824 that it seems likely that the officials, with or without the Fiscal's complicity, had started the search warrant rumour to strike a blow at Pringle. He was their adversary over the matter of the *South African Journal* and was also Somerset's particular *bête noire.*

It came also on top of their action, as Somerset's hatchet men, against Greig and the *South African Commercial Advertiser,* whose great offence, in the Governor's eyes, had been its reporting of the Edwards case.

By the end of May 1824 the *Journal, Advertiser* and Pringle's librarianship were all at an end, and Greig's deportation had been ordered (though it was later rescinded). The scoundrel Edwards had been sent back to Botany Bay. The placard incident and Greig's deportation order seem to have hit Pringle harder than all his tribulations at the hands of Government.

Pringle denounced, six months later, to Lord Bathurst at the Colonial Office Lord Charles's manifesting towards him 'such a spirit of hostility and vengeance as greatly to disturb my quiet, to impair my public reputation and to defeat my honest endeavours to gain a respectable subsistence in this colony'. He called upon Bathurst 'for protection and redress', writing more passionately of the placard incident than of any other action against him:

> I accidentally discovered to my inexpressible horror and annoyance that the Fiscal had been *authorised* to insert my name among others of a very disreputable description in such warrant *signed* by the *Governor* thereby tending to convey an indirect but disgraceful and disgusting slur on my reputation.[16]

The year 1824, such a calamitous one for Pringle, came to an end with two further blows to his status and well-being. The decline of the Academy was apparent in August with the withdrawal of sons of officials anxious not to cross the Governor. Pringle and Fairbairn had long planned the setting up of a literary and scientific society on the lines of the Literary and Philosophical Society of Newcastle-upon-Tyne, founded in 1793 and still flourishing, and of which Fairbairn had been an active member. Their high standing in the white community is clear from the short history of the planned society, its acceptability heightened by Fairbairn's articles in Nos 1 and 2 of the *Journal*.

On 11 July Pringle and Fairbairn met with nine friends at the house of the merchants George Thompson and Charles Stuart Pillans, elected a committee of three, with Pringle as secretary and Fairbairn charged with writing a constitution for the new society. 'Sixty-one of the most intelligent and respectable persons in South Africa'[17] (including Chief Justice Truter) were ready to join, but first the Governor's approval – and patronage – was sought. A public-spirited East India Company official on furlough William Thomas Blair, Advocate Henry Cloete and their delegated colleagues were sternly rebuffed by Somerset. He had already, wrote Pringle, 'given [Truter] such a rating for joining the society that Sir John, almost frightened out of his wits, anxiously entreated me to withdraw his name from the list of members, at the same time assuring me that he conscientiously believed the institution to be a most praiseworthy one'. Somerset told Cloete that he was 'fully determined to thwart and oppose, so long as he held the reins of Government, everything whatever in which Mr Pringle and Mr Fairbairn were concerned, or words to that effect'[18] (this to the Commissioners, and to Bathurst and Brougham, which can only have been quoted with Cloete's permission).

It may seem strange that Pringle and his friends thought for one moment that Lord Charles would countenance the new society, with Pringle as its secretary. Truter, who had been present at Pringle's confrontation with Somerset, denied to the Commissioners that Pringle had been 'censured in a manner both severe and insulting'. Pringle, furthermore, himself reported that at the end of the meeting Somerset 'softened down so far as to coax me with a few compliments and endeavoured to persuade me to go on with the publication of the Journal upon the terms of our original Prospectus'.[19] Ever the optimist, Pringle had some grounds for believing that Somerset's enmity towards him was not implacable. The search warrant after the placard incident proved to him otherwise.

Pringle bore Somerset's attacks with fortitude and, in his humbler station in life, lacked some of the weapons of retaliation of Donkin, who had been similarly anathematized by Somerset – Donkin held senior military rank and, from 1832, had a seat in the House of Commons. Pringle took his cause, with some effect, to Lord Bathurst at the Colonial Office, adding yet more evidence of Somerset's 'personal rancour and relentless hostility'.[20] He had learned that his friend the Revd William Wright, the Irish clergyman who had fallen out with others of the Anglican community and was known to Somerset somewhat contemptuously as 'Paddy' Wright, was warned 'by a gentleman in confidence of his Excellency' that he could expect no favour 'since it was observed that he was *still* in the habit of *visiting at my house*.'[21] Though a central figure in Scots circles in Cape Town, he was denied nomination to the committee petitioning the Governor for permission to erect what became St Andrew's Church, for Presbyterian worshippers, his name being 'obnoxious to his Excellency'.[22] Most ruinous financially, he and Fairbairn having been 'openly denounced as obnoxious' by Somerset, more than half the pupils of the Academy 'were gradually withdrawn from our school.'[23]

Was Somerset's autocratic treatment of Pringle and Fairbairn part of what Pringle was to call a 'reign of terror'? It has been suggested that Somerset's vendetta induced a paranoid reaction on Pringle's part. In his *African Sketches*, published ten years later and eight since he had left the colony to a complete change of circumstances and occupation, his indignation had no whit abated:

> Infuriated by the fear of exposure, the Colonial Government seemed determined to strike down every man who should dare even to *look* or *think* disapprobation of its deeds. A frightful system of espionage pervaded every circle of society … informers and false witnesses abounded …The state of society in Cape Town, and indeed throughout the colony at this period was truly deplorable. Mutual confidence was shaken, distrust, apprehension and gloom everywhere prevailed … The singular *audacity* of the Government … absolutely paralysed the mass of the community with terror.[24]

There is a lack of diaries, memoirs, even personal letters to bear this out, though the presence in Cape Town of the unsavoury William Jones, a Government spy and *agent provocateur* sent from England by Lord Charles's friends in the Tory government, fits the picture and his responsibility for the outrageous placard against Somerset (to be blamed on his enemies) remains a possibility.[25] There is also the record of Samuel Eusebius Hudson, who had come to the Cape in the entourage of Lord Macartney, and was not known to Pringle: his diary entry for 15 July 1824 read that there was 'no law in the Colony but the will of Lord Charles Somerset. … A most diabolical placard [accused Somerset of] unnatural practices with Dr Barry … it has thrown the whole Cape into consternation'. There were further placards: 'where this dangerous and shameful business will end I know not.'[26]

By September 1824 Pringle had realized that 'my prospects in the Colony were for the present entirely blasted and that to continue the struggle would only sink us deeper in ruin. I began therefore seriously to consider returning to England'. What clinched the matter was the withdrawal of pupils from the Academy, which, he wrote with an unconscious but prescient self-reference, 'now looked like a consumptive patient whose recovery is quite hopeless, though dissolution may be for a brief space protracted.'

It remained only for Pringle to 'see once more my relatives at Glen-Lynden'[27] and, leaving Margaret in Cape Town with her sister Janet, whose 'seminary for young ladies' continued to be listed in the *African Court Calendar* until 1825, and presumably supported the sisters financially.

On 8 October, with W.T. Blair, his associate in the literary society venture, and another East India Company officer, Captain W. Miller, on their way to inspect the settlers' conditions of life in Albany, he set off on the first leg of their journey to the frontier.

NOTES

[1] Pringle to Scott, 31.10.1822, Vigne (2011), p. 76. NLS MS 3895 f 201.
[2] Pringle to Mackenzie, 25.6.1823, Vigne (2011), p. 87. NLS MS 3896 f 203.
[3] *Government Gazette*, Cape Town.
[4] *African Court Calendar*, 1824.
[5] Pringle to Bathurst, 15.1.1825, Vigne (2011), p. 164. *RCC* 19, p. 443.

[6] Pringle to Mackenzie, 25.6.1823, Vigne (2011), p. 87. NLS MS f 203.

[7] Somerset to Wilmot Horton, 14.2.1823, *RCC,* 17, p. 267.

[8] *Ibid.*

[9] Greig to Somerset, 1 7.1823, *RCC* 16, pp. 161–3.

[10] Pringle (1966), p. 180.

[11] Somerset-Bigge correspondence Bodl. Lib. (Rhodes House), MSS Afr. S. 24.

[12] Millar, A.K., *Plantagenet in South Africa. Lord Charles Somerset* (1965), p. 154.

[13] Pringle to Commissioners of Inquiry, 2.6.1824, Vigne (2011), p. 102. *RCC* 17, pp. 363, 462–4. See Pringle (1966), pp. 187–90.

[14] *Ibid.*

[15] Pringle to Somerset, 18.5.1824, Vigne (2011), pp. 96–7. *RCC* 17, p. 325.

[16] Pringle to Bathurst, 15.1.1825, Vigne (2011), p. 163. *RCC* 19, pp. 442–52.

[17] Pringle to Commissioners of Inquiry, 16.9.1824. Vigne (2011), p. 163. *RCC* 18, p. 385.

[18] Pringle to Bathurst, 15.1.1825, Vigne (2011), p. 109. *RCC* 19, pp. 443–52.

[19] Pringle to Commissioners of Inquiry, 2.6.1824, Vigne (2011), p. 109. *RCC* 17, pp. 462–4.

[20] Pringle to Bathurst, 15.1.1825, Vigne (2011), p. 163. *RCC* 19, pp. 443–52.

[21] *Ibid.*

[22] *Ibid.*

[23] *Ibid.*

[24] Pringle (1966), pp. 195–7.

[25] Hattersley, A.F., *Oliver the Spy and Others. A Little Gallery of South African Portraits* (1959), pp. 1–15.

[26] *Quarterly Bulletin of the South African Library,* 8, 4–6 (September 1953).

[27] Pringle (1966), p. 199.

10
Vale of Grace

Pringle and his companions made their way on horseback through Stellenbosch and Fransch Hoek and over the Hottentots Holland mountains. On the third day of their journey, 10 October 1824, they reached the pioneer Moravian mission station Genadendal, or as Pringle headed his letters, in the German spelling, Gnadenthal, the 'vale of grace'.

'In distant Europe oft I've longed to see this quiet Vale of Grace', Pringle wrote in his sonnet a month later. He had met Bishop Latrobe through his friend and mentor the Revd Alexander Waugh in London and doubtless knew the heart-warming story of the revival in 1792 of Georg Schmidt's original station, closed down by the V.O.C. authorities in 1739, and of its progress, set in an idyllic mountain landscape. In *African Sketches* he recalled hearing, as they approached the village, the 'voice of sacred songs … ascending from the rustic chapel, in the midst of its venerable grove of oaks, harmonizing finely with the Sabbath-like seclusion of that beautiful spot'. They enjoyed all day the 'sweet repose of the scene' and the 'good missionaries' … characteristic courtesy' among their 'Hottentot disciples'.[1]

An introduction from Latrobe, who had visited the mission in 1816, and his own sojourn in Enon with Robert Hart in 1821 made Pringle specially welcome then – and later after disaster had befallen him.

They were some twelve kilometres on their way east next day when Pringle's horse, 'being bit or snapt at by an ill-mannered cur, in passing a boor's place … I was thrown violently from my saddle to the ground and had one of my thigh bones fractured'. He was taken back to Genadendal where he experienced 'every kind attention in the power of the benevolent brethren to bestow'.[2] The generous, forgiving side of Pringle's nature comes through in his reaction to the appalling inhumanity of the young farmer who refused to transport him to the mission unless paid the high price he demanded. He took pains to point out how untypical this was of the Boer farmers whose hospitality he had enjoyed on previous journeys.

He was in Genadendal for nine weeks and the picture we get from his twelve surviving letters to Fairbairn in Cape Town is in quite remarkable contrast to the scene depicted in those to the Commissioners, Lord Bathurst, and Henry Brougham before and after the Genadendal interlude. It seems almost providential that he emerged from the cauldron of his Cape Town troubles to the 'sweet repose' of Genadendal. Margaret joined him after only eight days and the 'repose and seclusion we here enjoyed were peculiarly delightful after the harassing turmoil to which we had been recently subjected'.[3]

The price was high. The injury was first thought to be 'a very severe contusion in my lame left thigh, by which the flesh appears to have been shaken from the bone for a considerable space along the tibia'.[4] In early November he wrote to Dr John Murray, an army surgeon in Cape Town: 'it turns out that I was right, the thigh bone was actually *fractured*…right through'[5] according to Brother J.H. Stein, whose medical experience was a great advantage.

Uncomplaining throughout, his suffering is admitted only in the last lines of the sonnet in praise of Genadendal: '… it hath been a Sabbath Home for me \ Through lingering months of solitude and pain'. He saw a doctor only once: Dr Edward Roberts, 'surgeon, apothecary, accoucheur', an Albany settler who had moved to Cape Town, ('Roberts says I may walk tomorrow' he told Fairbairn on 15 November). His relief throughout was a traditional local treatment – an embrocation of 'Buchu brandy', a tincture of brandy with the Cape shrub, Buchu (*Barosma betulina*).

At first able only to read, writing soon became possible and after a fortnight he wrote to Fairbairn that the superintendent of the mission, the Revd Hans Peter Hallbeck was 'a very agreeable and intelligent man and often relieves the monotony of my Kaamer by an hour's crack or so'. Better still, 'Now that I can write more easily', he had produced ten sonnets, 'a few of them tolerably good in my own conceit, … several love songs to my wife – a ballad in three parts entitled "The Ostler's Tragedy" and begun an Epic in the Spenserian stanza, opening with an address to the Mountain Winterberg'.[6]

Among the sonnets was 'Franschhoek', which appeared, without Pringle's permission, to his great annoyance, signed 'Agricola' in Bridekirk's *South African Chronicle* (vol. 2, nos 55 and 56) slightly changed from the holograph copies found in the letters to Fairbairn, though not referred to in them. How Jardine, acting editor of the *Chronicle* acquired them is a mystery: 'That skamp "Jargon" has put in another of my Sonnets and bedevilled it into the bargain', he complained to Fairbairn.[7]

Little more of this outpouring found its way into print. A sonnet, 'To Scotland', appeared as 'My Country' in *African Sketches* (1834) The 'Epic' eventually turned into the 47 nine-line stanza 'fragment entitled Glen-Lynden', intended as 'the first part of a Poem to be entitled "The Emigrants"' two or three times its length. The final nine quatrains of 'The Emigrants',[8] as it appears in *African Sketches*, recall the Scots settlers departure in 1820, escaping 'vile dependence in our native land', introduced by lines from Pringle's own experience:

> They gaze upon the fast receding shore
> With tearful eyes – while thus the ballad strain,
> Half heard amidst the ocean's weltering roar,
> Bids farewell to the scenes they ne'er shall visit more.

The quatrains end:

Our native Land – our native Vale –
A long, a last adieu!
Farewell to bonny Lynden-dale,
And Scotland's mountains blue.

The 'love songs to my wife' and 'The Ostler's Tragedy' may have stayed with the papers sent to Fairbairn by Margaret after Thomas's death, never again to see the light of day.

One piece of light-hearted versifying survived in the letters to Fairbairn and was first made known by Patricia Morris.[9] This was 'Auld Hurlbarrow', a drinking song with a rousing chorus. Pringle told Fairbairn it was 'not very elegant' and instructed him not 'to let it out of your hands as auld Scotch songs are apt to be misunderstood by English and Irish people.'[10] If this is a veiled reference to friends or enemies in Cape Town it is hard to identify the Irish among them. Dr O'Flinn and the Irish-born Dr James Barry were well disposed to him, though the latter was close to Governor Somerset. He might send it to their fellow Scot Benjamin Moodie and we suddenly catch a glimpse of a different Tam Pringle, who hoped, when they were all three together in Cape Town, to 'have a cheering Whisky Toddy and sing it all together in full chorus'.

He has 'some more "auld sangs"' and 'as I have tasted no wine nor strong drink' since his accident, 'I mean to have ae merry gae down at least by and by', but 'using the Cratur [Whisky], not abusing it'. He hopes Fairbairn's 'voice is improving'.

In good spirits throughout, Pringle wrote, after a fortnight: 'I cannot get out of bed yet – though otherwise in perfect good health and spirits'.[11] Margaret's health and spirits improved too, though the doctors were urged to keep the fracture from her – and from her sister Janet in Cape Town: 'The women make such a hully-balloo about such matters', he wrote to Dr Murray on 6 November. It seems slightly out of character for what we know of Margaret that Pringle asks for 'a few Lbs of good tea and coffee and half-a-dozen of sherry wine for Mrs Pringle'[12]

His greatest need was for a copy of *Redgauntlet*, repeatedly asked for, even of Dr Murray. Published in Britain in June 1824 it is the closest of the Waverley novels to being autobiographical, though it tells the entirely fictitious story of a second Jacobite plot. Not much more than half in jest he urged Fairbairn to cancel his visit to Genadendal with 'one old maid' [Janet Brown?], 'the Clergyman' [Wright?], 'one young Dr' [Murray?], medical items and 'pewter pisspots'. ('Bless your hearts I would rather have had *Redgauntlet* than the whole waggon load.').[13] Of course there were cares – expenses, the declining school enrolment ('Are any more officials withdrawing their children?' he asked Fairbairn.) And the dispute over the Distressed Settlers fund.

Yet there is more of the lightheartedness in the Genadendal letters than what has been called Pringle's 'almost paranoid distrust of anyone who was not a member of the close-knit opposition group'.[14] The battle lines had been drawn and those on the other side, and the waverers, were not to be spared. He was hungry for news of the Reformed Church synod, its first, distrusting the Scriba, Dr Thom, as an ally of the Governor's, but most concerned with the conflict over the distressed 'Albanians'.

The *Chronicle*, favoured by Somerset, had published on 28 August a letter signed 'Settler' which attacked Philip, Pringle and their friends and was highly critical of the Albany settlers' claims of hardship and want. It made much of an outrageous story that had found its way into the obscure *British and Indian Observer,* published in London by Capt. William White, Fifteenth Bengal Native Infantry. This news sheet was condemned by the Hon. East India Company as 'a tissue of falsehoods, calumny and slander'. Among these was a report which alleged that starving settler women were selling their virtue for food.[15] The 'Settler's' charge that the Philip faction had planted the story was furiously denied. Pringle suggested to Fairbairn on 22 November that the writing of this *canard* 'seems to be an imitation of Dr Philip's style'.

From a different quarter came a conflict which Somerset seized upon to discredit 'the conduct of a Person calling himself the Revd Dr Philip' and of Pringle and Fairbairn. Somerset's letter to Lord Bathurst[16] was intent upon revealing 'the mischievous intentions of these people.' Philip had met the Revd Andrew Murray in Cape Town and their conversation was confided to Commissioner Bigge in such a way, Murray claimed, as to commit him to views opposed to the emancipation of the Khoikhoi, and to tar Stockenstrom with the same brush.

Pringle sought to explain the quarrel to Stockenstrom, assuring him that 'no reflection at all' was cast on him to the Commissioners.[17] It was much later a triumph for Pringle that he was able to heal the wounds Somerset had reported to Bathurst, when, in August 1825, he brought Philip and Stockenstrom together, with Andrew Murray, in Graaff-Reinet.[18]

Somerset's account of the quarrel sent to Bathurst on 27 January 1825 consisted of a highly defamatory 'Biographical Sketch of John Philip, formerly a Journeyman Weaver and now the Head of the Missionary Society at the Cape of Good Hope and calling himself Dr Philip', followed by the Revd Andrew Murray's recall of his conversation with Philip and 'some interrogations' by the Commissioners regarding Philip's account ot 'the conduct of A. Stockenstrom Esquire, Landdrost of Graaff-Reinet'.[19]

Murray here denied that he had in any way derogated Stockenstrom's character or that either of them held views 'inimical to the freedom of the Hottentots' in their conversation about the 'contract system' from which the Khoikhoi had been freed. 'Deeply wounded and hurt in my mind', Murray wrote to Philip, at the latter's 'most unpardonable conduct', he refused 'further Communication' with Philip.

Somerset was clearly pleased to quote, in conclusion, a letter from Fairbairn to Pringle, written ten days after the accident near Genadendal. 'This letter', he explained, 'was sent by mistake, *unsealed,* from Harington House to a Gentleman in Cape Town, who embraced the opportunity of taking a copy of it'. Pringle's and Fairbairn's shared distrust of the Cape Post Office, '*as at present constituted*', as Fairbairn put it, was surely justified. It is possible, of course, that Somerset was told by the interceptors of the letter this most unlikely account of its provenance.

The letter concerned a pre-publication copy of the pamphlet defending the actions of the Governor and his officials towards the Albany settlers, produced by the Colonial Printing Office. Fairbairn had obtained a copy and Philip had taken it to the Commissioners. Publication of the pamphlet was a clear breach of the Governor's own proclamation forbidding such debate and when the officials knew of its reaching the Commissioners there was, wrote Fairbairn, 'a terrible uproar ... the Lord was storming, the Fiscal thundering, Richert [superintendent of the Printing Office] wailing, and the whole House in great perplexity'.

By insisting that printing was not publishing, the Commissioners saved Somerset from 'a foul and illegal act'. From their action Fairbairn deduced that the Commissioners were now Somerset's men and that 'Dr Philip has no favour to expect from them'.

Fairbairn's tirade against Somerset was every bit as vehement as Pringle's, if not more so. Somerset, 'by infringing the Proclamation for the purpose of gratifying personal malice has disgraced again the character of His Majesty's Representative, forfeited the Confidence of the Colony and given up all claims to public and private respect'.

The real sting, from Somerset's point of view, was in the tail. Fairbairn (or the copier of the letter?) ended: 'By the way the Doctor *is not a scrupulous man*, and is pretty well versed in the methods of managing people.'

It is curious indeed that as early as 25 October Pringle acknowledged receipt of the intercepted letter of the 20th. He was less dismissive of the Commissioners, who were possibly 'still carrying on the system of *make believe*'. For his part Pringle was 'inclined to *hope* the best – but to *trust* nothing'.[20]

On 27 November he told Fairbairn 'the waggon and Redgauntlet have not yet arrived. My limb is much stouter since Roberts was here and I now intend to start by Wednesday the 1st Dec.' and to reach Cape Town by the 6th.[21]

Thus ended his two-month absence from Cape Town, a respite despite the serious injury, which he had borne manfully. Back in Cape Town 'I found myself overwhelmed with debts to an amount quite ruinous and appalling in my then situation, as I had no means left even for the temporary support of my family',[22] he wrote in the *Narrative*. An immediate return to Britain was impossible.

Once he had found ways to overcome the worst of his financial problems and had set out upon a course of action that would enable him eventually to start again in London, he was ready to take up a new challenge. His admiration for both John Philip and Andries Stockenstrom, at odds with each other though they were, was partly due to their opposition to 'the Old System of compelling the Hottentots to bind themselves to the Farmers'.[23] This was but one factor that led Pringle to transform his lifelong sympathy for the underdog, in South Africa the oppressed indigenous people, and the imported slaves, to active campaigning for their full freedom.

NOTES

[1] Pringle (1966), p. 200.
[2] *Op. cit.*, p. 201.
[3] *Op. cit.*, p. 206.
[4] Pringle to Fairbairn, 20.10.1824, Vigne (2011), p. 126. LP, Fairbairn Papers, 1, 10.

[5] Pringle to Murray, 6.11.1824, Vigne (2011), p. 135. LP, Fairbairn Papers, 1, 22.

[6] Pringle to Fairbairn, 25.10.1824, Vigne (2011), p. 129. LP, Fairbairn Papers, 1, 14.

[7] Pringle to Fairbairn, 29.9.1825, Vigne (2011), p. 249. LP, Fairbairn Papers, 1, 96.

[8] Pringle (1838), pp. 112–13.

[9] Morris, p. 245

[10] Pringle to Fairbairn, 16.11.1824, Vigne (2011), p. 139. LP, Fairbairn Papers, 1, 26.

[11] Pringle to Fairbairn, 25.10.1824, Vigne (2011), p. 129. LP, Fairbairn Papers, 1, 14.

[12] Pringle to Fairbairn, 2.11.1824, Vigne (2011), p. 133. LP, Fairbairn Papers, 1, 18.

[13] Pringle to Fairbairn, 15.11.1824, Vigne (2011), p. 139. LP, Fairbairn Papers, 1, 28.

[14] Morris, p. 247.

[15] Prospectus calling for re-issue, 1828, UCL Special Collections.

[16] Somerset to Bathurst, 27.1.1825, *RCC* 19, pp. 481–90.

[17] Bodl. Lib. (Rhodes House), Philip Papers, Addnl. F394.

[18] See pp. 154–6, below.

[19] Somerset to Bathurst, 27.1.1825, *RCC* 19, pp. 525–6.

[20] Somerset to Bathurst, 25.1.1825, Vigne (2011), p. 129. LP, Fairbairn Papers, 1, 14.

[21] Pringle to Fairbairn, 27.11.1824, Vigne (2011), p. 144. LP, Fairbairn Papers, 1, 24.

[22] Pringle (1966), p. 202.

[23] Somerset to Bathurst, 27.1.1825. *RCC* 19, pp. 525–6.

11

On the Frontier

The Final Year

The Pringles were away from Cape Town and back on Eildon for a full year, from February 1825 to February 1826, just two months short of their departure from South Africa forever. Thomas had withdrawn to try and repair his totally shattered fortunes enough to pay his most pressing debts and finance their return to Britain.

He had written an eloquent appeal to Lord Bathurst on 15 January 1825. After listing the blows dealt to him by Somerset that had destroyed him, he asked that:

> Your Lordship shall be graciously pleased to view my humble but zealous services as the leader of one of the most orderly, and energetic parties that have come out to South Africa, as deserving of … moderate compensation and encouragement …I shall feel duly grateful for such favourable consideration, and willingly admit that all my claims on His Majesty's Government have been generously cancelled.[1]

The requested compensation was moderate indeed: 'a sufficient grant of land and competent means of occupying and improving it', willing as he was 'to try my fortunes as a settler in South Africa' – a new beginning after the 1820 settlement.

He then made what turned out to be a cardinal error, not in stating what he did but in carrying it out with the grant of land not yet decided. Lord Bathurst, he wrote

> will not be surprised at my adopting the only alternative that remains to me, namely, that of abandoning a colony where as a literary man I have been insulted and persecuted, as an instructor of youth openly discouraged and secretly calumniated and where as a Settler I have now no better prospects before me than poverty and distress.

He could expect no response for at least seven months so took himself and Margaret back to the frontier, her sister Janet staying in Cape Town with her 'seminary for young ladies' in what is now St George's Street. His frequent letters to Commissioners Bigge and Colebrooke in Cape Town must have been designed, in part at least, to strengthen his case when Bathurst came to seek their advice on his cry for help. This must needs have increased the time of waiting at least another six or seven months, and it did so.

After the tedious and distressing sale of their belongings – furniture, his pony, even his books – he advertised in the *Gazette* on Christmas Day 1824:

Mr Pringle, intending shortly to proceed to the Interior, with the view of making arrangements for returning to England, begs to announce that he has resigned his interest in the
Classical and Commercial Academy, Harington House, in favour of Mr Fairbairn, by whom
the Establishment will be conducted as usual.

The likelihood of his farming on the frontier, always ruled out by his disability, he
clearly discounted, though he had not yet appealed to Bathurst for means to try
his hand.

They were busy last weeks in Cape Town. His *Some Account of the Present State of
the English Settlers in Albany, South Africa* arrived from Underwood's (jointly
published with Oliver and Boyd in Edinburgh) in December 1824. Written before
the return of H.E. Rutherfoord from his fact-finding tour of the Albany settlement, it consisted of

a series of extracts from letters written by some of the most respectable heads of parties,
and by other trustworthy individuals residing in their vicinity, descriptive, chiefly, of their
more recent misfortunes and their present sufferings, or prospects. … The calamitous tale
they tell of disaster and destitution requires no aids of composition to enable it to reach
the hearts of Englishmen.[2]

Thomas Campbell's *New Monthly Magazine* of 1 June 1824 bore out the author's
claim, recommending it to

those who feel interested (and who do not !) in the state of our new colonists in South
Africa. Their situation is dreadfully afflicting. Their losses by bad seasons and inundations
are enough to break the spirit and destroy the hopes of those who have escaped with the
least injury to their stock and crops. What then must be the state of those who have lost their
all?

The manuscript had gone to Underwood's in January 1824 and was on sale at
Bridekirk's in the Heerengracht and Howell's at 10 Burg Street in December.
Pringle saw the sanctuary of the 'location' on the Baviaans River as the place to
live without expense and to make progress with his book, already begun, on his
time in South Africa, planned with the encouragement of Barrow before he left
England. On 1 January 1825, Bridekirk, at the *Chronicle,* produced a leaflet advertising *A Residence of Four Years in South Africa,* to be published at the end of 1825 or
the start of 1826.

Pringle soon found, as he told Fairbairn when long settled at Eildon, that the
work he had undertaken to do in writing up the merchant George Thompson's
notes on his travels to make a book, made it difficult to write his own account of
the same region. 'I have in fact found myself somewhat embarrassed between my
own book and Thompson's', he told Fairbairn' – and as I consider myself bound
in honour [and presumably to earn his fee] to do what I can for him I shall make
it forthwith.'[3]

Though two years had passed since the start of his stormy fifteen-month career
in Cape Town, he felt it 'difficult to write with perfect candour and good temper
on matters that mainly concern ourselves or friends until time has a little mellowed
them'. There was also the danger of libel, 'I mean therefore to lay aside my own

book for the present'. Thompson's *Travels and Adventures in Southern Africa* finally went into print in London in 1827 (and Pringle's hand in it was not made known until V.S. Forbes's 1966 edition for the Van Riebeeck Society, Cape Town, despite the appearance of seven of his poems in the book). His own *Narrative* did not appear until 1834.

His year on the frontier was spent on a range of activities. A two-month tour of the Albany district before reaching the 'location' on the Baviaans River, and a six-week absence in Graaff-Reinet and its surroundings left only a final three-month stay at Eildon before beginning the final return to Cape Town.

The Albany visit was a remarkable undertaking for a man who had so recently suffered a broken femur and endured the most severe mental stress as a chief victim of Somerset's 'reign of terror' and who was almost without funds.

After their 'tedious and sleepy voyage' they spent two days 'at Algoa Bay' and four in Bethelsdorp, which, he told Fairbairn, had assumed 'the aspect of a thriving European village in place of a Hottentot kraal'[4]. He wrote also to Dr Philip in some detail about 'the air of activity and intelligence about the people … the appearance of seriousness and sincerity in their religious assemblies … the excellent almshouses, the tanks, the smiths' shops, the stores and the missionaries' houses … all great and obvious improvements'[5] since his visit on his arrival at Algoa Bay in 1820.

That was not all: ten days earlier Bethelsdorp had been visited and much praised by the new Colonial Secretary, Colonel Bird's successor, Sir Richard Plasket, and even the landdrost Colonel Cuyler, who had neglected and disapproved of the mission, 'bore a reluctant testimony to the improvements at Bethelsdorp'. Of Plasket, Pringle wrote later, 'I hear several things … on my route which persuades me he is *honest*'.[6]

Plasket had urged Lord Charles Somerset, nearing the end of his first tour of the Albany settlement, to visit the mission – unsuccessfully, though Somerset had sought throughout his visit to conciliate the settlers, who had been so ill-used by his government since their arrival.

After Bethelsdorp the Pringles spent a few days with 'that excellent and upright man', the Revd Alexander Smith, a friend though he had been embroiled as an ally of the Revd Andrew Murray in his recent bitter dispute with Dr Philip. After Uitenhage, 'a pleasant, healthy and cheap village but wonderfully dull and disagreeable', they travelled to 'the romantic Moravian settlement of Enon',[7] with memories of his visit there with Robert Hart in 1821. From Theopolis, another L.M.S. mission, he wrote to Fairbairn, the Great Lama (Somerset, in Fairbairn's correspondence with Pringle) 'still maintains that they are rascally places and … he has hemmed in and curtailed this place and Bethelsdorp on every side by granting away to Settlers and Boors all the adjoining lands which they had long applied for and partly occupied'.[8]

In the next eight days Pringle visited 'nearly all of the Albany Radicals',[9] all of them party leaders: Thomas Philipps, former Pembrokeshire gentleman farmer and banker, settled near Bathurst, with a high opinion of the Pringles expressed in his letters; Major George Pigot of Pigot Park on the Blaauwkrantz River, natural son of Lord Pigot, Governor of Madras, perhaps the highest ranking settler in social terms, who 'knows little about political principles – but he detests the Lama and refuses to wait on him'; Donald Moodie, younger brother of Benjamin Moodie of Grootvadersbos; and Duncan Campbell, half-pay Royal Marines captain, of Thorn Park near Grahamstown , 'the only staunch, thorough Whig', who 'judged it prudent to conform outwardly in the demonstrations of loyalty to "Constituted Authority".'[10]

At Pigot's 'hospitable mansion' he met his fellow Scots Captain Campbell, Lieutenants Donald and John Moodie, also the young Carlisle brothers, the elder, John, from Staffordshire and 'other intelligent heads of parties'. Separate visits were made to the 'farm-cottages' of Thomas Philipps, Robert Dunn, father of the Zulu 'chief' John Robert Dunn; Lieutenant William Gilfillan, half-pay, 60th Regiment (the latter two having settled independently of the 1820 scheme); and Mrs Campbell, widow of Major-General Charles Campbell and stepmother of Dr Ambrose Campbell, whose book *The Wrongs of the Caffre Nation* (1837) outdid Pringle in the vehemence of his attack on colonial misdeeds against the Nguni. A poignant moment in their ox-wagon journey was the discovery, when crossing the Kowie River, that the ferrymen were two of the 27 survivors of the *Abeona* disaster who had succeeded in making their way to South Africa.

Despite the settlers' bad treatment by Somerset and his officials (the worst of whom was the Albany magistrate Harry Rivers) and the failed attempt to use the funds raised by Distressed Settlers Relief committee to build a church, 'Constituted Authority' in the person of Lord Charles was surprisingly well received. Major Dundas, who had become Pringle's friend on the voyage from Cape Town, was a popular replacement of Rivers and the £10,000 raised by the Relief committee under Rutherfoord's secretaryship, with Pringle acting in his absence, had been distributed among the settlers most in need in January 1825. Sir Richard Plasket was well received too and Somerset's conciliatory, albeit grandiosely appointed, tour, Pringle told Fairbairn, weakened the opposition.

> Though the 'Albany Radicals', with the exception of the rogues and the waverers, are neither cajoled nor committed, yet the late visit and the change of system has to a considerable extent neutralized or paralyzed them.[11]

Mixing his metaphors, he told Fairbairn that

> though the blandishments of the Lama, like those of Delilah have … despoiled them of their locks of strength for a season [he found himself] rather flattered to find that the Lama could not refrain from expressing in distinct terms his hatred and fear of me even here.[12]

With the break-up of the Somerset Farm his youngest brother John requested the continued services of a freed slave serving his apprenticeship at the farm. Somerset, however, as Pringle told Fairbarn, not without humour:

> expressed his anger and surprise that such a favour should be asked for the brother of 'such an inveterate enemy of the govt.' as me. The friend [Robert Hart perhaps] expressed ignorance and regret at hearing of my criminality. 'Yes,' said the magnanimous Lama, 'you cannot imagine the amount of the mischief his brother Thomas has done to me and my govt.' The friend took courage to say however that John Pringle was totally innocent of any participa-

tion in the wicked deeds or purposes of said Thomas, and added that indeed his education did not fit him for any share in such matters. 'Aye,' said the Lama with emphasis, 'and I assure you *the less education the better*'!![13]

Though Somerset's Albany visit was intended to count in his favour in the forthcoming Commissioners' report, his continued 'hatred and fear' of Pringle was unabated and gave Pringle even more ammunition in his letters to the Commissioners and to Lord Brougham. His personal feud with the Somersets, father and son, the latter leading 'commando' raids across the frontier, increased his commitment to the cause of the indigenous people, specifically of the Nguni communities on the Cape frontier.

Somerset felt able to write to Commissioner Bigge from Grahamstown that he was

> happy to confirm the favourable report of the general and unanimous feeling here ... they are only anxious how to show respect and goodwill towards me by every possible means [and, later, that] I was met by the whole company of Boors on my way to the Hantam Berg and who have also attended me here. Yesterday in spite of all the rain 100 more met me with cheers and salutes. In short it is impossible to see a better feeling towards the Government.[14]

Thomas and Margaret reached Baviaans River at the end of April, after nearly a month in Grahamstown, in all likelihood as guests of his eldest sister Mary and her husband William Williams of the Commissariat department, whom she had met on the voyage to South Africa in 1822 and married the following year. Mary gave birth to their first child on 22 March 1825, about the date of Thomas and Margaret's arrival. In his only surviving letter to Fairbairn while waiting for an ox-wagon and drivers to complete their journey he wrote of meetings with 'the Albanians', with pen pictures, not always kind, of the leaders. Duncan Campbell, 'a right true Whig – a decided liberal – a kindly Scot – an enthusiastic Highlander ... has faults – he is almost as procrastinating as yourself'. Thomas Philipps he found 'one of the most agreeable little men in the world – but somewhat vain – fickle and jealous and fond of popularity and the favour of the great'.[15] Philipps's account of the Governor's arrival in Grahamstown is telling:

> His Excellency's condescension very great, bowing etc., and standing at Mr Dietz's, nearly the first House on entering, about half-a-dozen of us stood opposite to it uncovered. Col. Somerset drew his Father's attention towards us and a most marked look and hat off was immediately the consequence. On passing the ex-Landdrost [Harry Rivers] he simply touched his hat in return to the Landdrost's courtesy. This sacrifice to popular feeling and no doubt designed, was excellent policy, for H.E. was watched by a hundred.[16]

The 'favour of the great' was manifested in an additional, personal grant to Philipps's Glendour estate of 4000 acres by the Governor and, not least, by being placed on Somerset's left hand at a state dinner.

Pringle wrote on 5 April 'I am quite sick of Grahamstown, and wish I was again "afar in the desert",' his best loved poem already well known enough to Fairbairn to be quoted to him, and soon to appear in full in Thompson's *Travels and Adventures*.

The lot of the Albany settlers had improved, and continued to do so, and they were no longer the underdogs that had called forth his active sympathy. In the *South African Journal*, in *Some Account of the Present State of the English Settlers* and in his work for the Relief fund he had crusaded for them, at great cost to his career and well-being in Cape Town. His two-month visit to them had been undertaken, in part, to collect

> authentic materials for an account of the British settlement intended for a volume which I then had in contemplation. But I afterwards abandoned, or at least postponed, this design, and furnished my friend Mr George Thompson, with most of my notes for his work.[17]

He does not reveal in the *Narrative* that he was 'ghosting' Thompson's book but six months later told Fairbairn that

> My correspondence with the Commrs. and with Greig's paper [the revived *Commercial Adver-tiser*], and scribbling poetry and writing my 'Residence' and Thompson's 'Researches' are far too many irons in the fire together. I have therefore resolved to abandon for the present, 1st poetry – 2ndly of my 'Residence' and 3rdly Greig, except when I can't help it . 4thly I mean to set tooth and nails to Thompson's book – and get it off my hands. And 5thly I mean in future to write very short and dry articles for HM Comrs.[18]

For the six months ahead these were some of the tasks that occupied him at Eildon and on his visits elsewhere in the region. These were his literary and epis-tolary tasks – which included some forty letters to Fairbairn. The attack on Somerset had not been blunted by the reception of the Governor on his eastern frontier tour. He told Fairbairn, nevertheless, half in jest:

> It remains for us and the doughty Doctor who have borne the brunt of the battle to disable and finally destroy the Hydra. If the Bogles [ghosts, i.e the Commissioners] are false or feck-less, let them fall without mercy. If they prove decoy ducks let them be spitted and roasted the same as wild game. No compromise or whitewashing must be tolerated.[19]

The duel with Somerset went on but more of Pringle's time was now to be spent as a Baviaans River settler leader and increasingly on his new crusade for the indigenous underdogs.

NOTES

[1] Pringle to Bathurst, 15.1.1825, Vigne (2011), p. 168. *RCC* 19, p. 452.
[2] Pringle (1824), p. 3.
[3] Pringle to Fairbairn, 14.10.1825, Vigne (2011), p. 261. LP, Fairbairn Papers, 1, 100.
[4] Pringle to Fairbairn, 1.3.1825, Vigne (2011), p. 170. LP, Fairbairn Papers, 1, 36.
[5] Pringle to Philip, -.3.1825, Philip, John, *Researches in South Africa*, 2 vols (1828), vol. 1, pp. 226–30.
[6] Pringle to Fairbairn, 13.3.1825, Vigne (2011), p. 170. LP, Fairbairn Papers, 1, 36.
[7] Pringle (1966), p. 203.
[8] Pringle to Fairbairn, 14.3.1825, Vigne (2011), p. 171. LP, Fairbairn Papers, 1, 38.
[9] Pringle to Fairbairn, 22.3.1825 , Vigne (2011), p. 173. LP, Fairbairn Papers, 1, 40.
[10] *Ibid.*

11 Pringle to Fairbairn, 28.3.1825, Vigne (2011), p. 175. LP, Fairbairn Papers, 1, 42.
12 *Ibid.*
13 Pringle to Fairbairn, 22.3.1825, Vigne (2011), p. 174. LP, Fairbairn Papers, 1, 40.
14 Somerset-Bigge correspondence. Bodl. Lib. (Rhodes House). MS Afr. S 24. Millar, p. 207
15 Pringle to Fairbairn, 5.4.1825, Vigne (2011), p. 179. LP, Fairbairn Papers, 1, 44.
16 Philipps, Thomas, ed. A. Keppel-Jones, *Philipps, 1820 Settler* (1960), p. 225. Millar, p. 205.
17 Pringle (1966), p. 218.
18 Pringle to Fairbairn, 14.10.1825, Vigne (2011), p. 261. LP, Fairbairn Papers, 1, 100.
19 Pringle to Fairbairn, 5.4.1825, Vigne (2011), p. 178. LP, Fairbairn Papers, 1, 44.

Part IV

The Frontier, Karroo

Rural Retreat and the 'Great Cause' (1825–1826)

12

Return to Glen Lynden

Pringle wrote of his return to Glen Lynden (he called it that, though the name had not been gazetted and was later to refer only to the parish):

> We had the satisfaction of finding our relatives in much more prosperous circumstances, as husbandmen, than any party of settlers that we had seen in Albany[1]

He and Margaret found that their beehive hut was now the kitchen of the 'commodious farm-cottage of stone and brick with a stone chimney', the first built in the Baviaans River sub-district. He revelled in furnishing his hut near William's house, 'putting my desk and table together and manufacturing bedsteads, chairs and cutty stools', he told Fairbairn, adding, in his usual mock-boastful style:

> My mechanical talents I am happy to say are still unsurpassed – and my cottage and furniture are the admiration of the Bavian's River. They even greatly surpass the grandeur and magnificence of my former state. Besides my own exquisite handiworks I even possess an iron bedstead and a cane bottomed sofa.[2]

Though William had taken his place officially as leader of the settlement, Thomas seemed – perhaps due to William's ill-health – to have resumed his old role. His first surviving letter from Eildon was in reply to the Graaff-Reinet magistrate Stockenstrom on 9 May 1825, recording the three servants – Mortimer (long gone), Souness and Eckhorn – articled to party members, and stating that of the twenty, the seven males had paid deposits for a hundred acres (40.47 ha) each, the total now enlarged to some 8,000 morgen, an eighteenfold increase. He clearly took pride in his 'sanguine hope' that

> the general and ultimate success of the party continues unimpaired, and that after an absence of three years during which their prosperity has been checked by many difficulties and disappointments I have the satisfaction of finding almost every family in a state of steady though slow progression.[3]

He rejoiced to Fairbairn, with more jocular boasting:

> I am a very great personage and my influence and reputation (in spite of my loss of court favour) are equal to my magnificence. I am patriarch, priest and King. I have Boors for clients and Bastaards for vassals.[4]

He ran a Sunday school in Dutch with a congregation of fifty men, women and children of 'the black chivalry of the Bavian's River' and was building a church (which has not survived) but admitted to Fairbairn that the unpaid labour involved may have been motivated less by 'pious principle' than by 'a considerable distribution of gunpowder among my congregation and ten days' hunting on the Mancazana as soon as the work is done'.

Despite these distractions he was working hard on Thompson's manuscript, a secret between Thompson, Fairbairn and himself, yet enjoying

> perfect leisure and perfect quiet. I am near my relations, I am on my own location – and I am able to work here at my desk without interruption or disquiet. I have no others near me – the last not the least of my privileges.

Rather this life than that under 'the tools of corruption and tyranny' in Cape Town. Fairbairn was instructed to write under cover to Major Dundas, the well-disposed landdrost in Grahamstown, knowing as he did the Post Office to be in the hands of the 'tools'.

In the first two years at Eildon he had been smiled upon by Acting-Governor Donkin, the Colonial Secretary Colonel Bird and the local officials. How different now! He wrote to William McDonald Mackay, landdrost of the new Somerset district, of which Baviaans River was part, in support of applications for land from Christian and Karel Groepe and 'a host of Bastaard clients all clamorous for memorials [for land allocations]',[5] among them Hans Blok and Klaas Eckhard who, like the Groepes, had considerable stock and were 'steadier and soberer men than most of the others'. He suggested for them a year on probation during which the 'exceedingly ignorant, drunken and disorderly' among them could be helped to mend their ways by means of the Sunday school and a ban on the '*Wine and Brandy waggons*' coming up this river'.

Perhaps he was rash to let Mackay know of his unacceptability to Cape Town officialdom. He doubted the wisdom of forwarding to the Colonial Office so many applications in one go. Most tellingly he did not think that 'under *present circumstances* it will be advisable that any should be forwarded in my handwriting'. The following month he made another land application for his Boer neighbour Diederik Muller, the intrepid lion hunter, this time to Sir Richard Plasket in Cape Town and not through Mackay 'as Muller is not in favour with Mr Mackay, the landdrost of Somerset'. Pringle was 'but slightly acquainted with Mr Mackay and will not insinuate any things to his prejudice without certain grounds'.

The memorial for Muller was again not in Pringle's hand, 'for any appearance of acquaintance with me is not I fear likely to benefit any person in the eyes of His Excellency the Governor'. As his acquaintance with Mackay became closer his respect for him diminished and, a further month later, he told Fairbairn that the landdrost at Somerset was

> a poor creature – a proper tool for the Beaufort interest – He is frightened even to speak to me or any other obnoxious person. I treat him with civil contempt and write him *official* letters now and then which he takes great care never to answer in writing for fear of getting

into a scrape. How amusing it is to see the terror of these tools when one comes near them, dreadfully afraid of either quarrelling with one or of showing one any civility for fear it be reported to their employers![6]

There was a sting in the tail of the 'poor creature' which was a severe affliction for Dr Philip and painful to Pringle in years to come (see p. 217–18).

Pringle was much concerned for Fairbairn's health, on Janet Brown's information from Cape Town, and his future. The academy was closed and Harington House disposed of. With the return of George Greig the battle for press freedom was largely won, and the *South African Commercial Advertiser* was revived, with Fairbairn as editor. At a humbler, personal level Pringle could contribute and in return his smaller debts were liquidated by Fairbairn.

Despite his fight for press freedom, however, Greig had lost Pringle's respect. He replied on 20 May 1825 to a letter from Fairbairn, written before Greig's return:

> What you state respecting Greig does not surprise me. It was always my apprehension. It would have been too romantic to expect patriotic principles from *him* if a sufficient temptation occurred. Nevertheless some use may be made of his press – if he is not pledged to be a tool of corruption altogether. He is vain and vindictive and may be turned perhaps to some better acct: than that dumpling hearted animal we have at present [Bridekirk, whose *South African Chronicle* had Somerset's favour].[7]

Fairbairn had considered a move to Stellenbosch but Pringle suggested instead that he travel with Dr Philip to Dithakong, fearing that 'the cold nights and sifting winds through the waggon will be too much for you',[8] or spend a month or two at Baviaans River or Graaff-Reinet 'and store up information for the day of retribution'. But of all options, his strong preference was that 'if we get all home together, you, the Dr and myself, we could I think make a prodigious impression on the public through the press *next session* of parliament.'

This despite his financial state, for 'in a matter in which my heart is set I am not very easily discouraged by difficulties, in this *cause* I am now too deeply embarked to recoil under any contingency.' He urged that if the move to England could not be effected

> let us make all the preparations we can in the meanwhile for there will be the tug-of-war and we must conquer or perish. We have not the cause of this wretched Colony to stand out for – but for the general cause of liberty – of humanity – of mankind.

The 'cause', in his sonnet 'To Oppression' which he sent to Fairbairn in July 1825,[9] is still the struggle against the oppression of absolute rule that had victimized and ruined him ('Oppression! I have seen thee face to face …'), and his vow

> Still to *oppose* and *thwart* with heart and hand
> Thy brutalizing sway – till Afric's chains
> Are burst, and freedom rules the rescued land.

relates as much to the white colonist as to the downtrodden Khoisan and Griqua, and the invaded and dispossessed Xhosa. The balance was soon to shift, when he came together with the two chief protagonists in the cause of the indigenous oppressed, landdrost Stockenstrom and missionary Philip.

Pringle's championing of the victims of colonialism was not that of a distant liberal, a 'do-gooder' who had no experience of the indigenous African as a threat, even to life itself. He wrote to Mackay on 29 May 1825:

> Having recently heard various alarming rumours of the approach of the *Mantatees* towards the Colony and an official Circular sent up by the Field Cornet Van der Nest a few days ago having stated that they were supposed to be approaching the Winterberg, – I thought it necessary for the safety of this location to endeavour to procure some precise intelligence respecting the movements of those marauders.[10]

He sent a party of his mixed-race (or Mulatto as he now called them) tenants on a fruitless three-hour ride towards the Winterberg. George Rennie, joined en route by Diederik Muller, after a five-hour ride to a Thembu settlement across the Black Kei River, learned from the Thembu chiefs Bawana of the amaTshatshu and Qwesha of the amaNdungwane, that

> the invading horde whom they call Ficani or *Fitcanees*, had been roaming about for a considerable time in the vicinity; and had about two months ago defeated the united forces of the Tambookie [Thembu] king [Ngubencuka] and Hinza [Hintsa, Xhosa king], with great slaughter, six of their principal Captains and a great number of warriors having fallen in the battle.

This early section of these fragmented, dispossessed people, known as the Mfecane,[11] were probably the amaBhaca under their chief Madikane from what is now KwaZulu Natal, and now on the Tsomo River, a tributary of the Great Kei.

Pringle's information tallied with roughly similar reports from the missionaries John Brownlee and W.R. Thomson. Major Forbes having also learned of the Mfecane's movements from Lieutenant W.H. Rogers after his reconnoitring their position, sent a small cavalry unit of the Cape Corps to protect the Baviaans River people, who had become 'apprehensive that our little settlement might be suddenly overwhelmed by an irruption of this moving host of 20,000 barbarians.'

Major Forbes received a severe reprimand from the Governor and the 'party of Dragoons ... for the protection of the Scottish Party was withdrawn by orders from headquarters as soon as they heard of it. It was strange he said to send 30 Dragoons to protect *one* individual! So the frontier must protect itself'.[12]

Happily, however, these Mfecane forerunners did not invade the colony but turned eastwards and after a spell on the Tsomo River were decimated in 1828 at the Battle of Mbholompo by Xhosa and Thembu armies, augmented by a British force under Colonel Henry Somerset.

This is but a sketchy fragment of the still unclear story of the great turbulence that wrought such havoc on the frontier, to the east of the Great Kei River, and further north. Pringle's own account to Mackay quotes Rennie's Thembu informants to the effect that

The horde had come from a country lying considerably to the north-east. They had been driven from their own land by a people of yellow complexion, with black beards and long hair, and who were armed with swords.[13]

Though Pringle speculated that this 'long-haired race' were Portuguese he showed some scepticism in that 'they were not described as carrying firearms rather than swords'.

In the *Narrative* he referred to 'the ravages of the people called Mantatees and Ficani, described in Mr Thompson's work'[14] of which he was the ghost writer. Pringle included in the book much of Rennie's report as quoted in his own letters to Mackay and Fairbairn, with a rather modified description of the aggressors who had expelled this early Mfecane horde from their own territory. They were rather 'a stronger nation, among whom were people of the colour of Hottentots, and with large beards and long hair'. All reports agreed that the Mfecane 'massacred without mercy all whom they met with'. George Rennie saw many of the Thembu warriors 'with dreadful gashes on their bodies not yet whole'.

Thompson, doubtless in Pringle's words, wrote:

It appears that this horde of ravagers had been within little more than two days' march of the Colony; nor was there any obstacle on their first advance, to prevent them from overwhelming the Scotch location and other frontier settlements. Fortunately, however, they contented themselves, at that time, with the plunder of the Tambookie kraals, and soon after retired again to the eastward.[15]

The neighbouring Thembu, particularly Bawana and his people, had shown themselves to be friendly to the Scots settlers, which may have reassured Pringle in his attitude to the Nguni, whom the settlers in Albany, alongside the Rharhabe section of the amaXhosa, resented as cattle thieves and even feared as a threat to their survival.

With the descent upon them of the Mfecane in full force in 1826–7, Bawana's amaTshatshu section of the Thembu were at even more serious risk and, through George Rennie, Pringle being by then in England, asked the colonial government for support against the Mfecane. Rennie told Mackay:

Having been always a sincere friend of the Colonists, he considers that he has very great claims on the Government. He certainly has been and still is a very great protection to that part of the Frontier which bounds his territory, and should he be forced down towards the coast it will leave a great part of the Frontier exposed to the inroads of *skellum* Caffers, Bush men and Ficani.[16]

Rennie called for 'a small Commando of 20 to 30 men' to expel the Mfecane, who were without firearms , but his request was refused. Six months later 3,000 Thembu with 12,000 cattle entered the colony to escape the Mfecane, the great majority returning to Bawana's territory across the Black Kei. By October 1827 Rennie reported to Mackay that they had withdrawn, leaving Bawana and a few of his people in the Tarka sub-district.

If Pringle's relationship with the Nguni, specifically the Thembu, was reasonably harmonious, he felt strong hostility from the earliest days of the settlement towards what he called the 'banditti', parties of Bushmen hunter-gatherers, dispossessed in an earlier period, and of Khoikhoi and mixed-race thieves, among them armed Cape Corps deserters and 'one or two runaway slaves'. The 'band of desperadoes' under attack in 1825 were led by Dragoener, a 'tame Bushman' who had fled a Boer's employ after a sjambok flogging, and 'sworn eternal enmity to the colonists'.[17]

The clash between his humane and would-be Christian attitude to the indigenous people, an attitude unsympathetic South African historians called 'philanthropic', and his need to safeguard the well-being of the settlers comes out clearly in his exchange with Fairbairn during this first part of his final stay at Baviaans River.

> The Bushmen on the Koonap continue to plague us — *ungrateful schelms*! Even after I have celebrated them in song.[18] They stole all my brother's riding possessions [three horses] last week and severely wounded a Bastaard Hottentot [Groenberg] with poisoned arrows. So I have declared war against them and have this day written to the Landdrost for a commando to attack them in their rocky dens. You see we back Settlers grow all savage and bloody by coming in continual collision with savages.[19]

He redeemed himself by requesting 'to have the wretches blockaded not massacred', adding, as if seeking further redemption, that these marauders were 'not genuine Bushmen but some of them Cape Corps deserters living by plunder'.

Fairbairn's lost letter of reproof with its 'denunciations against my Bushman Commandoes',[20] brought forth a sharp rejoinder. Unlike Lady Macbeth, 'there is no "damned spot" on my hands'. He had told Fairbairn that if attacked he would 'resist even to slaying the aggressor'. He pitied the Bushmen, 'those poor wretches', more than he blamed them, and almost threateningly warned Landdrost Mackay against bloodshed. He played the liberal card: 'Dr Philip is going to re-establish his missionaries among them and I trust will soon prove that it is a better policy to convert than extirpate them'.

As to Dragoener's band, after the failure of a Boer commando it was 'surrounded in one of their fastnesses by a strong party of military and burgher militia',[21] refused to surrender and in an attempted escape 'Dragoener and his boldest comrades being slain, the rest were taken prisoners'. The fate of the captives is unknown. His 'Song of the Wild Bushman' evoked the Bushman's Arcadian life, albeit 'mid the mountain rocks. The Desert my domain', and celebrated his proud independence.

> Thus I am lord of the Desert land
> And I will not leave my bounds,
> To crouch beneath the Christian's hand,
> And kennel with his hounds.

It was revolted 'tame Bushmen' that were led by Dragoener, one such himself.

The *Narrative* revealed the Pringle whose crusading had moved most determinedly to the cause of the indigenous people. He gave a harrowing account of the sufferings of the Bushmen through 'the barbarous acts of ancient times' to the atrocities of his own day.

The frontier colonists, be they Dutch or British, *must* of necessity continue to be semi-barbarians, so long as the *commando system* – the system of hostile reprisals – shall be encouraged or connived at; and so long as the colonists are permitted to make encroachments on the territory and the natural rights of the natives …mutual enmity and reciprocal outrage will proceed as heretofore.[22]

Despite continuing '*talk* of our boundless benevolence and our Christian philanthropy, fresh loads of that guilt which the Almighty has denounced in awful terms – the bloodstained guilt of OPPRESSION, will continue to accumulate upon our heads as a nation'.

The Hydra-headed oppression under Somerset's absolute rule, addressed in the sonnet 'To Oppression', had gone and a benevolent Governor, Major-General Bourke, had succeeded him, with the beginnings of representative government. Oppression now confined itself to the 'aboriginal race' in its various ethnic and mixed groupings and to the slave population. This was the cause which dominated the rest of Pringle's life.

And the 'Mantatees', the alternative name Pringle gave to the Mfecane of 1825? This was a portmanteau term for the remnants in flight from clashes with the Griquas, some themselves aggressors but many of them fugitives who took refuge in the colony and were encountered by Pringle in his six-week absence from Baviaans River in July-September 1825.

NOTES

1 Pringle (1966), p. 213.
2 Pringle to Fairbairn, 13.5.1825, Vigne (2011), pp. 180–1. LP, Fairbairn Papers, 1, 46.
3 Pringle to Stockenstrom, 9.5.1824, Vigne (2011), p. 180. *RCC* 21, p. 230.
4 Pringle to Fairbairn, 13.5.1825, Vigne (2011), p. 181. LP, Fairbairn Papers, 1, 64.
5 Pringle to Mackay, 14.5.1825, Vigne (2011), pp. 182–3. CA 1/SSE/8/98.
6 Pringle to Fairbairn. 22.7.1825 , Vigne (2011), p. 197. LP, Fairbairn Papers, 1, 54.
7 Pringle to Fairbairn, 20.5.1825, Vigne (2011), p. 184. LP, Fairbairn Papers, 1, 48.
8 *Ibid.*
9 Pringle to Fairbairn, 22.7.1825, Vigne (2011), pp. 197–8. LP, Fairbairn Papers, 1, 54.
10 Pringle to Mackay, 29.5.1825, Vigne (2011), p. 186. LP, Fairbairn Papers, 1, 50.
11 Unlike most present-day historians , Pringle and his informants and correspondents identified both the participants in the mass movement and the movement itself as Mfecane.
12 Pringle to Fairbairn, 22.7.1825, Vigne (2011), p. 197. LP, Fairbairn Papers, 1, 54.
13 *Ibid.*
14 Pringle (1966), p. 230.
15 Thompson (1967), vol. 1, p. 186.
16 G. Rennie to Mackay, 10.1.1827, CA 1/SSE 8/98, 67. See Rennie, vol. 2, p. 806; vol. 4, p. 1726.
17 Pringle (1966), p. 222.
18 Pringle (1838), 'Song of the Wild Bushman', pp. 11–12, 74.
19 Pringle to Fairbairn, 29.6.1825, Vigne (2011), p. 192. LP, Fairbairn Papers, 1, 52.
20 See pp. 76, 78 n20.
21 Pringle (1966), p. 223.
22 *Op. cit.*, pp. 229, 231.

13

Karroo Turning Point

On 29 June 1825 Pringle wrote to Fairbairn that he expected 'to meet Dr Philip in Somerset in three or four weeks and proceed with him to Graaff-Reinet where I will probably spend a week or two'.[1] Here was an exception to the full and frank exchange of information and ideas in their correspondence. No purpose was mentioned. Rather than to exclude Fairbairn from the intimacy of the talks ahead the object was surely to keep them away from Government through intercepted letters. Stockenstrom, landdrost of Graaff-Reinet, whom they were to meet, was seriously at risk as a government servant.

The date of the forthcoming meeting was accurate enough. On 22 July he wrote from what had been Somerset Farm and was now the village and magistracy of Somerset,[2] later Somerset East, that Philip was expected hourly, on his way to Dithakong. The Revd William Wright, who had set off from Eildon to visit the Thembu and Bushmen in the region and beyond, was to join them.

Pringle wrote next from Graaff-Reinet a fortnight later that Dr Philip had joined him in Somerset the week before and they, with Wright, who had visited the ageing Ndlambe at his Great Place near today's King William's Town, were house guests of the landdrost, Andries Stockenstrom.[3]

Pringle was asked by Fairbairn: 'But what are you doing at Graaff-Reinet?' and was given the evasive reply '*Much good*. All I can't explain to you at present – and Wright, though present, is not acquainted with all'.[4] With Dr Philip was the Revd James Read, son of the pioneer missionary Van der Kemp's first assistant, who is not mentioned by Pringle and nothing more is said of the 'good' that was achieved. He showers praise on both Philip and Stockenstrom – 'two of the best men in South Africa', who, rather than 'finding foes in each other are delighted with each other's talents and sentiments'.

He applauds Stockenstrom as 'hearty in the good cause and in the great cause of humanity. He is a decided advocate for the extinction of slavery and for the full emancipation of the Hottentots'. From Philip's example Pringle is 'awakened from my lethargy by the edifying example he exhibits of indomitable pertinacity. His hand, his heart and whole soul would be engrossed by his great and serious task'.[5]

The attack on slavery must have been a major topic before them. Pringle told Fairbairn three weeks later that he was setting about producing a pamphlet on slavery at the Cape.[6] This became the 'Letter from South Africa. Slavery', published first in Thomas Campbell's *New Monthly Magazine* in October 1826, soon afterwards in an entire issue of the *Anti-Slavery Society Monthly Reporter*, which led to Pringle's appointment as secretary of the Society nine months after his arrival in Britain. Wright, though excluded from the inner circle, also became a dedicated abolitionist, publishing his *Remarks on the Demoralizing Influence of Slavery* (London, 1828) and *Slavery at the Cape of Good Hope* (London, 1831). He also contributed a 'Testimony .. on Colonial Slavery' as an appendix to *Negro Slavery described by a Negro, being the Narrative of Ashton Warner*, published by Pringle for the Anti-Slavery Society in 1831.

Whatever the 'great and serious task' and 'the good cause' [7] addressed by Philip, Pringle and Stockenstrom in Graaff-Reinet there were lesser objectives: the ridding of the colony of Lord Charles Somerset as governor and the curing of the ills for which they blamed him, such as the 'commando system', exposure of the handing over of farms in the Neutral Territory to undeserving Boer intruders, combating press censorship, as well as combating the corruption inevitably gaining a hold under absolute rule. Dear to Pringle's heart was the reconciliation of the two major white champions of the downtrodden indigenous people of the colony and of the threatened Nguni and Sotho nations beyond its borders.

'Here Philip and Stockenstrom have met and learned to appreciate each other' he was able to write with great satisfaction..[8] He sets the scene for the objective that was achieved:

> The day after our arrival we all met in Church. Wright preached, Stockenstrom ushered Philip and me into Murray's pew and as soon as the service ended, Murray held forth his hand and shook the Dr's and mine almost cordially before all the congregation – all of whom even to the Snowberg boors had heard of the quarrel – so active have been the Dr's enemies endeavouring to widen the breach.[9]

Thus was staunched the bad blood which had flowed at the start of the year over Murray's accusation that Philip had disingenuously implicated him in the matter of the government's anti-settler pamphlet and spread the word that Murray and Stockenstrom were both 'inimical to the freedom of the Hottentots'.[10] The quarrel was bad enough but Somerset's use of Fairbairn's intercepted letter in reporting of it to Lord Bathurst was just as damaging. Pringle painted a rosy picture:

> Murray since he discovered his mistake has not been a party in spreading these slanders and is very happy at the opportunity of reconciliation. Mutual friendly calls have repeatedly passed among us and today we dine all together at Stockenstrom's, tomorrow at Murray's.[11]

He urged Fairbairn that he and Rutherfoord 'make all this known to the confusion of the workers of iniquity', so that, via Jardine and Peter Brink, 'it may reach the ears even of the Lama'.

Pringle found 'Stockenstrom, poor fellow, … in rather bad health and in very low spirits. … He has lately been fretted beyond endurance by the calumnies and indirect insults of the Somersets towards him'. He went on

> Here we all met again in friendship and cordiality – and dined all pleasantly together both at Stockenstrom's and Murray's. And on the subject of Hottentots, Bushmen and slaves Dr Philip and Stockenstrom found themselves absolutely agreed in everything essential.[12]

Stockenstrom's own account of the meeting varied a little: 'I found these gentlemen very agreeable society', he wrote and in their 'warm debates' judged that 'the liberty of the Press was of course paramount', with 'the aborigines came… next to, if not before, the press'.[13]

He harked back to the bitter dispute with Philip, who had told the Commissioners of Inquiry that 'being a Dutchman I was naturally in favour of the old system' of indentured Khoikhoi labour on the Boer farms. The visitors left 'tolerably satisfied that I was not so hostile to blacks and missionaries as I had been represented'.

Two major issues at the meeting, the bringing to an end of Somerset's rule and the exposure of the evils of slavery at the Cape, were, surprisingly, not mentioned by Stockenstrom. The former omission was surprising, since he had been subject to Somerset's wrath, five years earlier, over his dispute with Colonel Henry Somerset. He recalled, writing many years later, that 'they certainly tried my temper by the virulence with which they persisted in denouncing the present generation of the Colonists, or refused to make any allowance for their actual position, which rendered self-defence absolutely necessary for the preservation of both parties'.

Philip left on 6 August for Dithakong and Wright, though urged by Pringle to make his way to Algoa Bay and to face the hostile Anglicans of Cape Town, preached on two more Sundays. An extract from an unsigned letter among Pringle's to Fairbairn gives us a glimpse of the service:

> The old Dutch inhabitants of this place were lately not a little startled by the appearance of a clergyman of the Church of England (the Revd Mr Wright of Wynberg) with the white surplice in their Presbyterian pulpit. The formalities of the service, the kneeling etc., were all very strange to them … and it was a subject of much discussion … whether this service and dress did not retain some of the 'airs of Antichrist' and 'rags of Rome'!

Murray reassured them that 'the Church of England liturgy was the work of excellent men, both sound and pious', the surplice began to 'lose its horrors' and the peculiarities they witnessed were 'merely the *zonderling manier van den Engelsche kerk*'.[14]

The *zonderling manier* of the Irish clergyman William Wright was frequently despaired of by Pringle, who wrote of this gallant pioneer Anglican missionary: 'Poor Wright continues the same as ever, intangled, unteachable, making ten foes for every friend wherever he goes'.[15] Wright had arrived in Graaff-Reinet ahead of the others and Stockenstrom, who wrote that he 'had for some time been travelling on the Frontier and through Kafirland [and] was literally frantic about the injustice and oppression he had heard of and witnessed'[16]. He came under heavy attack from the Revd George Hough, the Governor's chaplain and strong supporter, and the Anglican community in Cape Town and made himself ridiculous by his lovesick quest after successive young women, with no result. Despite his repeated rejection as a bridegroom, he did marry, and promptly sailed for England with his bride, to the great displeasure of the Anglicans, disapproving to the last. Pringle, however, despite his criticisms of this 'wild Irishman', described him as 'the only clergyman of the Church of England in the colony … who was friendly to the freedom, or active in promoting, the improvement, of the coloured classes'.[17]

The Pringles' fortnight in Graaff-Reinet was followed by three weeks with Thomas's youngest brother John, farming at Melkrivier, near Graaff-Reinet, after his four years service at Somerset Farm. From both places, and the magistracy of Somerset, Thomas sent eleven letters to Fairbairn. In them, as in the three lengthy communications to the Commissioners of Inquiry, he went over and over the main points in their struggle with Somerset and his officials: the closing of the *Commercial Advertiser* and the treatment of Greig (now returning with Bathurst's imprimatur to publish his newspaper); Somerset's attempted censorship of the *South African Journal,* Pringle's rejection of which and the petition for press freedom constituted the inevitable declaration of war; the search warrant threat, the severest personal blow to Pringle; the proscription of the Literary Society, supported by the cream of mercantile and official society; the decline of the Classical and Commercial Academy through Somerset's disfavour; even the refusal of John Pringle's request for continued employment of the 'prize negro' apprenticed at Somerset Farm.

All this was summed up by Somerset's pronouncement to Advocate Hendrik Cloete of his anathema against Pringle and Fairbairn whom 'he was fully determined, so long as he held the reins of Government, to oppose and thwart [in] everything which emanated from them without exception or in which they were concerned'[18].

The Commissioners – the 'Bogles' (ghosts) as Pringle and Fairbairn mockingly named them – were preparing their report and the two wrote much of their possible partisanship towards Lord Charles. Pringle's 'three sheet' (3,500-word) letter to them from Graaff-Reinet, on 7 August ended with an accusation of Somerset's behaviour towards him:

> His open and inveterate denunciation of myself, as a turbulent and factious person, and a marked disturber of the Government – are rather too bad to be tamely submitted to. I do therefore respectfully solicit, Gentlemen, your rigid investigation into the truth of these stigmatising declarations of Lord Charles Somerset – in regard to me as I consider them unequivocal manifestations of that spirit of vindictive persecution of which I have especially complained to Earl Bathurst.[19]

Fairbairn was suffering from bouts of an unexplained illness, followed by convalescence in Dr Philip's holiday cottage (later added to and renamed Clifton House, on the Kloof Road to Camps Bay), yet despite this and Pringle's earlier complaints at his failure to answer letters, he kept Pringle fully informed with replies no longer extant, to the letters arriving with almost neurotic frequency in those final months on the frontier. Of Fairbairn's letter to the Commissioners Pringle wrote:

> Your proposed '*statement*' to them is a glorious step. It is far nobler and bolder than my appeal to Earl B. It is worthy of yourself. I wd envy you the glory of it – but am a married man and comparatively a coward. … Be cautious – but terrific in your onslaught. You will destroy them.[20]

Pringle was no coward save for his one terror – a fate that would be worsened by his married state: deportation to Botany Bay, on which he was later to consult Brougham.[21]

His attack was not only centred on his own victimization and ruin at Somerset's hands. He exposed 'frontier affairs', in which Colonel Henry Somerset was strongly criticized for his commando raids, and the apportionment of land in the Ceded Territory, from which the Scottish party was excluded. He exploded to the Commissioners in the middle of a long tirade:

> Am I then to consider my relations who had been accustomed to rank among the first class of Scottish farmers, as really inferior, in the estimation of Lord Charles Somerset, to the veriest vagabonds and off-scourings of the Colony, to whom he is at this instant signing grants of the choicest spots in the Ceded Territory, to the extent in some instances of three or four thousand morgen each?[22]

These 'vagabonds and off-scourings' included the 'unhanged rebels' of Slagtersnek, whose 'wild and parched and narrow location' had been allotted to the Scottish party in 1820.

While at Melkrivier Pringle witnessed the arrival of 'several hundred natives belonging to various tribes of the Bechuana [who] were driven into the Colony from the north-east, mostly in a state of utter starvation', fleeing from 'the wandering hordes called Mantatees and Ficani' and of Griqua bands.[23] They were apprenticed to farmers, several families to the Scottish location 'where I believe they still reside, and who proved very faithful servants'. To Thomas and Margaret Pringle at Melkrivier came a Tswana boy fugitive, Hinza, son of one Marossi, about ten years of age and 'alone in the world'. They took him in as a young servant but he became a much loved surrogate child, virtually adopted by them and accompanying them to England. He does not emerge clearly from Pringle's poem, 'The Bechuana Boy', written for the young, where his arrival is fictionalized by his leading a tame springbok, Pringle having seen such a relationship on a farm. The only other account of him is a eulogy after his death, from 'a pulmonary complaint', in December 1827 (see p. 185).

The poem was one of some fifteen Pringle wrote in his last frontier sojourn. He sent Fairbairn 'another sonnet for your criticism' – 'To Oppression', from Somerset before the meeting at Graaff-Reinet and asked his advice about sending it to Thomas Campbell for the *New Monthly Magazine*, thanking him twelve days later for his 'encomiums on my late rhyming attempts,' which he found 'very flattering'.[24]

He had written from Eildon 'I still indulge now and then in this "profane and profitless art of poem-making",' quoting their admired friend John Leyden, once reproached with these words, and sent him two poems for Campbell's journal 'if you and Rutherfoord pronounce them passable'.[25] To Campbell he also sent Fairbairn's 'The Nameless Spring', which he judged 'full of thought and feeling'. It was a rejoinder to his own 'Nameless Stream', a product of a bout of depression in his remote refuge.

Despite the pressures of 'the great task', his debts and lack of money, his actions for the mixed-race tenants of Baviaans River and his very demanding correspondence with the Commissioners of Inquiry, both to unseat Somerset and to obtain compensation for his losses, he found that 'I fly to versifying like a man with an evil conscience who flies to drink to drown remorse'. He confessed to Fairbairn:

I have always cherished at the bottom of my heart the ambition of writing some day or other a little volume of poetry worthy of being preserved. A very small proportion of which I have written is in my own sincere opinion worthy of that description.

He still hoped

to write something that may not dishonour Scotland. At present, however, I almost feel criminal in giving up any part of my heart or time to poetry ... sensible of the vast importance of the task I have undertaken and I will not flinch from it.

Written after the meeting with Philip and Stockenstrom had begun, he was guilt stricken in comparing himself with Philip, 'the good servant improving his ten talents while I am hiding my one in the earth'.[26]

From Melkrivier he sent Fairbairn a revision of 'The Nameless Stream', with his judgment of it: 'I did not think it good at first and now I despise it – though I still consider it good enough for *The New Monthly.*[27] He sent it, on a single page, with Fairbairn's 'sort of indirect satire upon it'. He was critical of the latter – 'the thought is very fine but has justice scarcely done to it, for the development of your idea is somewhat indistinct and defective in perspicacity'. He sensed 'some tendency to Wordsworthian mysticism about it', bearing out his 'suspicion ... of your heretical leaning that way'. Francis (later Lord) Jeffrey, the highly respected editor of the *Edinburgh Review,* condemned Wordsworth's metaphysics, especially in *The Excursion,* as 'silliness'.[28] 'The Nameless Spring' would nevertheless be sent to Campbell, who 'shall have springs and streams and nameless rivers enough for one batch from South Africa – not quite so dry and immelodious I hope as African themes usually are'.[29]

He took a very different tone, going cap in hand to Campbell, a very considerable figure in the literary scene:

I have no means of ascertaining whether any of these trifles [are] worthy of admittance ... the two signed JF and Q are by my friend Mr J. Fairbairn. ... The verses are later attempts of our own, some of them, perhaps all, unfit for your distinguished miscellany.

Campbell's biographer and the *de facto* editor of the review, Cyrus Redding, quotes the letter and adds that the poems were never received.[30] Perhaps in using 'a more direct channel' – he had sent poems before, presumably in the care of a traveller – he had reckoned without the long arm of the Cape Town post office, under his enemies' control.

Pringle's 'stream' was his life as a poet. After 'gliding free from uplands green ... through flowery meads, where snow-white lilies screen The wild swan's whiter breast', before reaching the ocean

It meets the thirsty desert – and is gone
To waste oblivion. Let its story teach
His fate who sung – and sunk like it unknown.[31]

The rapid succession of letters from Melkrivier and on his and Margaret's return, via a short stay in Somerset in early September, carried with it evidence of

Pringle's state of mind. He had been brought down by his clash with Somerset and his 'tools', was disillusioned regarding 'the Bogles', Bigge and Colebrooke, whom he had seen as his allies, and facing a future with no certainty of a return to the upward path he had embarked on five years before. Yet he was as fertile as ever and produced such material as an account, for Greig's revived *Commercial Advertiser,* of the 'internal districts', Graaff-Reinet, Somerset and Albany, with constructive ideas for their 'improvement'. His sympathy for the Boer inhabitants, still largely dismissed by the British colonists, who judged them much inferior to the Dutch-speakers of Cape Town and its hinterland, is well expressed. He compares their character to 'the superior enterprise of the British settlers' and finds them

> in general a very respectable class of men, and much superior, in some points, to what they have been represented … There is something sound, substantial and prudent in the character of the African Boor.

After judiciously adapting himself to the circumstances of his new situation, having built his house, grown some crops, and run cattle and sheep, the rural Afrikaner 'then sat still'. The 'new race from Europe … are enterprising and intelligent', while the Boers are 'more prudent and experienced'. He suggests a plan to bring them together, sinking 'reciprocal jealousy and dislike', and 'imitating what on either side is worthy of imitating'.[32]

The 'plan', originally Stockenstrom's idea and put forward a week later, called for the holding of twice yearly fairs at a common meeting point for the three districts, for the encouragement of trade. He proposed the establishing of an Agricultural Society, to meet at the fairs, the Society to conduct its affairs without the supervision of landdrosts and to hold cattle and produce shows and horse races. The fairs would be 'accompanied by balls and other festivities'. He proposed that 'the new district of Somerset' be the site of the fairs.[33] Six months later, while in Cape Town, he was appointed a steward at the first such fair, to be held at Somerset, but declined 'due to my departure from the frontier' and suggested that 'my name may have been inserted by mistake instead of my brother *John's* – who resides at Graaff Reinet'.[34] He had withheld his name at the outset for fear of its jeopardizing the scheme. He asked Fairbairn: 'Will the "muckle sumph" not conceive my project of an Agricultural Society on the frontier as another plot against him?'[35] Perhaps his identity as the original proposer was indeed known to the organizers.

The 'great cause' of emancipating the Khoikhoi and slaves and protecting the Griquas and neighbouring Nguni from military attack was thus not a total obsession for Pringle. He favoured Graaff-Reinet among the other 'interior districts' as 'free of disturbances from the Caffres', a judgment that could not have come, without qualification, from his idol Dr Philip or from William Wright

His fury at Somerset's rule continued unabated. In his biting denunciation of Somerset's claim that 'particular favours had been conferred upon me and my family' he found it difficult 'to restrain the open expression of my scorn and derision'. Rather than favour him Somerset had 'insulted, calumniated and persecuted me and I claim redress'.[36]

The same letter attacked again the Government's land grants in the most fertile parts of the Ceded Territory, to 'the unhanged rebels of Bavian's River and Bruintje's Hoogte' and others as undeserving. The latter included a group of settlers headed by Lieutenant William Proctor of Oude Wynberg, a farmer and horse-breeder, named in a corruption charge against Lord Charles, who was exonerated by the Commissioners in 1823.

His own shattered circumstances were never far from his mind. Trapped on the frontier by his penniless state and pressing debts, yet determined to get to England to pursue his case, he exploded to Fairbairn: 'Oh that cursed cash – that is the misery of miseries. Were I free of debt – I should not mind much any other difficulties'.[37] He was occupied with Thompson's book, 'my own book' (still not begun) and 'a pamphlet on Cape slavery',[38] which was later to change his life's course. A commission to put together the book of Captain W.F.W. Owen's African coastal explorations promised good payment, but not until the job was done. He politely declined to resume the co-editorship of the *Commercial Advertiser*, pleading his absence from Cape Town, which, unstated, he could not afford to remedy.[39] He had written to Fairbairn from Graaff-Reinet: 'You urge me again to come down. *I cannot.* A visit to Cape Town wd. cost me a thousand Rds – and I have not a stiver'.[40]

His poetry was an antidote to the 'misery of miseries' and he urged Fairbairn to criticize the verses he sent him: 'Criticism always does me good. If I don't adopt what is suggested it yet excites to something else'.[41]

NOTES

[1]   Pringle to Fairbairn, 29.6.1825, Vigne (2011, p. 191. LP, Fairbairn Papers, 1, 52.
[2]   Pringle to Fairbairn, 22.7.1825, Vigne (2011), p. 231. LP, Fairbairn Papers, 1, 54.
[3]   Pringle to Fairbairn, 5.8.1825 , Vigne (2011), p. 238. LP, Fairbairn Papers 1, 56.
[4]   *Ibid.*
[5]   *Ibid.*
[6]   Pringle to Fairbairn, 26.8.1825, Vigne (2011), p. 227. WUL, Fairbairn Papers, A653, Bb2.
[7]   *Ibid.*
[8]   *Ibid.*
[9]   *Ibid.*
[10] Somerset to Bathurst, 15.1.1825. *RCC* 19, 481–90.
[11] Pringle to Fairbairn, 5.8.1825, Vigne (2011), p. 199. LP, Fairbairn Papers, 1, 52.
[12] Pringle to Fairbairn, 13.8.1825, Vigne (2011), p. 214. LP, Fairbairn Papers, 1, 62.
[13] Stockenstrom, p. 243.
[14] Pringle to Fairbairn, n.d. (- 8.1825), Vigne (2011), pp. 217–18. LP, Fairbairn Papers, 1, 64.. 'The peculiar way of the English church'.
[15] Pringle to Fairbairn, 22.7.1825, Vigne (2011), p. 196. LP, Fairbairn Papers, 1, 54.
[16] Stockenstrom, p. 243.
[17] Pringle (1838), p. 87.
[18] Pringle to Fairbairn, 16.9.1825,Vigne (2011), p. 109. *RCC* 18, pp. 258–97.
[19] Pringle to Commissioners of Inquiry, 7.8.1825, Vigne (2011), p. 207. LP, Fairbairn Papers, 1,176. *RCC* 22, 453–62.
[20] Pringle to Fairbairn, 19.8.1825, Vigne (2011), p. 216. LP, Fairbairn Papers, 1, 66.
[21] Pringle to Brougham, 20.12.24, Vigne (2011), p. 153. UCL Sp.Coll. 12099.
[22] Pringle to Commissioners of Inquiry, 8.9.1825, Vigne (2011), p. 238. *RCC* 19, pp. 52–8.

23 Pringle (1966), p. 231.
24 Pringle to Fairbairn, 22.7.1825, 5.8.1825, Vigne (2011), pp. 197–8. LP, Fairbairn Papers, 1, 54, 56.
25 Pringle to Fairbairn, 29.6.1825, Vigne (2011), p. 192. LP, Fairbairn Papers, 1, 52.
26 Pringle to Fairbairn, 5.8.1825, Vigne (2011), p. 198. LP, Fairbairn Papers, 1, 56.
27 Pringle to Fairbairn, 24.8.1825, Vigne (2011), p. 218. WUL, Fairbairn Papers, A653, Bb 2.
28 Francis Jeffrey, 'The Excursion', *Edinburgh Review,* 24 November 1809, pp. 310–23.
29 Pringle to Fairbairn, 24.8.1825, Vigne (2011), p. 218. WUL, Fairbairn Papers, A653, Bb 2.
30 Pringle to Campbell, n.d.. Vigne (2011), p. 250. Redding, Cyrus, *Literary Reminiscences and Memoirs of Thomas Campbell,* 2 vols (1860), vol. 2, pp. 522–6.
31 The version in Pringle (1838), p. 69 is much changed. The final sentence reads 'Let its story teach \ The fate of one – who sinks, like it, unknown,'
32 *South African Commercial Advertiser,* Cape Town, 9.9.1825.
33 *SACA,* 21.9.25.
34 Pringle to Plasket, 28.2.1826, Vigne (2011), p. 297. CA CO 293/70/299..
35 Pringle to Fairbairn, 3.9.1825, Vigne (2011), p. 231. LP, Fairbairn Papers, 1, 76.
36 Pringle to Commissioners of Inquiry, 8.9.1825, Vigne (2011), p. 238. *RCC* 23, pp. 52–8.
37 Pringle to Fairbairn, 27.8.1825, Vigne (2011), p. 227. LP, Fairbairn Papers, 1, 64.
38 Pringle to Fairbairn, 24.8.1825, Vigne (2011), p. 219. WUL Fairbairn Papers, A53, Bb2.
39 Pringle to Fairbairn, 2.9.1825, Vigne (2011), pp. 229–30. LP, Fairbairn Papers, 1, 72.
40 Pringle to Fairbairn, 13.8.1825 , Vigne (2011), p. 216. LP, Fairbairn Papers, 1, 62.
41 Pringle to Fairbairn, 4.9.1825, Vigne (2011), p. 223. LP, Fairbairn Papers, 1, 78.

14

Last Months at Eildon

Thomas and Margaret returned to Eildon from their Karroo journeys in mid-September and 26 letters written by Thomas in the two months that followed have survived, 17 of them to Fairbairn, three to the Commissioners of Inquiry, two each to Sir Richard Plasket and the *Commercial Advertiser*, and single letters to Brougham and Thomas Campbell. The stream of letters then dries up and we do not hear from him again until a letter is sent to the Commissioners from Graham-stown on 12 January 1826 indicatng that he had left Baviaans River at the end of December.[1] His silence for the four weeks before his departure is unexplained but we shall find other evidence of his life at Eildon and his leaving the settlement in that time.

Pringle found a depressing scene at Baviaans River which was suffering the worst drought since 1821 and worse even than that, when no rain had fallen for eleven months. There would 'not be an ear of corn reaped on the river this season' unless rain fell speedily. At Eildon, William's 'twenty acres of corn' were 'mostly dead already and his garden like a barn floor', though unlike the aridity at Graaff-Reinet, there was 'plenty of old grass and the sheep and cattle are in good condition'.[2]

There had been serious clashes with the Bushmen. 'Why has the Government not established missions among the Bushmen?' he pondered accusingly, 'or taken some other measures to reclaim them from savage and predatory habits?' He showed a new understanding of their plight, the choice between 'predatory warfare ... or of servitude to the Boors'. The result of their situation was clear: 'spots in the woods entirely covered with the bones of hundreds of sheep and oxen they have slaughtered and left to the vultures'. Exposure to their murderous hostility was 'no joke': 'we cannot go a hundred yards from here without a gun'. Yet these 'Children of the Mist' worked on his literary imagination and he 'intended to write a Bushman's tale in prose some day'.[3]

The drought was unrelenting and they were not to see the end of it. Writing was a relief and Pringle, in the solitary life in his hut, became almost obsessive about his correspondence with Fairbairn, listing letters sent and complaining of the irregularity of his friend's replies. The letters, despite the depressing circumstance in which they were written, remain a pleasure to read, laced as they are with discussion of the poetry he is producing and of Fairbairn's journalism as editor of the *Commercial Advertiser*. ('Blackwoodian' is his term for censure of an intemperate leading article.) The conflict with Lord Charles Somerset is a constant theme. He sees Waterloo on the way, on the Press freedom issue, with himself as Blücher to Fairbairn's Wellington.[4]

The notoriety of the disaffected and deported former naval officer Bishop Burnett – 'a sort of Gentleman Swindler' and 'a *Schelm*' – is against their interest and his letter to Brougham, who had at last replied to one of his earlier approaches (the others were lost, perhaps intercepted) is a masterpiece of tactful damning. Burnett is not considered 'as a representative of the respectable class of settlers' or as 'their champion … whatever be his *real* grievances (and I believe they are very great).'[5]

He was very happy to find Brougham's 'appreciation of our magazine … exceedingly gratifying' – recalling the humiliation the Chaldee MS meted out also to its chief target, Archibald Constable, publisher of the *Edinburgh Review*, of which Brougham was a founding and major contributor. The *Edinburgh's* reviewers were also constantly abused by post-Pringle *Blackwood's*. Lockhart, in his third issue (September 1818) called them 'a set of cunning, dissembling, undermining, jeering, jesting, cynical antagonists of Christianity', which Pringle might well have remembered, as Brougham certainly would have done.[6]

The Commissioners of Inquiry were dealt with at inordinate length in letters averaging 2000 words. One answered Somerset's charges against him made to Bathurst of 'flagrant abuses' and on 'certain remarks' in the *South African Journal*, about the sufferings of the Albany settlers, which had led to the *Journal's* closure. He tackled in another the 'monstrous overcharge' inflicted by the Commissariat Department on the settlers for the rations issued to them in 1820–21. The debt of 1100 Rixdollars was subsequently waived.[7]

Pringle's letters to Sir Richard Plasket, Colonel Bird's successor in Cape Town, recall the good terms he had enjoyed with the colonial officials before Lord Charles's return from leave. Though William had succeeded him as leader of the Scottish party, he wrote enquiring officially whether the subdivision of the location needed to be reconsidered at his departure and a new survey undertaken. The approach towards obtaining land for the Scottish party's mixed-race tenants – Christian and Karel Groepe, Hans Blok and Klaas Eckhard – first made in May via the new Somerset landdrost Mackay, a mere 'tool' of Lord Charles and of his son the Colonel, in Pringle's view, was repeated for four more in October. Its terms showed a confidence that Plasket would share his liberal view of the matter.[8]

The new memorialists were Klaas Eckhard (again), Philip and Nicolas Blok and Joseph Arendse. He described them as

> people of colour, or *Bastards* [*sic*], according to the phraseology of the colony. In other respects I consider them quite as respectable as the generality of the Burghers of this neighbourhood – more so indeed than many who have lately got grants of land … their attachment to the Government and their respect for constituted authority [are] unquestionable.

He reported that he had spoken about the applications to Mackay who 'seems to have doubts on the subject. Indeed Captain Stockenstrom is the only provincial magistrate … who appears to entertain judicious and liberal views on such points.' He urged Plasket to refer to Stockenstrom, if he were still on a visit to

Cape Town. 'I am not aware that he knows the memorialists personally, but it is in regard to the general principle of granting lands to this class of men that I particularly refer.' He assured Plasket that he had no object but 'to further, as far as I can, the interests of the community and of deserving individuals whom prejudice , or other circumstances, have placed in the background'.

No response to the applications has been traced. By 1830 Christian Groepe and Klaas Eckhard were both leading members of the Kat River Settlement, Groepe as Field-Commandant. Sir Richard Plasket, for all his ability and liberal views on colour, left the colony in 1827, after only three years as Colonial Secretary, and was able to make small impact.

Life at Eildon is seldom described. Pringle tells Fairbairn of his and Margaret's riding to see his father on his up river farm, Clifton, of his Sunday morning services, attended mainly by the mixed-race tenants and Khoikhoi servants of the settlers, and by his 'school for the Hottentots'.[9] He was much preoccupied with postal arrangements. A letter of 22 October 1825 he sent 'through a circuitous route under cover to Mr Paton' [army and general agent in Strand Street, Cape Town], which he took to be 'a safe and unsuspected channel'. An impressive number, perhaps fourteen, of his African poems were produced at this time in their original forms (he was an incorrigible reviser – even after publication). Several were sent to Fairbairn for his criticism, or for publication in the *Commercial Advertiser*.

At Somerset, Graaff-Reinet and Melkrivier he wrote 'To Oppression', 'The Bushman's Song' (later renamed 'Song of the Wild Bushman'), clearly inspired by the meeting with Philip and Stockenstrom. Like 'The War Song of Lynx' (later 'Makanna's Gathering', 'The Kosa' (later 'The Caffer'), 'The Hottentot' and 'The Bushman' were inserted in Thompson's *Travels*, with which he was toiling throughout this period. They show the same inspiration and commitment to the cause of emancipation and protection of the indigenous underdogs. 'The Korana' is an exception. Beyond the writ of colonial rule this Khoikhoi community, encountered by Thompson on the Orange River in 1823, was described, presumably in his notes, in similar terms to Pringle's verse:

> Midst all his wanderings, hating toil,
> He never tills the stubborn soil,
> But on the milky dams depends,
> And what spontaneous nature sends.

The text in the *Travels* reads: 'They lead an indolent, wandering life, living chiefly on the milk of their cattle'.[10] The poem is explained as 'one of Mr Pringle's African sketches to diversify my pages'. The contrast with the poems about the victims of colonial rule is telling.

He inserted also 'Afar in the Desert' and 'The Lion and the Camelopard' (later 'The Lion and Giraffe'), both from the *South African Journal*, No. 2. They recall his pre-Graaff-Reinet preoccupation – the landscape, Africa's people and its varied and plentiful fauna. 'The Caffer's Song' (*South African Journal*, No. 1) presents an Arcadian, idyllic, carefully recorded scene:

> By the streamlet my heifers are grazing;
> Prone o'er the clear pool the herd-boy is gazing,
> Under the shade my Ileza is singing –
> The shade of the tree where her cradle is swinging.

Less than two years later he sees the 'Caffer' as a Xhosa cattle-thief: 'Lo! Where he crouches by the Kloof's dark side, \ Eyeing the farmer's lowing herds afar'. Then comes the polemic, full of passion and commitment:

> He is a robber? – True, it is a strife
> Between the black-skinned bandit and the white.
> A savage? – Yea, though loth to aim at life,
> Evil for evil force he doth requite.

'The Caffer's Song' (later 'The Brown Hunter's Song') and 'The Caffer' have in common the Xhosa subject as the centre of the poem, as in 'The Hottentot' and 'The Bushman'. The former, placed after Dr Richard Heurtley's drawing of a Khoikhoi herder holding 'the boor's huge firelock', was written 'by my friend Mr Pringle … in the interior of the Colony long before. He had seen it … *from life*'.[11] It reveals a defeated people: 'the shields \ And quivers of his race are gone, he yields, \ Submissively, his freedom and his lands'. 'The Bushman', though, 'His secret lair, surrounded, echoes to the thundering gun, \ And the wild shriek of anguish and despair!', leaves, dying, 'to his sons a curse should they be friends \ With the proud "Christian-men" – for they are fiends !'

Pringle, in a footnote in the *Travels*, introduces 'The Song of the Wild Bushman' as 'designed to express the sentiments with which these persecuted tribes may be supposed to regard the colonists'.[12] Defiance dominates. 'Thus I am Lord of the Desert Land' ends, in the third person:

> No, the swart Serpent of the Rocks
> His den doth yet retain:
> And none who there his sting provokes
> Will find its poison vain.

The 'swart Serpent' in the *Travels* and the *Commercial Advertiser* (21 September 1825) becomes the 'brown serpent' in *Ephemerides* (1828), whether as closer to the Bushman's colouring ('swart' means swarthy in English but black in Dutch and Afrikaans) or to eliminate the archaic poeticism 'swart' is arguable.

'The War Song of Lynx' (later 'Makanna's Gathering') breathes similar defiance:

> Then come, ye Chieftains bold,
> With war-plumes waving high;
> Come, every warrior young and old,
> With club and assegai,
> Remember how the spoiler's host
> Did through our land like locusts range!
> Your herds, your wives, your comrades lost –
> Remember – and revenge!

Last Months at Eildon

In *African Sketches* Pringle added to the poem a lively narrative of the Battle of Grahamstown, making use of the Revd James Read's personal account of Makhanda and the recollections of his friend Captain Harding who 'communicated to me … details relating to these campaigns', in which he took part. It is curious that he had to ask Fairbairn: 'I am not quite sure whether the attack on Graham's Town was in 1818 or 1819? Inquire and correct.' Evidence that news of the battle had little or no deterrent effect on Pringle and his party members as they prepared to leave for the very battle zone only months after the attack, which took place on 22 April 1819. The poem itself was to enrage many readers among the Albany settlers when published in *African Sketches* in years to come.

Fairbairn's comments are referred to in some of Pringle's letters and they were sometimes harsh in the extreme. 'A Noon-day Dream' leads the reader from the dreamer's (i.e. Pringle's) blissful childhood 'through Cheviot's valleys, to pluck the flowers \ Or chase with young rapture the birds through the bowers' and a surfeit of both, plus shepherds, milk-maidens and 'sweet voices that called me aloud by my name' to 'a grim Spectre enthroned on high \ And its name was written – TYRANNY!' Its victims are 'swart Afric's tribes with their woolly hair, The enslaved Madagass, the dejected Malay.' To Robert Wahl 'Pringle's sonnet on "Slavery" is one of the worst he wrote, and his poem "The Slave-Dealer" … is sheer melodrama'.[13] 'A Noon-day Dream' ranks with both. Fairbairn evidently thought so too. Pringle replied jocularly, recalling the 'Scotch reviewers' lethal criticism in the *Edinburgh Review*: 'You surpass John Dennis – and even Francis Jeffrey – you are a perfect mohawk'.[14]

He accepted uncomplainingly Fairbairn's 'critical scourge' and 'philippic' and made no objection to his frequent failure to acknowledge what he was sent or to use it in the *Advertiser*. He even allowed Fairbairn, on occasion, to 'alter anything you like'[15] and relied on his judgment on which poems to send to Thomas Campbell for the *New Monthly Magazine*. His modesty, even diffidence, about his poetry is plainly not false and he hopes only for the survival of 'a very small portion'. He found the sonnet 'so easy, notwithstanding the rhyme', adding that he did not 'care much to read other people's, and believe as few will care to read mine'[16]. He had his hopes raised, nonetheless, when Fairbairn praised 'my late rhyming attempts', that he would one day to produce that 'little volume of poetry worthy of being preserved'.

His poetic imagination was ever present, despite the stresses of his life and voluminous correspondence from Eildon. Many late September days were lost in writing a forty-page 'article' for the Commissioners, which is no longer extant. Without John Bluck, the amanuensis he and Fairbairn employed in Cape Town[17] copying his own letters was 'not only an intolerable drudgery but a wretched waste of time' (and no copy was made of the forty pages). Despite Thompson's *Travels*, the laborious arguments to the Commissioners, Plasket and Brougham, and haunted by his destitution and debts, his poetry flowed out. There was also preparation for the paper on slavery at the Cape, which would be written while waiting for a ship to Cape Town and which would change his life after publication in the *New Monthly Review* the following October.

167

NOTES

1 Stockenstrom, vol. 1, pp. 251–4.
2 Pringle to Fairbairn, 22.9.1825, Vigne (2011), p. 244. LP, Fairbairn Papers, 1, 88.
3 *Ibid.* See p. 221.
4 Pringle to Fairbairn, 4.11.1825, Vigne (2011), p. 279. LP, Fairbairn Papers, 1, 114.
5 Pringle to Plasket, 3.11.1825, Vigne (2011), pp. 256–7. UCL Spec. Coll. 1201.
6 Christie, William, *The Edinburgh Review in the Literary Culture of Romantic Britain* (2009), p. 152. *Blackwood's* 3.9.1818, p. 694.
7 Pringle to Commissioners of Inquiry, 5.10.1825, Vigne (2011), pp. 252–6. *RCC* 23, p. 13.
8 Pringle to Plasket, 5.10.1825, Vigne (2011), pp. 256–7. CA CO 8458, 137.
9 Pringle to Fairbairn, 22.10.1825, Vigne (2011), p. 269. LP, Fairbairn Papers, 1, 108.
10 Thompson (1966), vol. 1, p. 123.
11 *Op. cit.*, pp. 29–30. See also Pringle (1838), p. 64 for a later version.
12 Thompson , vol. 2, p. 54. See also Pringle (1838), pp. 11–12 for a later version.
13 Pringle (1970), p. xxii.
14 Pringle to Fairbairn, 10.11.1825, Vigne (2011), p. 290. LP, Fairbairn Papers, 1, 122. John Dennis (1658-1734), controversial critic and writer on criticism.
15 *Ibid.*
16 Pringle to Fairbairn, 19.10.1825, Vigne (2011), p. 267. LP, Fairbairn Papers, 1, 102.
17 Was he the unusually named, once admired engraver in England, reduced to doing copying work at the Cape?

15
Return of the Settler

Visitors to Baviaans River were few. Before the Graaff-Reinet meeting, the missionary he most admired, the Revd John Brownlee, who had come to the frontier from Lanarkshire in 1817, visited Eildon from his mission station on the Gwali, a tributary of the Tyhume river, forty miles to the south-east. He made 'many valuable suggestions in regard to measures for promoting the civilization of the Caffer tribes',[1] as did Wright both at Eildon and at Graaff-Reinet shortly afterwards. Even in his idealized portrait of Brownlee, 'The Good Missionary', dated 'Cafferland 1825' in *Ephemerides*, the battle lines are drawn. Brownlee had served as a very reluctant 'government agent' on the frontier, earned Somerset's disapproval and was supplanted in 1821 by the Revd W.R. Thomson. Just before the Graaff-Reinet meeting Dr Philip persuaded him to rejoin the London Missionary Society, from which he had resigned in 1818, before Philip's arrival. In 'The Good Missionary' Pringle wrote:

> The credit of the arduous work he wrought
> Was reaped by other men who came behind.

The sonnet was sent to Fairbairn for the *Commercial Advertiser* on 19 October 1825, a few days after its composition. Brownlee, Pringle felt, 'had been vilely used by the Cape Govt. and not very well by some whom it and Dr Thom have recently set *over him*. I would like it indicted on this act.'[2] Like other material Pringle sent, Fairbairn did not publish 'The Good Missionary'.

Another diversion was the wedding in June 1825 of Thomas's half-sister Catherine to his cousin (but not hers) John Brown Rennie, second son of the widow Rennie. Thomas's elder sister Mary and her husband Captain Williams of the Commissariat visited the family from Grahamstown at the end of September. Fairbairn was told on 29 September 1825: 'Margt. is well and rides up with me tomorrow', perhaps to a family gathering for the Williamses at Robert Pringle's farm, Clifton.

His closeness to Mary, whose music accompanied his songs in their early days in Scotland, seems to have lessened. He was later to complain of her neglecting to reply to his letters. We learn from Professor Rennie (vol, 3, p. 1181) that Mary's collection of 'several important manuscripts and other material connected with the life, family interests and literary output' of her brother passed to her grandson who in old age gave away or sold numerous items, in the 1950s. A copy of *Albyn's Anthology* was bought off a wheelbarrow by Eric Pringle, the family historian at that time. The handsome volume, inscribed 'To Mrs Williams from her affectionate brother Tho. Pringle, Cape of Good Hope, Oct. 1st. 1824', would have been with Pringle's baggage forwarded to Grahamstown when, on 8 October, he set off on his ill-fated horseback journey to the eastern frontier which ended at Genadendal..

He must have been more cheered than he lets us know in informing Fairbairn of the response, on 14 October 1825, to the second of his 'Agricola' letters on bringing the three 'internal districts' together and proposing agricultural shows (or fairs) to that end. Exactly a month after it had appeared in the *Commercial Advertiser,* he wrote that the letters 'have produced some effect',[3] though not as he should have wished it to be.

> The functionaries at Somerset (which are much of the caliber of the wise men of Gotham) have had divers meetings on the subject of *Fairs* and I am threatened with a visit of the Landdrost and Heemraden in a horse waggon to consult with me and the Scotch party about the matter. The owls want (as usual) everything to be done by *them* and the *Government.* I want *them* to do nothing but proclaim the facts, withdraw obstructions and let things take their course. The likes of Stockenstrom and Dundas might do some good in setting things agoing but this Mackay is such a weak creature and such a miserable tool of Col. Somerset that he'll put his foot in it.

The first fair was held in late March 1825 at Somerset, the *Gazette* announcing the setting up during the fair of 'an Agricultural Society for the Eastern Province of the Colony'. Stockenstrom took the chair and Landdrosts Dundas and Mackay were among the twenty-five founding members, as were Thomas's two brothers, the two surviving Rennie brothers and their friends Robert Hart and John Meares Devenish and, from Albany, Thomas Philipps. It had been Stockenstrom's idea but Pringle had brought the idea into the public domain, albeit under a pseudonym to save it from Governor Somerset's proscription.

He was in demand also by the Albany 'radicals', British country gentlemen translocated to the Zuurveld of South Africa and forced by a heartless regime in Cape Town to setting themselves up in opposition to Governor Somerset and his 'tools'. He told Fairbairn on 4 November 1825:

> The Albany Radicals are awaking from their slumbers and are pressing me, Pigot, Campbell and Philipps – to come down and write down their information. I have charged them to be busy and I'll be among them ere long.[4]

His knowledge – and recording – of the state of affairs in Albany was much increased before his meeting, six weeks later, with the 'radicals' there. Thomas Philipps, the leader among them, arrived at Eildon on 7 December 1825, with 'our mutual friend' H.E. Rutherfoord who was on a tour of the eastern districts. 'I had long an intention of visiting Mr Pringle'[5] and at last Philipps did so, with Rutherfoord, a strong supporter, and their interpreter the Christian convert, Diyani Tshatshu, son and heir of the Ntinde chief Tshatshu, whom he was to succeed. He later appeared before the Parliamentary Select Committee on Aboriginal Tribes

(British Settlements), know as the Aborigines Committee in London, in 1837.

They travelled by way of Somerset, visited Robert Hart en route, called briefly at Groot Willem Prinsloo's 'fine farm'. At Mrs Graham's farm, 'now occupied by a Bastard by the name of Classaker [Klaas Eckhard]' the farm people 'were particularly attentive to us, notwithstanding the presence of a Brandy Waggon from the District of George, to which most of them had been applying with visible effect'. This despite Pringle's efforts, through the unsympathetic landdrost, to forbid the brandy wagons access to Baviaans River. It took them more than two hours to reach Eildon, where they 'had the pleasure of meeting our good and amiable friends' and their hosts, William Pringle and his wife. Thomas and Margaret Pringle were preparing 'to leave the Colony, Mr Thomas Pringle intending to follow his literary pursuits in England'.

Philipps, Rutherfoord and Tshatshu were with the Pringles from 5 to 13 December. Philipps's journal recorded the second day, spent

> at home conversing on the past and passing political events, the success which had attended our mutual exertions, the gradual realization of almost all our hopes and wishes, the Recall, and the steady prospect of an entire change from despotism to freedom, to all of which Mr Pringle had very materially contributed, and was still continuing his exertions by representations to the Commissioners of Inquiry.

The 'Recall' of Lord Charles Somerset by Lord Bathurst, of which Philipps had learned in Grahamstown, was for Somerset to answer the many charges against him and he left for England in March 1826, when Pringle was awaiting his own departure.

Philipps, it must be said, had acted somewhat equivocally towards the Somersets, father and son. Of an influential landed family in Pembrokeshire he had planned to move from banking to politics as a loyal Whig until he fell out with the head of his family, Lord Milford, a staunch Tory. At the Cape he again found himself seeking the favour of a Tory patron, Lord Charles, despite the Whig principles that had led to his taking a party of settlers to the Cape in 1820. Pringle first referred to him, on hearing that he had received a further grant of land during Somerset's visit to Albany in 1825, as 'Radical or Courtier Philipps (I don't know which he is at present)'. A magisterial appointment had been hinted at in return for an address in praise of Somerset's administration but Philipps did not deliver and was duly passed over.

Philipps included in his journal a brief, wholly factual account of Pringle's career, much of it doubtless learned from Pringle himself, and said of him:

> Both Mr Pringle and Mr Rutherfoord are men of mild and philanthropic dispositions, with well cultivated minds, consequently their society is most interesting.[6]

Next day Rutherfoord and one of the Rennie brothers rode up to the Winterberg, Philipps and Pringle accompanying them as far as 'the source of the River, where his father resided'. They breakfasted with Robert Pringle 'a fine patriarchal character with snowy locks, surrounded by his Children and his grandChildren' and returned to Eildon later in the day. Next morning Pringle took 'some memoranda on the subject of past occurrences', since 'he might publish some account of the Cape when he went home'.

There was much talk of drought (but 'enough corn in rick to last a couple of years'), of locusts and lions. Philipps, Rutherfoord and Rennie rode over to Devenish's farm, Doornkroon, with 'the finest field of wheat I have ever seen in Africa' and on to the military post and an 'excellent dinner' with Dr Duncanson (the commanding officer, Major Rogers 'was gone to Grahams Town to a Ball') at which 'the claret was circulating'. They were back at Eildon in the morning, having stopped an hour with Georg Ludwig Krebs who had come to the Cape in 1817 as 'collector to the King of Prussia' in search of birds and animals and served zoologists well in his 25-year stay. He and the Pringles had been shipmates in their 'tedious and sleepy' voyage from Cape Town in April 1825.

On Sunday 11 December Philipps observed Pringle's

> usual congregation and it was pleasing to see them arrive, principally on horseback. Besides his own family it consisted of Classaker and his friends. Mr Pringle read chapters of the Bible in Dutch and it was gratifying to hear several of them afterwards, both men and women, read verses in turn, they sang two hymns in the same melodious voice for which the Hottentots are so celebrated.[7]

After the service Eckhard 'expressed his great regret to us that they would be so soon deprived of their Teacher'.

They continued their journey on 13 December after stopping 'to see some rude paintings done by Bushmen when they formerly occupied this Country, certainly not *less* than 30 years ago ... really singular when we reflect that they were done by an untutored savage race'. Thomas and Margaret, with Hinza Marossi, were to make their own departure less than a week later and their leave taking of the family at Clifton was painful:

> As I left the house I found it difficult to suppress my feelings when I viewed this assembly of Relations, who for the last time were associating together without the probability both from Age and distance of their ever again meeting in this World.

Though asked to share the last meal together they rode on so missed 'the last heart-rending, last farewell, between the Father and the Son and the Brother'.

Philipps and Rutherfoord's onward journey took them through Tembuland to Brownlee's mission on the Gwali which he and his family were about to leave for the Buffalo River, near Chief Tshatshu, where King William's Town now stands. Their last calls were at King Ngqika's Great Place and the fair at Fort Willshire.

On the eve of the fair they were told by arriving traders that Colonel Somerset had led a commando raid on 'some part of Cafferland, but on what part no one knew, as the object was kept a profound secret ... Surprise and sorrow were depicted in the countenances of all [white] ranks who heard the news', which was not told 'to the Caffres and thus lead to confusion at the Fair in the Morning'. This was the ill-famed 'blundering commando' on Ngqika's headman Nyoka, which put an end to Pringle's planned journey into independent Xhosa territory, due to begin that same day.

Philipps reached his farm, Glendour, on Christmas Eve, at the end of his 800–kilometre journey and was soon to see Thomas and Margaret Pringle again. They had left Eildon by ox-wagon, with Hinza Marossi and Khoikhoi drivers, on 19 December. They intended to 'cross the eastern frontier on my route and to spend a week or two visiting the various Missionary stations, and some of the principal Chiefs in the Amakosa territory – an object I had long in view'.[8] As they neared the frontier they learned that 'Colonel Somerset, with 200 men of the Cape cavalry and a party of boors, [had] made a sudden dash into Cafferland on the very day before that on which I meant to have crossed the border'.

It was a malign irony that Pringle's plans were thwarted by 'one of those execrable commandos' which he had attacked so vigorously, to the exasperation of Governor Somerset, who could tolerate no criticism of his son the Colonel.

The target of the raid, Neuka [Nyoka], Pringle likened to the robber-chief Donald Bean Lean, an anti-hero in *Waverley*. Not one but two Xhosa villages were attacked, the first that of Chief Bhotomane, previously on good terms with officials in the colony, where several women and children were shot dead. When their mistake was clear, captured cattle were returned and apology offered. One of King Ngqika's villages was then invaded, again unconnected with Nyoka. 'Amidst all this wretched blundering and murderous havoc' Nyoka and his men lay low in the forests and were not found. Five hundred cattle were driven off and later distributed 'among the burghers of Bavian's River and Bruintjes Hoogte', who had done all the shooting of 'the unresisting Caffers in breach of express orders to the contrary' but with complete impunity, as Pringle learned later in Grahamstown.

The visit to 'the Amakosa territory' had to be abandoned, with 'the unoffending population, throughout the whole frontier, … for the sake of a few stolen horses, thrown into a state of the most violent alarm and exasperation'. Two European stragglers from the returning commando were killed 'by the enraged Caffers. Had I happened to have been a single day earlier on my route, this might have been my own fate.'

The Philippses gathered the 'Albany Radicals' Pigot and Moodie and their wives to meet the Pringles and Philipps subsequently wrote to his widowed sister Catherine Richardson in Pembrokeshire in terms that he would not have used in the journal, intended, as it clearly was, for publication. Pringle advised Philipps that Fairbairn's infant *New Organ,* for which it had been written, had ceased publication, thwarted by Government after its single 6 January issue, and volunteered to convey the 'three full sheets' to England. Philipps gave Thomas and Margaret a letter of introduction to Catherine and told her:

> You will find them worthy people, downright Scotch. She laments excessively that she could not come round here in order to have *another* sight of the Ladies in order to give [you] the latest account of them.

He observed that Pringle's 'anxiety to get out of the Colony is so great that he cannot spare time. He is, and will be, a sharp thorn in Lord [Charles's] side'. Pringle was to see Catherine's 'compilation [of her brother's and sister-in-law's letters]' from which 'he may if possible glean a little' for his own book.

The reverse was to happen: Pringle contributed considerably, and anonymously, to Catherine's also anonymous *Scenes and Occurrences in Albany and Cafferland* (1827). The book was well received, the *Literary Gazette* calling it 'a delightful little volume written with great liveliness and observation … a treat for fireside travellers … bringing the scene completely before your eyes'.[9] The lion hunt, as in the journal, fills four columns. Even Theal, in 1913, found it 'pleasantly written' but having perhaps detected the hand of Pringle, whose writing he never failed to condemn, at least in part, added 'but there is nothing in it of any particular value'.[10] Philipps ended a letter to his sister: 'They are very plain people, he is lame and uses crutches … he is highly estimated by us all'.[11]

Pringle found time to send to the Commissioners from Grahamstown a full report of the 'blundering commando' raid on Nyoka, which formed the basis of his account in the *Narrative*. In two previous letters to the Commissioners Pringle 'refrained from offering any remarks upon the recent Commando of Col. Somerset' but did so on 12 January, having, surprisingly, heard Henry Somerset's description of the raid and checked it with several of his officers and also 'some of the Chumie Missionaries I have met with here'.[12]

He and Margaret reached Uitenhage by 17 January and from there 'sent a messenger to the [Algoa] Bay to get us a passage' to Cape Town, as he told Fairbairn, enclosing an article on the commando raid 'which I have taken some pains to have correct. I have heard Col. Somerset describe it *himself*' and mentions Brownlee as another source. He ended 'Mr Smith [Revd Alexander Smith, Presbyterian minister at Uitenhage, presumably the Pringles' host] sends his respects. So does Mrs P.'[13]

They eventually sailed in the brig *Mary* on 18 February 1825, listed as 'Mr and Mrs Pringle and one servant',[14] the latter being Hinza Marossi who became to them their much loved child, and were in Cape Town six days later. Pringle certainly worked on the Cape slavery paper for the *New Monthly Magazine* and doubtless made progress with Thompson's *Travels* in this enforced five weeks' leisure.

His commando report did not appear in the *Advertiser* but that to the Commissioners of Inquiry survived in Stockenstrom's *Autobiography* (1897).[15] It may also have been the basis of the account by Cory, who, despite his unswerving pro-settler position, showed a scientist's concern for facts. He sums up:

> Though the Eastern Province in subsequent years was greatly indebted to Colonel Somerset for his self-sacrificing devotion to the continued defence of the frontier, this unfortunate affair, at the time it happened, served to add to the obloquy which had been accumulating around the name of Somerset during the last four years of Lord Charles's reign.[16]

Lord Charles Somerset and his family sailed from Table Bay seven days after the Pringles' arrival. Thomas shared Fairbairn's amusement at the farewell dinner for Lord Charles, one of several, and the eulogies reported in the pro-Somerset *South African Chronicle*.[17] Bridekirk's *Chronicle*, edited by the equivocal Jardine, was to 'fold' in December of that year, while the *Advertiser,* revived in August 1825 with Fairbairn as editor, survived until March 1827 before temporary suppression on Earl Bathurst's orders in response to an anti-Somerset article reprinted from the London *Times*. Fairbairn and Greig soldiered on, and freedom of the press was finally legalized in the colony the following year. In the *Narrative* Pringle's praise was unstinting for Fairbairn's 'eminently influential' role in winning press freedom and in sowing what would become a 'goodly harvest of liberal principle, of generous sentiment, of humane feeling, of Christian goodwill … in the long neglected fields of Southern Africa'.[18]

Pringle spent seven weeks 'arranging our affairs'. As he also put it in the *Narrative*, 'some circumstances occurred which, with the kind aid of friends in Cape Town, enabled me so to arrange matters'[19] so that he could return to England. To have done so despite the losses amounting – by his account – to 'about £1000' is evidence of the trust in him shown by his creditors, *inter alios* his father, the Underwoods in London, Fairbairn, Greig, Philip, Rutherfoord and George Thompson and of the generosity of the last three named. Somehow he raised the passage money for Margaret, himself, Janet Brown and Hinza Marossi.

He had some 'very satisfactory interviews with the Commissioners of Inquiry and with General Bourke', acting for Somerset and later his successor, with whom a bond was formed which was later to serve their common purpose. With Sir Richard Plasket he settled the final assignment of lands to his fellow Scottish settlers on 31 March 1826, as 'head or representative of the Party of British settlers located at Bavians River in the District of Somerset and with the concurrence of all the heads of families'.[20] The settlement included 'to my Brother William Pringle the allotment in his possession called *Eildon*'. By arrangement with William when Thomas sold Eildon to him in 1825, he retained some 2,000 morgen of mountain veld on the western side of Eildon, known as Eland's Kloof.

He obtained also General Bourke's permission to take Hinza Marossi, then a seven- or eight-year-old, to England, through Plasket's good offices, 'to bring the boy up as a servant' but also 'to give him as good an education as his capacity and my circumstances may admit of, and to return him to the Colony when of adult age, should he then desire it'. Hinza, he wrote, 'appears perfectly contented to go any where with me'. He did not reach 'adult age', to Thomas and Margaret's great sadness, so was never to return.

Their outlook in England was bleak but, eternal optimist, despite his debts and lack of 'cursed cash … the misery of miseries', Pringle (now in his late thirties) expected good earnings from Captain Owen for ghosting his *Voyages*, compensation from Government for his losses due to Somerset's victimization, from the book he had been encouraged by Barrow to write six years earlier, and from literary work in London through Thomas Campbell, John Murray and others. Covertly editing Philipps's letters for his sister to publish as *Scenes and Occurrences in Albany and Cafferland* awaited him too and was not mentioned even to Fairbairn.

He remained committed to the struggle against Somerset, still governor though 'on leave' for questioning in Whitehall where attacks on his governorship were becoming an embarrassment. After 1823 'numerous petitions, protests and complaints against the Governor' began to 'pour into the Colonial Office'[21] and into the public prints. Somerset's sun was clearly setting.

The 'great cause' which Pringle championed with Philip, Stockenstrom, Fairbairn, Rutherfoord, Wright and others, remained the emancipation of the indigenous and the slaves in the colony and the protection and uplifting of those over the frontier. Support from the 'philanthropists' by the Albany settlers was in jeopardy, despite their past successful efforts for the settlers in their time of distress. Pringle was at a loss to understand 'a most furious letter from Capt. Campbell accusing Greig [i.e. the *Commercial Advertiser*] of making war on the settlers' and urged Fairbairn to 'come in today and consider whether it may be proper to notice their wrath or not'.[22] Were they 'mad or wrong headed' to be 'so violently annoyed by the plain facts of their situation being made known'? Far worse was to come and there were to be disappointments, but opportunities of promise loomed larger in Pringle's mind as his life in South Africa came to an end and he took the fight to the heart of the empire. Fairbairn came to see Thomas and his little family off in the brig, *Luna*, on 16 April 1826. They sailed next morning. Janet Brown wrote to him after their arrival in England, heedless of the correct grammar one might expect from a schoolmistress: 'When Mr and Mrs Pringle and me parted with you, you said you would see us again next day. I suppose we set out too early in the morning for you to get to town.'[23] Here was a small manifestation of Fairbairn's occasional lack of concern for his friend's interests, which was to do Pringle's memory infinite harm in time to come.

They arrived in London on 6 July 1826 after 'a rather tedious voyage of nearly twelve weeks', relieved by Pringle's making a friend of Captain Knox, as was his way, and 'all in pretty good health'.[24] Another temptation to providence, though unsuspected, as the third and final chapter of his stormy life began.

NOTES

[1] Pringle (1966), p. 217.
[2] Pringle to Fairbairn, 19.10.1825, Vigne (2011), p. 266. LP, Fairbairn Papers, 1, 102.
[3] Pringle to Fairbairn, 14.10.1825, Vigne (2011), p. 264. LP, Fairbairn Papers, 1, 100.
[4] Pringle to Fairbairn, 6.11.1825, Vigne (2011), p. 285. LP, Fairbairn Papers, 1, 116.
[5] Philipps (1960), p. 258.
[6] *Op. cit.*, p. 262.
[7] *Op. cit.,* p. 285. Dr James Duncanson, medical staff officer. Philipps has 'Duncannon'.
[8] Pringle (1966), p. 333.
[9] *Literary Gazette,* Cape Town, 26.5.1827, pp. 322–3.
[10] Theal, G.M., *Catalogue of Books and Pamphlets relating to South Africa South of the Zambezi* (1912), p. 263.
[11] Philipps (1960), p. 255.
[12] Stockenstrom, vol. 1, pp. 251–4.
[13] Pringle to Fairbairn, 17.1.1826, Vigne (2011), p. 294. LP, Fairbairn Papers, 1, 134.
[14] *Gazette,* 3.3.1826; Rennie, vol. 2, p. 610.
[15] Stockenstrom, vol. 1, pp. 251–4.
[16] Cory, vol. 2, pp. 238–9.
[17] Pringle to Fairbairn, -. 2.1826, Vigne (2011), p. 296. LP, Fairbairn, 1, 128.
[18] Pringle (1966), p. 332.
[19] *Ibid.*
[20] Pringle to Plasket, 13.3.1826, Assignation memorandum, CA CO 8459/66, Rennie 2, p. 619, Vigne (2009), p. 298. CA CO 293/83/375.
[21] Cory, vol. 2, p. 325.
[22] Pringle to Fairbairn, -.2.1826, Vigne (2011), p. 296. LP, Fairbairn Papers, 1, 128.
[23] Brown to Fairbairn, 1.9.1826, LP, Fairbairn Papers, 2, 76.
[24] Pringle to Fairbairn, 12.7.1825, Vigne (2011), p. p. 298. LP, Fairbairn Papers, 1, 132.

Part V

London Literary Life and the Anti-Slavery Campaign

(1826–1833)

16
London Journalist and Editor

On arrival in London, Thomas had £5 in his pocket, debts to meet in London as well as the mountain of them at the Cape, and four mouths to feed, with the Owen manuscript his only prospective source of income. The publishing trade was in a 'shocking state',[1] he told Fairbairn in his first letter, just six days after landing, having heard all the bad news at dinner at Longman's in Paternoster Row just before writing.

There had been 'great failures in London and Edinburgh. Hurst and Robinson here for half a million. Constable also for not much less. Constable's fall has brought down James Ballantyne and Ballantyne has involved Sir Walter Scott for about £40,000.' With his sterling capacity for sympathy for the plight of others when himself in a dire state, he added: 'Scott is said to be quite reduced – his estate, library, everything sold. This is hard after a laborious life – and he seems to be generally pitied.' We know now that Scott's mighty cash demands from his publisher Ballantyne, which, in secret, he partly owned, contributed to their, and his, financial ruin. Ruin it was, nonetheless, and his recovery from it heroic indeed.

Pringle borrowed £10, probably from his agents, Underwoods, though his debt to them had reached £380 and they 'seem somewhat vexed that I have no more cash for them'. The lodgings he found in Arundel Street, then a rather squalid lane running from the Strand to the river, cost only a guinea a week and he and Margaret said good-bye to her sister Janet, who returned to Scotland. A younger sister, Susan, a teacher like Janet, soon took her place. Poor Hinza, to whom Margaret had become deeply attached, was already suffering from the 'pulmonary complaint' which was soon to end his short life.

Pringle found himself cut off from his South African affairs. Though he saw Rutherfoord, Eaton and Dr Samuel Silverthorne Bailey of the Somerset Hospital in his first week, they were all near the end of their visits and had less news from the Cape than he had. On the English scene, he found that 'nothing at all had been done – the last session – on Lord C's business'.[2] Colonel Bird sailed back to Cape Town without their even meeting. Dr Philip, he told Fairbairn, hoped for 'a full exposé in the ensuing session' but Pringle did not think 'Dr Philip or any other of the Cape men know more than I do. Our general information is that the Home Government will, with the aid of the Commissioners of Inquiry, white wash the Lord if possible'.[3] Dr Philip had been in England since April 1826 and was to stay another year.

Pringle had his own future to concentrate on, his case for redress to pursue at the Colonial Office, as well as his present need: the housing and feeding of his wife, her sister and their surrogate child, the already ailing Hinza Marossi.

He managed at last to finish Thompson's *Travels and Adventures in Southern Africa* but his pleasure was taken away by Captain Owen's proving not the gentlemanly fellow he had taken him to be. Owen 'shuffled out' of their arrangement[4] and gave the ghosting of his book to another, Thomas Boteler, who had served under Owen as lieutenant in H.M.S. *Leven*. His *Narrative of a Voyage of Discovery in Africa, Asia and Madagascar* did not appear for another three years and Pringle, with uncharacteristic pique, spoke very ill of it.[5]

It was a small substitute for him to work with Mrs Catherine Richardson, sister of his Albany friend Thomas Philipps, on turning her brother's letters into one of the very few attractive and pleasing accounts of the settlers' life and environment. The anonymously published *Scenes and Occurrences in Albany and Cafferland, South Africa,* published early in 1827, shows numerous signs of Pringle's work on it: names corrected, such as Classaker in the transcribed letters, rectified as Klaas Eckhard, one of Pringle's mixed-race tenants, and Stockenstein as Stockenstrom. He greatly increased the exotic charm of the book by inserting his account of the Baviaans River lion hunt which he wrote and rewrote so many times, first in the *South African Journal* and finally in his *Narrative of a Residence in South Africa* at the end of his life. This time he added George Rennie's accounts of his encounters with elephants. Another insertion describes, in lyrical natural terms, Philipps's journey from Grahamstown to Somerset, with detail better known to Pringle than Philipps, nowhere to be found in Philipps's letters and scarcely covered in his own *Narrative*, perhaps to maintain concealment of his hand in the *Scenes and Occurrences*. Both make lively reading and the little book's attraction was further enhanced by the addition of a hand-coloured aquatint of the mouth of the Kowie River, commissioned by Pringle.

Scenes and Occurrences was well received, not least by Philipps himself who wrote to thank Pringle for 'the assistance you rendered to my sister in her undertaking. She speaks of it in the warmest terms'. To his sister he wrote 'now, my dear Kate, how shall I express my obligation to you and all able assistants for the trouble you have had in ornamenting my simple tales and ushering them into the great world?'[6] The assistants were presumably Pringle, the unknown artist and the publisher, William Marsh, London. Major-General King, later Kate's second husband, was thanked for his 'elegant introduction to my narrative'.

Thompson's *Travels and Adventures* had allowed Pringle scope to express the liberal sentiments towards the indigenous people that he shared with Thompson. Philipps's liberal views were more moderate but Pringle did not forget 'the cause' in his preface to *Scenes and Occurrences*. The *Monthly Review,* first of the journals to publish book reviews, maintained the Whiggish views of its founder in 1749, the non-conformist bookseller Ralph Griffiths. The reviewer singled out Pringle's pro-African stance in a ten-page review and was

happy to find our author confirming the opinion which we have long presumed and entertained of the native South-African tribes. We have lifted up our voices against the cruelties

which have been committed against that people under ...our colonial laws. ... whatever crimes they may have perpetrated were much more to be attributed to the harsh, and frequently inhuman policy which was adopted towards them, both by their Dutch and British masters, than to any incorrigible propensity to wickedness inherent in their own nature.[7]

He quoted 'the author' on the Bantu-speaking Africans who were Philipps's and Pringle's neighbours on the eastern frontier:

The natives of this part of Africa ... are a fine race of people, infinitely superior in phys-ical energies and in manly appearance to the other tribes of that quarter of the globe, and possessing mental capabilities which may hereafter render them a flourishing and happy people.

He found them

capable of receiving and justly appreciating the blessings of civilization; ... to be susceptible of gratitude for favours received as well as deserving of confidence bestowed.

These were views that would have found little support in white South Africa and which showed an intensifying of his own feelings towards the abaThembu and amaXhosa with whom he had had dealings.

The entertainment value of Pringle's contribution was clearly to be seen in the *Literary Gazette* of 26 May 1827, where *Scenes and Occurrences* was seen as

a delightful little volume, written with great liveliness and observation. It will be a treat indeed to fireside travellers for the author possesses to a great degree the faculty of bringing the scene completely before your eyes, witness the following lion hunt.

and there were two columns containing the entire text of the oft-told tale.

Pringle divided his time between such light relief (albeit inserting some polemic for 'the cause') and his campaigning. His major article on slavery at the Cape which he had written in Uitenhage in January while waiting for a ship from Algoa Bay appeared in Campbell's *New Monthly Magazine* as 'Letter from South Africa: No 1 Slavery' in October 1826. It did not take long to create a turning point in his life and lead to his first paid employment since his days with Thomas Thomson at the Register House in Edinburgh eight years earlier and his year as sub-librarian in Cape Town. This time it was to be an employment in a cause to which he was totally committed, the abolition of slavery.

His breadwinning journalism went on. The literary contacts he had made in his few weeks in London before sailing to the Cape and his occasional correspondence with Thomas Campbell, his friendship with Dr Waugh, which doubtless led to the latter's son-in-law, the bookseller Thomas Underwood, serving as his agent, had, probably more than his Edinburgh journalism, all kept his name alive. He was approached by editors and publishers needing to fill the need for good copy for the magazines and review journals. Many had sprung up despite the great slump in the booktrade that had impoverished Scott and brought down others.

The energetic and ever busy Alaric Watts, who had edited the *New Monthly Magazine* for Campbell during Pringle's Cape years, sent him an 'elegant present' in August 1926, the *Literary Souvenir,* one of the best of the new Christmas annuals that had followed the vogue begun by Rudolf Ackerman's *Forget-me-not,* the first and longest lasting of them (1823–60). The collection of illustrated prose and verse had proved very marketable in Germany and the formula soon caught on in England. He sent Watts seven unpublished poems but advised him that two of them, 'a sonnet and song about the Bushman' would appear in 'the little volume of poems relating to South Africa' he planned to bring out that winter.[8]

He told Watts that he hoped to produce 'some South African tales to illuminate the character and condition of the Native tribes', but was 'so pressed by other engagements that he could not promise them even for the Christmas 1828 *Souvenir,* though Watts was offering 'more substantial remuneration'. Money was clearly coming in, though in his letters to Fairbairn he continued to ask for his friend's help in meeting his creditors' demands at the Cape. He was finding it very hard 'to make up the £25' he was paying Underwoods' quarterly, a debt incurred by the requirements for the academy, now in other hands. His time was soon to be taken up, and his finances modestly improved, by the impact of his *New Monthly Magazine* 'Letter from South Africa: No 1 Slavery'. *Ephemerides; or Occasional Poems, written in Scotland and South Africa* did not appear until the spring of 1828.

Another contact he had maintained at the Cape was with the flamboyant maverick James Silk Buckingham, whose monthly *Oriental Herald* he was contributing to by October 1826 and putting his South African case (but not his own). He told Fairbairn that he expected to write for 'two or three other journals in various shapes to assail the vagabonds'.[9] He was assailing them alone, having 'no communion with Burnett and his set' and finding Dr Philip concerned only with the Khoisan (and presumably with writing at top speed his *Researches in South Africa*), while the London Missionary Society were 'paralysed for fear of being branded "politicians".' He had 'put my fist into the Press, however, and will give them [Somerset and his 'tools' in the Cape Government] a rounding up before I cease with them'.

His work for the *Oriental Herald* went on for two years until Buckingham closed the magazine down. Of the many magazines he started and closed the *Oriental Herald* survived the longest – 1824 to 1829 – perhaps because it promoted his personal campaign against the Hon. East India Company's trade monopoly with the sub-continent.

It was typical of Pringle to bear no grudge towards Buckingham for stopping a source of his income. His abiding grievances over his victimization by Lord Charles Somerset and his 'tools' in the Cape Government were in strong contrast and indicate the deep hurt he had suffered at their hands, both morally and materially.

He published in the *Oriental Herald* fourteen of his own poems and ten articles critical of the Cape Government, as well as the anonymous eight-pager, 'Slavery at the Cape of Good Hope'. This was clearly the work of his friend, the socially maladroit clergyman William Wright, who was able to call Dr John Philip as a witness to the 'treatment of the Hottentot race generally',[10] Philip's *Researches in South Africa, illustrating the Civil, Moral and Religious Condition of the Native Tribes* having appeared in 1828. A paper on the disastrous commando against Chief Nyoka written by Pringle's half-pay officer friend Hugh Huntley, then farming near Uiten-hage, followed. Pringle had told Fairbairn as early as 30 September 1826 'You will see by the *Oriental Herald* for Oct. what I am about there [i.e. in the press]', but he was now ready to move on. Relinquishing the editorship, he told Fairbairn, 'led me to more important and more agreeable pursuits'.

Of these, the most to his credit was his editorship of one of the best of the annuals, *Friendship's Offering*, in which his poem 'A Noon-day Dream' had already appeared. He was now able to commission prose, verse and illustrations with an authority he had lacked in his time with *Blackwood's* and Constable's *Edinburgh Magazine* ten years before, with William Blackwood interfering and politically hostile and his co-editor, the abrasive and disliked Cleghorn, a major handicap. This time his old *Blackwood's* adversary John Wilson, who had so heartlessly humiliated him in the 'Chaldee MS' spoof in 1818, welcomed his editorship, most surprisingly as this was in the 'Noctes Ambrosianae' series where scorn and insult were more common than praise.

'The Shepherd' (an often unkind caricature of James Hogg) asks 'Christopher North' (John Wilson) during their nightly revels at Ambrose's tavern: 'What say you to your auld frien' Pringle the editor o' the Friendship's Offering, sir?' 'North' replies:

> I say, James, that Mr Pringle himself is a pleasing poet and amiable man, that he possesses peculiar qualifications for being the Editor of an Annual, and I have no doubt that his will be one of the best of the whole set.[11]

For several pages the discussion included the *Bijou, Christmas Box, Forget-me-not, Gem, Keepsake* and *Souvenir*, with appreciation rather than sarcasm. Other journals and many writers were equally pleased and respectful. *The Literary Gazette*, praising 'the little annual books that have become so much in the fashion during the last three or four years' found 'the embellishments of the *Friendship's Offering* mostly admirable' in 1828, but was distinctly cool two years later. The writer took Pringle to task being 'at a loss to discover in what it is so much superior to its competitors'. The poetry was 'rather in want of originality', with exceptions noted in William Kennedy and the Revd George Croly,[12] very minor figures today in comparison with John Clare, Hogg, Mary Russell Mitford and Pringle himself, who all contributed to the 1830 issue. Pringle had gone to great pains to reprint the ballad revived by Lady Anne Barnard, 'Auld Robin Gray', with the help of Sir Walter Scott – and his permission since it had been published before only by the Bannatyne Club in Edinburgh, of which Scott was chairman. 'The history of the ballad, and the ballad "Auld Robin Gray" are too well known to have needed repetition' the *Literary Gazette* complained. The prose too was 'below standard'.

Perhaps Pringle was experiencing an envious attack by a supporter of a rival annual. He wrote to James Hogg that he and his friend and fellow Borderer Allan Cunningham, who launched his own annual, *The Anniversary,* that year, 'though editors of rival Annuals have agreed to write for each other, in scorn of the paltry jealousy which activates some of our compeers'.[13]

The annuals became very popular, the most successful selling upwards of ten thousand copies, and few writers kept aloof. Charles Lamb did so, as did Wordsworth, until he sent poems in 1827 to *Winter's Wreath* at the request of Joanna Baillie. The profits were to go to charity but both were unaware that *Winter's Wreath* was 'to be periodical'. Wordsworth's polite refusal of Pringle's invitation to contribute to *Friendship's Offering* in 1828 pointed out that he had been 'betrayed if I may so – with an apparent breach of a Rule I had laid down to myself'. He had the grace to end the letter with 'acknowledgments for an elegant sonnet you have done the honour of addressing to me'. The letter was addressed to '9 Flask Walk, Hampstead' though the Pringles were still living in Solly Terrace, Pentonville.[14] He knowingly broke his rule in 1828 when, needing the money, he wrote a poem, 'The Country Girl', for *The Keepsake*.

The annuals catered for a middle-brow, mainly female readership and strove for the highest standards of text and illustration, the engravings being a major feature. Pringle made sure that his issues would bring no blush to the reader's cheek – a phrase he used in returning to Hogg a poem (for the 1830 edition) which might do so. *Blackwood's* published Hogg's riposte in a comic poem, in which the narrator decides to write some verses called 'The Miser's Grave' and sell them to *Friendship's Offering, Forget-me-not* (edited by Shoberl), the Halls' *The Amulet* or A.A. Watts's *Literary Souvenir.*

> The title will secure a ready market
> Into the Annuals. Pringle has applied.
> I don't like Pringle, he's too finical,
> And so pragmatical about his slaves.
> I'll try the German Shovel-Board. He pays.
> Or Hall. But then his wife's the devil there!
> And Watts is ruin'd by false self-conceit.[15]

Friendship's Offering was praised for its embossed leather binding and the quality of its engravings, the latter commissioned by Pringle rather than his publishers, and fellow Scots, Smith, Elder and Co. Perhaps it was they and not Pringle who conceived for that 1830 issue what has in the past few years been proclaimed as the first dust jacket, discovered by a keen-eyed librarian at the Bodleian Library in Oxford in 2009.[16] The production of the annuals was seldom commented on, with praise or blame, by contemporary critics, though the quality of the engravings was a common theme. A.A. Watts's memoir by his son, many years later, recalled that

> by 1828 *Friendship's Offering* had ceased to be a pocketbook [*taschenbuch*] at all and in its new and improved form had become a formidable rival. It had always been ably conducted and survived to receive in latter days contributions from Mr Tennyson and Mr Ruskin.[17]

Both Tennyson and Ruskin had, by 1884 when the memoir was published, become great men of the Victorian age, but both had been recruited by Pringle at the start of their careers, in the quieter reign of William IV. The seven issues of his editorship brought in some of the major writers of that earlier age and most of the minor ones who were shared among the many competing annuals.

Of the many minor poets there are names remembered today, like Barry Cornwall (B.W. Proctor), Allan Cunningham, Mrs Ellis (Sarah Stickney), Felicia Hemans, the prolific Quakers William and Mary Howitt and William's brother Richard, Letitia Landon (L.E.L.), Mary Russell Mitford, James Montgomery (in whose 'Cry from South Africa' Pringle had to correct the facts), Caroline Norton, and, better known for their prose writings, Agnes Strickland and her sister Susanna, later Moodie, perhaps beginning her friendship with the Pringles.

Many of them appeared in rival annuals as did their editors and publishers, such as J.S. Buckingham, Josiah Conder (Pringle's earliest biographer), S.C. Hall (of *Forget-me-not*, perhaps in part the original of Dickens's odious Mr Pecksniff), W.H. Harrison (a later successor of Pringle as editor), T.K. Hervey (Pringle's predecessor), William Jerdan, Charles Knight, Cyrus Redding, Leitch Ritchie (editor of the *Englishman's Magazine*, and another early biographer) and Thomas Roscoe.

After much cajoling he published Fairbairn's 'The Nameless Spring' and 'The Heart's Confession' in 1830 and even Dr Philip's brief description, in prose, of tropical sunsets. Some of his authors appeared in more than a few issues and often with more than a single contribution. The highest score – 34 contributions – was his own, beginning with 'A Noon-Day's Dream' in 1828 and his 'Spenserian epic' begun at Genadendal in 1824, 'Glen-Lynden: a Tale of Teviotdale' the following year, covering 17 pages, after its publication in 1828 as a single slim volume. 'The Bechuana Boy' in 1830 after Hinza Marossi's death, reduced a correspondent, quoted by Leitch Ritchie, and his mother to tears. Pringle's response to these

> tributes, which I highly prize, not from any particular vanity but because it satisfies me that my aim to attain the simple language of truth and nature has not been entirely unsuccessful. *Condensation* and *simplicity* are *now* my great aim in my poetical attempts, for without these I am satisfied that nothing I may write will live or deserve to live.[18]

Most of his contributions had been published before, like 'O, the Ewe-bughting's Bonny' in 1834, dating back to his discovery of Lady Grizel Baillie's lines in 1816. His verse was generally praised as 'elegant' but the *Literary Gazette's* very brief review of the 1832 issue, though it praised the binding as 'handsome and lasting' found Pringle's 'Dream of Fairyland' 'not among his happiest efforts'.[19] He himself called it 'wishy washy' to Susanna Strickland.[20]

Despite the lasting effects of the long succession of his detractors, from the days of Lockhart and Wilson, through William Blackwood's biographer, Mrs Oliphant and down to the American Professor E.L. Griggs in 1951, his name has been kept alive in European and American literary scholarship by his association, as their editor, with some of the major poets and writers of his day. His letters to Sir Walter Scott, James Hogg and John Clare have survived, and much about his friendship, near the end of their lives, with Samuel Taylor Coleridge, from the latter's praise of 'Afar in the Desert' in 1828 until their last days. He published the Poet Laureate, Robert Southey's 'Funeral Song' in 1828, Edward George Bulwer-Lytton in 1832, John Galt in 1831 and 1832, and in 1833 an early manifestation of what became Victorian triumphalism, 'The Armada', by Thomas Babington (later Lord) Macaulay, son of Zachary, his co-editor of the *Anti-Slavery Monthly Reporter*. From its start: 'Attend all ye who list to hear our noble England's name', Macaulay's ringing iambic heptameters seem to herald the coming age.

Asked by Fairbairn at the Cape for 'some literary news. Who are the illustrissimi of the day?'[21] he could name only two unfamiliar to Fairbairn, 'Tennyson and Elliott … two new poets of very considerable powers, though with a great mixture of alloy'. The work of Ebenezer Elliott, an iron-founder, whose *Corn Law Rhymes* had great success in 1830 is unread today but the young Tennyson, 22 when Pringle published his sonnet, 'Me my own fate to lasting sorrow doometh' in 1832 and reprinted (from the *Englishman's Magazine*, probably arranged with the owner, Edward Moxon, Dr Waugh's son-in-law) 'Check every outflash', but the latter against Tennyson's wishes. His friend Arthur Hugh Hallam had submitted it and, Tennyson wrote to Pringle, 'for more reasons than one I could wish it had been suffered to moulder in the dead body of that ex-periodical, but the stars rule all things'.[22] He had written a month earlier 'I will receive your *Friendship's Offering* with open arms' and that he lived in hope 'of being introduced to your *Ephemerides*'. In the December letter he thanked Pringle for the pleasure the book, published in 1828, had given him, and ended: 'The volume is without doubt faulty, but certainly not so much so as that of mine [*Poems, Chiefly Lyrical,* 1830] … I like the evening Rambles and that sonnet on the Missionary better than anything else in the book; the last is very perfect'. His judgment here was faulty too: 'The man who could write it will not flow an altogether nameless stream, through the nineteenth century'.[23] He wrote the same day to Edward Moxon to send Pringle a copy of his new *Poems*, already published, though dated 1833.

His appreciation of Pringle reappears in 1837 in a letter to Moxon, publisher of Pringle's *Poetical Works* in that year: 'You may put me down for one copy of Pringle's Works. But for my poverty I would order more'.[24]

The biography of George Smith of Smith, Elder tells us that their annual had a circulation of eight to ten thousand copies and gives us a glimpse of the actual publication of *Friendship's Offering,* which

> was a notable event. For two or three days before its appearance everybody remained after the shop had closed. Tables were set out, and we sealed up each copy in a wrapper [that first dust jacket?]. When the work was all over we were regaled with wine and cake, and sang songs.[25]

The partners were both Scots, as was their young shop-boy, Charles Richardson. Perhaps Pringle joined in with one of the lays he had hoped to enjoy with Fairbairn after Genadendal.

It was Charles Richardson who brought Pringle into the life of another great Victorian-to-be, who wrote of him, however, with a not altogether good-natured condescension, so unlike Tennyson's pleasant relationship, or Coleridge's warm friendship. Richardson the 'shop-boy' told Pringle, regularly in Smith, Elder's offices as editor and author, 'wonderful things of his little student-cousin', John Ruskin, not yet in his teens. Pringle was invited to lunch at the Herne Hill home of the prosperous sherry importer, John James Ruskin of Ruskin, Domecq and Co., and, his 11- or 12-year-old son John wrote late in life, 'partly in the look-out for thin compositions of tractable stucco wherewith to fill interstices in the masonry of *Friendship's Offering,* Mr Pringle visited us … and sometimes took away copies of [my] verses in his pocket'.[26]

Pringle he described as 'a pious Scotch missionary and minor – very much minor – key poet ..., mentioned once or twice with a sprinkling of honour in Lockhart's Life of Scott'. Young Ruskin found him

a strictly conscientious and earnest, accurately trained, though narrowly learned, man, with all the Scottish conceit, restlessness for travel, and petulant courage of the Parks and Living-stones; with also some pretty tinges of romance and inklings of philosophy to mellow him, he was an admitted, though little regarded, member of the best literary circles, and acquainted, in the course of catering for his little embossed octavo, with everybody in the outer circles, and lower, down to little me.

Pringle, Ruskin wrote from what he learned later, had had Scott as a patron and corresponded politely with Wordsworth and Rogers and enjoyed 'familiar intercourse with the Ettrick Shepherd'. In his 'book of poems on the subject of Africa' [presumably *Ephemerides*, published at this time], Ruskin continued in this belittling vein 'antelopes were called springboks and other African manners and customs carefully observed.' Pringle, he continued, and the story is worth telling as a clue to his reason for such disparagement:

was the first person who intimated to my father and mother, with some decision, that there were as yet no wholly trustworthy indications of my one day occupying a higher place in English literature than either Milton or Byron, and accordingly I think none of us attached much importance to his opinions.

Nevertheless, recognizing John James Ruskin's 'high natural powers and exquisitely romantic sensibility', and Margaret Ruskin's evangelical beliefs which – wrong again – 'he set himself apart to preach', he 'became an honoured, though never quite cordially welcomed, guest on occasions of state Sunday dinner; and more or less an adviser thenceforward on the mode of my education'.

Pringle, recognizing the boy Ruskin's love of nature and versifying skill, duly took him on a 'Delphic pilgrimage' to visit the revered poet Samuel Rogers. In his *Praeterita* (1899), Ruskin does not mention that he had been given Rogers's *Italy*, with its superb Turner engravings for his twelfth birthday.

The old man ... was sufficiently gracious to me, though the cultivation of germinating genius was never held by Mr Rogers to be an industry altogether delectable to genius at its zenith. Moreover, I was unfortunate in the line of observations by which, in return for his notice, I endeavoured to show myself worthy of it. I congratulated him with enthusiasm on the beauty of the engravings by which his poems were illustrated, – but betrayed, I fear me, at the same time, some lack of an equally vivid interest in the composition of the poems themselves. At all events, Mr Pringle – I thought at the time, somewhat abruptly – diverted the conversation to subjects connected with Africa. These were doubtless more calculated to interest the polished minstrel of St James's Place.

Young John was guilty of a further misdemeanour when paying court to the great man by:

allowing my own attention, as my wandering eyes too frankly confessed, to determine itself on the pictures glowing from the crimson-silken walls; and accordingly, after we had taken leave, Mr Pringle took occasion to advise me that, in future, when I was in the company of distinguished men, I should listen more attentively to their conversation.[27]

He tells somewhat grudgingly that his shop-boy cousin brought with him to Herne Hill Smith, Elder's 'most ambitious publications, especially choosing, on my behalf, any which chanced to contain good engravings' such as by Clarkson Stanfield and James Duffield Harding, his drawing master in the 1840s. Neither of these were used as illustrations by Pringle. Ruskin gave most credit to the 1827 *Forget-me-not*, a present from an aunt, 'with a beautiful engraving' of a painting by Prout, which was the 'most precious and continuous in deep effect upon me'. Collingwood's biography, however, credits *Friendship's Offering* where Ruskin does not: 'Mrs Ruskin in a letter of 31 October 1829, finds "the poetry very so-so" but John evidently made the book his model'.[28]

Margaret Ruskin was slighting all round. In November 1829 she wrote to her husband, away travelling with Mr Domecq: 'the plates are well done but they are not interesting, the tales are horrible enough … upon the whole it does not improve'.

Did Pringle's reproof after the meeting with Rogers rankle after all those years? For so he recalled it in his rightly celebrated but often erroneous memoir, *Praeterita*. He gave no thanks for Pringle's guidance, for the meeting with Rogers, whose *Italy*, with its engraving after Turner which 'set the entire direction of my life's work', nor for commissioning the 15-year-old's first published work.

Pringle wished to use a particularly fine engraving of Salzburg in his last issue of *Friendship's Offering*, dated 1835, which he was putting together in the early summer of 1834. Knowing of the Ruskins' continental tour in 1833, he asked John for some verses to go with the plate. They were, according to Collingwood, 'written and rewritten' and sent to Pringle.[29] Before Christmas 1834 the 1835 issue arrived and 'on opening it, there were his "Andernach" and "St Goan" [under the title 'Fragments from a Metrical Journal', chosen by Pringle from Ruskin's MS in his care] and his 'Saltzburg' [*sic*] opposite a beautifully engraved plate … in Turner's manner more or less, "Engraved by E. Goodall from a drawing by W. Purser"'. He contributed to *Friendship's Offering* for many years to come and hailed Pringle's successor-but-one, W.H. Harrison, as his first editor and literary master. He delighted, jocular and unfeeling to the last, that 'The rigidly moral muse of Mr Pringle had by this time gone to Africa, or, let us hope, Arabia Felix, in the other world'.[30]

Pringle's only surviving reference to his encounters with the Ruskins is in an undated letter to Fairbairn, which hardly bears out Ruskin's depiction of him as a narrow and earnest 'Scotch missionary':

Dr F.

I send you this which I have just rec'd. Read and review it in your paper and tell the Colonists that I have sent it for their improvement. It is full of valuable information. This reprint is published here by my friend Mr Ruskin of the house of Domecq and Co., so often mentioned by the author. They are the greatest sherry merchants in England. I have drunk at Mr Ruskin's table sherry 80 years old, and which sells at 26 shillings a bottle. I think this book is full of facts which the Cape Wine Growers might greatly profit by. What should hinder Greig from reprinting it at the Cape? Only 500 copies have been printed here. The

Editor's Preface was written by me at the request of my friend Mr Ruskin. T.P.

If the Cape wine farmers don't exert themselves to improve their wine I have no doubt they will be entirely cut out in a short time by the Australians – just as they were in merino wool.

Poetic justice in every sense, perhaps, that the letter does not mention the 12-year-old prodigy John Ruskin. Mr Ruskin's, or his author's, expert account of sherry is lost to us, as is Pringle's preface: the archives of the House of Domecq were disposed of in recent years and no copy of the little book or the reprint has been found.

Poetic justice too that Pringle is remembered as a friend, even a hero, of the people of South Africa, black and white, while Ruskin's only link with them is a distasteful one in today's judgment. His inaugural lecture at Oxford in 1870, three years before Cecil Rhodes entered the university but still circulating in print, is thought by many to have inspired Rhodes's imperialist ambitions. England, Ruskin had declaimed, 'must found colonies as fast as she is able … seizing any piece of fruitful waste ground she can set her foot on, and teaching the colonists that … their first aim is to be to advance the power of England by land and sea'.[31] The border Scot, born only a few miles from Flodden field, would have been revolted by such English vainglorious jingoism.

NOTES

[1] Pringle to Fairbairn, 12.7.1826. Vigne (2011), p. 299. LP, Fairbairn Papers, 1, 132.

[2] *Op. cit.,* p. 298.

[3] Pringle to Fairbairn, 30.9.1826. Vigne (2011), p. 302. LP, Fairbairn Papers, 1, 134.

[4] *Op. cit,* p. 303.

[5] Pringle to Napier, 31.10.1833. Vigne (2011), p. 357. BL Add. MS 34616.

[6] Philipps to Pringle; Philipps to C. Richardson. Philipps to Maj. Gen. King, 22.8.1827. Philipps (1960), p. 320.

[7] *The Monthly Review,* September 1827, pp. 201–02.

[8] Pringle to Watts, 10.8.1826, Vigne (2011), p. 301. J. Rylands Lib. Eng MS 382/1650.

[9] Pringle to Fairbairn, 30.9.1826, Vigne (2011), p. 303. LP, Fairbairn Papers, 1, 134.

[10] *The Oriental Herald,* No 64, April 1826, pp. 323–33.

[11] *Blackwood's,* November 1828; *Noctes Ambrosianae,* ed. R.S. Shelton (1854), vol. 3, p. 173.

[12] *Literary Gazette* No 718, 28.10.1830, p. 960.

[13] Pringle to Hogg, NLS MS 2245 f 101–2.

[14] Wordsworth to Pringle, 21.6.1828. Paver letters, Cory Lib.

[15] *Blackwood's,* June 1831, p. 96. In contemporary usage (see *OED*), 'pragmatical', as used here, denoted officious or interfering, and 'finical' excessively punctilious.

[16] *The Guardian,* London, 24.4.2009, 'Earliest known book jacket discovered in Bodleian Library'.

[17] Watts, A.A., *Alaric Watts: a Narrative of his Life,* 2 vols (1884), vol. 2, p. 268.

[18] Pringle (1838), p. cxliii.

[19] *Literary Gazette,* No 769, 15.10.1831, p. 664.

[20] See p. 211, n. 21.

[21] Pringle to Fairbairn, 19.1.1833, Vigne (2011), p. 349. WUL, Philip Family Papers, A85.

[22] Tennyson to Pringle, 13.12.1832; Sotheby's Catalogue, 29.10.1969.

[23] *Ibid.*

[24] Tennyson to Moxon, 2.7.1832; Fitzwilliam Museum MS; Ledbetter, p. 85.

[25] Smith, G.M., 'Recollections of a long and busy life', NLS MS 23191; B. Bell, 'George Murray

Smith'. *ODNB* (2004).

26 Ruskin, John, *Praeterita. The Autobiography of John Ruskin* (1896 ed.), p. 127.

27 *Op. cit.,* pp. 126–9.

28 Collingwood, W.G., *The Life of John Ruskin* (1893), p. 5; *The Ruskin Letters*, vol. 1, p. 208.

29 Collingwood, p. 43.

30 Lutyens, M., *Millais and the Ruskins* (1967), p. 45.

31 Rotberg, R.I., *The Founder. Cecil Rhodes and the Pursuit of Power* (1988), p. 94.

17

The Literary Life and Cape Achievements

Pringle reached the age of forty on 5 January 1829, a year that was to be in many ways a turning point in his life. His financial plight was still a sore trouble to him. He wrote to Hogg in March 1829 that he had been 'absolutely overwhelmed with work, all the forenoon with my office and my evenings occupied' with editorships of both the *Oriental Herald* and *Friendship's Offering,* Owen's MSS and 'scribbling for two other periodicals … This is too much on my hands – but I am scribbling to make all the Siller I can to clear off old scores'.[1] Nevertheless, there was much to please him. Lord Charles Somerset had resigned when Bathurst and Lord Liverpool's other high Tory ministers had left office on Canning's succeeding Liverpool as Prime Minister in 1827. Somerset had escaped punishment and even censure, but had been discredited in the public mind.

He was succeeded by Lieutenant General Sir Richard Bourke, who shared the determination of Dr Philip and his friends to emancipate the Khoikhoi. He was to work closely with Pringle in their attempt to repatriate the 'last chief of the Hottentots', David Stuurman, from New South Wales, to which he had been transported as a convict in 1823. Stuurman died in 1830 a year before his release was effected. Bourke's and Pringle's interaction came about from an unusual overlap of Pringle's literary and humanitarian commitments. Bourke had arrived at the Cape as Lieutenant Governor of the Eastern Districts in 1825 and was acting governor in Somerset's absence 'on leave' – polite fictions for Bourke's being in place to succeed Somerset.

Having read Pringle's account of Stuurman's case in the *New Monthly Magazine,* with its trenchant statement on Stuurman's transportation to Botany Bay: 'Such was the fate of the last Hottentot chief who attempted to stand up for the rights of his countrymen',[2] Bourke immediately wrote to the governor of New South Wales (whom he was to succeed in 1831) and obtained a 'ticket of leave' for Stuurman. Sadly, as Pringle wrote in his *African Sketches,* 'the "last chief of the Hottentots" had been released by death before General Bourke reached his new government'.[3] The efforts of the 'upright and benevolent General Bourke' and of Pringle, who had raised the funds for Stuurman's return to South Africa, had been in vain.[4] This melancholy incident nevertheless put Pringle in a relationship with the Governor of the Cape the very opposite to that which he had suffered with Somerset.

The literary-political overlap was to be seen also through his connexion with

Samuel Rogers, a dominant figure among English poets and writers and at the centre of the social world (a status the young John Ruskin seems not to have valued). Pringle, to whom Rogers showed much kindness, was unable to attend one of Rogers's 'breakfasts' and was told by him when they met next day:

> I am sorry you were not with us yesterday. We had your old friend Wilmot Horton with us. In the course of conversation I asked him if, among the changes that were taking place, we were to have Lord Bathurst and himself back again at the Colonial Office. Mr Horton, starting to his feet, exclaimed with great vehemence: 'No! that d—d *Times* has turned us out of office and will keep us out of office'.[5]

Dr Philip, in a letter of 1831, continued the story: 'The paragraph in the *Times* to which he referred was a series of strictures on the Government of Lord Charles Somerset and they were all supplied by Mr Pringle'. Pringle nowhere claimed to have fed the *Times* the 'strictures' that helped bring down Liverpool's ministry.[6]

And yet he had, he was to write in *African Sketches,* 'published a detailed account of the whole of these frontier transactions in a periodical work of extensive circulation' in order to 'add my feeble voice to the far more powerful ones, which, I trust, will soon be raised to claim for the injured African JUSTICE and REDRESS'.[7] With Parliamentary Papers for 1827 (the Commission of Inquiry report), Sir Rufane Donkin's and Colonel Bird's pamphlets he listed the *Oriental Herald*, 1826–8 and Saxe Bannister's *Humane Policy, or Justice to the Aborigines of New Settlements* (London, 1830) as 'additional evidence' of the 'flagitious injustice which has been done to the Native Tribes of South Africa'.

As victorious for Pringle and his friends as the resignation of Somerset was Bourke's promulgation in August 1827 of Ordinance No 50, the *Magna Carta* of the Khoisan. Its second clause could have been drafted at the Graaff-Reinet meeting of Philip, Stockenstrom and Pringle, with Murray, Read and Wright, in July 1825:

> And whereas by usage and custom of this Colony, Hottentots and other free persons of colour have been subject to certain restraints as to their residence, mode of life, and employment, and to certain compulsory services to which others of His Majesty's subjects are not liable: be it therefore enacted that from and after the passing of this Ordinance, no Hottentot or other free person of colour, lawfully residing in this Colony, shall be subject to any compulsory service to which other of His Majesty's subjects therein are not liable, nor to any hindrance, molestation, fine, imprisonment, or punishment of any kind whatsoever, under the pretence that such person has been guilty of vagrancy or any other offence, unless after trial in due course of law; any custom or usage to the contrary in anywise notwithstanding.[8]

Other clauses established the right of Khoisan and other 'free persons of colour … to purchase or possess land in this Colony', and dealt with contracts of employment, wages, apprenticeships, safeguarding the rights of the formerly oppressed Khoisan and others. The ordinance was drafted by Judge William Westbrook Burton, but Pringle argued convincingly that Stockenstrom 'had the merit of strongly advocating this important measure' and recommending to Governor Bourke 'the total repeal of all the laws which imposed peculiar disabilities on the coloured classes. Pringle also recognized the influence on Bourke of the Revd

William Wright, so often the subject of Pringle's exasperated criticism, raising his awareness of 'the oppressions endured by the natives' and the need for 'immediate enactment of a protective ordinance'. Stockenstrom's and Wright's persuasion led to 'a measure to which the General's own benevolent feelings strongly disposed him'.[9]

Pringle wrote also that Sir George Murray at the Colonial Office in London added only a clause to the Order in Council 'that it should not be competent for any Governor or other Colonial Authority to alter or abrogate any of its provisions'.[10] Was this clause due to Pringle's influence, exercised through Henry Brougham whom he took pains to keep fully informed, and due to his bitter experience of Somerset's absolute rule? He wrote to Fairbairn in August 1829 that Murray 'appears fair': with him as Colonial Secretary 'our anti-slavery cause looks rather more promising.'[11] There had clearly been no contact between the two. Dr Philip was in England at this time but was careful to avoid accusations of political activity, which included actions to the discredit of Lord Charles Somerset.

Pringle's closeness to Thomas Fowell Buxton must certainly have been a major factor in Parliament's emancipation of the Khoisan and the other 'free persons of colour'. By a remarkable coincidence this was enacted by an unopposed motion by Buxton, with Murray's concurrence, only two days before Bourke's promulgation of Ordinance 50 in Cape Town. Buxton's memoirs give credit for his motion and the resulting Order in Council to Dr Philip, who had 'urged Mr Buxton to bring the cause of the Hottentots before Parliament'.[12] Pringle had had a hand in this too. He wrote to Philip: 'By the way you should stir up Buxton … a most excellent man but he is dilatory and somewhat irresolute when he has to deal with *civil* persons … he trusts too much to their good *intentions*'.[13]

A bare month before Buxton achieved the emancipation of the Khoisan in Parliament, Mrs Philip wrote to her husband, after attending a meeting of missionary and evangelical societies at Exeter Hall in London that she wished Buxton would 'stir himself a little in behalf of the Hottentots'.[14] Philip, and surely Pringle in his Anti-Slavery Society office in Aldermanbury, saw to it that he did so.

In Cape Town Sir Lowry Cole, Bourke's successor as Governor, bowing to a storm of protest from the white colonists, was on the point of amending Ordinance 50 to negate the Khoisan's equality when, by another providential coincidence, the Order in Council, with its veto on such action, reached Cape Town, and the Khoisan and 'other free persons of colour' remained equal with the white population in the sight of the law. The Order in Council became law at the Cape on 15 January 1829, at the start of Pringle's 'turning point' year.

His private life had reached a new level of stability and some comfort. We have a picture of this in a letter to Fairbairn of 15 July 1829. A far cry from the guinea-a-week lodgings in Arundel Street near the river, the Pringles and Margaret's sister Susan Brown were now in 'a pleasant and airy residence up here at Pentonville'. He found himself 'already much the better of walking daily from Aldermanbury, and rising early. I am writing this before 6 a.m. I may add Mrs P and Miss B's kindest regards though they are not awake to send them'.[15] Rutherfoord, he told Fairbairn, was about to return to Cape Town and would bring with him 'a complete set of Anti-Slavery Reporters bound up for your Lit. Society', marking both the re-emergence of the literary society Somerset had forbidden and Pringle's own paid employment and co-editing, with Zachary Macaulay, of the important and influential *Anti-Slavery Reporter.*

Old concerns remained. The settlement at Baviaans River continued in moderate prosperity and Pringle was still anxious to gather the rest of the family there. He wrote to his sister Mary on 19 December 1828, in one of the very few surviving family letters, that there had been 'no new intelligence from our brother Alexr' but more cheerfully that he was editing 'one of the elegant works' called annuals, 'which has somewhat improved my income', that he was 'on friendly terms with [Thomas] Campbell' and that his 'literary acquaintance is now very extensive.'[16]

Campbell's fame went back to his and Mary's childhood, when Thomas had declaimed to his new friend Story on the eve of their departure for Edinburgh University: 'Hope, for a season, bade the world farewell, And freedom shrieked – as Kosciusko fell!' With Bourke and Murray, not to mention Buxton, on their side he could now see freedom's rebirth for the Khoisan at the Cape.

He wrote also to Hogg, in May 1828, that his *Ephemerides, or, Poems Written in Scotland and South Africa* had been 'favourably received by most of the periodicals' but like all his verse 'does not sell well'. His habitual modesty about his poetry conceals the fact that the reception of *Ephemerides* was much more than just 'favourable' in the literary press.[17] It was acclaimed.

As one humbly born Scot to another, he told Hogg that it had put him 'on a pleasant footing with many literary men to whom I was previously unknown – among others with Sam Rogers, Coleridge, Southey, Montgomery, Croly, Allan Cunningham and some others well known to fame'. All of these had contributed to *Friendship's Offering.*

The *New Monthly Magazine* of March 1828 judged *Ephemerides* to be 'a volume of delightful poetry' and carried a Smith, Elder advertisement for the book which bears out Pringle's claim for it (and shows the appreciation of Pringle's muse, much less regarded today). To the *London Magazine* it had 'freshness and origi-nality' and its 'peculiar vein of poetic tenderness and sweetness ... strongly remind us of Allan Ramsay and Logan' (Scottish nature poets of the 18th century, Logan, though praised by Pringle in a letter of 1832, is not to be found in Margaret Drabble's *Oxford Companion to English Literature,* 6th ed., 2000). The *Athenaeum* wrote that Pringle's poetry 'flows like the natural language of a heart gushing over with the healthy sensibilities of humanity' and to the *Gentleman's Magazine* he was 'a poet of great power'. In Scotland the *Caledonian* praised the book's 'stream of poetry, original and singular'. The *Kaleidoscope, or, Literary and Scientific Mirror,* a 'cheap weekly' published in Liverpool by Egerton Smith found it 'independent of the intrinsic merit of the poetry ... peculiarly valuable on account of the notes contained, which are so interesting'. Pringle's South African years were recalled, his 'manly and uncompromising' opposition to the Governor praised, and the sonnet 'To Oppression' quoted in full.[18]

'Afar in the Desert' was the most admired poem in the collection. It had first appeared in the second issue of the *South African Journal* in 1824 and later in enough places to warrant a study of the many changes Pringle made to it, by George W. Robinson of the University of California, Los Angeles, published by *Papers of the Bibliographical Society of America* (17.1) in 1923.

With six other poems of his, Pringle had included 'Afar in the Desert' in his ghosting of Thompson's *Travels and Adventures in South Africa*. Somewhat disingenuously, he noted, as if he were Thompson, 'a few weeks before I set out on this journey', on 24 July 1824, it was included 'though somewhat long for a footnote' because it 'expresses so well the feelings of a traveller in the wilderness and contains such lively and appropriate sketches of African scenery'.[19]

Its inclusion led to the accolade which was bestowed by a giant of English literature and has given the poem and Pringle a measure of fame outside South Africa (where his status was assured), despite the radical changes in taste and style poetry has undergone in our time. Samuel Taylor Coleridge, old at 55 and ailing but still a massive presence, wrote to Pringle on 20 March 1828, in reply to a note from him, perhaps accompanying a review copy of *Ephemerides,* a letter worth quoting at some length:

> It is some four or five months since G. Thompson's Travels etc. in Southn. Africa passing its book-club course through our house, my eye by chance lighting on some verses, I much against my Wont was tempted to go on – and so I became first acquainted with your *Afar in the Desart* – Tho' at that time so busy that I had not looked at any of the new Books, I was taken so completely possession of, that for some days I did little else but read and recite your poem now to this group and now to that – and since that time have either written or caused to be written, at least half a dozen copies.[20]

He bought the two volumes and sent a copy of 'Afar in the Desert' to his son and daughter-in-law and then found it had been reprinted in the *Athenaeum.* He ended his eulogy:

> With the omission of about four or at the most six lines I do not hesitate to declare it, among the two or three most perfect lyric Poems in our Language —. Praecipitandus est *liber* Spiritus, says Petronius: and you have thoroughly fulfilled the prescript.

The letter concluded with an invitation to Pringle to visit him at Highgate 'any time after One o'clock in the morning [afternoon, surely] for I am an invalid', and any Thursday evening, when 'we commonly see a few intelligent friends from Town'.

'Among two or three perfect lyric poems in our language' with that very small qualification about omitting 'at the utmost six lines' was quoted by Leitch Ritchie in the *Poetical Works* (1838)[21]. The editor of Coleridge's *Collected Letters* (Oxford, 1971), Earl L. Griggs accused Ritchie of distorting the qualification by replacing the full stop after 'Athenaeum' with a semi-colon and placing it after 'six lines', a charge noted in later studies. Griggs, though a consummate scholar, saw fit to express his faint praise of the poem as 'not without merit' after quoting Coleridge's eulogy.[22]

Pringle published eight poems of Coleridge's in *Friendship's Offering* 1834, which he would have put together in 1833. The Pringles and Susan Brown had moved, in March 1833, from Pentonville to a charming little house with a garden behind it (in which Margaret planted an olive tree) in secluded Holly Terrace, a few hundred yards from Coleridge at Dr Gillman's house, The Grove, and their friendship blossomed.

Pringle had, in fact, in one of his many kindnesses as a 'good Samaritan', while still in Solly Terrace, Pentonville and overwhelmed with his anti-slavery work, sought to restore the annual stipend of £100 granted in 1824 to Coleridge and eight others from the Royal Literary Fund, paid by George IV from the Privy Purse. The stipend lapsed two years after the accession of William IV in 1830 and Pringle at once enlisted three well-placed interceders. Samuel Rogers saw Prime Minister Earl Grey about it, with good effect. The politician and writer Sir James Mackintosh, an old associate of Coleridge's replied, that though he took 'a strong interest in poor Coleridge's case' to get a pension from the present government was 'like trying to pull down the moon'[23] (as Pringle himself was to find in his own time of need). He would talk it over with Rogers. Pringle's old friend Colonel C.R. Fox – 'gay-humoured Captain Fox' of 'The Emigrant's Cabin' – was best placed, as brother-in-law of William IV's natural son, the Earl of Munster, and equerry to Queen Adelaide. Munster, however, was discouraging. The stipend was not renewed but Lord Grey found £200 to be paid to Coleridge over two years.

Rogers wrote to Pringle on 27 May 1831 that he had seen Lord Grey and that Coleridge 'is still to receive his annuity, so it must give you double pleasure, for it is in a great degree your work'[24]. Coleridge's friend, the merchant and *Blackwood's* contributor Joseph Hardman, who was also seeking the restitution of the Royal Literary Fund stipend, was equally congratulatory: 'I shall always consider that Mr Coleridge is indebted *to you* for this important benefit, for *by you* and *your friends* alone has the impulse been given'.[25] Hardman assured Pringle that he would 'be rewarded in this world and in a better one, for your active benevolence on this occasion'.

Coleridge's view was different. While grateful to those who had won him this charity from government, he regarded the £200 (later increased to £300) as payment to a pauper to keep him from want and not to an honour bestowed by the Sovereign in recognition of his work and to free him to continue it. Others had pleaded for the restitution of his 'royal associateship' – led by Brougham, they had included the author and classicist William Sotheby, Daniel Stuart, editor of the *Morning Post*, Charles Lamb, and Hurst, publisher of the *Englishman's Magazine* – and the only success had been the £200 grant secured by Rogers, recruited by Pringle.

Earl L. Griggs's cogent summary of the matter quotes Coleridge's statement 'a few months before his death' on 25 July 1834, that he had not had 'a shilling of my own in the world since King William the Fourth took my poor gold chain with a hundred links – one hundred pounds'.[26] The two survivors of the nine former 'royal associates' received civil list pensions in 1835, but Coleridge was no more – and might, had he been alive, have rejected this also as eleemosynary and not an honour.

Griggs, who wrote dismissively of Pringle's editorship of *Blackwood's* impugned Leitch Ritchie for misquoting Coleridge in Pringle's favour and belittled Coleridge's view of 'Afar in the Desert', also demolished Ritchie's claim that 'the restoration of a fund which was the sole support of a man of genius in his last days was mainly the work of Pringle'.[27] The fact remains that Pringle did restore the 'sole support' of the man of genius. It was the man of genius who refused the support because it was an act of charity and no longer the recognition of his genius he felt was his due. Griggs's judgment of Pringle has been unchallenged in biographical and literary studies that have followed.

Pringle and Coleridge were no more than acquaintances with mutual respect at the time of the Royal Literary Fund matter. By May 1833 Pringle was able to write of 'my friend and neighbour the Wizard Coleridge'[28] and Coleridge, sending his poem 'Love's Apparition and Evanishment' to Lockhart, wrote that it 'will with 4 or 5 other scraps appear in the *Friendship's Offering* (an Annual edited by my friend, Pringle)'.[29] By October 1833. Coleridge could sign himself 'Your afflicted but very sincere friend and thorough *esteemer*, with friendly affection'.[30] His letters to Pringle have survived only because Margaret Pringle gave both Ritchie and Conder access to his papers, and they were duly transcribed for their biographies. A few originals have survived in British, South African and American libraries, and two, not listed by Griggs, were lent by Margaret to the naturalist Adam White and found their way in 1968, via Sotheby's auctioneers, appropriately, to the National Library of South Africa in Cape Town, the renamed, much enlarged and rebuilt South African Library of Pringle's day.

The letters of 1833 reflect two aspects of the relationship of these near neighbours in Highgate – Coleridge's contributions to *Friendship's Offering*, 1834 (that of October 1833 acknowledged payment, presumably for them, though he 'never had the slightest thought of any remuneration of this kind');[31] and the question of slavery in philosophical as well as practical terms. From Adam White's estate came also proofs of pages 1 to 16 of *African Sketches*, with Coleridge's suggested changes to 'The Bechuana Boy', and the recently renamed 'Afar in the Desert'.[32]

The changes are very minor and most were adopted. The most radical was to the final stanza of 'Afar in the Desert', where the original has, as lines 5 and 6:

And feel as moth in the Mighty Hand
That spread the heavens and heaved the land.

Coleridge substituted

And feel the unprisoned soul expand
To freedom in the Eternal's hand.

Doubtless torn, Pringle deleted the couplet, reducing the stanza from ten to eight lines.

Though Pringle amended many of his poems numerous times, these are the only changes suggested by another that he is known to have accepted. In 1834 Charles Lamb, whose adopted daughter Emma Isola was married to Edward Moxon, publisher of *African Sketches*, suggested revisions to the proofs of 18 pages of *African Sketches*, in which were 'The Emigrant's Cabin', 'The Incantation' and 'The Caffer Commando'. Sotheby's cataloguer (the proofs were also Adam White's, given to him by Margaret) took it upon himself to pronounce that the majority were not accepted. 'though most readers would probably consider that they are improvements on Pringle's original'.[33]

Lamb's undated letter to Pringle reveals his ignorance of the setting of the African poems[34] – probably a general condition, even in the world of letters – since he wrote that the book 'seems calculated for Sierra Leone or the Plantations'. Like Ruskin, he objected to 'the gun, and the whip, and the gemsbok, and the oribi' (he called them 'choke pears') for 'home circulation'. If the book is to be 'a Colonial volume, I do not object', he conceded. Explanations in notes there were but 'poetry requires instant sympathy'. He ended 'I shall have pleasure in seeing you at Highgate a few weeks hence'. Lamb was a lifelong friend of Coleridge's, since their schooldays as 'bluecoat boys' at Christ's Hospital.

Moxon had published – his first venture – Lamb's unprofitable *Album Verses* in 1830 and Lamb, in a somewhat misplaced jest, suggested for Pringle's poems the title 'Nigrum Verses' adding 'and I wish it a whiter fate than my *Album Verses*'. His view was not all critical however: '"The Lion Hunt" is spirited but the "Evening Rambles" is my favourite'.

In January 1833, at a party for Moxon's authors Pringle had met Lamb, with Barry Cornwall (Proctor), Allan Cunningham, Thomas Hood, Leigh Hunt, Leitch Ritchie and others.[35] Margaret, White noted, 'did not seem to love Lamb', his essay 'Imperfect Sympathies' (*London Magazine,* 1821; *Essays of Elia,* 1823) being the reason. 'I have been trying all my life to like Scotchmen and am obliged to desist from the experiment in despair', Lamb had written.[36]

Coleridge's letters to Pringle on slavery were much sterner stuff. As 'an ardent and almost lifelong Denouncer of Slavery',[37] he nevertheless cast serious doubt on the whole question of human rights, on the capacity of the West Indian economy to survive abolition, and drew on deep religious sources to consider the guilt not only of the slave owner but of the beneficiaries of slavery in England. 'I and others', he wrote, 'consider [the West Indian proprietors] as only the Executive Ministers and Functionaries of a National Act'.[38]

Pringle's replies have not survived but his pamphlet of 1834, *Suggestions occasioned by the Act ...respecting the Apprenticeship of Negro Children* went beyond Coleridge's view: 'Slavery – i.e. the perversion of a Person into a Thing, is contrary to the spirit of Christianity. ... It is the duty of Christians to labour ... for its ultimate removal from the Christian world'.[39]

Pringle's income took a turn for the better with the emergence of a publishing phenomenon of the 1830s and '40s. This was the Society for the Diffusion of Useful Knowledge or 'SDUK', a brainchild of the polymath Whig reformer Henry Brougham and driven by the energetic publishing entrepreneur Charles Knight, who had been an editor of *Friendship's Offering.* Among its offshoots was the Library of Entertaining Knowledge, for which, Pringle, in September 1829, told Macvey Napier, Jeffrey's successor as editor of the *Edinburgh Review,* he was 'preparing a little volume on "The Native Tribes of South Africa",' the plan for which Brougham had approved.[40]

In November, however, he wrote to Fairbairn that this work 'lies over'. He had been 'rather seriously ill of late' and was 'not yet quite well'. He was 'debarred by the Doctor from any hard fagging at present'.[41] Was this the early pulmonary trouble that came to a crisis five years later? The 'Native Tribes' seems not to have been taken up again. Knight was a generous payer: he could afford to be when SDUK publications reached sales of 200,000. Pringle was to benefit from his many contributions to the mass circulation, working-class-oriented *Penny Magazine,* on African, mainly natural history, themes, and a major study of Sir Walter Scott in the Monthly Supplement for October 1832.

The end of that turning-point year, 1829, saw also the arrival from the Cape of John Wedderburn Dunbar Moodie, half-pay lieutenant of the Royal North British Fusiliers, youngest of Benjamin Moodie's younger brothers. Moodie lodged with the Pringles in Pentonville, where he met, the following year, Susanna Strickland, whose friendship was to bring much pleasure to Thomas in his last years. She also brought profit to the anti-slavery campaign which was to intensify in those years and lead to much 'fagging' for Pringle, perhaps with fatal consequences.

NOTES

1. Pringle to Hogg, 9.3.1829. Vigne, 'Additonal Letters' (2011), p. 11. NLS 2245 f 100.
2. *New Monthly Magazine,* January 1828, 'The British Government at the Cape of Good Hope', pp. 168–70.
3. Pringle (1966), p. 245.
4. *Ibid.*
5. Rogers to Pringle, – 1.1831; Macmillan, W.M., *The Cape Colour Question* (1927), p. 220.
6. *Op. cit.,* pp. 204–05.
7. Pringle (1966), p. 299n.
8. *Gazette,* 25.7.1828; Macmillan (1927), pp. 211–12n.
9. Pringle (1966), p. 249n.
10. *Op. cit.,* p. 249.
11. Pringle to Fairbairn, 25.8.1829.Vigne (2011), p. 321. LP, Fairbairn Papers, 1, 138.
12. Buxton, Charles, *Memoirs of Sir Thomas Fowell Buxton* (Everyman, 1925), p. 105.
13. Pringle to J. Philip, 23.8.1834, Vigne (2011), p. 367. WUL Pringle Family Prs MS A85.
14. Jane Philip to Philip, 10.5.1828; Macmillan (1927), p. 56.
15. Pringle to Fairbairn, 15.7.1829, Vigne (2011), p. 317. LP, Fairbairn Papers, 1, 136.
16. Pringle to M. Williams, 19.12.1829, Vigne, 'Additional Letters' (2011), p. 24. NELM 93.2.1.32.
17. Pringle to Hogg, 22.5.1828, Vigne, 'Additional Letters' (2011), p. 6. NLS MS 2245 f 118–10.
18. *New Monthly Magazine,* 1828; *Kaleidoscope,* 12.4.1828, p. 352.
19. Thompson (1968), vol. 2. pp. 17–19.
20. Coleridge to Pringle. Endorsed 20.3.1828; Griggs, vol. 6 (1971), p. 732.
21. Pringle (1838), p. cxliii.
22. Griggs, E.L. *Quarterly Bulletin of the South African Library,* vol. 6, No 1, September 1951, p. 1.
23. Pringle (1838), pp. cviii-cix.
24. *Op. cit.,* p. cix.
25. *Op. cit.,* pp. cix-cx.
26. Griggs, E.L., *Collected Letters of Samuel Taylor Coleridge,* 6 vols (1956–71), vol. 6, letter 1809.
27. Pringle (1838), p. cviii.
28. Pringle to Fairbairn, 22.5.1843, Vigne (2011), p. 171. LP, Fairbairn Papers, 1, 150.
29. Coleridge to Lockhart, -.11.1833. Griggs (1971), pp. 971–3.
30. Coleridge to Pringle, 24.10.1833, Griggs (1951), p. 6.
31. *Ibid.*
32. Sotheby's Catalogue, 29.10.1833.
33. *Op. cit.,* p. 114.

34 Lamb to Pringle, n.d. WUL MS A759.
35 Pringle to Fairbairn, 21.1.1833, Vigne (2011), p. 350. LP, Fairbairn Papers, 1, 146.
36 Lamb, Charles, 'Imperfect Sympathies', *Essays of Elia* (1835), p. 65. First published in the *London Magazine*, August 1821.
37 Coleridge to Pringle, -.6.1833. Griggs, vol. 6, p. 940.
38 Coleridge to Pringle, endorsed 13.8.1833. Griggs, vol. 6 (1971), p. 953.
39 Jackson, H.J., *The Collected Works of Samuel Taylor Coleridge, Marginalia*, 6 (2001), p. 29. Griggs (1951), p. 4.
40 Pringle to Napier, 25.9.1829, Vigne (2011), p. 324. BL Add MSS 34614 f 1822.
41 Pringle to Fairbairn, 23.11.1829, Vigne (2011), p. 325. LP, Fairbairn Papers, 1, 140.

18
Emancipation and After

Five Thomas Pringles are known to history: the founding editor of *Blackwood's*, the Scots settler leader to the eastern Cape frontier, the 'father of South African poetry', the champion of freedom of the Press in the Cape Colony, of the settlers in need and of the oppressed indigenous people, and, most historically memorable, the secretary of the Anti-Slavery Society at the triumphant climax of its campaigning. Yet it is this last seven-year role that is the least recorded, the most obscure.

In the nineteenth and early twentieth centuries offices in organizations in what is today called 'civil society' were held by the socially prominent, by public men, parliamentarians, peers, baronets and knights. A second rank of officials, known as 'servants' (a usage surviving in 'civil servants') performed the day-to-day clerical work that enabled their organization to function.

Pringle first encountered these 'officers' when he was recruited by the Anti-Slavery Society in May 1827, four months after the *Anti-Slavery Monthly Reporter* had published his *New Monthly Magazine* article on Cape slavery in October 1826. They were Thomas Fowell Buxton, well-to-do landowner, brewery proprietor and Member of Parliament, successor to the ageing and ailing William Wilberforce as leader of the abolition movement; Henry Brougham, Whig politician, polymath, future Lord Chancellor; and Wilberforce's lieutenants in the successful campaign which in 1807 ended the slave trade in the British Empire: Thomas Clarkson, Stephen Lushington, Zachary Macaulay and James Stephen.

Pringle as the paid servant of the Society is rarely mentioned either in its records or in later histories of its great work. Pringle worked most closely with Zachary Macaulay whose grand-daughter, Viscountess Knutsford's biography of him makes no mention of Pringle.[1] Macaulay and Pringle were joint editors of the *Monthly Reporter* from 1828, when it was in its fifth year of publication. 'Monthly' was later dropped from its masthead as it produced frequent supplements and Pringle, from 1832, had the further duty of editing the cheap, mass produced *Anti-Slavery Record*. His name appears only in connection with his South African material, and his initial 'Letter from the Cape' is announced as 'authentic details which have been furnished by a colonist now in this country, on whose information we place implicit reliance'.[2]

The target of anti-slavery campaigning was, of course, the West Indies, the sugar-producing islands and mainland territories of Berbice and Demerara (today's

Guyana), with occasional references to the Cape, contributed by Pringle, and to Mauritius, the subject of impassioned accusations in 1831–3.

After their hard-won victory in 1807 the stalwarts, mainly Quakers, of the Society for the Abolition of the Slave Trade had set up the African Institution as a watchdog against the inhumanity of surviving slavery and to work towards abolition of the 'system', as it was called, in its entirety. In 1823 the slow-pace of its diffuse activity was accelerated by the establishing of a new body, its aims and objects revealed by it name: the London Society for the Mitigation and Gradual Abolition of Slavery throughout the British Dominions. In September 1827, using its emollient original name, Pringle wrote from the Society's office at 18 Aldermanbury, in the City of London, to the Committee of the South African Public Library requesting their 'acceptance of the accompanying three volumes of pamphlets and a few loose tracts for the South African Library'[3]. It was already known simply as the Anti-Slavery Society, as a growing number of its supporters throughout the country were demanding total and immediate abolition.

In May 1827 he had written to Hogg that he was 'at present so engrossed with my official duties as secretary of the "Abolitionists" that I have little leisure for mere literary labours'. He hoped to have more time when Parliament rose. Four months later he wrote to Scott that his appointment, 'though not a very lucrative one is highly respectable and affords me also, except at certain periods' – presumably when copy date for the *Monthly Reporter* approached —'a good deal of leisure to devote to literary pursuits'.[4] In November 1829 he told Fairbairn that 'the Anti-Slavery office occupies the forenoon pretty fully',[5] so his duties seem to have been undemanding. And his correspondence at this time was full of his 'literary pursuits'.

He was also able to involve himself, and Buxton, in the emancipation of the Khoisan, with great success. He had advised Dr Philip to 'stir up' Buxton, who was 'somewhat irresolute' in dealing with such as Spring-Rice, parliamentary ally of Buxton's, and Colonial Secretary in 1834.[6] He later said of Buxton that he had a weakness for setting up committees rather than going into action.

There is no hard evidence that Pringle sided with the radical element demanding total, immediate abolition, but as the latter's campaign gathered pace he made approving noises. In August 1829 he told Fairbairn 'our anti-slavery cause looks rather more promising. Sir Geo. Murray [colonial secretary, 1828–30] appears fair. But much, much remains to be done – and old Zachary as you will see by the Reporters is not idle'.[7]

He continued with comments on the public anger aroused by revelations of continuing slave trading in Mauritius, taken from France in 1810. Sir Lowry Cole was a successor to Sir Robert Farquhar, Governor until 1823. It was Farquhar who urged the Colonial Secretary to exempt Mauritius from the Act abolishing the slave trade so that the sugar industry, introduced in those years, could flourish. This was refused but slaves continued to be brought in, mainly from nearby Madagascar, in defiance of the Act, and treated with great harshness and cruelty. Slavery in Mauritius, wrote the *Monthly Reporter*, 'wore its most disgusting and horrid form'.[8] James MacQueen's rejoinder in *Blackwood's* outdid even his attack on Pringle as publisher of *The History of Mary Prince*. According to MacQueen, the author of this vile publication possesses an advantage over every honest man, as he can tell so many lies on a page as will require a volume on the part of the accused to answer. … It would be easy for me to knock the head of Mr Pringle against the brains of Mr Macaulay, and to smash them with their own contradictions.[9]

Mauritius had been a major stick to beat the pro-slavery lobby, used by Buxton with great effect in Parliament. Disappointed by Farquhar's record (though he attacked French slaving ships with good effect) and Sir Lowry Cole's half-hearted attempts at improving the conditions of slavery on the island, the Anti-Slavery members' hopes rose with the appointment of the francophone Guernsiaise judge John Jeremie as attorney-general of Mauritius. Pringle wrote to Fairbairn on 31 December 1831 rejoicing at the appointment of a confirmed anti-slavery judge – Jeremie of St Lucia –

as attorney-general of the outrageous colony where he will have very important and arduous duties to perform. He is a decided and valuable person, and thoroughly with us.[10]

Jeremie was forced out of the 'outrageous colony' by the white officials and colonists, became a hero to the Anti-Slavery Society and to Buxton a useful martyr to colonial oppressors and reactionaries. He was later appointed to the bench in Ceylon. The slaves, in time, were freed and the sugar industry saved by the importing of indentured Indian labourers.

Pringle's extant letters make no reference to the Society's campaign against slavery in the West Indian colonies, by far the most important of the Society's fields of action. His identifiable contributions in the *Monthly Reporter*, unlike his publication of *The History of Mary Prince*, are to do with the Cape and Mauritius: his 'great cause' was not put aside. Both within and outside the Society's work, nevertheless, he took action of great value where his skills as a writer were put to use.

Pringle's authorship is difficult to detect in the *Monthly Reporter* but his January 1827 'Slavery at the Cape of Good Hope' article, and a second major contribution in January 1828, 'Remarks on the Demoralizing Influence of Slavery' are demonstrably his. The latter, published as a pamphlet the same year, bases its arguments on the situation at the Cape.[11] They are clearly derived from Pringle's first-hand experience. On page one of the *Remarks* he wrote:

It has been remarked by Tacitus, one of the most shrewd observers of human nature, that there is nothing so sweet to the human heart as the gratification which arises from the consciousness of having the life of a fellow-creature at one's disposal. And it is this prevailing love of power which presents, perhaps, the greatest obstacle to the abolition of slavery in our slave colonies. Power, in the hands of men, is in no instance so much subject to abuse as in its exercise over their own species which, of itself, forms no inconsiderable argument against slavery.

The *Remarks* is a remarkable case study of the relationship of master and slave at the Cape, written partly as a rejoinder to the *Quarterly Review* (vol. 20, p. 435) which had asserted that 'since the emigration of British settlers in 1820, the influx of labourers from Europe will be a great means of hastening the abolition of slavery in that settlement'. Pringle destroyed this argument by pointing out that in South Africa, where slaves 'form more than nineteen parts out of twenty of the labouring class, the value of slaves and consequently the system of slavery existing in that colony are not likely to be materially affected by any importation of free labourers'[12]

He went on to substantiate this argument, with many examples of cruelty to slaves by English as much as Dutch masters or mistresses of otherwise blameless character, and ended with the last words, 'as he ascended the scaffold', of Wilhelm Gebhardt, son of the Dutch Reformed minister at Paarl, who had beaten a slave to death. Asked by Pringle's friend, the Revd William Wright, for his opinion on slavery, the condemned man replied: 'Sir, slavery is a bad system, it is even worse for the masters than it is for the slaves.'[13]

Pringle's other contributions were based on the experiences of slaves, all but one from the West Indies. In 1831 his friend, and lodger, Susanna Strickland (later to be 'given away' at her marriage to the Pringles' guest from the Cape, Captain J.W.D. Moodie, took down the life story of a Bermudan slave, Mary Prince, brought to England from Antigua by her owners, John Wood and his wife. She was denied manumission and abandoned by them in London. She found her way to 18 Aldermanbury in 1828 and in 1829 moved in with the Pringles in Pentonville as their domestic servant. *The History of Mary Prince, a West Indian Slave, Related by Herself* was an instant success and ran to three editions in 1831. Pringle's preface makes it clear that the Society had 'no concern whatever with this publication' and that he had 'published the tract, not as their Secretary, but in my private capacity'.[14] Any profit from sales was to go to Mary Prince herself.

He did the Society the further service of adding the five-page 'Narrative of Louis Asa-Asa, a Captured African', which balances the wickedness of the white slave trader and of many masters, with that of the black enslaver. 'While Mary's narrative shows the disgusting character of colonial slavery, this little tale explains with equal force the horrors in which it originates.'[15] Louis Asa-Asa was taken by African slavers from a hostile tribe in Sierra Leone, bought and sold 'six times over, sometimes for money, sometimes for cloth, sometimes for a gun' and it was six months before 'we got a ship, in which we first saw white people: they were French. They bought us'[16]. The ship was driven by a storm into St Ives harbour and Louis was freed, with others, after a writ of Habeas Corpus was obtained by George Stephen.

The success of *Mary Prince* coincided with the upwelling of anti-slavery passion among women's organizations throughout Britain. Pringle was in touch with the committees concerned, such as the Birmingham Ladies' Society for the Relief of Negro Slaves, through whom he negotiated the freedom of a slave from St Vincent's, Nancy Morgan, at a cost of £80, raised by himself.[17]

He gave personal help to a number of slaves who had been brought to England by their 'owners'. Among them was the 24-year-old Ashton Warner, freed as a child but re-enslaved and seeking to recover his freedom. Susanna Strickland produced his *Negro Slavery described by a Negro: being the Narrative of Ashton Warner, a Native of St Vincent's, with an Appendix containing the Testimony of four Christian Ministers, recently returned from the Colonies, on the System of Slavery as it now exists.* Ashton

Warner died, in Pringle's arms, in the London Hospital, before publication. Pringle wrote to Susanna Moodie, as she had become, in December 1831: 'The story of Ashton Warner has sold indifferently and there will be, I expect, from £15 to £20 of loss, which of course falls on me as it was all my own management'.[18]

One of the 'four Christian ministers' in the appendix was the Revd William Wright, a Jonah perhaps. Wright, now married and living in Ireland, had published his own *Slavery at the Cape of Good Hope* in 1831, but Pringle told Mrs Moodie, it 'has not sold at all – and there is a great loss on it – which I am not responsible for'[19]. Its failure is surprising since it had the imprint of Longman (and partners), London, and Westley in Dublin, though probably not at the publishers' risk. Five hundred words of the book, 'in the Press', are quoted in the *Ashton Warner* appendix.

Susanna was the youngest of the five Strickland sisters, four of whom made their marks as novelists, biographers and poets. Pringle became her close friend and to her he was 'Papa' Pringle, and his letters were to 'My dear bairn',[20] though he was only fourteen years her senior. She must have brightened his struggling, penurious London life, with Margaret's poor health, his burden of debt, lack of a positive response to his claim on the Colonial Office and the grim stories of the cruelty and suffering that he daily encountered in his work against slavery.

His letter to Susanna of 20 December 1831 displays his resilience: 'The health of Mrs P is just *so so* as Mary [Prince] says. My own is tolerable. I am lucky as usual'. A postscript was frank about his 'Dream of Fairyland' which he had included in *Friendship's Offering* 1833. It was 'rather wishy washy stuff. Had it not been my *own* I suppose it would have had a bad chance of insertion – but one is always kind to one's own poetry and one's bairns even though they be rickety brats'.[21]

He went much deeper in an undated letter which survives, in part, in Susanna's papers in Canada, where she and John Moodie had settled in 1833 and where she and her sister Catherine Parr Traill are recognized as significant literary figures. He wrote that she valued his friendship too highly. He was

> A poor, weak, inconsistent mortal, variable in my temper, hasty and sometimes harsh to those I love, but … the best I can … say for myself – I am naturally frank, honest and simple – I think – I hope, always so with those I esteem and love.[22]

Did he think Susanna was too fond of her 'Papa'? He went on to praise Margaret, and to give us a rare sense of her character:

> I love similar qualities in others; my wife has these qualities in perfection. My excellent deceased friend, Dr Waugh, used to say of her, that 'she was the [truest] woman I know'. She is an honest kind-hearted woman, and beloved by all who know her.

The early 1830s were a time of almost frantic activity among the abolitionists, with what present-day historians call the 'immediatists' challenging and overtaking the 'gradualists'. Joseph Sturge and other leading Quakers, with George Stephen in support, eventually formed the Agency Committee, sharing 18 Aldermanbury with the founders of the Anti-Slavery Society and conducting nationwide meetings, employing 18 lecturers and organizing the petitions that Parliament and Downing Street could not ignore. Nor could the Agency Committee ignore Buxton, the Macaulays father and son, Clarkson, Lushington and the other pioneers of the abolition movement, Pringle's loyalty seems to have lain with the latter, and the work he refers to in letters to Fairbairn and others has more to do with the campaign in Parliament than outside it. His surviving correspondence in those years is scanty and contains no hard evidence of his attitude to the division in the movement..

Nor do we have evidence of his participating in the packed meetings, some with audiences in the thousands. His letter of 14 January 1832 to his brother William describes his visit to their ancestor's grave which he may have made after meetings in Edinburgh and Kelso earlier in the month.[23] Their cousin, the Revd Alexander Pringle, was a main speaker at a meeting in Perth in October 1831. Thomas wrote to his childhood nurse, Mary Potts, and to Mrs Morrison, daughter-in-law of the Secessionist minister in the Morebattle of his early schooldays, in December 1833 and January 1834, recalling his visit to Morebattle in 1832 but there is no mention of anti-slavery campaigning in Scotland (see Chapter 21 below). He would not have shied away from rowdy meetings in crowded halls, which would have revived memories of his student days and his organized *claque* in support of Joanna Baillie.

A third anti-slavery memoir, in 1833, was possibly the most telling of all. Charles Buxton recalled its origin, which was due to Pringle's prompt action. It was to 'call forth a burst of public feeling',[24] most opportunely for the 'immediatists':

> Mr Buxton, being one morning at breakfast, surrounded as usual by papers, and deep in discussion with Mr George Stephen, a young man named Whiteley was brought in and introduced to him by Mr Pringle as a book-keeper who had just returned from the West Indies. He told what he had seen, a tale of cruelty and suffering such as Mr Buxton had heard a hundred times before. The young man took his leave; but scarcely was he gone, when the thought struck Mr Buxton that such a picture fresh from the very spot was the very thing they needed.[25]

He caught Whiteley on the corner of Portland Place, having pursued him 'without his hat', persuaded him to write down his story and 'in a few days the pamphlet was in print'.

'The effect was prodigious' wrote Charles Buxton, and quotes a letter to his father: 'Whiteley, nothing but Whiteley, is the order of the day; the sensation it creates is immense; the printers can scarcely supply the demand. Mr Pringle says ten thousand have been ordered today'. In two weeks nearly 200,000 copies of *Three Months in Jamaica in 1832, comprising a Residence of Seven Weeks on a Sugar Plantation* were sold. In its 'homely but graphic style' it conveyed a picture of the slave-owners cruelty and indifference with 'truth stamped on every word'. Here was an exposure of the horror of slavery by an Englishman to the people of Britain. The case he made struck a chord with many. Whiteley said of himself that he had been:

> one of those individuals who believed that there is more *real* slavery in England than in any of her colonies. Many a time I have blamed such gentlemen as Mr Buxton and Dr Lushington and others for making so much ado in Parliament about slavery and neglecting (as I

conceived) the story of the poor factory children at home with whose condition I was well acquainted.[26]

He ended: 'Between the case of the factory child and plantation slave there can be no just comparison. The former is very bad, the latter is INFINITELY worse'. Thanks were due to Pringle who, on his crutches, made that long early morning walk, with Henry Whiteley, from the City, or even Pentonville, to Buxton's house in Marylebone.

Buxton received much assistance, in the research into the pro-slavery and official statements he had to deal with, from Zachary Macaulay and from Pringle, 'whose poetical writings are well known', wrote his son. 'Mr Pringle's originality, his admirable English style, his diligence, tact and temper rendered good service to the cause.'[27]

Charles Buxton described the vastly increased activity of the abolitionists in these final years of their campaign:

'Now was the time ... to sweep away all the obstacles by an irresisitible impulse of public feeling', he wrote. '... the meeting in Exeter Hall and the publication of Whiteley's pamphlet had led the way. These first steps were followed up by the most vigorous proceedings, under the direction chiefly of Mr George Stephen and Mr Pringle, whose services were of essential value at this critical juncture.'[28]

At Exeter Hall in the Strand on 18 April 1833, 330 delegates from committees from all over the country agreed an address to the Government and next day, in a body, presented it to the Prime Minister, Earl Grey, in Downing Street. On 14 May Thomas Fowell Buxton brought to the House of Commons a petition signed by 187,000 women of Great Britain and had to be assisted by four members in carrying it into the chamber. Buxton then proceeded to open the debate which led to the enactment, after a long battle over compensation of the slave-owners and compulsory apprenticeship of the freed slaves, to the enactment of the Bill for the Total Abolition of Slavery throughout the British Dominions. The Royal Assent was received on 28 August 1833, emancipation took place a year later, on 1 August 1834.

The pace of change had been unexpectedly rapid. Pringle wrote to Dr Philip in January 1833: 'If I survive the settlement of the Slavery Question I have little or no doubt (if the Whigs are in power) of being properly provided for ... there is no *near* prospect of that however'.[29] Yet by May the great Abolition debate had begun and total abolition had become law in August.

One who did not 'survive the settlement' was its early champion William Wilberforce, who died on 29 July 1833, four days after the Second Reading of the Abolition Bill had been passed and a fortnight before it was enacted. He was told the good news, the result of his labours since, in 1787, William Pitt had recruited him, then aged 28, to bring the 'Slavery Question' to Parliament. He handed over active leadership to Buxton in 1823 but was always kept informed and often consulted. A confirmed 'gradualist', he had nevertheless shown much kindness to Pringle, the penurious paid servant of the Society, so unlike his fellow Clapham Sect evangelical Anglican campaigners and the equally well-to-do Quaker abolitionists. Leitch Ritchie quotes two of Wilberforce's letters to Pringle, one of them concerning the copy of Scott's Annotated Bible he was donating to the library Pringle was assembling for Glen-Lynden (the library, and the Bible, survive in the Cory Library in Grahamstown). Somewhat ironically, accompanying the Bible was a parcel to Wilberforce's cousin in Cape Town, W.W. Bird, with whom Pringle had fallen out, of which the sender was probably quite unaware.

That letter, dated 2 February 1830,[30] suggests that there had been a difference between Pringle and Wilberforce which the latter was seeking to repair. It may only have been that Wilberforce was surprised that Pringle had left Highwood Hill, the Wilberforces' house near Mill Hill, where he had been a guest for only one night, on 23 January, leaving Wilberforce with the 'suspicion that you would have stayed longer if pressed … I hope I am mistaken'. Pringle's letter to Margaret shows that he clearly was mistaken.[31] He was delighted by his reception and by his host's welcome, not least in being given, ever the tenant farmer's son among his 'betters', 'the *best* bedroom – a mark of polite attention to a visitor without any of the attribution of worldly consequence, and especially when so many other visitors were in the house'. Pringle brought with him 'the news of Lord William Bentinck … prohibiting in future the burning of widows throughout the British dominions in India'. Wilberforce appeared silently to thank God 'for this great triumph of Christian philanthropy', an ideal of which the emancipation of the slaves was only a part.

A letter from Elmwood House, near Birmingham, in January 1832 praised Pringle's 'exertions in our great and good cause', ending 'whenever, D.V., I am in London again, I shall feel it an act of friendly regard if you will do me the favour to come and shake me by the hand'[32].

Pringle, like the other Abolitionists and Wilberforce, was disappointed in the Bill's clauses which committed the freed slaves to lengthy 'apprenticeships', whereby they would work most of the day without pay for periods varying from five to fifteen years according to circumstances and locality. Children of six and under were freed (with an exception later to be attacked by Pringle and the Society). The 'immediatists', now led by Buxton in the Commons, fought back and reduced the period to a uniform five years (four at the Cape).

The Agency Committee were equally disapproving of the compensation to the slave-owners for the loss of their 'property', which was raised from a loan of £15 million to a gift of £20 million. Wilberforce, however, said, when brought the news of the passing of the Second Reading, a few days before his death: 'Thank God that I should have lived to witness a day in which England is willing to give twenty millions sterling for the abolition of Slavery.'[33]

Almost the last statement from Pringle on slavery is an eight-page statement entitled: *Suggestions … respecting the Apprenticeship of Negro Children*.[34] This is a vigorously-worded plea for the 'apprenticing' of children under six who are 'not properly supported by their parents [or others] disposed voluntarily to undertake the support of such children' for a period of 21 years. Pringle argued forcefully that it would be 'an act of extreme cruelty to the children, as well as of folly and improvidence on the part of parents or relations, if they should be induced … to forego the immense advantage which the law happily gives them.' Such children must be saved 'from the possibility of undergoing their second bondage of from 15 to 21 years, which would be an infliction equal to that of the worst felons'.

His final signed statement, on 27 June 1834, published the Abolition Act in full and ascribed 'the hour of the triumph of the Almighty'. It called upon the public 'to devote the approaching 1st of August – the appointed day of manumission – to His service and praise'.[35]

It has been claimed that the name 'Anti-Slavery Committee' used by Pringle in the November 1833 *Suggestions* was a face-saving euphemism for the Agency Commttee. It is more likely that he was anticipating the demise of the Society. He sent the *Suggestions* to Fairbairn on 4 November, predicting 'that we may not issue many more [papers] as an Anti-Slavery Society. Nothing is yet absolutely fixed as to the period of our dissolution but my impression is that it will *be soon*'.[36]

The final meeting of the Society did not, in fact, take place until 5 August 1834 when it was agreed that 'the salary of Thomas Pringle, the Secretary, be fixed at £100 per annum [i.e. halved] from the next quarter'. It was minuted that 'the Committee feel it only an act of justice to record the great satisfaction which the Committee derives in looking back at the zeal and prudence and industry with which the Secretary and Clerk [Thomas Hart] have discharged their respective duties'.[37]

The recognition of Pringle's role that came from Zachary Macaulay was well-earned, and well-judged since he had worked so closely with Pringle for so many years. The Committee, he wrote:

felt themselves fortunate in being able to engage him as their Secretary; and in that capacity, for upwards of seven years he continued to labour with signal assiduity and devotedness until … the extinction of colonial slavery, [to which] Mr Pringle greatly contributed, by his practical knowledge of the evils of that iniquitous system, and by the unwearied exertion of his talents in the service of the Society.[38]

Macaulay wrote privately to Brougham when forwarding to him Pringle's letter of 27 June 1833 seeking the 'recommendation of yourself and other friends' for the 'employment of my services in South Africa', with his anti-slavery work almost at an end. Macaulay endorsed 'the claim of a very deserving person which I would be most happy to see gratified', Pringle being 'a man of genius and talent and yet distinguished by calmness and solidity of judgment and sound principle'.[39]

Josiah Conder quoted from the circular quoted above (which he believed to have been drafted by Macaulay) the Committee's acknowledgment that Pringle had been 'for years one of the most meritorious, efficient and disinterested of their fellow-labourers'.[40]

George Stephen, son of the early campaigner James Stephen, honorary solicitor to the Society and initiator of the Agency Committee, took a different view. Asked by Harriet Beecher Stowe about his fellow campaigners twenty years after abolition, he regretted, half in jest perhaps, that she had not been among them, lacking as they did anyone capable of 'mingling a little humour with the appalling gravity of the anti-slavery truth … None of our Parliamentary leaders had an interesting pen'. He listed them all, with a critical word for the literary style of each, ending 'Even Mr Pringle, long the Secretary of the Anti-Slavery Society, and well known in literature, could never infuse a drop of amusing interest into colonial topics'.[41] Perhaps 'The Emigrant's Cabin' was the exception that proved the rule.

Light hearted and humorous, it was completed, from an early draft, and published only when the anti-slavery cause had triumphed. It is serious too. The emigrant, Pringle himself, finds that 'in this wilderness there's work to do'.

> Something for the sad Natives of the soil,
> By stern oppression doomed to scorn and toil;
> Something for Africa to do or say –
> If but one mite of Europe's debt to pay –
> If but one bitter tear to wipe away.

His poetry must have reached many unwilling to read lengthy tracts about slavery, and was often published in them. 'The Slave-Dealer' (1828), a searing cry of remorse by a wielder of the lash on a dying woman slave and the sonnet 'To Oppression' (1825, see p. 149) were much reproduced. The latter is clearly about South African slaves and the Khoisan and about Pringle's treatment by Somerset and his 'tools', despite some critics' view. Even his sonnet 'Slavery' (1823) ('one of the worst he wrote', in J.R. Wahl's judgment)[42] reappeared after publication in *Ephemerides* (1828) and makes the point that it is the master who 'quakes with secret dread', knowing that punishment will ultimately come to him and not to the slave.

His poetry was harnessed not only to the cause of abolition but to bringing South Africa, its human and natural landscape, to the Anglophone world of the northern hemisphere. In *The Bow and the Cloud*, an anthology compiled by his fellow campaigner Mary Anne Rawson in 1834, he published 'The Forester of the Neutral Ground', recognized by J.R. Wahl as concerned 'for the first time in South African literature with the now familiar figure of a man who becomes an outcast because of his love for a coloured woman'[43] – and she a slave.

NOTES

[1] Knutsford, Viscountess, *Life and Letters of Zachary Macaulay by his Grand-daughter* (London, 1900).

[2] 'Slavery at the Cape of Good Hope. Letters from the Cape: 1. Slavery', *Anti-Slavery Monthly Reporter*, No 20, 31.1.1827, p. 289.

[3] Pringle to Committee of South African Public Library, 8.9.1827. Vigne (2011), p. 311. NLSA CT MSD 193 (1) 1.

[4] Pringle to Hogg, 19.5.1827, Vigne (2011), p. 309. NLS MS 2245 f 100–01; Pringle to Scott, 10.12.1827. Vigne (2011), p. 312. NLS MS 3905 f 202.

[5] Pringle to Fairbairn, 23.11.1829, Vigne (2011), p. 325. Fairbairn Papers, LP 1, 140.

[6] Pringle to J. Philip, n.d. (?1827), Vigne (2011), p. 307. Macmillan, W.M., *Bantu., Boer and Briton* (1929), pp. 102–07.

[7] Pringle to Fairbairn, 25.8.1829, Vigne (2011), p. 321. LP, Fairbairn Papers, 1, 138.

[8] *Anti-Slavery Monthly Reporter* 62, vol. 3, no. 14, 1 July 1830, p. 299.

[9] *Blackwood's*, 76, vol. 29, no.1, February 1831. MacQueen, editor of the *Glasgow Courier*, had

managed a plantation in Grenada and sided, often intemperately, with the slave-owners. His attack on Pringle and Mary Prince was in *Blackwood's,* 81, vol.30, no. 2, November 1831.

10   Pringle to Fairbairn, 31 December 1831, Vigne (2011), p. 336. LP, Fairbairn Papers, 1, 114.

11   A Resident at the Cape of Good Hope, *Remarks on the Demoralizing Influence of Slavery* (London, Bagster and Thomas, 1828).

12   *Op. cit.,* 5.

13   *Op. cit.,* p. 15.

14   Prince, Mary, *The History of Mary Prince, a West Indian Slave,* ed. S. Salih (2000), p. 5.

15   *Op. cit.,* p. 66.

16   *Op. cit.,* p. 69.

17   Midgley, Clare, *Women against Slavery. The British Campaigns,* 1780–1870 (1992), p. 87.

18   Pringle to S. Moodie, 20.12.1831. Library and Archives, Canada.

19   *Ibid.*

20   Pringle to S. Moodie, 7.1.1829. Lib. and Archives, Canada,

21   Pringle to S. Moodie, 20.12.1831, Lib. and Arch., Canada.

22   Pringle to S. Moodie, -.1832., Vigne (2011), p. 344. *Palladium of British America,* 2.1.1839, Lib. and Arch., Canada.

23   Pringle to W. Pringle, 14.1.1832. Vigne, 'Additonal Letters' (2011), pp.18–21. Cory Lib., Pr 2736A.

24   Buxton, C., p. 147.

25   *Ibid.*

26   Whiteley, Henry, *Three Months in Jamaica in 1832* (1833), p. 2.

27   Buxton, C., p. 123.

28   *Op. cit.,* p. 149.

29   Pringle to J. Philip, 19.1.1833, Vigne (2011), p. 347. WUL Philip Family Papers A85.

30   Wilberforce to Pringle, 2.2.1830. Pringle (1838), p. xcv.

31   Pringle to M. Pringle, 23.1.1830, Vigne (2011), 'Additional Letters' (2011), p. 15. Pringle (1838), pp. cii-cv.

32   Wilberforce to Pringle, 23.1.1832. Pringle (1838), p. xciv.

33   Buxton, C., p. 159.

34   *Suggestions occasioned by the Clause of the Act of 3 and 4 William IV. Chap. LXIII respecting the Apprenticeship of Negro Children.* By Order of the Anti-Slavery Committee. Thomas Pringle, Secretary, Anti-Slavery Office, 18, Aldermanbury, November 1, 1833 (London, S. Bagster, Junr).

35   Pringle (1838), p. cxii.

36   Pringle to Fairbairn, 4.11.1833, Pringle (2011), p. 358. LP, Fairbairn Papers, 1, 148.

37   Anti-Slavery Papers, Bodl. Lib. RH, quoted in Meiring, Jane, *Thomas Pringle. His Life and Times* (1968), p. 150.

38   Pringle (1966), p. xxxiii.

39   Pringle to Macaulay, 27.6.1833, note to Brougham. Vigne (2011), p. 352. UCL Sp. Coll. Brougham MSS 36245

40   Pringle (1966), p. xxxiii n.

41   Stephen, G., *Antislavery Recollections in a Series of Letters addressed to Mrs Beecher Stowe written by Sir George Stephen at her Request* (1854), p. 116.

42   Pringle (1970), p. xxii.

43   *Ibid.* See also p. 230 below.

7. Susanna Moodie, born Strickland (1803–85), one of six literary sisters, of Reydon Hall, Bungay, Suffolk, writer, transcriber of *The History of Mary Prince,* married John W.D, Moodie from the Pringles' house in 1830 and settled with him in Canada where she became a major figure in Canadian literature. (Portrait by Thomas Cheesman)
(Library and Archives Canada, NL–15557)

8. Sir Thomas Fowell Buxton (1786–1845), leader of the anti-slavery movement in Britain from 1823, and campaigner for African rights at the Cape, moved the Abolition Bill in the House of Commons, 1833. Engraved by James Thomson after a drawing by Abraham Wivell.
(National Portrait Gallery, London)

9. 7 Holly Terrace, 'our
hermitage in Highgate ... at
once cheap and delightful',
home of Thomas and Margaret
Pringle, with Susan Brown,
1832–4.
(*Simon Wheeler*)

10. Thomas Pringle,
posthumous engraving by
Edward Francis Finden,
frontispiece of Pringle's
Poetical Works, 1838.
(*National Library of South Africa,
Cape Town*)

Part VI

Scotland and Highgate

A Poet Returns to his Roots and Last Works (1830–1834)

19

'A Little Doctoring'

In character with so much of Pringle's somewhat star-crossed life, his fate was revealed the very day after he had signed the Society's announcement of the Abolition Act. He wrote from Holly Terrace, Highgate, on the morning of 28 June 1834 to Dr James Kennedy, whose patient he had been for several years.

> I must have a little doctoring. Last night, in taking some slight supper, a crumb of bread seems, as we say, to go down the wrong throat. This induced a violent coughing, and I assume lacerated some small blood-vessel in the lungs, for a litte blood – not very much – came up: that soon ceased, but I feel this morning a sensation as if there was a small abrasion of the part; so I suppose you had better come out and prescribe.[1]

There was still so much to do – above all the book of his African experiences suggested by Barrow fifteen years before, his literary life resumed – and money to be earned – and claimed from government – now that he was no longer 'engrossed in slavery' and without the income that supported him.

The build-up to the final abolition needed intense work by Buxton and his colleagues on the parliamentary front, with major national issues – the great Reform Bill of 1832, Ireland and church reform – in the way of the attack on slavery. An active, powerful and well-funded pro-slavery lobby was another obstacle and by May 1826 Buxton was in a state of collapse, after bringing the horrors of slavery in Mauritius to the House of Commons. He was, he recorded, 'seized with a fit of apoplexy',[2] with several days unconscious and a long recovery from what might today be labelled a nervous breakdown.

The strain on Pringle, already perhaps in the early stages of his fatal 'pulmonary complaint', must have been heavy, and intensified by the work he undertook, much of it with Zachary Macaulay, to supply the information that underpinned Buxton's leadership of the anti-slavery cause.

The exhausting experience of litigation was no help and he was lucky to be an ocean away from a case in which he was involved at the Cape in 1830. So strong was the growing anti-slavery community in his favour – as it was of Dr John Philip, the defendant – that his reputation seems to have suffered no harm and the pro-slavery lobby to have been unaware of it or it might have added material to the vicious attacks that were to follow.

Dr Philip's years in London had resulted in the publication in 1828 of his two-volume and highly influential *Researches in South Africa*. Among many charges Philip brought against officialdom at the Cape was an accusation that in December 1825 Landdrost Mackay of Somerset had imposed a harsh punishment of flogging and imprisonment on a Khoikhoi wagon driver who had helped himself out of a cask of brandy he was transporting for Mackay. Philip wrote that Mackay had pocketed the wages the driver received from the farmer, to whom Mackay had contracted him for three years.[3]

Mackay sued Philip for libel and Philip's counsel, Advocate Henry Cloete, argued that the case should be heard in England where the book had been written and published, and that, Mackay not being named, no libel had been intended or taken place.[4] Judges Burton and Kekewich (Judge Menzies was absent on circuit) found for Mackay who was awarded damages of £200 (he had asked for £1000) and costs, which were assessed at an exorbitant £900. Curiously, Menzies' report of the case quotes Cloete as naming Philip's informant as 'John Pringle, of London, now or late Secretary of the Anti-Slavery Society',[5] an error perpetuated by Cory, normally scrupulous as to facts, whatever his opinions, though he omits the reference to London and the Society.[6]

There was much public sympathy for Philip in Britain and the damages and costs were quickly raised. Some donors even feared for Philip's liberty. Pringle wrote to Philip in November 1830 that

> Buxton … and his daughter have written anxiously enquiring about you and what we are doing for your aid. … I have letters also from … other friends throughout the country with anxious enquiries. There is a report among them that you are *in prison*.[7]

Theal, quoted by Cory with obvious approval, wrote that 'it was asserted by men of high position in society that Dr Philip was suffering persecution on account of the noble efforts he was making to secure humane treatment for the poor oppressed natives in South Africa'.[8] Though meant ironically, this was not far wide of the mark.

By 31 May 1831 Pringle was able to tell Philip that £2000 had been raised.[9] In neither letter does he mention having fed Philip the wrong information that led to the libel action. As he was on his way to Cape Town in December 1825 and his brother John was farming near Somerset it may well be that Philip's informant was indeed John Pringle, and the attribution to Thomas was Judge Menzies' blunder. Whether John told Thomas who told Dr Philip we shall never know. In any event, Thomas's reputation in Britain seems not to have suffered. The damage to it came from his West Indian connexions.

Pringle's work was often on his own initiative and his *History of Mary Prince* was a very considerable contribution to that multiplying of popular support needed to bring abolition into the forefront of parliamentary politics. The book cost him dear, and not just financially. James MacQueen, former Grenada plantation manager turned geographer and journalist, became, as editor of the *Glasgow Courier* and contributor to *Blackwood's*, a strident, often abusive champion of the pro-slavery lobby. His open letters in *Blackwood's* to the Whig Prime Minister, Earl Grey and to the Tory Duke of Wellington went beyond all limits in championing the slave-owning colonists and King Sugar by vilifying the abolitionists.

His riposte to a detailed study of slavery in Mauritius in the *Monthly Reporter* in

February 1831 was a nasty foretaste of things to come. In the February letter MacQueen merely threatened 'to knock the head of Mr Pringle against the brains of Mr Macaulay, and to smash them with their contradictions'.[10] The anti-abolitionists often matched the cruelty of the system of slavery with the scurrility of their attacks on the anti-slavery spokesmen. The Mary Prince affair aroused the Society's adversaries, MacQueen at their forefront, to new levels of libellous invective.

Blackwood's published in November 1831 an open 'letter to Earl Grey'[11] in which MacQueen went far beyond the knockabout stuff of the February letter. The only compensation for John Wood, Mary Prince's 'owner', who had refused her manumission after bringing her to England, and was the victim of Pringle's 'lies', would be 'to come and take Pringle by the neck, and with a good rattan or Mauritius *ox* whip, lash him through London'. The most scurrilous abuse was his reference to Pringle's 'secret closeting and labours with Mary: … servants are not removed from the washing tub into the parlour without an object'[11] – elsewhere he characterized Mary as a prostitute.

The same month the virulently pro-slavery *John Bull* spread the same *canard,* claiming that Pringle 'as is also *well known*, keeps in his house a black —— hush! Offend not the classic ear of Mr PRINGLE by giving utterance to a word of undoubted import'[12].

Pringle wrote to Fairbairn, with remarkable restraint, on 31 December 1831:

> Do you see how MacQueen is abusing me in Blackwood? I will ere long reply to his misrepresentations (not his abuse) in a fourth edition of "The History of Mary Prince". Meanwhile I am prosecuting him for libel. Abuse is what we must all expect – and in truth it is a distinction to be calumniated in such a cause.[13]

There was no fourth edition (though the book is in print today, published by at least one American and two British houses). The libel action came to the Court of Common Pleas in London on 21 February. As both MacQueen and Blackwood were in Scotland, the defendant was Thomas Cadell, Blackwood's London agent, an unoffending man who had not even read the article, and was proud to have been the publisher of the highly moral religious writer Hannah More. When he had done so he agreed with his defence counsel that he had no case. Mary Prince gave evidence that it was she and not Pringle who had written the *History* and was not cross-examined. The judgment was awarded to Pringle, with damages of only £5 – he had asked for £2000. More important, he was awarded costs, assessed at £435, with which sum MacQueen reimbursed Cadell. George Stephen had acted for Pringle, without fee.[14]

Only six days later Pringle found himself the defendant in a libel action brought by John Adams Wood in the Court of King's Bench. The London *Times* tells a very different story, making much of Mary Prince's cross-examination, and punctuating its report by the telling insertion '(laughter)'.[15] MacQueen had called her a 'prostitute … addicted [to] immoral habits' and the cap seemed to fit, not least in her story of finding a rival in Captain Abbot's bed and giving her a 'licking'. The court found that the story of her ill-treatment by the Woods had been 'exaggerated' and judgment went to Wood, with damages of £25. Pringle was awarded costs, in the region of £250, and was again represented by George Stephen, with no fee, as before.

Domestic service and her memoirs were far from the only connection between Mary Prince and the Pringles. Thomas, through Dr Lushington, tabled a petition in Parliament seeking 'relief' so that Prince could return to her husband Daniel James, himself free, in Antigua. He corresponded with the Moravians in Antigua to win support for Prince's case, as did others he recruited to her cause, and did his best, again with Stephen Lushington as his spokesman, to persuade the obdurate Wood to grant Mary her liberty. His statement of her case, as a supplement to the second edition of the history is evidence of his tireless efforts for her, of Wood's manipulations and hypocrisy employed to make Mary suffer. He obtained opinions of others who knew her, notably Joseph Phillips, an Anti-Slavery Society member from Antigua and expressed in the supplement his own view of her character, warts and all. She was, he ended, 'on the whole as well-behaved and respectable a person in her station as any domestic, white or black, (and we have had ample experience of both colours) we have had in our service'.[16]

Mary Prince disappears from the scene, leaving the stigma, recently discovered, that her re-admission to the Moravian church, which she had joined in Antigua in the early 1820s, was refused by its Fetter Lane congregation in July 1832. Their records show that as she had been suspended from the Moravian church in St John's, Antigua, for 'immoral conduct' and after Pringle's friend Bishop C.I. Latrobe had 'stated what he knew of her character and circumstances', while she was still with the Pringles.[17]

On the credit side, it may be said that she was a guest at the wedding of Susanna Strickland and Captain Moodie in 1832 and is mentioned with kindliness and some humour in Strickland's and Pringle's letters. And it is Mary Prince who, whatever her faults, is admired today. Her *History* did much to destroy the myth of the happy slave and that Africans were a human sub-species. 'Her narrative is not just a record of her personal experiences, it is also a protest on behalf of all those who were forced to suffer the abuse of their human rights during the era of transatlantic slavery.'[18] This verdict by a very recent editor of *The History of Mary Prince* would have been approved by Thomas Pringle, the first editor and publisher of Susanna Strickland's transcription of the slave Mary Prince's life story.

Even through the intense anti-slavery activity of the early 1830s Pringle maintained both his literary life and his close involvement with South African affairs, not least with the Baviaans River community. He put a great deal of hard work into his editorship of *Friendship's Offering*, and was pleased with both its success and the necessary addition to his income, meagre indeed at £200 per annum from the Anti-Slavery Society. He felt keenly that it distracted him from the 'great cause'. He wrote to a friend (unnamed in Leitch Ritchie's brief 'Memoirs of Thomas Pringle'):

> I do not feel satisfied at devoting my leisure hours to an object which has no higher aim than the mere entertainment of lovers of light literature. ... Should I agree to edit another volume I shall certainly insert a story as the illustration of the condition of the colonial population in South Africa, though my immediate objective ... is to eke out an otherwise scanty income.[19]

He wrote just such a story but clearly realized that it was strong meat that would not be acceptable to the refined, largely feminine readership of *Friendship's Offering*. He had had to reject Hogg's poem contributed to the 1829 issue for just that reason: he could not admit 'a single expression which could call up a blush on the cheek of the most delicate females if reading aloud to a mixed company'.[20] His story – the only one he wrote in prose – described the life of Pangola, a Bushman herder who, though his Boer master was kindly, was flogged cruelly by the Field Cornet Van Bronkhorst in his master's absence. Swearing revenge, he led a band of 'other fugitives from the colony as desperate and destitute as himself' in the neutral territory 'adjoining to the Koonap River and the Winterberg Mountains', making 'predatory inroads into the Colony in order to wreak his vengeance on the oppressors of his race'. Their depredations ended with a commando raid in which his former master, an English officer and the Field Cornet took part and Pangola met his end, though 'the English officer humanely offered to have his wound examined'. He preferred not 'to be doomed, by laws which I disclaim, to a more ignominious death. I die in arms against the Christians – the murderous Christians who destroyed my race'.

The story is harrowing but well told, though marred for a modern reader by the high-flown rhetoric in Pangola's exchanges with Diederik Kruger, his master. The action displays Pringle's personal knowledge and experience and is a stinging rebuke to his fellow Christians for their near-genocide of the Bushman and their virtual enslaving of those they did not kill. It was published in his friend Thomas Roscoe's collection, *The Remembrance* in 1831 as 'Pangola, an African Tale, by Thomas Pringle, Esq.' Dedicated to Queen Adelaide, this was a superior publication with many of Pringle's literary circle contributing: Mrs Hemans, Richard Hill, James Hogg, Mary Howitt, Mary Russell Mitford, James Montgomery and several others.

Characteristically, Hogg appears to have parodied his friend, whom he had so mistreated in the days of the Chaldee MS and the *Poetic Mirror*, in publishing in *Blackwood's* in November 1829 his story 'The Pongos', subtitled, like Pringle's articles in the *New Monthly Magazine*, 'A Letter from Southern Africa'. Did Hogg pick up the local colour he needed from Pringle? Much of his background material might have come from reading Pringle's *New Monthly Magazine* articles from 1825 to 1827 or the *Oriental Herald*, or from seeing an early draft of 'Pangola'.

The 'Letter' is from one 'Wm Mitchell , Vander Creek near Cape Town' and tells the story of the abduction of first his infant son and then his wife Agnes from their farm among the Kousies, whose chief is 'the great Karoo'. One night 'a tribe of those large baboons called ourang-outangs, pongos or wild men of the woods' invaded the Mitchells' settlement and made off with the baby, William. Mitchell gathered a force to search for the child and then for his mother when she was also taken by the Pongos.

His friend Captain Johnstone sent out two companies of the 72nd Regiment, the Duke of Albany's Own Highlanders, to frighten Chief Karoo, the suspected kidnapper. (The 72nd Foot had, in fact not fiction, served at the Cape off and on from 1806 to 1822. Later, a 'disbanded serjeant' Hozie had wanted to shoot, while they were at their supper, five Xhosa warriors to whom Pringle's father Robert had given shelter and food.

Angered by Mitchell's refusal to sell him Agnes for four oxen, Karoo had threatened retribution, in a scene which is a caricature of the visit of the Thembu chief Bawana to the Pringles in 'The Emigrant's Cabin':

> It is Powana from Zwart-Kei, I ween.
> The Amatembu chief. He comes to pay
> A friendly visit, promised many a day;
> To view our settlement in Lynden Glen,
> And smoke the Pipe of Peace with Scottish men.

In Hogg's account:

> The chief Karoo came to me one day, with his interpreter, whom he caused to make a long palaver about his power and dominion and virtues and his desire to do much good … he concluded with expressing his lord's desire to have my wife to be his own..

When the Pongos are revealed, two years later, to have taken Agnes and William, a local force was raised. Its composition is a curious mixture of Hogg's imagination and information, much garbled, from Pringle:

> We raised in all fifty Malays and Koussies, nine British soldiers and every one of the settlers that could bear arms were with us, so that we had in all a hundred men, the blacks being armed with pikes and all the rest with swords, guns and pistols.

The story ends with the Mitchells' departure for a new life in a 'little wigwam five miles from Cape Town' and planning a move to Australia. The settlers had ended up on good terms with the Pongos and with the recovery of Agnes and William. A forerunner of Edgar Rice Burroughs, Hogg casts Agnes as a leader of the Pongos, and little William as the adored surrogate son also of the Queen, whose own infant did not survive the raid on the Mitchells. William behaves like a white boy with black playfellows in Pringle's South Africa, 'cuffing them and ordering them … to do this, that and the other thing and they were not only obedient but seemed flattered by his notice and correction.'

Mitchell's final judgment on the Pongos reads as if Hogg were having a final dig at the Whig abolitionist Pringle, from his own apolitical, Tory-inclined standpoint: 'I cannot help having a lingering affection for the creatures. They would make the most docile, powerful and affectionate of all slaves'. Present-day criticism, with 'alterity' and 'subaltern' studies in vogue, judges the story to be Hogg's subtle attack on colonial behaviour, with its similarity to 'the artificiality of such classification systems', which include British class categorizing of which 'the Ettrick Shepherd' was at the receiving end. This came, wrote one such study, from Hogg's 'association with such settlers as Pringle who were both abolitionist and deeply concerned about the treatment of natives by settlers'.[21] True of Thomas Pringle but hardly befitting his friend James Hogg.

Careful study could tell us which of the mass of material in the *Anti-Slavery Monthly Reporter* was Pringle's and which Zachary Macaulay's, and doubtless some of it came from both. The story of the mistreatment of the Jamaican slave Kitty Hilton by her clergyman master, the Revd G.W. Bridges, and the transcription of the appeal on her behalf by Pringle for the Anti-Slavery Society to the Colonial Secretary Sir George Murray, in the *Reporter* of 1 September 1830 was clearly Pringle's, as was Betto Douglas's case, fully reported in No 25, June 1827. He wrote further about this ill-treated woman slave, kept in the stocks for a year by Lord Romney's overseer in St Kitts, in his shortlived *Anti-Slavery Record* in March 1832. On 6 March 1833 he wrote to Allan Cunningham: 'I am just sitting down to show up a *lord*' about Betto Douglas, whom 'he refuses to emancipate *on any terms*'.[22] Romney yielded, before the Abolition Act was passed three months later.

In addition to the *Reporter*, the *Record* and the many pamphlets he wrote or edited for the Society, Pringle's writing appeared in *The Tourist, or Sketch Book of the Times*, which described itself as 'a literary and anti-slavery journal under the superintendence of the Agency Anti-Slavery Society', providing further evidence of his association with the Agency committee, though employed by its parent body. His most significant contribution was his essay 'The Wrongs of the Amakosa', bylined 'by Thomas Pringle, Esq.', in the issue of 14 January 1833. He set out to apportion blame for the 'wars between the European colonists and the native tribes in South Africa'. He adjudged 'if the balance were fairly adjusted … an enormous preponderance of wrong must be placed to the account of the less excusable party – the enlightened and powerful'. The article is memorable for its quotation (or reconstruction) of the statement to Colonel Willshire, recorded by Captain Andries Stockenstrom, of a follower of Makhanda after the Battle of Grahamstown. The eloquent *induna* proclaimed that 'this war, British Chiefs, is an unjust war for you are striving to extirpate a people whom you forced to take up arms' by imposing the unacceptable suzerainty of Ngqika over Ndlambe's followers, of whom Makhanda was a war leader and prophet. Pringle ended by applauding the meeting of the Rharhabe chiefs at the Wesleyville mission on 21 March 1832 at which promotion of Christian missions was accepted.

'The Wrongs of the Amakosa' reappeared in *Friendship's Offering*,[23] in 1833, only a year before the outbreak of the Sixth Frontier War, which Pringle did not live to see and to regret. It brought an angry response from among the Albany settlers, though Fairbairn's *Advertiser* leaders condemning settler and government actions on the frontier were even more extreme. The settlers were roused to fury by *African Sketches* very soon after.

Pringle expressed the same view in the *Edinburgh Review* on the Methodist missionary Revd Stephen Kay's *Travels and Researches in Caffraria* in January 1834, praising the book's thorough coverage of the Nguni nations and their way of life and its pro-African, pro-missionary stance. Yet he found it 'ill-digested and confusedy arranged', with 'large portions mere repetition' with 'whole chapters consisting almost entirely of extracts from recent well-known publications on the Cape'. He found it 'more reprehensible' that 'many of the quotations are not duly acknowledged'. Some of these extracts were from his own work. To Fairbairn he described Kay as a 'shameless thief'.[24]

The 'mere entertainment' he regretted in the contents of *Friendship's Offering* was at least of educational value – and far more remunerative – in his work for the *Penny Magazine of the Society for the Diffusion of Useful Knowledge* in 1832 and 1833. These were crisply-written brief accounts of African wild-life: the baboon, buffalo, leopard, ostrich, snakes; of human society: Khoisan and settler, 'A Party of Emigrants Travelling in South Africa' (the Scots party's journey from Algoa Bay in 1820), 'Sabbath in the Wilderness', 'A Settler's Cabin in South Africa' and 'An African Judge and European Slave-holder'.

Of greater length and at a higher level is the eight-page Supplement to the issue of 29 September to 31 October 1832 – the 'Biographical Sketch of Sir Walter Scott'. Space limitations had prevented Pringle 'from fully employing his original materials'. It is, in effect, an obituary of Sir Walter, who had died, aged 61, on 21 September 1832, and was buried in Dryburgh Abbey, near the graves of Pringle's forebears. In a fine study, full of whole-hearted praise of Scott's character and towering literary stature, Pringle admitted some 'foibles and faults', of which the writer (anonymously) had 'neither space nor inclination [for] impartial delineation'. What were they? His lack of religion perhaps, or the commercial ruthlessness and acquisitiveness that brought him down.

He gave much space to describing his first visit to Abbotsford in 1819, 'having been acquainted with Sir Walter in Edinburgh for a year or two previously, recalling Scott's *bonhomie* and his revealing 'the personal history of this extraordinary man', who was totally without 'egotistical assumption or literary vanity'. His guests, after dinner, enjoyed 'an intellectual treat of the richest and most racy description'.

Pringle dwelt on Scott's 'acts of friendship to literary men whom he found struggling in obscurity or diversity', citing James Hogg, Allan Cunningham and 'Mr T. Pringle (another of his Border acquaintance), who was warmly recommended by him when he went abroad in 1820, for a government appointment at the Cape'. The old deference remained: the writer never presumed to claim Scott as a friend.

Scott's generous 'acts of friendship' to Pringle seem never to have been shared by his son-in-law Lockhart and his friends, who as late as 1828 were still joking about Pringle's lameness and his crutches, so heartlessly targeted in the Chaldee MS. Lockhart recorded that on 7 October when Scott was visiting London, 'Mr Pringle, the Lamb of the Chaldee MS, of all people, paid a visit', recalling that 'the Lamb and the Bear [Cleghorn] came skipping on staves'[25]. Andrew Lang, Lockhart's biographer, sought some mitigation by adding 'Lockhart later did what he could for a book by his old victim, reviewing it in the *Quarterly*',[26] a review which had faults that somewhat marred the mitigation.

Lang himself shared the joke about Pringle's disability, recalling that during Pringle's dispute with Blackwood 'we find Scott trying to help a (literally) lame dog over a style'.[27]

Lockhart did recognize Scott's closeness to Pringle, whom he thanked, on 1 November 1832, for 'the very graceful and feeling tribute you have paid in the paper you enclosed to the memory of dear Sir Walter'. Already busy with his lengthy life of Scott, he asked Pringle to send him 'any particulars respecting either yourself, or poor Allister Campbell, or any other individual of whose relations with Sir W you had equal cognizance'.[28]

'Poor Allister Campbell' was Alexander Campbell, in whose *Albyn's Anthology*, four of Pringle's early poems (three of them later in *Ephemerides*) were published in 1816 and 1818. Campbell fell on evil days and late in life scarcely supported himself by copying Scott's manuscripts and would take no charity. Scott's diary entry after Pringle's London visit in his absence was somewhat grudging: 'he might have done well [at the Cape] could he have scoured his brain of politics, but he must needs publish a Whig journal at the Cape of Good Hope! He is a worthy creature but conceited withal – *hinc illae lachrymae*'.[29] Lockhart's footnote, despite errors – 'lame in both legs', 'died … in very distressed circumstances' – made some recompense for past ill-use with what Ruskin called 'a sprinkling of honour': *African Sketches* is 'a charming little volume' and Pringle 'a man of amiable feelings and elegant genius'.

NOTES

[1] Pringle to J. Kennedy, 28.6.1834. Pringle (1838), p. cxiii.

[2] Buxton, C., p. 97.

[3] Menzies, William, *Cases decided in the Supreme Court of the Cape of Good Hope as reported by the late Hon. William Menzies* vol. 1, pp. 455–6; J. Philip, *Researches in South Africa,* vol. 1, p. 266.

[4] Menzies, pp. 456, 459.

[5] *Op. cit.,* p. 461.

[6] Cory, vol. 2, p. 420.

[7] Pringle to J. Philip, 16.11.1830, Vigne (2011), p. 382. LP, Fairbairn Papers, 1, 142.

[8] Theal, G.M., *History of South Africa from 1795 to 1872,* 4 vols (1915), vol. 1, p. 432; Cory, vol. 2, p. 420.

[9] Pringle to J. Philip, 31.5.1831, Vigne (2011), p. 330. Bodl. Lib. (R.H.), Addns. 1793–1839 f 311a.

[10] See p. 203 above.

[11] *Blackwood's,* 87, November 1831, p. 744. See n. 14.

[12] *John Bull,* 26.12.1831, p. 27. Letter from 'Expositor'.

[13] Pringle to Fairbairn, 31.12.1831, Vigne (2011), p. 337. LP, Fairbairn Papers, 1, 114.

[14] Thomas, Sue, 'Pringle v Cadell and Wood v Pringle: the Libel Cases of *'The History of Mary Prince', Journal of Commonwealth Literature,* 49, March 2005, pp. 13–35. See also n. 17 for Prof. Thomas's further contribution.

[15] *The Times,* 1.3.1833.

[16] 'Supplement to the History of Mary Prince, by the Editor', *History of Mary Prince,* 2nd edition, 1831. See also Prince, pp. 39–63.

[17] Thomas, Sue, 'More Information on Mary Prince in London', *Notes and Queries,* vol. 256, no. 1, March 2011, pp. 82–5.

[18] Prince, p. xxxii.

[19] Pringle (1838), p. xcii.

[20] Pringle to Hogg, 28.5.1828. NLS MS 2245 f 122.

[21] Alker, Sharon and Nelson, Holly Faith, 'The Limits of Language in Hogg, " The Pongos".' In *James Hogg and the Literary Marketplace,* Alker, S., Nelson, F.H. eds (Farnham, Ashgate, 2009) p. 203.

[22] Pringle to Cunningham, 6.3.1833, Vigne (2011), 'Additional Letters' (2011), p. 23. J. Rylands Lib., Eng. MS 415/140.

[23] *Friendship's Offering,* 1833, pp. 80–91.

[24] Pringle to Fairbairn, 4.11.1833, Vigne (2011), p. 359. LP, Fairbairn Papers, 1, 148.

[25] Lockhart, J.G., *Memoirs of the Life of Sir Walter Scott, Bart.* (1844 ed.) p. 640.

[26] Lang, A., *Life of John Gibson Lockhart* (1897), p. 412.

[27] *Op. cit.,* pp. 145–6.

[28] Lockhart to Pringle, 1.11.1832. LUL, Brotherton Library. 5515.

[29] *The Journal of Sir Walter Scott,* ed. W.E.K.Anderson, 23.10.1826. Ruskin, *Praeterita,* p. 128.

20

African Sketches

Responses

Overshadowing all Pringle's prose writings in these and earlier years is his *Narrative of a Residence in South Africa,* first published as Part 2 of *African Sketches* in May 1834, seven months before his death. His publisher Edward Moxon reissued the *Narrative*, posthumously, the following year as a separate volume, with Josiah Conder's 'biographical sketch'. Pringle wrote to Fairbairn on 22 May 1834:

> The little book of which I now send you a copy was published two days ago. You will find that I have *spoken out*. … I am sure you will suffer for it by the excited rage of the *vermin* around you, who will no doubt pour forth their puny malice on you along with myself and the Dr in consequence of what I have said of them. But what signifies *their* enmity. They cannot harm you, I think, more than they have already – and *our names* and what is better our *deeds* will survive when they and all that belongs to them will be swept into the gulf of oblivion.[1]

Was this Thomas Pringle in the conceited mode observed by Scott and hard to find elsewhere in his words or deeds? The *Narrative* has survived, though a book of such quality deserves to be better known and appreciated in South Africa. Unlike Philip's *Researches in South Africa*, it has been reissued in our time, in an edition limited to 750 copies in 1966, and there was a much abbreviated school edition in the 1920s. It has not taken its place among the Barrows and Burchells, its light extinguished by the South Africa presented by Theal and Cory, from which the country's historiography has slowly moved on.

As with Philip's *Researches*, the author's attitude to the colonists has kept the *Narrative* in the shadows. His reference to the politicians and officials among them as 'vermin' makes it clear that the book would be anathema to them and their descendants down to the *apartheid* era. The book would have been even better had this animus not run through the last four chapters. The years of conflict with the pro-slavery spokesmen, some, like MacQueen, extreme in their abusive tirades, had infected Pringle, who showed more tolerance towards his fellow colonists when at the Cape. The equally abusive response from the colonists was as Pringle predicted but he had gone from the scene before this would have been known in Britain.

His implacable attitude to the military and civil authorities and the majority of the colonists on the frontier was not new. In the radical journal founded by Jeremy

Bentham, the *Westminster Review,* he reviewed in the January-April issue, a slight but influential account of the Cape of the late 1820s, *Four Years in Southern Africa* by Cowper Rose, then a young Royal Engineers officer. He praised the book but objected to Rose's belief that 'in and about Cape Town … cruelty [to slaves] is rare', and referred to the *Anti-Slavery Reporter* Nos 20, 32 and 54 as reasons why he, Pringle, was 'constrained to adopt a very opposite position'. He quoted the Colonial Secretary Huskisson's dispatch to the Governor, General Bourke, in 1827, requiring particulars of a case in which a slave was given 125 lashes and two months working in irons for making a complaint against his master.

He was as critical of Rose's claim that 'the English' were not guilty of 'wanton cruelty' in their military operations against the amaXhosa. Rose's letter, from the Office of Woods and Forests in London, in January 1830, expressed his gratitude for the 'very kind and handsome terms' in which Pringle had reviewed the book, but defended his dismissal of 'wanton cruelty' allegations, in terms that might have tempered Pringle's attitude. Rose wrote:

> I have never by a single word attempted to defend the system pursued towards the Kaffers. That system was a short-sighted one of intimidation – cruel and sometimes treacherous but still not wantonly cruel.[2]

The object of the system, perhaps erroneous, was 'connected with the safety of the colonists'. The consequent actions were oppressive 'but I still think that there is a distinction between them and acts of wanton cruelty'.

Narrative of a Residence in South Africa, part two of *African Sketches,* had been fifteen years in the making, from the idea warmly taken up by Barrow in 1819 to the approaching end of slavery in 1833, when, as Pringle told Fairbairn in November 1833: 'I am preparing at last a book on the Cape, in verse and prose, comprising all my old scraps worth collecting and a good deal not yet in print.'[3]

Much of what had been written earlier had been put aside until Pringle's crowded days allowed him a few hours of leisure. Pages 40–1, 63–5 of the 1966 edition are a straight transcription of the journal he kept in the Baviaans River days, more still was recycled from the *Penny Magazine* and the *Tourist.* The last four – out of 15 – chapters, a little over one-third of the book, were rushed out with the printer's devil waiting at the door. As he wrote to Fairbairn on 16 July: 'I had only a couple of chapters written when I began to print, and the rest was written as the printer required copy, with the exception of passages formerly printed in periodicals'.[4]

The result is a book of enduring interest, a flowing narrative, lit up by passages of real beauty and charm, and in its final chapters a passionate response to immediate events on the frontier, learned from a file of the *Commercial Advertiser* up to 1 March 1834, barely two months before publication, and just 'as I am sending these, the last sheets of my volume, to press' as the final lengthy footnote reads. He applauded Fairbairn's leaders urging an assembly of 'the Amakosa chiefs west of the Kei River (about ten in number)' to meet the Governor and his officers and advisers. The object would be to agree a treaty 'such as we enter into with civilized nations' by which 'the boundaries will be defined and distinctly marked

– the channels of communication between the Governor and the Chiefs specified'. The Chiefs would be cemented 'in a regular confederacy' to prevent 'the further breaking down of the Caffer nation into weak and mischievous fragments'.[5] This was 'in singular accordance with the views I have expressed'.[6]

None of this was to be. The Governor, Sir Benjamin D'Urban, was a 'facile man', as Pringle had commented to Fairbairn,[7] and dilatory. There was no assembly, instead there was war, and *African Sketches* reached the colony while the frontier settlers were suffering in the first all-out conflict on the frontier since their arrival in 1820.

Part 1 of *African Sketches,* entitled 'Poems Illustrative of South Africa' gave greater offence to the settlers than did the lengthy diatribes in the closing chapters of the 'Narrative', which were perhaps less read. 'The Caffer Commando', previously published in *Ephemerides* (1828) began:

> Hark! – heard ye the signals of triumph afar!
> 'Tis our Caffer Commando returning from war:
> The voice of their laughter comes loud on the wind,
> Nor heed they the curses that follow behind.
> For who cares for him, the poor Kosa, that wails
> Where the smoke rises dim from yon desolate vales –
> That wails for his little one killed in the fray,
> Or his herds by the Colonist carried away?

And proclaims

> For England hath spoke in her tyrannous mood,
> And the edict is writing in African blood!

His naming 'England' as the tyrant suggests that Pringle, the Border Scot, recalled the history of his home region, but, like most contemporaries, he used 'England' to connote the British state.

Its first publication, in the *Oriental Herald* in 1827, had four more stanzas which rebuked the English more harshly, quoting the Commandant:

> 'Promotion will follow – and as for the rest.
> 'Tis *powder and ball* suits these travellers best: –
> You may cant about Missions and Civilization –
> My plan is to shoot – or enslave the whole nation.'

> Thus spoke the gay Chief, in his arrogant mood –
> And his words are now writing in African blood![8]

'Makanna's Gathering' was as reviled by the settlers' spokesmen. Makhanda hears 'the voice of HIM who sits on high, and bids me speak his will!'

> He bids me call you forth,
> Bold sons of Káhabee,
> To sweep the White Men from the earth
> And drive them to the sea.

Pringle made many such changes and revisions in his poems with their reappearance in later journals and books. With 'Makanna's Gathering' there was perhaps an intention to reduce the offence to the settlers rather than to improve scansion or choice of words or images.

The milder version said enough to provoke such objections as those in Godlonton's outspokenly pro-settler *Graham's Town Journal,* the most vicious, to use Rennie's epithet, being the letters of one C.J. Gray, whom Rennie identified as a Grahamstown land surveyor.[9]

On 2 January 1835, a few days after the beginning of what Godlonton called 'the irruption of the Kafir hordes', Gray described 'Makanna's Gathering' as

> an address to the Kafir nation supposed to be delivered by one of its seers, in which the great God of mercy and truth is solemnly mocked, and his dread majesty made to issue his commands to drive the English from this country, or else into the sea. Not the most zealous 'Makanna', nor the most ferocious Kafir chief … could have spirited up his countrymen to the remorseless warfare of revenge and extermination more effectually or more earnestly than has this ungrateful viper, Thomas Pringle.[10]

Godlonton's leaders were almost as angry at the *Narrative* and correspondents kept up the attack on Pringle for months to come. Philip's *Researches,* which Pringle was accused of co-authoring, and Fairbairn's editorials in the *Commercial Advertiser,* took much abuse, though there were letters in their defence, particularly of Fairbairn – one from 110 signatories, albeit beside another attacking him by 234 Grahamstown residents.[11]

The *Narrative* contains many passages of great quality. Chapter 10 tells the story of Pringle's Cape Town years, from his high hopes to 'the ruin of the author's prospects' in 25 pages. The rest of the book is based on the frontier, with much natural description of the quality of the ride with Robert Hart, from the Somerset farm to Enon.[12] The final chapters deal with the Mfecane, Bushmen, Khoikhoi and Xhosa, with understanding enlivened by passion. In a final, memorable five pages, near the end, Pringle gave praise to Fairbairn, who,

> with a courageous consistency, a patient perseverance, a lofty disregard of temporary interests … he has devoted the powers of his mind and the purpose of his life … to the unflinching advocacy of the great principles of Justice, of Freedom, of Christian Philanthropy, as paramount to all accidental or conventional distinctions of station, lineage, colour or caste.[13]

He recalled that in 1828 'the wealthier class' at the Cape had, in the words of an address, testified that Fairbairn 'had consistently advocated and protected the best interests of the Colony' and especially evinced 'their gratitude for procuring for them the blessings of a FREE PRESS'. He had been presented with 'a handsome piece of plate, two-thirds nearly of those grateful subscribers being Cape-Dutch slave-holders'.[14]

Many turned against Fairbairn as slavery came under serious threat and even more when it was abolished five years later. They poured 'unmeasured vituperation' on him, 'on Dr Philip and other colonial friends of the coloured classes, and of the "Saints and Philanthropists" in England',[15] of which Pringle, unnamed, was the most active in the Cape interest.

Pringle had written to Dr Philip in November 1830: 'I have had no letters from Fairbairn nor have I heard any sign of him – fear that he was unwell which gives me great concern. He has fought nobly in the good cause'.[16] Then, and at the end, Fairbairn's neglect of his friend, who had brought him to South Africa, mars his otherwise shining reputation. Their correspondence resumed in 1831 and both, with Philip and Stockenstrom, continued to pursue the 'good cause' in those final years.

Their correspondence resumed when Fairbairn wrote in April 1831 that he had married Elizabeth, John and Jane Philip's second child. Pringle's December 1831 letter was full of anti-slavery news and asked 'Why has our old intimate correspondence broken off? It ought not to be so'. He mentioned 'several literary schemes on my hands' – *African Sketches* was one of them – but they must wait until his 'hands and head' were no longer 'full of "slavery"'.[17]

When that time came he found he had to feed the printer with copy so sent in the 'Poems Illustrative of South Africa' which thus forms Part I of the book. Most were about the South African landscape, people and wild life and all but a very few had appeared most recently in *Ephemerides, The Penny Magazine* and *The Tourist* in 1828, 1832 and 1833. Some had seen the light of day in the *South African Journal, Commercial Advertiser* and *South African Chronicle* in Cape Town. Only 'The Emigrant's Cabin' and 'The Forester of the Neutral Ground' made their first appearance in *African Sketches*. The latter was written for a 'collection of original contributions in prose and verse, illustrative of the evils of slavery and commemorative of its abolition in the British Empire' entitled *The Bow in the Cloud, or the Negro's Memorial* and edited by Mrs Mary Ann Rawson, a leading woman abolitionist, with help from Pringle. The touching story is told in Chapter 7 above.

'The Emigrant's Cabin' as Pringle explained to Fairbairn came about when 'turning over some old scraps one day I found the rough commencement of a rhyming epistle to you … I set to and with a little labour extended it to the thing you see, … I really think it improves my African Collection considerably by giving a view of our familiar and domestic condition.' He judged it 'not the worst of my attempts in my own opinion' and was pleased to add his 'friend and neighbour the Wizard Coleridge's' fondness for it.[18]

'The Emigrant's Cabin' reads well today, lacking as it does the poetic language of the day, but for repeated 'o'ers'. (The modern reader has to get past 'Afar' before enjoying 'Afar in the Desert'.) 'The Emigrant's Cabin' takes the visitor Fairbairn through an imagined visit to, and luncheon at, the Beehive Hut, served by the Khoikhoi maid, Vytjie Dragoener, with conversation between the two friends, with 'Mrs P and her Sister … round the table' until *Exeunt Ladies*. Fairbairn challenges his host:

> Come now, be candid: tell me, my dear friend,
> Of your aspiring aims is *this* the end?
> Was it for Nature's wants, fire, shelter, food
> You sought this dreary, soulless solitude?

and ends his examination:

> Be frank, confess the fact you cannot hide –
> You sought this den from disappointed pride.

Pringle's countering argument is spirited:

> You've missed the mark, Fairbairn: my breast is clear.
> Nor wild Romance nor Pride allured me here:
> Duty and Destiny with equal voice
> Constrained my steps: I had no other choice.

Against Fairbairn's

> *Here!* – save for Her who shares and soothes your lot,
> You might as well squat in a Caffer's cot':

he defends his life 'Mid Afric's deserts rude':

> I have my farm and garden, tools and pen:
> My scheme for civilising savage men.

And continues with four pages of lively description of the region, his friends, and, last, a visit from the Thembu chief, Bawana, quoted above.

There is an extra dimension, and pleasure, in the copious notes added, the longest, a page and a half *exposé* of the 'injury and insult' suffered by the Revd William Wright in the colony and the 'supercilious disregard' by the SPCK in England, which Pringle 'witnessed with disgust'.[19] This despite his letters repeatedly complaining to Fairbairn of Wright's maladroit and counter-productive behaviour, beside his undoubted 'good works'. The note displays Pringle's outrage at ill-treatment of an undeserving victim, whatever faults the victim may have had.

Pringle's poetry, though its phrasing and metre may be a barrier today, has been the subject of much study in South Africa – by Attwell, Coetzee, Shaw, Shum, Voss, Wahl and others – which excuses the biographer from straying into esoteric literary fields. Even 'the Wizard Coleridge' spoke out on the barrier of Pringle's poetic language. The proofs of Part 1, pages 1 to 16, with Coleridge's marginalia, are referred to on page 197 above.

His poetic output was considerable, if varied in quality and substance – published in *The Institute, The Autumnal Excursion, Glen-Lynden, Ephemerides,* Part One of *African Sketches* and finally the *Poetical Works*. He claimed a modest ranking among Scottish, not English, poets. His short life lacked the tranquillity in which – as Wordsworth wrote – emotion might be recollected and so create the 'spontaneous overflow of powerful feelings'.[20]

The four months at Genadendal and the final year in the 'reed hut in the wilderness' gave him time but he had throughout both periods 'a battling time of it', facing the misery of debt and poverty, and preoccupation with his struggle against his enemies in the Cape government, Somerset and his 'tools'. It is remarkable that poetry flowed from him. Though it may have brought remorse at the diverting of his energies from 'the great cause', his 'Duty and Destiny' remained inviolate.

NOTES

1 Pringle to Fairbairn, 22.5.1834, Vigne (2011), p. 361. LP, Fairbairn Papers, 1, 150.
2 Rose, Cowper, *Four Years in Southern Africa* (1829). *Westminster Review,* vol, 12, No 23, pp. 232–46. Rose to Pringle, 8.1.30. Paver letters, Cory Lib.
3 Pringle to Fairbairn, 4.11.1833, Vigne (2011), p. 359. LP, Fairbairn Papers, 1, 148.
4 Pringle to Fairbairn , 16.7.1834, Vigne (2011), p. 365. LP, Fairbairn Papers, 1, 54.
5 Pringle (1966), p. 332.
6 Pringle (1966), p. 319n.
7 Pringle to Philip, 23.8.1834, Vigne (2011), p. 367. WUL Philip Family Papers MS A85.
8 *Oriental Herald,* 30.4.1827, pp. 39–40.
9 Rennie, vol. 3, pp. 1029–30; vol. 4, p. 1779.
10 *Op. cit.,* p. 1030; *Graham's Town Journal,* 2.1.1835.
11 Rennie, vol. 3, p. 1032. *Graham's Town Journal,* 13.2.1835.
12 Pringle (1966), pp. 77–85, 81–5. ; see above pp. 84–5.
13 *Op. cit.,* p. 330.
14 *Ibid.*
15 Pringle (1966), p. 331.
16 Pringle to Philip, 16.11.30, Vigne (2011), p. 329. LP, Farbairn Papers, LP 1, 42.
17 *Ibid.*
18 Pringle to Fairbairn, 22.5.1834, Vigne (2011), p. 361. LP, Fairbairn Papers, 1, 150.
19 Pringle (1838), pp. 87–8.
20 Wordsworth, William, *Lyrical Ballads,* with S.T. Coleridge, 2 nd ed. (1800).

21

On Scottish Ground

Before the accelerated pace generated by the Agency group made a long absence from his Anti-Slavery office in Aldermanbury too difficult, Pringle wrote to Sir Walter Scott, on 14 June 1830:

> I have almost resolved to make an excursion to Scotland this autumn, for the sake of my health, which has of late somewhat failed me; but it is not very likely that I shall be in Roxburghshire. I have not set my foot on Scottish ground since I embarked for the Cape eleven years ago.[1]

He and Margaret duly went north that autumn but left no record of their travels. By his own account we know only of his visits to Selkirkshire, and to Morebattle in Roxburghshire, the adjoining county of his childhood. He wrote at length to his brother William in his South African Eildon about their immediate Pringle ancestors.

This was not simply a letter but the opening pages of a well-bound volume, its pages otherwise blank, but with *Family Memorials Vol. I* on the spine and 'Family Memorials &c.' at the top of page 1. The letter is unsigned and is followed by the 28–line 'Inscription' quoted at the foot.[2] The volume found its way to the Ainslie family of Braeside in the Fort Beaufort district of the Cape Colony, descendants of Thomas's sister Jessie. It survives in the Cory Library in Grahamstown

Thomas's immediate family had sprung from a small farm, once the orchards of Dryburgh Abbey, a noble ruin since destroyed by English invaders in the mid-16th century. The Scottish Eildon hills lay a few miles west of Dryburgh. Further back the Blaiklaw family descended from the Pringles of Yair, to the west, north of Selkirk. Sir Walter Scott's Abbotsford lies between Dryburgh and Yair and Scott himself is buried in the Abbey ruins.

In the grounds of the Abbey Pringle found the grave of their great-grandfather, William, its gravestone gone (and found in the Abbey cellars by the family's South African historian, Eric Pringle of Glen Thorn, Cape in 1969).[3] Thomas planned to erect a new one with an inscription 'as a memorial to our family'. In his usual tetrameter in rhymed couplets its 28 lines survive in his letter to William, with revisions in *Friendship's Offering* for 1832 and in *African Sketches*. The lines include a brief account of the 'venturous race' of Robert Pringle, grandson of old William, and his offspring:

Another band beneath the Southern skies
Have built their homes where Caffer mountains rise,
And taught wild Mancazana's willowed vale
The simple strains of Scottish Teviotdale.

He was able to assure his brother that the connection of old William's father, also William, to the Laird of Whytbank of that time was confirmed by 'the present worthy representative of the house of Whytbank, Alexander Pringle MP for Selkirkshire'. The 9th Laird of Whytbank, he identified the old Peel Tower on the banks of the Tweed, the home of their great grandfather William and his son.

Of their traditionally held relationship to the Lairds of Whytbank Thomas would go no further than to describe it as 'rather distant if not altogether imaginary'.[4] A legal document of 1663, however, published in 1921 by a later Alexander Pringle described the first William Pringle as 'natural son to James, third Laird of Whytbank'. Thomas's fame in the Borders was still great enough for this Alexander to say of him that 'there is no greater scion of the house of Yair, nor indeed of the Surname, than Thomas Pringle',[5] yet suggested he would have seen the document when at the Register office and suppressed any reference to it. It was, in Rennie's sound judgment, a 'genuine failure'[6] by Thomas in his quest for his family's origins.

His local fame certainly brought Thomas into friendly contact with Alexander Pringle MP, and with John Pringle, 9th Laird of Clifton, whom he met after visiting Mary Potts, his old nurse at Morebattle. He also met Mrs Morrison, the widow of his schoolfriend David Morrison, son of the Secessionist Minister at Morebattle during Pringle's schooldays there. The Laird of Clifton, the last of his line, wrote from Clifton Park that he had bestowed a little charity on Nanny Potts.[7] The rest of the Scottish visit is silence.

Pringle was back in London in early November, to find a backlog of mail. He replied to a letter from Jeremy Bentham that 'owing to my being in Scotland ... I was not able to give that proper attention to it which my great respect for you would have commanded'.[8] Bentham, at the height of his fame in the world of reform, had written a pamphlet on the undesirability of colonial expansion, entitled *Emancipate your Colonies!*,[9] and sought contact with an Anti-Slavery committee member, the Revd Robert Walsh, author of *Notices of Brazil*[10], an attack on Brazilian slavery. Pringle's dealings were now with both the great and the far-flung.

His activities seem almost frenzied in the first years of the 1830s, as he entered his forties. Despite his anti-slavery commitment, the libel cases, his publishing, editing and journalism, research and writing for the Anti-Slavery Society, as well as pursuing his claim against the Colonial Office, Pringle kept faith with the growing family settlement on the Baviaans River. He sent books to the Glen Lynden library – the first lending library in South Africa – and gave much time to finding a minister for the church the Scots settlers were to share with their Calvinist Boer neighbours.

The Revd John Pears, an MA of Aberdeen University, ordained in 1817, was carefully selected, after Lord Bathurst had accepted a memorial from the settlers and had undertaken to pay the transport costs and stipend of the right man.[11]

Pringle gave him detailed instructions about his post and he sailed for the Cape in 1829 with Pringle's sister Isabella as a fellow passenger, and bringing with him the first stock of books for the library. He found the church wrongly sited, the congregation too small and the stipend half what Dutch Reformed Church ministers received so left after only 13 months' service, to become Professor of Classics at the newly founded South African College in Cape Town.

In Glen Lynden the Church council were deeply disappointed that 'a congregation so lately established [should] so unexpectedly be left destitute of the Gospel'.[12] Despite lack of support from the Governor, Sir Lowry Cole, the Church council – four Afrikaners and two Scots – urged Pringle to intercede with the Colonial Office in London on their behalf. R.W. Hay, secretary to Viscount Goderich (later Earl of Ripon and Prime Minister), asked Pringle to find a suitable man[13] and after a long search, with the 'assistance of my clerical friends in Scotland, the Revds Drs Chalmers, Gordon, Burns and others' the Revd Alexander Welsh, of Dundee, a former teacher and ordained only in 1832 after 15 years in a poor parish in Glasgow, was appointed and committed to a stay at Glen Lynden for five years.[14] Pringle had told Dr Burns that the new pastor should learn Dutch, which Pringle himself had 'learned to write and speak *tolerably* well in a very few weeks'.

With his wife Elizabeth, son Elias, 14, and two daughters and another son, between 7 and 2 years of age Welsh sailed from Liverpool in the *Jane Henry* on 19 July 1832. They made landfall in Table Bay only on 25 March 1833. His account of the calamitous voyage[15] must rank high among the stories of suffering and sacrifice made by missionaries to distant lands in the days of sail. It perhaps bears retelling for that reason. They suffered cramped quarters, shortage of food and water but plenty of liquor, a drunken, violent captain (tried and gaoled in Cape Town), incompetent mates, drunken quarrels among the crew and the 64 steerage passengers, most of them army pensioners bound for Tasmania, and, worst of all, sickness and the deaths of the Welshes' children Janet, 7, and Alexander, 4.

At Loango, on the coast of today's Congo Brazzaville, seeking food, there was a skirmish with local people and the *Jane Henry* put to sea, leaving nine of her compliment on shore, Elias Welsh among them. They were recovered after nine weeks, Elias at the point of death from fever. He lived, settled among the Pringles, his descendants marrying a Pringle and a Rennie. Catherine Brand Welsh grew up to marry Thomas's nephew William Scott Pringle, 2nd of Eildon.

During those nine weeks, they put in at Fernando Po, today's Bioko and part of Equatorial Guinea. Passengers and crew were succoured by the British superintendent of the island, leased from Spain as an anti-slave-trade naval base. On Christmas day Welsh preached a sermon, the first, he was told, 'ever delivered on that island'. The huge congregation included three to four hundred captured slaves 'all cleanly habited'. He baptised four adults and 24 children and married three couples. He also established a prayer meeting but resisted the urgent pleas that he remain as their minister, at a high stipend, and kept to his duty as minister at Glen Lynden. John Beecroft, the superintendent, whom he calls Governor, Welsh described as 'one of the most amiable men I ever conversed with and well qualified, in my opinion, for the honourable station which he occupies'.

After rescuing Elias and his three shipmates, five having died, and further misadventures Alexander and Elizabeth Welsh with their three surviving children ended their 'long and disastrous voyage' after 250 days at sea, and were much helped in Cape Town by his Glen Lynden predecessor, Professor Pears. Welsh was finally inducted as Glen Lynden minister in August 1833, serving there as pastor and teacher through three frontier wars, until his death in 1856.

Pringle might have surveyed the South African scene with some satisfaction at the time of the Revd Alexander Welsh's arrival. A pastor was at last installed at Glen Lynden, the family settlement was still growing in number, enlarged in area and prospering. In the colony as a whole, a free press had been achieved. Fairbairn, his newspaper and Literary Society were flourishing, General Bourke's 50th Ordinance had emancipated the Khoisan and slavery was nearing abolition. Most remarkably, Philip and Stockenstrom were acceptable to the Cape government and influential at the Colonial Office in London.

In England too, a stocktaking would reveal that he could take pride in his central position in both the anti-slavery campaign and in South African affairs seen from Whitehall. The failed and humiliated founding editor of *Blackwood's* was now in his fifth year of editing one of the most admired annuals, *Friendship's Offering*, commissioning the major writers of the day, a friend to some of the most respected of them – Thomas Campbell, Samuel Rogers, Robert Southey and, most intimately, Samuel Taylor Coleridge. His own poetry collection of 1828, *Ephemerides*, had won much praise.

In Scotland in 1830 he had been received warmly by Pringle kinsmen of a higher status than his Blaiklaw family, the Lairds of Clifton and Whytbank, his friendship with Scott was recognized by Lockhart, the great man's son-in-law and biographer, after Scott's death in September 1832. Lockhart had asked for his memories of their relationship[16] and he had been prominent in the warm reception given that year to James Hogg, the Ettrick Shepherd, as a literary celebrity down south.[17] At a higher level than the many literary magazines that accepted his work, the *Edinburgh Review* published his lengthy review of Kay's *Travels and Researches* in 1834.

He even touched the fringe of the monarchy, through his friendship from Eildon days with 'the gay-humoured Captain Fox, \ With whom I roamed 'mid Koonap's woods and rocks'.[18] Now a Colonel and a Whig MP, Charles Richard Fox was married to Lady Mary FitzClarence, natural daughter of the Duke of Clarence, who became King William IV in 1830. Fox renewed their friendship when he and Pringle met by chance in London in 1828. Pringle was permitted to dedicate the 1831 *Friendship's Offering* to Queen Adelaide, and Fox's father, the prominent Whig politician Lord Holland, wrote warmly to him,[19] with a P.S. 'Your friend Colonel Fox is in Turin with his brother'. The FitzClarence connection enabled him to put the case for the restoration of Coleridge's cancelled annual royal grant, despite Griggs's dismissal of Conder's claim and the failure of E.K. Chambers, Coleridge's biographer, to mention his role in this or any other context.[20] Despite his long friendship with Thomas Clarkson, Coleridge's strongly held and often expressed views on slavery, as in his letters to Pringle, are similarly unmentioned by Chambers.

The Pringles' home life was happy, though, as he wrote to Susanna, now Moodie, at this time, he was 'variable in my temper, hasty and sometimes harsh to those I love'.[21] Margaret was a devoted wife, 'Our hermitage at Highgate', their home from spring 1832, was, he told Fairbairn a year later 'at once cheap and delightful'. His health benefitted: 'Going out and in daily on the top of the stage is expensive but it has done me a world of good and saved me much in Doctors' bills.'[22]

Old friendships stood firm. On 31 December 1831 he recalled old Hogmanays with his friend Fairbairn,[23] adding, with some self-congratulatory phrases, that 'God's good providence has conducted both of us forward' as 'recognized champions of human rights and promoters ... of human virtues and happiness'. They had 'toom [empty] purses' but were 'far more honoured than if we had attained worldly honours and riches'.

He wrote also, in February 1832, to an unidentified 'dear friend'[24] proposing to write him a weekly letter about his past and present life, the collected letters to form 'a little sketch of my biography to prefix my "Poetical Remains".' He acknowledged an element of self-glorification – '"Ah, Tamas! Tamas! – vanity and egotism!" I hear you exclaim!' Yet he recognized that he was no 'Aonian swan' and ranked himself 'among those "minors" who have indited ... a few things their countrymen "would not willingly let die".' He likened his 'poetic trifles' to those of Bruce, Logan, Beattie, Grahame and Leyden, all of them Scots and all of them unquestionably 'minor'.[25]

Who was the friend? Internal evidence rules out Fairbairn, though he is named as John. Was he John Hunter, Writer to the Signet, of Edinburgh, twelve years Pringle's junior so not a contemporary at the university, but an executor of his will in 1834? The letter appears not to have been sent and is quoted by Leitch Ritchie, who had access to Pringle's papers, which included copies of letters sent and, in this case, unsent.

He did send a letter to John Hunter in February 1831, enclosing 'a little anti-slavery tract of mine just published', with a copy for 'your friend Weir' asking for the latter to notice it in 'his Journal' (presumably the *Edinburgh Magazine* launched by the radical bookseller William Tait in 1832) and hoping that Hunter would notice it himself. He enclosed a copy also 'for our worthy friend Dr Morehead', Pringle and Cleghorn's successor as editor of their *Edinburgh Magazine*, and a cousin of Francis Jeffrey. The letter is evidence that he had been in touch with Hunter and the others when in Scotland the previous autumn and that he had made friends among Edinburgh's Whig intelligentsia. A sister of Hunter's was married to John Jeffrey , brother of Francis, and Robert Morehead was their cousin.

We meet John Hunter in a letter from Jane Welsh Carlyle to her friend Mrs Susan Stirling, another sister of Hunter's, to whom she wrote in 1840: 'What a likeable man your brother in Edinburgh is: so intelligent and so unpretentious, so quietly clever and so quietly kind'. Carlyle adds a footnote: 'John Hunter, a worthy and prosperous law official in Edinburgh, residence Craigcrook (Jeffrey's fine villa)'.[26] A man after Pringle's heart, in character if not in social ranking. Perhaps this friendship went to his head a little and accounts for the 'vanity and egotism' of the letter, which he thought better of and kept, unposted.

There were serious flaws in what he had attained in the six years since he had arrived in England with five pounds in his pocket, a huge debt in South Africa and a very depressed literary market-place for his sole source of income. His health was bad. He lamented that he was 'enfeebled by dyspeptic and nervous complaints of long standing'.[27] He had 'felt the misery of debt too severely', though he was able to tell Dr Philip in January 1833 that he was 'gradually emerging from my pecuniary distress' and had insured his life for £100 and lodged the policy with Fairbairn 'for what I owe you'.[28] He knew that abolition would come soon and his income would be much diminished. His hopes of compensation or even relief by the state had virtually ended with Bathurst's decision, conveyed by R.W. Hay in November 1826,[29] that 'as you have quitted the Cape you have placed it out of his Lordship's power to assist your views in the manner that might have been done if you had remained in the colony'. Bathurst was 'not disposed to reject your application altogether' but Pringle came to recognize that these words meant nothing to Bathurst's Whig successors as he had hoped they might.

Perhaps his greatest disappointment, despite all he had gained, was his awareness of what he saw as the wrongs endured by the amaXhosa as victims of the 'commando system' and what he saw as the aggressive hostility of the colonial, forces, with Boer and some British irregulars, towards their black neighbours. Was he conscious of childhood memories of John Turnbull, the Blaiklaw shepherd's tales of the wrongs the Scots had suffered from their more powerful neighbours the English, of Flodden, and of aggression from the south over the centuries?[30] Did he unwittingly share Turnbull's 'hereditary prejudices of his rank and nation', with the colonists replacing the 'southrons'? But he had worked hard for their relief, though this was when he might have seen them as the victims of an English nobleman, Somerset.

Pringle's news from Fairbairn and the *Commercial Advertiser* continued bad and enabled him to supply Buxton with the ammunition he let fly in Parliament on 1 July 1834:[31]

> The treatment of the Aborigines by the colonists is one of the darkest and bloodiest stains upon the page of history, and scarcely any are equal in atrocity to the conduct of the Dutch Boers, ably seconded of late, according to Pringle, by some of the more degraded of the English settlers.

Such attacks were not made only at a safe 6,000-mile distance. Fairbairn wrote in Cape Town on 18 July:[32]

> The conduct of the Colonial forces had been unjust and ferocious beyond parallel. ... The atrocity of the proceedings of the colonists is without a parallel among civilized people. The Kaffirs are termed savages, but it is the colonists who are most entitled to the appellation.

Colonel Wade, acting governor of the Cape before the arrival of Sir Benjamin D'Urban, described the recently deceased Pringle to the Aborigines Committee of Parliament in August 1835[33] as an authority mainly relied upon by those who deemed it impossible to promote the welfare of the aborigines without assailing the character of both the colonists and the Colonial Government.

Despite his bitter sense of wrong, Pringle knew he had the ear of the Whig leadership in England, both directly and through Philip and Stockenstrom, though so little was being done to right the wrongs he sought to expose. Altogether, when in June 1834 the slaves were at last freed, albeit to a long 'apprenticeship', Thomas Pringle, despite poor health and worse finances, was at the pinnacle of his career as a public figure and a man of letters.

NOTES

[1] Pringle to Scott, 14.6.1830, Vigne (2011), p. 327. NLS MS 3913 f 1911.

[2] Pringle to W. Pringle, 14.1.1832. Vigne, 'Additional Letters' (2011), pp. 18–21. Cory Lib. PR 2736a.

[3] Rennie, vol. 1, p. 87.

[4] Pringle to W. Pringle, 14.1.1832. Vigne, 'Additional Letters', (2011), p. 18. Cory Lib. PR 2736a

[5] Rennie, vol. 1, p. 83.

[6] Pringle, Alexander, 'Ancestry of Thomas Pringle, Poet', *The Border Magazine,* 26, 1921, p. 180. Rennie, vol. 1, p. 83.

[7] Pringle to Potts, -.12.1830, Vigne, 'Additional Letters' (2011), p. 25. Fairbairn Papers, LP 2, 21 8 J-M.

[8] Pringle to Bentham, 11.11.1830, Vigne, 'Additional Letters' (2011), p. 15. BL Add. MSS 33546 f 465.

[9] *Emancipate your Colonies! Address to the National Convention of France, Ao. 1793, showing the uselessness and mischievousness of distant dependencies to an European state* (London, 1830).

[10] *Notices of Brazil in 1828 and 1829* (London, 1830), 2 vols.

[11] R. Bourke to Earl Bathurst, 24.3.1826 *RCC* 26, 205; Earl Bathurst to R. Bourke, 27.6.1826, *RCC* 27, 11; Pringle to R.W. Hay, 27.10.1826, Vigne (2011), p. 305. Cory Lib., Lynedoch Papers, 13f; Pringle to J. Pringle, 26.5.1828, Vigne (2011), p. 314. Northumberland M and A ZAN M12; Rennie 2, pp. 641–2.

[12] Rennie, vol. 2, p. 672

[13] Pringle to R.W. Hay, 29.11.1831, Vigne (2011), p. 333; Pringle to R. Burns, 16.2.1832, Vigne (2011), pp. 341–2; Rennie 2, pp. 672–7.

[14] Pringle to A. Welsh, 19.4.1832, Vigne (2011), p. 343. Cory Lib. Lynedoch Papers, 13K.

[15] Welsh, A., 'Extracts from the diary of Alexander Welsh', *Coelacanth,* East London, 6.1, April 1968, pp. 17–38.

[16] J.G. Lockhart to Pringle, 1.11.1832, LUL Brotherton Library 5515.

[17] Parr, N., *Hogg at home, being the domestic life and letters of the Ettrick Shepherd* (Dollar, 1980), pp. 47, 95, 100–03.

[18] 'The Emigrant's Cabin', Pringle (1970), pp. 41, 140.

[19] Lord Holland to Pringle, 30.9.1834, LUL Brotherton Library 4359.

[20] Griggs, E.L., 'Samuel Taylor Coleridge and Thomas Pringle', *QBSAL* 6.1, September 1951; E.K. Chambers, *Samuel Taylor Coleridge, a biographical study* (Oxford, 1938), pp. 332–3 and *passim.* Coleridge's 'minor verse and prose' in *The Literary Souvenir, The Keepsake* and *The Amulet* are noted but not that in *Friendship's Offering,* p. 309.

[21] See p. 211, n 22.

[22] Pringle to J. Fairbairn, 21.1.1833, Vigne (2011), p. 350. LP, Fairbairn Papers, 1, 146.

[23] Pringle to J. Fairbairn, 31.12.1831. Vigne (2011), p. 336. LP, Fairbairn Papers, 1, 114.

[24] Pringle to unknown, 3.2.1832.Vigne (2011), pp 335–41. Pringle (1838), pp. cxxxviii-cxli.

[25] *Ibid.*

[26] Pringle to Hunter, 17.2.1831. NLS MS 8998. *Letters and Memorials of Jane Welsh Carlyle,* ed. Thomas Carlyle and J.A. Froude, 2 vols (1883), vol. 1, p. 131. Pers. comm. Professor William Christie.

[27] *Ibid.*

[28] Pringle to J. Philip, 9.1.1833. Vigne (2011), p. 347. WUL Philip Family Papers A85.

[29] R.W. Hay to Pringle, 6.11.1826. Pringle (1838), p. lxxxix.

[30] P. 4 above.

[31] Cory 3, p. 176.

[32] *Op. cit.,* pp. 177–8.

[33] *Op. cit.,* p. 303. Pp. 170–1 above.

22
Journey's End

Thomas Pringle's call to Dr Kennedy for 'a little doctoring' was made the morning after his signing the announcement, from the Aldermanbury office, of the emancipation of slaves in the British Empire. That 'crumb of bread' going down 'the wrong throat' on 27 June 1834[1] was the beginning of the end.

In January 1833 he was able to tell Dr Philip, at the Cape,[2] that he was 'generally emerging from my pecuniary distress' and had 'got nearly over the embarrassment by Underwood's failure' – a further financial setback not mentioned elsewhere. He had hoped, 'if I live a few years longer, of paying off every shilling I owe'. Dr Philip was clearly a major creditor, and Pringle added:

> Fairbairn I doubt not has long ago informed you that I lodged with him my life insurance for £200 for what I owe you – so that in case of my death before the debt is paid off your family will not suffer.

It seems curious, in our time, that a man of only 44 years should foresee the possibility of an early death, though he had complained of the 'hypochondriasis' which had long plagued him (this was a term that, as in Boswell's *Life of Johnson* denoted chronic depression and anxiety, not simply morbid fears about one's health). Interesting too that the schoolmaster-turned-journalist John Fairbairn was already concerned with the quite unrelated activity which led to his founding, a dozen years later, one of South Africa's major corporations, the internationally stock-exchange quoted 'Old Mutual' life insurance company.

Pringle was sanguine that when 'the Slavery Question' was settled he had 'little doubt (if the Whigs are in power) of being properly provided for – either at home or abroad – and if I go abroad at all I will go to *your* colony'.

The Whigs, under Lord Grey, had come to power at the end of 1830 after nearly fifty years in opposition. Pringle wrote to an unnamed member of the Government,[3] with words that might not have appealed to a hard-headed bureaucrat recipient. He sought employment, he wrote, in 'service to the cause of humanity, *in which I consider myself solemnly enlisted for life*', either in London or in South Africa, which 'next to my native country, has the strongest claim upon me both of duty and affection'. He thought himself best fitted 'in connection with the protection of the slaves or the improvement and civilization of the native races'.

As abolition came into view he wrote, in mid-1833, to Zachary Macaulay[4] suggesting 'an appointment on the Eastern frontier of the colony where no slave holders exist, where consequently prejudices on that score would form no bar to my usefulness'. Here he could exert himself 'in the general cause of Christian humanity'. He sought, in particular, the magistracy the Commissioners of Inquiry had recommended for the former Ceded Territory 'of which the Kat River valley forms a portion'. In August 1833 he asked of Brougham,[5] who had become Lord Chancellor as Baron Brougham and Vaux in 1830, to recommend his appointment as 'resident magistrate of the new (and still *unnamed*) district upon the border of Cafferland'. Here he would promote

> The interests of humanity and civilization by the encouragement of general instruction, of infant schools, of religious missions, of temperance associations and other sound practical means, for gradually elevating long-degraded races of men in the moral and intellectual scale of being.

The consequences of neglect of what became the Kat River settlement were 'imminent peril to the peace of the Colony, and manifold acts of cruelty and oppression towards the natives'.

Those lobbied included his old supporter Francis Jeffrey, editor of the *Edinburgh Review*, now an MP (and Lord Jeffrey a year later). Jeffrey wrote [6] that he would 'certainly mention you to the Chancellor with any recommendation in my power and shall also confer with Mr Macaulay on the best way of promoting your wishes'. He regretted that Pringle had 'again to seek employment at so great a distance'.

In October 1833 and again three months later Pringle wrote to his brother William[7] at Eildon that he had approached the Colonial Secretary Edward George Stanley, who had carried the Abolition Act and was, as Lord Derby, later to become Prime Minister. Despite a lack of response he assured William that 'if this ministry remains in power something I dare say will be done for me. They all admit my claims'.

In July 1834 he told Fairbairn[8] that 'all is still in statu quo about my own future destination'. Nothing would happen 'until the Colonial department obtain more correct views of things'. By the end of July, however, his hope of an appointment at the Cape was no more and the 'prospects of the future are more than ever dark and cloudy'. He told a correspondent[9] that he had heard from Spring Rice, Stanley's successor at the Foreign Office, that 'great reductions' were taking place at the Cape and that 'those reduced from the government service must have a preferable claim' to appointments there.

To Pringle it was, of course, most galling that 'those reduced were amongst the vilest tools of Lord Charles Somerset's administration'. As bad that

> to have been persecuted by a Tory government for maintaining Whig principles, or rather the principles of truth and justice, seems, even under a Whig administration, to operate rather to one's disadvantage, than otherwise.

He justly blamed this on the 'under-secretaries and clerks ... who determine most of the Colonial appointments, who were put in office by Lord Bathurst and who, to this day, act … on the wretched system of his administration … and thus things go on year after year'.

In low spirits as his illness advanced, he found himself 'tired with the wear and tear of town life, and struggling in straitened circumstances for ever'. He told Ritchie: 'If I had a few hundred pounds I would go out to the Caffer frontier, buy and stock a farm, and settle myself in the wilderness.'

His hopes of an appointment for Fairbairn had also come to naught, he told his friend's father-in-law, Dr Philip,[10] since 'Whigs in power are *generally* as weak and bad as Tories I see. Nothing is to be expected on the grounds of merit. Such are politicians'.

Despite the good friends in high places who had supported his case, as he wrote to Macvey Napier[11] in September 1834:

> all my promises from the Great have ended in nothing – and my hopes of obtaining an appointment at the Cape have ended in empty air, in spite of all the influence I could exert through Mr Buxton, Lord Brougham, Lord Holland (who was most zealous on my behalf), Lord Jeffrey, Mr Rogers and others.

He saw his relatively humble origins as the root of his problem, despite such connections: 'The fact is, a person like me, without political interest or personal weight in Society is almost sure to be set aside for applicants of another caste'.

In any event, he told Napier, 'my health has received such a shock' that he might 'never again be capable of active duty'. He had 'resolved, if possible, to go to the Cape', where he might 'either regain my health or find a not unmourned grave and leave my wife among kind friends'.

His claim for restitution of his losses at the Cape had been refused him, as had employment, however well qualified for and deserving of it he might be, and he would now try 'to obtain from Mr Spring Rice some sort of compensation for the grievous losses I suffered under Lord Charles Somerset, which have kept me steeped in poverty ever since'. Surely Spring Rice, a Whig Colonial Secretary, abolitionist and friend of Buxton's, would not deny him whatever Lord Bathurst, a Tory 'was willing to give me eight years ago – "any reasonable encouragement as a settler".'

He asked Spring Rice, he told Leitch Ritchie,[12] for 'a grant of land and a grant of money to stock it with, in consideration of my losses and and ill-treatment under Lord Charles Somerset', an appeal 'zealously backed by Mr Buxton and Lord Holland'.

Holland, a very influential Whig and father of Pringle's friend from Baviaans River days, Charles Richard Fox, wrote at the end of September 1834[13] that he would 'do his best to promote your wishes' but gave a coded warning: he 'did not wish to imply that my application and not his own great desire to oblige as well as his sense of your merits, were with Mr Rice the chief motives on which you have to rely'.

The blow fell at the beginning of November when poor Pringle heard from Spring Rice's private secretary, Richard Earle:[14] 'It is with much regret that Mr Secretary Spring Rice acquaints you of his inability to comply with your application for a grant of land' or 'to advance you a sum of money to assist you on your return to the Cape'. The minister was bound by rules governing the disposal of waste lands that 'are very strictly adhered to'. No reason was given for the refusal of financial help. There was a sop: Earle enclosed a letter to the new Governor, Sir Benjamin D'Urban, who '*may* have it in his power to render you assistance'.

Pringle replied[15] that the letter 'has, I must confess, mortified and disappointed me not a little'. Spring Rice's decision was 'far less favourable than that of Earl Bathurst in 1826'. He generously acceded that 'change of circumstances in regard to land' might account for the refusal of the land grant. He sent 'my best acknowledgments' for the letter of recommendation to Governor D'Urban.

He now had only his literary labours to fund his little household should he regain his health. The printer's deadline for the 384–page *Friendship's Offering* for 1835 was 1 August and it was duly put to bed. Dedicated again to Queen Adelaide and with a prefatory sonnet by the Editor, it included such regulars as Barry Cornwall, Mary Howitt, Moir, St John, more rarely John Clare and John Herschel, and, rarest of all, Fairbairn, with an evocation of the restored ruins of Melrose Abbey. Unusually he published only one poem of his own: 'To the Ostrich', which appears nowhere else, unsurprisingly.

His *African Sketches* had been published in May 1834, a month before his illness began and he remained concerned to get copies to South Africa, with advertisements by Greig, quoting the many good reviews in the English press. In late September he was able to write to his publisher Edward Moxon[16] regretting having missed him on 'the day I was in town', his only visit since the beginning of July, and urging 'a conference ere long about my book … I wish I could see my way *clearly* to a *second* edition!' He told Moxon he was about to leave Highgate 'for milder air … about Leatherhead in Surrey'.

He spent some time revising *African Sketches* but no changes are to be found in the separate editions of the *Narrative* or the *Poetical Works* published by Moxon in 1835 and 1838, the latter 'entirely for the benefit of Mr Pringle's widow'.

He had written to Macvey Napier[17] to beg a notice or at best a review in the *Edinburgh Review*, which would make it possible for him to publish 'a second and enlarged edition', but neither appeared until the separate editions were noticed after his death.

Certainly the most important and influential review was to appear in December 1835 in the Tory and unsympathetic *Quarterly Review*,[18] edited by his old, highly equivocal acquaintance John Gibson Lockhart, who must have written the review or at least had a hand in it. While praising the elegance of his verse, and itself a polished piece of prose, the review was a mean-spirited and error-filled farrago. Ritchie's rejoinder in his memoir with the *Poetical Works* does it justice but as so often it is the original that is remembered and the corrections forgotten. Pringle, son of a small farmer, suffering 'woeful physical deformities', becomes 'a parochial schoolmaster in his native district' until his head is turned by the deserved success of his (mis-titled) *Autumnal Excursion* ('The fatal word "genius" is wrung about the village, and the clearest head and humblest heart run a risk of being dazzled and inflated.'). Taken up by Scott, he moves to a literary life in Edinburgh and then a pioneering one in South Africa where, 'weary of the pastoral life', overweening ambition takes him to Cape Town and well-deserved ruin. Even his appearance, manners and way of speech are ridiculed.

Ritchie's rebuttal[19] asserted that 'the article, though in some respects just, is in the greater part grossly and cruelly incorrect'. When it goes on to aver 'that the journal afterwards conducted by Pringle at the Cape became dangerous to the well-being of the colony.... The writer does no more than pursue his calling as a political partisan'. Pringle did not live to read this continuing character assassination in the *Quarterly* but a letter from his friend Allan Cunningham of 28 August 1834 [20] would have reminded him of his *Blackwood's* traducers' belittling of him:

> There has been I see a grand dinner spread on the Border to our friend the Ettrick Shepherd with Wilson in the chair. They did not remember us, Thomas my friend, but we cannot help that: we have done what we could to deserve notice and we must hope for it from other quarters.

Having sympathized with Pringle's illness 'and rejoiced in your recovery' Cunningham ended with his love to Mrs Pringle, adding his wife's, 'for she loves the house of Pringle'.

The following day a warm, admiring letter from Mary Russell Mitford,[21] whose successful *Our Village* had appeared in 1832, must have cheered him. After expressing her 'sincere hope that you have entirely recovered from the severe accident' she told him of her delight with *African Sketches,* though knowing 'little of that part of the world, having read Vaillant and Barrow as a girl and ... no work on South Africa since'. She urged him to add minute details, perhaps of the first year or two of the settlement, adding a little poetry and developing the story of the settlers and the natives, who are 'the charm of the book'. Perhaps her letter inspired the enlarging of the book he planned for a second edition. She saw Pringle himself as 'the manly Resister of that base Oppressor ... a Hero more to my mind than all the Wellingtons that ever fought battles'. She ended 'when one thinks of all that Mrs Pringle must have braved and borne for his sake one feels proud of the sex'. The book had much increased her estimation of both Pringle's talent and character, great as these were before.

Neither knew that his recovery was now unlikely without a change of climate and that his anti-slavery friends were raising money to make this possible in the hope of saving his life. The disease of the lungs as diagnosed by Dr James Kennedy in his final report[22] had run its course unchecked after that 'accidental circumstance', as Pringle thought, of 'laceration of some small vessel in the lungs'.[23] Kennedy had reported that

> Mr Pringle's general health appeared quite good ... but as copious spitting of blood continued to recur during several days, grounds of suspicion were afforded ... that organic disease had commenced in the lungs ... although the bleeding was permanently checked in less than a fortnight, he began soon afterwards to lose flesh and strength, and to suffer from frequent cough, etc.—the ordinary signs of consumption.

With his habitual positive, optimistic view Pringle persuaded himself, six weeks after the 'accident', that 'I have had no return of alarming symptoms, and am, as the doctors tell me, doing extremely well: only they still keep the crutches from me and confine me to the sofa'.[24] He expected 'to get out again in about a fortnight, and trust I shall experience no permanent bad effects from this attack, as it appears to have been entirely accidental and my lungs appear to be otherwise sound'. Either Kennedy had not yet diagnosed tuberculosis, or had withheld the diagnosis from his patient. More than three weeks later he had 'not yet been out of the house' though his 'health has been slowly improving' as he told Dr Philip.[25]

By mid-September he was having to face the necessity of going to a milder climate before the winter set in. At the Cape he would 'have a climate equal to the best parts of Spain and Italy'.[26] He had been so advised after a visit from Dr James Clark, 'a physician of great eminence', who had first seen him when he was seriously ill in July and now, in mid-September, insisted that he 'could not remain in England during the ensuing winter without the greatest risk'.[27] Clark, a fellow Scot and former naval surgeon, was an early believer in what his widely read publication of 1829 called *The Influence of Climate on the Prevention and Cure of Chronic Disease.* He had, when practising in Rome, treated the dying Keats in 1820–21 (and had kept from him the death sentence of his diagnosis).

Pringle's situation was desperate and he struggled to raise funds 'for our passage, but after disposing of my little furniture, and settling household and other accounts I should not have one shilling remaining – but even be in debt'.[28] So he sent copies of Clark's report to Buxton and Zachary Macaulay. 'Never was anything more affectionate, delicate and generous than the conduct of these invaluable friends', he wrote to Ritchie. In less than a week they had 'raised funds (from among the affluent members of the Society) ample for our outfit and passage', with 'I understand, after I am gone something on a larger scale. ... No man in my circumstances could expect greater kindness and liberality than this'.

From Leatherhead, where Clark had seen him, Thomas and Margaret awaited embarkation in the *Sherburne* at the end of October and lodged at 6 Portman Square in Marylebone (Susan Brown remaining as tenant of 7 Holly Terrace). It was in the Portman Square house that he received Spring Rice's negative reply which so mortified him.

They were never to board the *Sherburne*. Pringle wrote to Dr Philip on 17 November 1834[29] that she was 'now, I suppose, on her way down the river, while we are *here*, having abandoned our passage in her'. Severe diarrhoea had set in, and he was simply too ill to face 'the cold and exposure in the vessel'. He explained to Dr Philip that

> about ten days before we should have actually embarked ... my doctors ... urged me in the most earnest terms to abandon the voyage by this vessel altogether. I yielded of course – what could I do?

Ever hopeful he added that 'within these two or three days symptoms of mitigation of the distemper have appeared (which have been very tenacious) and my doctors appear sanguine in the hope of relieving me of it ere long'. He thought that his strength was 'rapidly recovering ... I could not have written a letter half the length of this only four days ago'. He gloried in his faith but tried not to parade it other than to the man of God, John Philip: 'Oh! The privilege of being able to repose *all our concerns* …on Him, "who ordereth all things well"'! These remarks are for your own eyes'.

A fortnight later, he had moved to 28 Bryanston Street, off Portman Square, a house belonging to Arthur Gurney, perhaps a Quaker relative of Buxton's wife, born Hannah Gurney. The Revd John MacDonald, minister of the Scottish church in Islington, and an old friend, who attended him in these last weeks, recorded[30] that 'his mental activity triumphed over the combined effects of disease and medicine … he continued to exert himself in writing letters to different relations and Christian friends in various parts of the world'. Sadly, none of these has come to light.

On 1 December 1834 he signed his will,[31] witnessed by Dr Kennedy, 'being weak and infirm in body but in whole and sound possession of all my intellectual faculties'. He affirmed that 'the sole dependence for the salvation of my soul rests upon the atonement of our Lord and Saviour Jesus Christ'. He bequeathed all his estate to 'my dear wife Margaret', with Margaret, Zachary Macaulay and one John Hunter 'of Edinburgh Esquire Writer to the Signet', as executors. For probate the estate was valued at £450,[32] thought to be in part 'given to Pringle by friends and sympathizers … to enable him to go out to the Cape'.[33] The cost of the Pringles' passage was, charitably, refunded by the shipping company..

Kennedy[34] wrote: 'although made quite aware of the near approach of death, many days before it took place, he retained to his latest hours the greatest cheerfulness and resignation; his characteristic *firmness* never for a moment deserted him'.

On the evening of Friday 5 December, Macdonald wrote, 'he gently passed out of life'. He went on 'thus peacefully and in the faith of Christ died this devoted and unwearied friend of the slave and the oppressed. … His was no mercenary, though an official, advocacy of the rights of the African race'. He ended, using St Paul's words[35]: 'He lived for others, and he died poor, yet having contributed to "make many rich"; having in this world "nothing, and yet possessing all things".'

He was buried in Bunhill Fields, the non-conformist graveyard a short walk from Aldermanbury, the scene of his victory in the part of his 'great cause' that had occupied so much of the last seven years of his life. On the 150th anniversary of the arrival of the British settlers in Algoa Bay in 1820, after a major effort to perform this act of family piety, his remains were reinterred in a memorial chapel erected on his South African Eildon in the Baviaans River valley.

The gravestone was brought to the chapel from Bunhill Fields. The inscription was by his fellow poet and editor, Ayrshire-born William Kennedy. Pringle had sent Brougham his own articles on slavery, published by 'my friend Kennedy' in the *Englishman's Magazine* in 1830. The inscription bears reading today, as a just tribute to Pringle's life and work, despite its outdated elegiac style:

SACRED TO THE MEMORY
OF
THOMAS PRINGLE,
A HUMBLE DISCIPLE OF CHRIST
WHO DEPARTED THIS LIFE THE 5TH DAY OF
DECEMBER, 1834
IN THE 46TH YEAR OF HIS AGE.
IN THE WALKS OF BRITISH LITERATURE HE WAS
KNOWN
AS A MAN OF GENIUS:
IN THE DOMESTIC CIRCLE HE WAS LOVED
AS AN AFFECTIONATE RELATIVE AND FAITHFUL
FRIEND:
IN THE WIDE SPHERE OF HUMANITY HE WAS REVERED
AS THE ADVOCATE AND PROTECTOR OF THE
OPPRESSED.
HE LEFT AMONG THE CHILDREN OF THE AFRICAN
DESERT
A MEMORIAL OF HIS PHILANTHROPY
AND BEQUEATHED TO HIS FELLOW-COUNTRYMEN
AN EXAMPLE OF ENDURING VIRTUE.
HAVING LIVED TO WITNESS THE CAUSE IN WHICH HE
HAD ARDENTLY AND ENERGETICALLY LABOURED
TRIUMPH IN THE
EMANCIPATION OF THE NEGRO,
HE WAS HIMSELF CALLED FROM THE BONDAGE OF
THE WORLD
TO THE ENJOYMENT OF ETERNAL LIBERTY
THROUGH THE MERITS OF HIS REDEEMER

NOTES

1 See p. 217.
2 Pringle to Philip, 10.1.1833, Vigne (2011), p. 208. WUL Philip Family Papers A 85.
3 Pringle to 'A member of H.M. Government', 30.11.1831, Vigne (2011), p. 334. Pringle (1838), p. xxxvn.
4 Pringle to Z. Macaulay, 27.6.1833, Vigne (2011), p. 352. UCL Sp. Coll., Brougham MSS 36245.
5 Pringle to H. Brougham, 24.8.1833, Vigne (2011), p. 334. Pringle (1838), pp. cxvi-viii
6 F. Jeffrey to Pringle, 5.6.1833. Pringle (1838), p. cxviii.
7 Pringle to W. Pringle, 30.1.1834, Vigne (2011), p. 359. Robert Pringle Esq
8 Pringle to J. Fairbairn, 16.7.1834, Vigne (2011), p. 364. LP, Fairbairn Papers, 1, 154.
9 Pringle to unknown, 29.7.1834, Vigne (2011), p. 365. Pringle (1838), pp. cxiv-xvii.
10 Pringle to J. Philip, 23.8.1834, Vigne (2011), p. p. 367. WUL Philip Family Papers, MS A85.
11 Pringle to M. Napier, 15.9.1834, Vigne (2011), p. 369. BL Add MS 34616 f 398.
12 Pringle to L.Ritchie, 3.10.1834, Vigne (2011), p. 369. Pringle (1838), p. cxviii.
13 Lord Holland to Pringle, 30.9.1834. LUL Brotherton Library 4359.
14 R. Earle to Pringle, 23.10.1834. Pringle (1838), p. cxxi.
15 Pringle to R. Earle, 4.11.1834, Vigne (2011), pp. 373–4. Pringle (1838), p. cxxii.
16 Pringle to E. Moxon, 20.9.1834, Vigne, 'Additional Letters' (2011), p. 28. EUL Dc 4 101–3.
17 Pringle to M. Napier, 15.9.1834, Vigne (2011), p. 369. BL Add. MSS 34616 f 398.
18 *Quarterly Review*, vol. 55, No 109, December 1835–February 1836, pp. 74–96. The same article reviews J.W.D. Moodie, *Ten Years in South Africa* (1835).
19 Pringle (1838), pp. lxviii-lxxi.
20 Pringle to A. Cunningham, 28.8.1834. LUL Brotherton Library 3481.
21 M.R. Mitford to Pringle, 29.8.1834. LUL Brotherton Library 16839.
22 Pringle (1838), pp. cxiii-cxiv.
23 Pringle to J. Kennedy, 27.6.1834. Pringle (1838), p. cxiii.
24 Pringle to unknown, 29.7.1834, Vigne (2011), p. 365. Pringle (1838), pp. cxiv-cxvii.
25 Pringle to J. Philip, 23.8.1834, Vigne (2011), p. 366. WUL Philip Family Papers MS A85.
26 Pringle to M. Napier, 15.9.1834, Vigne (2011), p. 369. BL Add. MS 34616 f 398.
27 Pringle to unknown, 3.10.1834, Vigne (2011), p. 370. Pringle (1838), pp. cxix-cxxi.
28 *Op. cit.,* p. 374.
29 Pringle to J. Philip, 17.11.1834, Vigne (2011), p. 374. LP, Fairbairn Papers, 1, 156.
30 Pringle (1966), p. xxxviii.
31 Prerogative Court of Canterbury, 10 April 1835, PROB 11/1846. Vigne (2011), p. 375.
32 For further provision for Margaret Pringle and her sister Susan Brown see Pringle (1838), pp. cxxxiii-cxxxv; Rennie, vol. 3, pp. 1037–9.
33 Rennie, vol. 3, p. 1013.
34 Pringle (1966), p. cxxv.
35 Pringle (1966), p. xxxviii; 2 Corinthians 6:10.

Bibliography

Primary Sources

African Court Calendar and Directory for 1819–29, The, ed. G. Ross, Cape Town

British Library, London, Additional MSS

Bodleian Library, Rhodes House Library, MSS Afr., Addns.

Cases decided in the Supreme Court of the Cape of Good Hope, as Reported by the Late Hon. William Menzies, vol. 1 (Cape Town, Solomon, 1868–70; Juta, 1903)

Catalogue of Books and Pamphlets Relating to South Africa South of the Zambezi, compiled by George McCall Theal (Cape Town, Maskew Miller, 1912)

Catalogue of the Collection of Books in the English Language in the South African Public Library, A., compiled by Thomas Pringle (Cape Town, South African Public Library, 1825)

Cory Library, Rhodes University, Grahamstown, Lynedoch Papers, Paver Letters, 'Arrival of the Scots Party at Roodewal, July 1820', Charles Lennox Stretch, 1877

Croker Papers, The, The Correspondence and Diaries of the late Rt Hon John Wilson Croker, 3 vols (London, Murray, 1884)

Edinburgh University Library, Gen. MSS

Fitzwilliam Museum, Cambridge, Ledbetter MSS

Government Gazette of the Cape of Good Hope, Cape Town, 1820–34

John Rylands Library, Manchester, Eng. MSS

Leeds University Library, Brotherton Library, Pringle Album

Library and Archives, Canada, MSS 1829, 1831

Library of Parliament (Mendelssohn Collection), Cape Town, Fairbairn Papers, 1,2

National English Literary Museum, Grahamstown, Pringle letterbook

National Library of Scotland, Edinburgh, MSS

National Library of South Africa, Cape Town, Pringle letters, South African Public Library Minute Book, Vol 1 (1820–36)

Northumberland Museum and Archives, Woodhorn, Northumberland, MSS

Records of the Cape Colony, 1793–1831. Compiled by George McCall Theal, 36 vols (1897–1905), vols 12, 14–19, 21–23

Sotheby's Catalogue, London, 1968

University College, London, Library, Special Collections, Brougham MSS

Western Cape Archives and Records Service, Cape Town, CO (Colonial Office) Correspondence, 1820–34

Witwatersrand University Library, Johannesburg, Fairbairn Papers, Philip Family Papers

Secondary Sources

Ayliff, John, ed. P.B. Hinchliff, *Journal of John Ayliff, 1821–30* (Cape Town, Balkema, 1971)

Ayliff, John, *Memorials of the British Settlers of South Africa* (Grahamstown,1845; Cape Town, William Hiddingh Reprint Series, No 2, University of Cape Town, 1954)

Baillie, Joanna, *The Family Legend: a Tragedy* (Edinburgh, Ballantyne, 1810)

Ballstadt, C., Hopkins, E., Peterman, M., *Susanna Moodie: Letters of a Lifetime* (Toronto, Toronto University Press, 1993)

Bannister, Saxe, *Humane Policy or Justice to the Aborigines of New Settlements …* (London, Underwood, 1830)

Barnard, Lady Anne, *The Cape Diaries of Lady Anne Barnard, 1799–1800,* 2 vols (Cape Town, Van Riebeeck Society, 1999)

Barrow, John, *An Account of Travels into the Interior of Southern Africa in the Years 1797 and 1798,* 2 vols (London, Cadell and Davies, 1801, 1802)

Barrow, Sir John, *An Auto-Biographical Memoir of Sir John Barrow, Bart., late of the Admiralty* (London, Murray, 1847)

[Bird, W.W.], *State of the Cape of Good Hope in 1822, by a Civil Servant of the Colony* (London, Murray, 1823)

Botha, H.C., *John Fairbairn in South Africa* (Cape Town, Historic Publications Society, 1984)

Burchell, W.J., *Hints on Emigration to the Cape of Good Hope* (London, Hatchard, 1819)

Burchell, W.J., *Travels in the Interior of Southern Africa,* 2 vols (London, Longman, 1822, 1824)

Buxton, Charles (ed.), *Memoirs of Sir Thomas Fowell Buxton, Baronet* (London, Murray, 1848; Everyman, 1925)

Campbell, Alexander, *Albyn's Anthology, or a Select Collection of the Melodies and Vocal Poetry Peculiar to Scotland,* 2 vols (Edinburgh, Oliver and Boyd, 1816, 1818)

Campbell, Ambrose ('Justus'), *The Wrongs of the Caffre Nation* (London, James Duncan, 1837)

Carswell, Donald, *Walter Scott, a Four-Part Study in Biography* (London, Murray, 1930)

Chambers, E.K., *Samuel Taylor Coleridge. A Biographical Study* (Oxford, Clarendon Press, 1938)

Chambers, Robert, *The Scottish Songs, Collected and Illustrated,* 2 vols (Edinburgh, William Tait, 1829)

Christie, William, *The Edinburgh Review in the Literary Culture of Romantic Britain* (London, Pickering and Chatto, 2009)

Coetzee, J.M., *White Writing. On the Culture of Letters in South Africa* (New Haven, CT, Yale University Press, 1988)

Coetzee, J.M., *Stranger Shores. Essays 1986–99* (London, Secker and Warburg, 2001)

Collingwood, W.G., *The Life and Work of John Ruskin* (London, Methuen, 1893)

Constable, Thomas, *Archibald Constable and his Literary Correspondents, a Memorial,* 3 vols (Edinburgh, Edmonston and Douglas, 1873)

Cory, Sir G.E., *The Rise of South Africa,* 5 vols (London, Longman, 1910–39)

Cowan, R.M.W., *The Newspaper in Scotland, 1815–60* (Glasgow, Outram, 1946)

Crockett, W.S., *Footsteps of Scott* (Edinburgh and London, Foulis, 1905)

Cutten, T.E.G., *A History of the Press in South Africa* (Cape Town, NUSAS, 1935)

Davenport, T.R.H. and Saunders, C.C., *South Africa. A Modern History* (Basingstoke, Macmillan, 2000 ed.)

Dictionary of South African Biography, 5 vols (Pretoria, Human Science Research Council, 1968–87)

Dooling, Wayne, *Slavery, Emancipation and Colonial Rule in South Africa* (Pietermaritzburg, Universiity of KwaZulu Natal Press, 2007)

Douglas, Sir George, *Poems of the Scottish Minor Poets from the Age of Ramsay to David Gray* (London, Walter Scott, 1891)

Doyle, John Robert, *Thomas Pringle* (New York, Twayne, 1972)

Dracopoli, J.L., *Sir Andries Stockenstrom (1792–1864). The Origins of the Racial Conflict in South Africa* (Cape Town, Balkema, 1969)

Dugmore, H.H., *Reminiscences of an Albany Settler* (Grahamstown, 1871; ed. F.G. van der Riet and L.A. Hewson, Rhodes University, 1958)

Ellis, William, *Christian Keepsake and Missionary Annual* (London, Fisher, 1833)

Etherington, Norman, *Great Treks. The Transformation of Southern Africa, 1815–54* (Harlow, Longman, 2001)

Fawcett, John, *An Account of Eighteen Months' Residence at the Cape of Good Hope* (London, Nisbet, 1836)

Feneysey, S.F., *Die Niederduits-Gereformeerde Gemeente, Glen Lynden gedurende 'n Honderd Jare* (Cape Town, Nasionale Pers, 1930)

Gifford, Douglas; Dunnigan, Sarah; McGillivray, Allan, *Scottish Literature in English and Scots* (Edinburgh, Edinburgh University Press, 2002)

Giliomee, Hermann and Mbenga, Bernard (eds), *A New History of South Africa* (Cape Town, Tafelberg, 2007)

Gillies, R.P., *Memoirs of a Literary Veteran,* 3 vols (London, Bentley, 1851)

Goldswain, Jeremiah, *The Chronicle of Jeremiah Goldswain, Albany Settler of 1820,* 2 vols (Cape Town, Van Riebeeck Society, 1946, 1949)

Grant of Laggan, Anne, *Memoir and Correspondence of Mrs Grant of Laggan,* 3 vols (London, Longman, 1844)

Griggs, E.L., 'S.T. Coleridge and Thomas Pringle', *Quarterly Bulletin of the South African Library,* 16.6 (September 1951), pp. 1–6

Griggs, E.L., *Collected Letters of Samuel Taylor Coleridge,* 6 vols (Oxford, Clarendon Press (1956–71)

Hattersley, A.F., *Oliver the Spy and Others. A Little Gallery of South African Portraits* (Cape Town, Maskew Miller, 1959)

Hay, James and Belfrage, Henry, *A Memoir of the Rev. Alexander Waugh, D.D.* (Edinburgh, Oliphant, 1830)

Hay, William, *Thomas Pringle, his Life, Times and Poems* (Cape Town, Juta, 1912)

Hogg, James, *The Poetic Mirror, or, the Living Bards of Britain* (London, Longman; Edinburgh, Ballantyne, 1816)

Hogg, James, *Altrive Tales* (London, Cochrane, 1832)

Hogg, James, *The Collected Letters of James Hogg,* eds. Douglas S. Mack, Gillian Hughes, 2 vols (Edinburgh, Edinburgh University Press, 2004, 2006)

Hughes, Gillian, *James Hogg, a Life* (Edinburgh, Edinburgh University Press, 2007)

Johnston, H.J.M., *British Emigration Policy, 1815–30* (Oxford, Clarendon Press, 1972)

Jones, Stanley, *Hazlitt, a Life. From Winterslow to Frith Street* (Oxford, Clarendon Press, 1989)

Kay, Stephen, *Travels and Researches in Caffraria* (London, Mason, 1833)

King, Hazel, *Richard Bourke* (Melbourne, Oxford University Press, 1971)

Knutsford, Viscountess, *Life and Letters of Zachary Macaulay by his Grand-Daughter* (London, Arnold, 1900)

Lang, Andrew, *The Life and Letters of John Gibson Lockhart*, 2 vols (London, Nimmo, 1897)

Latrobe, C.I., *Journal of a Visit to South Africa in 1815 and 1816* (London, Seeley, 412)

Lockhart, John Gibson, *Memoirs of the Life of Sir Walter Scott, Bart.,* 7 vols (Edinburgh, Cadell; London, Murray, 1837–8)

Lutyens, Mary, *Millais and the Ruskins* (London, Murray, 1967)

McCrie, Thomas, *Life of Rev. Thomas McCrie,D.D. by his Son* (Edinburgh, Williams, Young, 1840)

Macmillan, W.M., *The Cape Colour Question. A Historical Survey* (London, Faber and Gwyer, 1927)

Macmillan, W.M., *Bantu, Boer and Briton* (London, Faber and Faber, 1929)

Malherbe, V.C., 'David Stuurman "The Last Chief of the Hottentots"', *African Studies*, 39.1, 1980, pp. 47–64.

Marchand, Marion, *Index to the Poems of Thomas Pringle* (Johannesburg, School of Librarianship, University of the Witwatersrand, 1960)

Meiring, Jane, *Thomas Pringle. His Life and Times* (Cape Town, Balkema, 1968)

Merriman, N.J., ed. D.H. Varley, *The Cape Journals of Archdeacon N.J. Merriman* (Cape Town, Van Riebeeck Society, 1957)

Meurant, L.H., *Sixty Years Ago, or Reminiscences of the Struggle for the Freedom of the Press in South Africa …* (Cape Town, Solomon, 1885)

Midgley, Clare, *Women against Slavery. The British Campaign, 1780–1870* (London. Routledge, 1992)

Millar, A.K., *Plantagenet in South Africa. Lord Charles Somerset* (Cape Town and Oxford, Oxford University Press, 1965)

Moodie, J.W.D.,*Ten Years in South Africa* (London, Bentley, 1835)

Morris, Patricia, 'A Documentary Biography of Thomas Pringle', Ph. D. thesis, University of London (1982)

Morris, Patricia, 'A Periodical Paternity Claim: Pringle v. Hogg', *English Studies in Africa,* 25.1 (1989)

Nash, M.D., *The Settler Handbook. A New List of the 1820 Settlers* (Cape Town, Chameleon Press, 1987)

Oliphant, Margaret, *Annals of a Publishing House: William Blackwood and his Sons, their Magazine and Friends,* 2 vols (Edinburgh, Blackwood, 1897)

Oxford Dictionary of National Biography, 60 vols (Oxford, Oxford University Press, 2004)

Parr, N., *Hogg at home, being the domestic life and letters of the Ettrick Shepherd* (Dollar, 1980)

Peires, J.B., *The House of Phalo. A History of the Xhosa People in the Days of their Independence* (Johannesburg, Ravan Press, 1981)

Pereira, Ernest and Chapman, Michael, *African Poems of Thomas Pringle* (Durban, University of Natal Press, 1989)

Philip, John, *Researches in South Africa* (London, Duncan, 1828)

Philip, Peter, *British Residents at the Cape, 1795–1819* (Cape Town, David Philip, 1981)

Philipps, Thomas, *Advantages of Emigration to Algoa Bay and Albany, South Africa* (London, Wilson, 1836)

(Philipps, Thomas), Anon., *Scenes and Occurrences in Albany and Cafferland, South Africa* (London, Marsh, 1827)

Philipps, Thomas, ed. A. Keppel-Jones, *Philipps, 1820 Settler. His Letters* (Pietermaritzburg, Shooter and Shuter, 1960)

Pigot, Sophia, ed. Margaret Rainier, *The Journals of Sophia Pigot, 1819–21* (Cape Town, Balkema, 1974)

Prince, Mary, *The History of Mary Prince, a West Indian Slave. Related by Herself, with a Supplement by the Editor. To which is added the Narrative of Asa-Asa, a Captured African* (London, Westley and Davies; Edinburgh; Waugh and Innes, 1831)

Prince, Mary, ed. S. Salih, *The History of Mary Prince, a West Indian Slave* (London, Penguin, 2000)

Pringle, E., M.E. and J.A., *Pringles of the Valleys. Their History and Genealogy* (Adelaide, Privately printed, 1957)

(Pringle, Thomas, with Story, Robert) Anon., *The Institute. A Heroic Poem in Four Cantos* (Edinburgh, McWilliam, 1811)

Pringle, Thomas, *The Autumnal Excursion, or Sketches in Teviotdale, with Other Poems* (Edinburgh, Constable; London, Longman, 1819)

Pringle, Thomas, *Some Account of the Present State of the English Settlers in Albany, South Africa* (London, Underwood; Edinburgh, Oliver and Boyd, 1824)

Pringle, Thomas, *Ephemerides, or Occasional Poems Written in Scotland and South Africa* (London, Smith, Elder, 1828)

Pringle, Thomas, *Glen-Lynden. A Tale of Teviotdale* (London, Smith, Elder, 1828)

Pringle, Thomas, *African Sketches* (London, Moxon, 1834)

Pringle, Thomas, *The Poetical Works of Thomas Pringle. With a Sketch of his Life by Leitch Ritchie* (London, Moxon, 1838)

Pringle, Thomas, *Narrative of a Residence in South Africa. To which is Prefixed a Biographical Sketch of the Author by Josiah Conder* (London, Moxon, 1835; Cape Town, Struik, 1966)

Pringle, Thomas, ed. J.R. Wahl, *Poems Illustrative of South Africa* (Cape Town, Struik, 1970)

Redding, Cyrus, *Literary Reminiscences and Memoirs of Thomas Campbell* (London, Skeet, 1860)

Rennie, J.V.L., *The Scottish Settler Party of 1820*, 4 vols (Grahamstown, National English Literary Museum, 1991)

A Resident of the Cape of Good Hope, *Remarks on the Demoralizing Influence of Slavery* (London, Bagster and Thomas, 1828)

Robinson, George W., *Bibliography of Thomas Pringle's Afar in the Desert* (Chicago, Bibliographical Society of America, 1923)

Rogers, Charles, *The Modern Scottish Minstrel, or the Songs of Scotland of the Past Half Century*, 6 vols (Edinburgh, A. and C. Black, 1855)

Rose, Cowper, *Four Years in Southern Africa* (London, Colburn and Bentley, 1829)

Rotberg, R.I., *The Founder. Cecil Rhodes and the Pursuit of Power* (Oxford, Oxford University Press, 1988)

Ruskin, John, *Praeterita. The Autobiography of John Ruskin* (London, Allen, 1899)

Sales, J., *Mission Stations and the Coloured Community of the Eastern Cape, 1800–1852* (Cape Town, Balkema, 1975)

Scott, Walter, *A Legend of Montrose* (Edinburgh, Constable, 1819; A. and C. Black, 1860 ed.)

Scott, Sir Walter, *Letters of Sir Walter Scott*, ed. H.J.C. Grierson, 12 vols (London, Constable, 1932)

Scott, Sir Walter, *The Journal of Sir Walter Scott,* ed. W.E.K. Anderson (Oxford, Clarendon Press, 1972)

Sellick, W.S.J., *Uitenhage Past and Present. Souvenir of the Centenary 1804–1904* (Uitenhage, Uitenhage Times, 1904)

Shaw, Damian, 'The Writings of Thomas Pringle', D. Phil. thesis, University of Cambridge (1996)

Shaw, Damian, 'Thomas Pringle's "Bushmen": Images in Flesh and Blood', *English in Africa*, 25.2 (1998), pp. 37–62

Shaw, Damian, 'Thomas Pringle's Plantation', *Environment and History,* 5 (1999), pp. 309–23

Shaw, Damian, '"Papa Pringle": the Relationship between Thomas Pringle and

Susanna Moodie', *Quarterly Bulletin of the National Library of South Africa,* 63.1–2 (2009), pp 31–8

Soga, J.H., *The South-Eastern Bantu (abe-Nguni, aba-Mbo, ama-Lala)* (Johannesburg, Witwatersrand University Press, 1930)

Souvenir in Commemoration of the Centenary of the 1820 Settlers of Albany (East London. East London Daily Dispatch, 1920)

Stockenstrom, Sir Andries, *The Autobiography of the Late Sir Andries Stockenstrom, Bart.,* ed. C.W. Hutton, 2 vols (Cape Town, Juta, 1887)

Story, Robert H., *Memoir of the Life of the Rev. Robert Story* (Cambridge, Macmillan, 1862)

Stretch, C.L., ed. Basil le Cordeur, *The Journal of Charles Lennox Stretch* (Cape Town, 1988) p. 58

Strout, A.L., 'The "Noctes Ambrosianae" and James Hogg', *Review of English Studies,* 13.50 (April 1937), pp. 179–83

Strout, A.L., *The Life and Letters of James Hogg, the Ettrick Shepherd*, vol. 1, 1770–1825 (Lubbock, Texas, Texas Technological College, 1946)

Strout, A.L., 'James Hogg's Chaldee Manuscript', *Publications of the Modern Language Association of America,* vol 65 (September 1950), pp. 695–718

Swann, Elsie, *Christopher North (John Wilson)* (Edinburgh, Oliver and Boyd, 1934)

Theal, G.M. *History of South Africa from 1795–1872,* 4 vols (London, George Allen and Unwin, 1915)

Thomas, Sue, 'More Information on Mary Prince in London', *Notes and Queries,* vol. 256 no.1, March 2011

Thomas, Sue, 'Pringle v Cadell and Wood v Pringle. The Libel Cases over The

History of Mary Prince', *Journal of Commonwealth Literature,* 40.1, March 2005, pp. 13–15

Thompson, George, *Travels and Adventures in Southern Africa*, ed. V.S. Forbes, 2 vols (Cape Town, Van Riebeeck Society, 1967, 1968)

Tredrey, F.D. *The House of Blackwood 1804–1954. The History of a Publishing Firm* (1954)

Van der Riet, F.G., 'An 1820 Settler Circulating Library at Glen Lynden, Eastern Province', *South African Libraries,* vol. 19 (1952)

Vigne, Randolph, 'Thomas Pringle at the South African Public Library', *Quarterly Bulletin of the National Library of South Africa,* 61.3 (2007)

Vigne, Randolph, ed. 'Additional Letters to *The South African Letters of Thomas Pringle',* www.vanriebeecksociety.co.za (2011)

Vigne, Randolph, ed., *The South African Letters of Thomas Pringle* (Cape Town, Van Riebeeck Society, 2011)

Voss, A.E., '"The Slaves must be Heard": Thomas Pringle and the Dialogue of South African Servitude', *English in Africa,* 17.1 (May 1990), pp. 61–8

Warner, Ashton, *Negro Slavery Described by a Negro, being the Narrative of Ashton Warner, a Native of St Vincent's,* ed. Susanna Strickland (London, Samuel Maunder, 1831)

Watts, A.A., *Alaric Watts. A Narrative of his Life* (London, Bentley, 1884)

Welsh, Alexander, 'Extracts from the Diary of Alexander Welsh', *Coelacanth,* 6.1, April 1968, pp. 17–38

Whiteley, Henry, *Three Months in Jamaica in 1832* (London, Hatchard, 1833)

Wright, William, *Slavery at the Cape of Good Hope* (London, Longman,1831)

Journals

Anti-Slavery Monthly Reporter, London, 1826–34

Blackwood's Edinburgh Monthly Magazine, 1817–21, 1831–5

Cape, The, An Independent Review of South African Life and Politics, Cape Town, January 1922

Cape Monthly Magazine, Cape Town, July 1856

Courier, The, London, 23 May 1821

Edinburgh Magazine, 1818–19

Edinburgh Review, 24 November 1819

Friendship's Offering. A Literary Album and Annual Remembrancer, London, 1827–35

Graham's Town Journal, 1835

Guardian, The, London, 24.4.2009

Literary Gazette, London, 26.5.1827, 28.10.1830, 15.12.1831

New Monthly Magazine, London, 1826–8

Notes and Queries, London, November 1855, March 2011

Oriental Herald, London, 1824–9

Palladium of British America: Palladium of British America and Upper Canada Mercantile Advertiser, Toronto, vol. 2, no 1 (1839)

Penny Magazine, The, London, 1832–45

Quarterly Review, London, 55.109, December 1835, pp. 74–85

South African Commercial Advertiser, The, Cape Town, January-May 1824, August-December 1825, 1826, 1833–5

Scots Magazine and Edinburgh Literary Miscellany, The, 1817

Scotsman, The, Edinburgh, 1820

Star, The, Edinburgh, 1817–18

Times, The, London, 1833

Tourist, The, London, 1832–3

Index

Index

Index

Index